Bridging the Education Di
Technologies

Somprakash Bandyopadhyay · Arina Bardhan ·
Priyadarshini Dey · Sneha Bhattacharyya

# Bridging the Education Divide Using Social Technologies

## Explorations in Rural India

 Springer

Somprakash Bandyopadhyay
Social Informatics Research Group
Indian Institute of Management Calcutta
Kolkata, West Bengal, India

Arina Bardhan
NexConnect Ventures Pvt. Ltd.
Kolkata, West Bengal, India

Sneha Bhattacharyya
Social Informatics Research Group
Indian Institute of Management Calcutta
Kolkata, West Bengal, India

Priyadarshini Dey
NexConnect Ventures Pvt. Ltd.
Kolkata, West Bengal, India

ISBN 978-981-33-6740-1      ISBN 978-981-33-6738-8   (eBook)
https://doi.org/10.1007/978-981-33-6738-8

# Preface

This book is primarily derived from our research at the Social Informatics Research Group, Indian Institute of Management Calcutta. For the last five years, we have been working on different projects with the aim to utilize the potential of social technology (an umbrella term used to capture a wide variety of terminologies depicting internet-enabled communications, platforms, and tools, e.g., web 2.0, mobile 2.0, social media, social software, etc.) in addressing problems related to marginalization and social exclusion of Indian rural communities. In an attempt to bring marginalized Indian rural communities in the mainstream, our research effort strives to empower the target group with sufficient knowledge and livelihood options necessary to pronounce their socio-economic status. While empowering marginalized communities happens to be our macro research focus, in the context of this book, we have attempted in providing a socio-technical framework towards optimally deploying social technologies for addressing the issue of education divide of marginalized communities. The book begins by conceptually postulating the ideas of education divide and education ecosystem theoretically, followed by providing a social technology-enabled framework to overcome the issue of education divide faced by marginalized learners. The proposed framework offers a transition from traditional content-centric, teacher-centric and centralized education ecosystem to a connection-centric, learner-centric, and decentralized education ecosystem of the socio-digital age.

Education divide, referring to the divide between one having education and the one devoid of it, forms the base of our research, which we wish to address using contemporary digital technologies. In this book, we have conceptualized education divide along three dimensions: access divide, capability divide, and opportunity divide. This implies that education divide not only exists in terms of lack of access to education. The monstrosity of the divide also gets manifested in terms of the lack of quality education, which disallows nurturing the capability of learners on a desired level. Moreover, lack of quality education and appropriate skill development trainings create an opportunity divide, which denies the ones on the disadvantageous side the ability to explore pronounced and enhanced opportunities. In this book, we have attempted to understand, analyze, and mitigate this education divide from an ecosystemic perspective.

In order to develop an ecosystemic perspective to understand the issues of education divide, it is first important to know what education ecosystem is and the operations and interactions of different elements within an education ecosystem. In the domain of education, ecosystems are understood as the network of living (*biotic*) and the non-living (*abiotic*) entities that are essential for quality teaching and learning. These living entities or actors include learners, parents, family, peer group, entrepreneurs, government agencies, religious bodies, content developers, institutional bodies, education associations, and curriculum developers who form the immediate biotic entities of an education ecosystem. An education ecosystem also nurtures the non-living (abiotic) entities which includes all available material means such as school infrastructure including IT infrastructure at school, teaching-learning materials, assessment tools, etc. These abiotic components have the capability to directly influence the nature of interactions among the biotic actors within an education ecosystem.

An education ecosystem is dependent on the mutual and reciprocal relationships and interconnectedness between biotic and abiotic entities that are influenced by the changing socio-cultural and political environment at large. Hence, apart from the biotic and abiotic components, education ecosystem is shaped by a set of external factors that act as *enablers* or *influencers*, which can be categorized under four dimensions: *social, economic, political, and socio-psychological*. These external influencers set the context and heavily determine the performance of an education ecosystem in inculcating effective and quality learning. These external factors in a geographic context determine whether the interaction of biotic and abiotic components will yield positive outcome or not in imparting quality education.

This ecosystemic approach to analyse educational process enables us to study teaching-learning processes as the outcome of interactions between biotic and abiotic entities and external influencers within an education ecosystem. Discarding the notion that education is based on the linear process of knowledge dissemination from teachers to students, an ecosystemic lens helps us to understand the several factors which are at play and contribute to the sustenance of unequal distribution of educational resources on a holistic scale. This book attempts to highlight that improving biotic and abiotic components of an education ecosystem will remain inadequate in mitigating education divide, if the said improvement is not done by taking into account the contextual specificities of external influencers, which crucially shape the conditions of effective education dissemination. In this book, we have attempted in devising a social technology-enabled online blended learning platform to bridge education divide, by triggering purposive collaborations between biotic, abiotic, and external influencers within an education ecosystem.

We have executed pilot studies in a few villages of West Bengal, India to demonstrate how our proposed online blended learning platform can mitigate education divide through promoting effective interactions between biotic and abiotic entities of the education ecosystem under the contextual influence of the four external influencers (social, economic, political, and socio-psychological) of the education ecosystem. However, despite the demonstration of positive outcomes of the proposed framework in bridging access, capability, and opportunity divide in a pilot scale, issue of sustainability and scaling up of such framework cannot be concluded from this research study. From an ecosystemic perspective, these pilot studies, for a short period of time, has only taken into consideration the interaction between biotic and abiotic entities and did not have a scope to experience and analyze the contextual impact of four external influencers (i.e., social, economic, political, and socio-psychological) on a long-term basis.

To scale up or sustain such interventions in different rural locales, it becomes imperative for external agents such as social enterprises to take up the responsibility. Thus, to investigate further on the scalability and sustainability issues we have come up with a social entrepreneurial venture named NexConnect, which is a start-up venture of our research group. NexConnect, as an example of a social entrepreneurial venture and as a transition intermediary to facilitate and enable use of the digital platform among rural population, has taken the initiative to practically implement our framework in several rural areas in collaboration with several local NGOs and government agencies. The experiential narrative of this social venture highlights, how crucially important it is to optimally coordinate with biotic–abiotic entities and negotiate with the external influencers in order to become effective in disseminating education to rural population through this platform. The Indian rural sector is facing several disadvantages in terms of social, economic, political, psychological dimensions, which cannot be encountered through a technology-driven platform alone to ensure betterment in learning in rural areas on a sustainable basis. In order to smoothen the integration of technology with the existing social system, the presence of transition intermediaries like Nexconnect play a vital role to manage this socio-technical transition process in nurturing effective educational practices in the context of rural India using digital platform.

The unique contribution of the book rests not only in an attempt to understand, analyze and mitigate education divide from an ecosystemic perspective, but also in providing a design and operational principles of a social technology-enabled online blended learning platform to mitigate the education divide. The proposed framework attempts to transform extant education system from a linear "pipeline" model to a networked education ecosystem, based on collaborations and connections between teachers, students, teaching-learning materials, learning environment, and facilitating agencies. This decentralized and democratic framework is premised on mobilizing crowd-based knowledge capital using social technologies, bringing in key enablers or agents, and focusing on specific needs that are aligned with the twenty-first-century learning skills. The need for *collaborative connectivity* makes an ecosystematic view both unique and indispensable to bridge extant education divide. The theorization illustrated in the book to utilize contemporary digital technologies in mitigating education divide is supplemented and practically realized through a proposed digital platform, architected to impart effective education for the underprivileged. Since the developing nations feature to be the context of the theorization, Indian rural sector accounts to be our practical research context, where the effectivity of the proposed platform in disseminating education following an ecosystemic approach is tested. The theorization and practical implementation of a framework to mitigate extant education divide makes the book a perfect blend of theory and practice, which in itself is a unique offering in the field of education.

* * *

We would like to express our deepest gratitude to Mr. Jayanta Basak, a co-researcher in our Research Group, for his support and cooperation in writing this book. We would like to express our great appreciation to our research partner Prof. Kalyan Sankar Mandal, ex-professor at Public Policy and Management Group of IIM Calcutta, for his valuable and constructive suggestions during the course of our research work. We would also like to acknowledge the support of Dr. Siuli Roy, Professor, Heritage Institute of Technology, Kolkata, and Dr. Souvik Basu, Asst Professor, Heritage Institute of Technology, Kolkata for making valuable contributions in our Research Study. We are much thankful to our Research Assistants and Field Workers, Mr. Anik Roy Chowdhury, Mr. Rajarshi Biswas, Mr. Santosh Pal, and Ms. Sujata Naiya, who, at different time-periods within the five-year span of our Research work have been immensely helpful for conducting extensive field studies in rural Bengal, India.

This work would not have been possible without the financial support from our Institute, Indian Institute of Management Calcutta. This study was conducted in close collaboration with Kandi Federation (Kandi Block Mahila Cooperative Credit Society), several NGOs, and Social Organisations, namely, Siksa Niketan, Bagaria Relief Welfare Ambulance Society (BRWAS), Calcutta Rescue, Chandanpiri Sri Ramkrishna Ashram, Sunnay Foundation, and Transform Rural India. We are grateful to all of them for helping us enormously in conducting our field studies. All our rural micro-entrepreneurs and classroom coordinators, whom we trained during our work in villages of West Bengal and Jharkhand, deserve special mention. We are especially thankful to all our student interns from different academic institutes, who have helped us in our primary data collections. Last, but not least, the unconditional support of our family members in the journey of writing this book, has served to be a true inspiration in making our journey successful.

Kolkata, India                                                                       Somprakash Bandyopadhyay
September 2020                                                                                       Arina Bardhan
                                                                                                    Priyadarshini Dey
                                                                                                 Sneha Bhattacharyya

# Contents

# About the Authors

**Prof. Somprakash Bandyopadhyay** is a Professor in Management Information Systems Group and Research Director of Social Informatics Research Group at Indian Institute of Management, Calcutta. He is also Founder-Mentor of a social start-up, Nexconnect Ventures Pvt. Ltd. He is a Ph.D. in Computer Science from Jadavpur University and B.Tech in Electronics and Electrical Communication Engineering from Indian Institute of Technology Kharagpur. He was a fellow of the Alexander von Humboldt Foundation, Germany and fellow of the Japan Trust International Foundation. He has around 40 years of experience in teaching, research, and development in several organizations of international repute and more than 150 publications in journals and conferences of international repute. Prof Bandyopadhyay is the Founder-Director of Social Informatics Research Group at Indian Institute of Management Calcutta. The objective of Social Informatics Research Group is to develop and evaluate Internet-enabled Social Information Systems and to investigate their applications for societal benefits. One of his research interests is "social inclusion through digital inclusions" and he works extensively on application of social technologies for development. https://www.iimcal.ac.in/faculty/centers-of-excellence/social-informatics-research-group.

**Ms. Arina Bardhan** has completed her Graduation and Post Graduation in Sociology from St. Xavier's College, Kolkata and University of Hyderabad, Hyderabad, respectively. In 2013, she joined Social Informatics Research Group at Indian Institute of Management Calcutta as a Research Associate and has submitted her Ph.D. thesis in Jadavpur University, Kolkata in 2020. She is a co-founder-Director of a social start-up, NexConnect Ventures Pvt. Ltd., which is incubated in Indian Institute of Management Calcutta Innovation Park (IIMCIP) in 2017. NexConnect is working towards solving problems in rural India through social technologies (www.nexconnect.co.in) using an online teaching-learning platform connecting senior teachers with rural learners. She publishes regularly in journals and conferences of international repute.

**Ms. Priyadarshini Dey** has completed her Bachelor's from Lady Brabourne College, Kolkata and her MA and M.Phil. in Sociology from Jadavpur University, Kolkata. Her research area is enhancing quality of rural education through ICT. In 2013, she joined Social Informatics Research Group at Indian Institute of Management Calcutta as a Research Associate and has submitted her Ph.D. thesis in Jadavpur University, Kolkata in 2020. She is associated with Transform Rural India (TRI), a subsidiary of Tata Trust as a Consultant, aiming towards creating sustainable education centers in rural Jharkhand. She is also the Co-founder and Director of the social start-up NexConnect Ventures Pvt. Ltd. She publishes regularly in journals and conferences of international repute.

**Ms. Sneha Bhattacharyya** has completed her Bachelor's in Sociology from Presidency University, Calcutta and Masters in Sociology from Jawaharlal Nehru University, New Delhi. She did her M.Phil. in 2017 at the Center for Studies in Social Sciences, Calcutta. In 2017, Sneha joined Social Informatics Research Group, Indian Institute of Management, Calcutta, as a Research Associate. Rural development accounts to be her primary research interest. At present, Sneha is currently working on socio-technical frameworks, through which contemporary digital technologies can be employed to address the issue of rural marginalization.

# Chapter 1
# Introduction

## 1.1 Preamble

The primary attempt of our book is to deploy the collaborative and connective spirit of contemporary digital technologies in mitigating extant education divide. Education divide, referring to the divide between one having education and the one devoid of it, forms the basis of our research, which we wish to address using contemporary digital technologies. In today's world, digital technology has enabled us to interact, innovate, and share knowledge in ways, which were previously unthinkable. This paves the path toward emergence of the *Networked Society*, enabled by internet-enabled communications, platforms, and tools, that include regular personal computers, embedded computers, and mobile personal devices (Cell-phones, PDAs, Tablets), connected together using computer networking technologies. We call them *social technology*, an umbrella term used to capture a wide variety of terminologies depicting internet-enabled communications, platforms, and tools, e.g., web 2.0, mobile 2.0, social media, social software, etc., which has the potential to establish collaborative connectivity among billions of individuals over the globe. This concept of connected world using social technology has the potential of transforming the way we innovate, produce, govern, and sustain (Fitzgerald et al. 2013). This internet-enabled digital economy has already started transforming the organization of firms, industries, markets, and commerce (OECD 2008).

Education is a social process and just like any other social processes, its prevalence is not uniform throughout society. Therefore, a clear divide exists between the ones privileged to acquire education and the ones devoid of it. Our book begins by explaining the concept of education divide and goes on to identify factors which shape and sustain such a divide. In doing so, it discusses the attempts undertaken to bridge the education divide. Such attempts include efforts to bring equality by giving open access to education to all, efforts to bring equity, which focuses on imparting quality education by shaping the curriculum in accordance to the needs of the learners, and providing opportunity-based education to enable the learners to compete in the competitive market. However, majority of the attempts undertaken

© The Author(s), under exclusive license to Springer Nature Singapore Pte Ltd. 2021
S. Bandyopadhyay et al., *Bridging the Education Divide Using Social Technologies*,
https://doi.org/10.1007/978-981-33-6738-8_1

along both physical and digital lines have remained insufficient in successfully mitigating extant education divide. The limitations of both physical and digital measures in holistically addressing the education divide will be discussed in detail throughout the book. This inadequacy of extant measures can be traced to the lack of ecosystemic approach to understand the social process of education (Railean 2019), which have majorly restricted the schemes in effectively mitigating education divide.

In order to develop an ecosystemic approach to understand the issues of education divide, it is first important to know what education ecosystem is and the operations and interactions of different elements within an education ecosystem. In the domain of education, ecosystems are understood as the network of living (*biotic*) and the non-living (*abiotic*) entities that are essential for quality teaching and learning (Renya 2011). These living entities or actors include learners, parents, family, peer group, edupreneurs, government agencies, religious bodies, content developers, institutional bodies, educational associations, and curriculum developers who form the immediate biotic entities of an education ecosystem. An education ecosystem also nurtures the non-living (abiotic) entities which include all available material means such as school infrastructure including communication infrastructure at school, teaching–learning materials, assessment tools, IT resources, etc. These abiotic components have the capability to directly influence the nature of interactions among the biotic actors within an education ecosystem.

An education ecosystem is dependent on the mutual and reciprocal relationships and interconnectedness between biotic and abiotic entities that are influenced by the changing sociocultural and political environment at large. Hence, apart from the biotic and abiotic components, education ecosystem is shaped by a set of external factors that act as *influencers,* which can be categorized under four dimensions: *social, economic, political, and socio-psychological.* These external influencers set the context and heavily determine the performance of an education ecosystem in inculcating effective and quality learning. These external influencers in a geographic context determine whether the interaction of biotic and abiotic components will yield positive outcome or not in imparting quality education.

Attempts dedicated to address the issue of education divide must take into consideration all the three factors of an education ecosystem, namely, biotic, abiotic, and four external influencers. In order to usher effective teaching–learning practices, improvement in biotic and abiotic educational parameters must be done in accordance to the context, nature, and specificities of these external influencers operative in a given scenario. It is to such a holistic ecosystemic focus, to which majority of the initiatives undertaken to mitigate education divide suffer from. Even though existing efforts have attempted in improving biotic and abiotic entities in the process of addressing education divide, they have devised their pathways by neglecting the operating context, determined by specificities of external influencers, which crucially influence effective education dissemination. In our research effort, we have attempted in devising a social technology-enabled solution to bridge education divide, by triggering purposive collaborations between biotic, abiotic, and external influencers within an education ecosystem.

Our framework is derived from Connected Learning Theory, which is based on the premise that learning and development are embedded within social relationships and cultural contexts. We have proposed a digital framework toward creating a digitally connected learning environment and analyzed the proposed framework from the perspective of education ecosystem in the socio-digital age (i.e., a digital age driven by social technologies and socially enabled applications). The proposed social technology-enabled framework offers a transition from traditional content-centric, teacher-centric, and centralized education ecosystem to a connection-centric, learner-centric, and decentralized education ecosystem of the socio-digital age. The operative intricacies of traditional education ecosystem has mostly attempted in cultivating and nurturing passive learners. Marking a departure from that, our research efforts attempt in creating an education ecosystem characterized by an alternative learning environment, which promotes education through dialogue and collaboration between teachers, learners, and other actors of the education ecosystem. This paradigm considers every learner to be a potential resource and attempts in imparting education, by virtue of which the learners are expected to gain academic and vocational credentials.

While the framework of such an education ecosystem characterized by collaborations between different actors is universal, its effective adoption is contextual, where contextual specificities of four external influencers should be considered in an attempt to practically realize the framework. Therefore, our framework for such a collaborative education ecosystem is supplemented by a digital platform, designed to practically implement the principles of the framework. The effectivity of the platform in realizing the framework is tested in Indian rural context, which is described in detail in part III of the book. It bears in-depth reference of the empirical validation of our proposed platform in rural India to show how a community-driven blended learning platform can mobilize knowledge capital of domain experts to teach underprivileged rural Indian children as well as help forming communities of practice to enable lifelong learning for rural adult population. In this context, we narrate the experience of a social entrepreneurial venture NexConnect, an initiative of our Research Group, that has scaled up the implementation and execution model of our proposed online blended learning platform and attempted to sustain the venture in different rural locations of India. By narrating the social entrepreneurial journey of our research study through NexConnect, we explain the challenges encountered by this social entrepreneur in mobilizing different biotic entities in coordination with the abiotic components of the proposed collaborative learning environment in varied operating context, determined by specificities of external influencers. The book concludes by spelling out the need for transition intermediaries like NexConnect to help in the process of technology adoption. Those intermediaries will be entrusted with the responsibility of bridging those divides by moderating symbiotic interactions between biotic, abiotic, and external influencers of an education ecosystem. It is only in the presence of such intermediaries that the proposed digital framework will be able to attempt in mitigating the education divide of marginalized segments by enabling effective virtual collaborations between different participating entities.

While so far we have discussed the primary objective of our book, now we will embark on a chapter-wise journey that will help the readers in navigating it.

## 1.2  Organization of the Book

The book is divided into three parts: *Part I (Education Divide and Education Ecosystem: A Conceptual Perspective), Part II (Education Ecosystem in a Digitally Connected World: Bridging the Education Divide)* and *Part III (Exploring Impact of Social Technologies on Education Ecosystem: Some Empirical Studies in Rural India)*.

Part I is divided into two chapters: Chapter 2 (*Education Divide: Concepts and Dimensions*) and Chap. 3 (*Education Ecosystem: A Chronological Perspective*). Chapter 2 is dedicated to explore the conceptual and practical dimensions of education divide. Education and its unfair distribution is the product of social factors, conventions, and regulations, which heavily determine the logic of distribution of education. The chapter begins by exploring the concept of education as a social process. Oxford dictionary defines education as systematic instructions disseminated to inculcate specialized academic knowledge and moral values to learners. Going beyond this definition, we identify education to be a holistic process, which has the ability to *improve multi-faceted credentials* among the learner (improved capability to learn and internalize), by virtue of which he/she can be a *responsible and able citizen* (ability to exploit given opportunity structure and contribute toward satisfying societal needs). Explaining the definition of education as a social process, the chapter proceeds onto narrating the unequal prevalence of education in society. Being governed by social conventions, distribution of education to a great extent is guided by the dictates of social hierarchy (Francisco and Jeremie 2014). Although several attempts, both nationally and globally, have been undertaken to promote equitable distribution of educational resources, the chapter critically explores how, in spite of undertaken initiatives, education divide continues to be a persistent problem of contemporary society.

Further, the chapter characterizes education divide along three dimensions: access, capability, and opportunity divide. This implies that education divide not only exists in terms of lack of access to education. The monstrosity of the divide also gets manifested in terms of the lack of quality education, which disallows nurturing the *capability* of learners on a desired level. Moreover, lack of quality education creates an *opportunity divide*, which denies the ones on the disadvantageous side the ability to translate acquired knowledge in pursuit of exploring and enhancing opportunity scopes. The characterizations of the education divide along these three dimensions stem from our conceptualization of education in terms of its applicability and ability in preparing the learner in accordance to twenty-first-century socio-economic needs. After exploring the concept of education divide, the chapter sheds light on the initiatives undertaken globally to resolve the issues originating because of the existing divide. However, in spite of several initiatives undertaken across diverse levels to mitigate education divide, the problem of education divide still haunts contemporary society. The chapter concludes by critically evaluating the outcomes of existing schemes and traces their inadequacy to the lack of an ecosystemic approach to comprehend the social process of education.

To conceptualize an ecosystemic approach to understand educational process, Chap. 3 (*Education Ecosystem: A Chronological Perspective*) is dedicated to apply the concept of ecosystem in the field of education, in order to view the educational process as a network of relationships between different biotic (learners, teachers, government bodies, educational associations, institutional bodies, etc.) and abiotic (infrastructure, teaching–learning materials, etc.) entities shaped by a set of external influencers, defining the social, economic, political, and socio-psychological contexts. These external influencers heavily determine the performance of an education ecosystem in inculcating effective and quality learning in a specific geographic context. This ecosystemic approach to education is in direct contrast to the conventional narratives of education, which views production and distribution of education along a linear axis. Subsequently, the chapter proceeds onto demystify the evolution of education ecosystem, starting from ancient and medieval society to the modern education ecosystem, the education ecosystem of the Industrial Age. The chapter concludes by narrating the limitations intrinsic within the modern education ecosystem, which marks the incapacitation of the same in meeting the emerging demands of twenty-first century.

*Part II* (*Education Ecosystem in a Digitally Connected World: Bridging the Education Divide*) is divided into three chapters: Chapter 4 (*ICT in Education*), Chap. 5 (*Emergence of Social Technologies: Social Meets E-Learning*), and Chap. 6 (*A Digital Framework towards Bridging Education Divide using Social Technology*). We have reserved this part to discuss about the education ecosystem in a digitally connected world and have proposed prospective solutions along digital lines to address the issue of education divide. In doing so, this part begins with Chap. 4, wherein we discuss in detail how ICT has been introduced and utilized in the field of education to usher effective teaching–learning practices. The chapter begins by tracing an evolutionary journey of deploying ICT in the field of education, where it narrates the three generation of ICT usage in teaching–learning process. The first generation refers to the pre-internet era, when computers were getting used in a standalone mode to provide digital content only (Voogt and Akker 2001); the second generation characterized by the internet era, when computer and communication got converged, giving rise to a digitally connected world through internet (Major 2015); and, the third generaion of *Social Internet* era, where social technologies and socially enabled tools and platforms facilitate anytime-anywhere social interactions using internet-enabled mobile devices. Although this chapter bears reference to the three generations of computer usage in the field of education, third generation, characterized by the deployment of social technologies has been taken up in greater detail in Chap. 5. Chapter 4 primarily builds on to the first and second generation of ICT usage in education and how the education ecosystem in the information age got impacted due to these two generations. To do so, the chapter illustrates the education ecosystem in digital age, postulating the potential of ICT in improving biotic and abiotic parameters of education ecosystem (Bindu 2016). However, while improving biotic and abiotic entities and their interactions using ICT are necessary to improve educational performance, it is not sufficient to mitigate extant education divide unless we take into consideration the contextual influence of four external influencers (social, economic, political, and socio-psychological) of an education ecosystem. Providing online digital content and online expert teachers, supporting asynchronous and synchronous mode of learning over the web, which was done in the first and second generation of deploying ICT in the field of education, remains incapacitated in meeting education divide. It is only when purposive and collaborative digital connections are established among different educational agents by optimally negotiating with the external influencers we can attempt in addressing the issue of education divide on a holistic scale.

This paves the path for Chap. 5 (*Emergence of Social Technologies: Social Meets E-Learning*), where we have attempted in exploring the potential of social technologies in maintaining collaborative interactions between biotic, abiotic, and external influencers of an education ecosystem. In order to establish a coherent interaction pattern between biotic, abiotic, and external influencers, it is important for e-learning initiatives to transcend from providing digital content (in asynchronous mode) or online teachers (in synchronous mode) to establishing contextually effective digital connections among the participating entities of the education ecosystem (Watwood et al. 2009). Chapter 5 discusses at length the potential of social technologies in establishing purposive digital connections within an education ecosystem. Endowed with the potential to establish collaborative connectivity among billions of individuals across the world, the chapter begins by narrating a conceptual perspective of social technologies. Subsequently, the chapter attempts in demystifying the impact of social technology-enabled tools and platforms in teaching–learning processes.

Social technology-driven tools and platforms have altered the socio-economic arrangements through the emergence of platform and sharing economy, where socio-economic activities take place through virtual collaborations (Sundararajan 2016). To analyze the effectivity of social technology in the field of education, the chapter examines various initiatives undertaken across the globe to conduct teaching–learning activities with the help of social technologies. In doing so, the chapter critically explores the contextual incapacitations of social technology in facilitating effective coordination among different participating agencies in an education process. It is only in the presence of a social technology-enabled integrated platform that incorporates collaborative interactions among different biotic and abiotic entities and considers context-specific influence of external influencers, prospects can be laid to deploy the spirit of social technology in mitigating education divide.

The need for an integrated social technology-enabled platform and the urgency to moderate digital connections between different educational agents within an education ecosystem by keeping in mind the contextual specificities of external influencers make it crucial to have a digital framework, which will be effective in addressing the issue of education divide on a holistic scale. Chapter 6 (*A Digital Framework towards Bridging Education Divide Using Social Technology*) takes on this issue, where we have explicitly propounded the functional and operational architecture of our proposed social technology-enabled digital framework to effectively address the issue of education divide. The chapter begins by narrating how Connected Learning Theory forms the premise of our proposed digital framework. Connected learning theory upholds that learning and development are embedded within social relationships and cultural contexts (Penuel et al. 2016). Premised on connected learning, our proposed digital framework attempts in creating a digitally connected learning environment, where in this chapter, we have tried to explore and analyze our proposed framework from the perspective of education ecosystem in the socio-digital age (i.e., a digital age driven by social technologies and socially enabled applications). After narrating the functional architecture of our proposed digital framework, the chapter subsequently proceeds onto narrate the functional intricacies of a digital platform premised on the framework. In this context, it is to be noted that the digital platform has been architected to give a practical shape to the postulated digital framework effective in mitigating education divide.

Since the proposed digital platform is driven by internet and internet-enabled devices, implementation and successful operationalization of this platform for underprivileged community is fully dependent on bridging three forms of digital divides: (i) access divide; (ii) capability divide; and, (iii) opportunity divide. The chapter concludes by spelling out the need for transition intermediaries to help in the process of technology adoption. These intermediaries will be entrusted with the responsibility of bridging those divides by moderating symbiotic interactions between biotic, abiotic, and external influencers of an education ecosystem. It is only in the presence of such intermediaries that the proposed digital framework will be able to attempt in mitigating the education divide of marginalized segment by triggering effective virtual collaborations between different participating entities.

While part I and part II of this book is dedicated to narrate the theoretical and conceptual foundations of our research, part III is mainly reserved to provide empirical insights of our research, where we have recorded our research experience in practically implementing our proposed digital framework to improve educational practices for marginalized rural Indian learners. Part III is divided into four chapters: Chapter 7 (*Exploring Rural–Urban Education Divide in India*), Chap. 8 (*Online Blended Learning Platform for Educating Underprivileged Children: Creating Active Learners Using Social Technologies*), Chap. 9 (*Online Blended Learning Platform for Rural Adult Learners: Bridging the Opportunity Divide through Community Formation*), and Chap. 10 (*Implementation Challenges of the Online Blended Learning Platform in Rural India: An Experiential Analysis from Ecosystemic Perspective*).

Before delving into the detailed intricacies of our empirical insights, this part begins with Chap. 7 (*Exploring Rural–Urban Education Divide in India*), where we have attempted in providing a clear picture of our practical research context, the Indian rural sector, and the problems faced by the marginalized inhabitants in acquiring quality education. Chapter 7 seeks to explore the rural–urban education divide in India, in terms of access, capability and opportunity divides that exist between rural and urban India. This chapter defines our research context where we have conducted our empirical studies and highlights how the socio-economic, political, and socio-psychological context of rural learners hinder effective educational practices in terms of providing access, nurturing capabilities, and securing opportunities for rural learners. The chapter bears explicit reference to the numerous attempts undertaken both by private and public organizations to implement ICT-driven teaching–learning practices among rural learners. These efforts have primarily been dedicated to provide access to educational resources both along physical and digital lines to rural learners. Apart from being sporadic, such initiatives majorly lack the credibility to enhance the capability of rural learners through disseminated education. While physical measures are restricted by territorial hindrances, digital measures have also been unable to reap desirable results because of the rural target group's alienation from the digital medium. The adopted measures, although have attempted in improving educational practices in rural India by improving biotic and abiotic parameters, have mostly ignored the context of implementation and remained negligent of the external influencing factors, namely, social, economic, political, and socio-psychological, that marks the disadvantages of rural India and subsequently hamper effective educational practices in rural areas.

A critical understanding of our research context has enabled us to design our research intervention by keeping in mind the specificities of rural India. In Chap. 8 (*Online Blended Learning Platform for Educating Underprivileged Children: Creating Active Learners using Social Technologies*), we have attempted in implementing our social technology-enabled digital framework, derived from Connected Learning Model as postulated in Chap. 6, to disseminate quality education to rural learners with the help of ICT. This chapter bears in-depth field insights of our experience in implementing our blended learning platform, by negotiating with the external influencers operative in rural India, to disseminate quality education to rural learners. Keeping in mind the inquiry of education divide in India, this chapter bears reference to the conducted benchmarking study of evaluating and comparing the existing quality of education in 33 schools, which are located across four districts in West Bengal, India. The administrative responsibilities of these schools rest with both private and public entities. The schools are scattered across rural, semi urban, and urban areas. The cost structure of these schools range from government-sponsored free schooling to high-cost private schooling. Followed by the benchmarking study, in this chapter we have conducted an empirical study where attempts have been made to implement the proposed framework in underprivileged schools from three rural areas of West Bengal, India. This social technology-enabled blended learning platform is based on the principles of sharism and collaboration, aiming to mobilize multiple agents/mediators who play crucial role in transforming the learning environment of the rural learners. The objective of the implementation of the online learning platform is to evaluate change in quality of education in low-cost/free public schools in rural areas. This chapter thus focuses on the impact and challenges of such an ecosystemic approach using blended learning platform model in a rural set up and proposes greater involvement of social entrepreneurs and the government. The findings reveal the effectivity of a blended learning platform in classroom settings coupled with expert online teachers, quality digital instructional content, and on-site class coordinators. The above-stated fusion has the potential in ushering a learning environment endowed with the capacity to improve learning achievements and well-beings of students. The attained benefits are analyzed to have inclusive impact, equally benefitting students from varied socio-economic status. While the impact of blended learning framework in improving educational practices of rural children has been dealt in this chapter, in the next chapter, we have attempted in exploring the effectivity of our framework in mitigating the opportunity divide of rural adult learners through community formation.

Focusing on the problem of opportunity divide existing in India, Chap. 9 (*Online Blended Learning Platform for Rural Adult Learners: Bridging the Opportunity Divide through Community Formation*) discusses the need to disseminate twenty-first-century-oriented skill-based learning among rural adults using social technologies. The unavailability of quality skill-based and competency-based training opportunities for the underserved populations, especially women in rural areas, have urged us to conduct empirical studies of implementing the blended learning platform in rural locales of West Bengal, India. It has been demonstrated that the ecosystemic approach of analyzing the learning environment followed by implementing the blended learning environment enables the rural mass with the opportunity to imbibe essential life skills through various lifelong learning programs. The chapter bears in-depth reference to field insights of how rural adult learners, from age 20 to 65 years, were trained in low-cost garments and jewelry designs, fabric paintings, digital literacy, and spoken English. Based on the learning framework, the adult learners were regularly trained using WhatsApp communications, live online training sessions, and offline trainings. These interventions were based on community mobilization, leading to possible market linkages with urban consumers and traders.

Chapters 8 and 9 insightfully reveals our research experience in implementing our proposed blended learning framework in mitigating access, capability, and opportunity divide of rural learners belonging to different age groups. However, it needs to be remembered that attaining quality educational practices in rural India via the proposed blended learning platform is the outcome of a pilot study, which has been obtained in a controlled setup, managed by our research group. However, scaling up and sustaining such an initiative by coordinating with biotic and abiotic entities and optimally negotiating with the external influencers, is indeed a challenge, which has been taken up in detail in the final Chap. 10.

Chapter 10 (*Implementation Challenges of the Online Blended Learning Platform in Rural India: An Experiential Analysis from Ecosystemic Perspective*) attempts to present evidences, instances, and experiences of scaling up of the already discussed blended learning platform by a social entrepreneurial venture NexConnect Ventures, an entrepreneurial initiative of our Research Group. NexConnect is a social business aiming toward addressing issues of social exclusion by introducing the potentials of social technology and by exploiting the knowledge capital of the crowd. The objective of this social business is to make social technology-enabled tools and platforms available to rural masses and in such remote rural locales of the country where there is serious dearth of access to right kind of knowledge, information, and opportunity.

By introducing the social entrepreneurial journey of our research study, this chapter focuses on the activities taken up by NexConnect in mobilizing different biotic components in coordination with the abiotic components of the proposed collaborative learning environment. The chapter begins by highlighting the specific roles and activities taken up by the biotic components of the education ecosystem in the proposed framework in different rural localities. The preliminary observations on the implementation of this blended learning platform highlights certain issues and problems which are examined through analysing detailed experiential narratives of each of the biotic components of learning such as the online teachers, para-teachers, learners, parents, and local entrepreneurs. Each of these experiences has been viewed from an ecosystemic perspective to explain the biotic-abiotic interactions and the contextual impact of the four external influencers of the education ecosystem.

Although our research journey using the blended learning platform, as postulated in the preceding chapters (Chaps. 8 and 9), has been successful in a pilot scale in disseminating quality education in rural India, our entrepreneurial journey through NexConnect has indicated the need to solve several operational challenges and to devise practical strategies to optimally coordinate with biotic-abiotic entities and negotiate with the external influencers in order to become effective in disseminating education to rural population through this platform. The Indian rural sector is facing several disadvantages in terms of social, economic, political, socio-psychological dimensions, which cannot be encountered through a technology-driven platform alone to ensure betterment in learning in rural areas on a sustainable basis. In order to smoothen the integration of technology with the existing social system, the presence of transition intermediaries like NexConnect plays a vital role in nurturing effective educational practices in the context of rural India.

Chapter 10 ends with providing a socio-technical framework on how to optimally use a social technology-enabled digital framework in a socio-economic context to address the issue of education divide on a sustained basis. However, the proposed model can only yield desirable impact on a long term and at a widespread scale if this social technology-driven platform is integrated within the social system by several transition intermediaries like NexConnect, who will moderate the exchanges between biotic, abiotic, and external influencers of education ecosystem on an optimal level, keeping in mind the contextual specificities of external influencers operative in a given scenario. The book concludes with Chap. 11 (Conclusion) where we have summarized the key findings of our book.

## References

Bindu, C. N. (2016). Impact of ICT on teaching and learning: A literature review. *International Journal of Management and Commerce Innovations, 4*(1), 24–31. ISSN 2348-7585.
Fitzgerald, M., Kruschwitz, N., Bonnet, D., & Welch, M. (2013). Embracing Digital Technology: A New Strategic Imperative. *MIT Sloan Management Review*. Retrieved from https://sloanreview.mit.edu/projects/embracing-digital-technology/.

Francisco, F., & Jeremie, G. (2014). The measurement of educational inequality: Achievement and opportunity. *World Bank Economic Review, 28*(2), 210–246. https://doi.org/10.1093/wber/lht004.

Major, C. H. (2015). *Teaching online: A guide to theory, research, and practice.* Johns Hopkins University Press.

OECD. (2008). *The future of the internet economy, Policy brief.* Retrieved from www.oecdminis terialseoul2008.org.

Penuel, W. R., Daniela, D., Katie, V. H., & Ben, K. (2016). A social practice theory of learning and becoming across contexts and time. *Frontline Learning Research, 4*(4), 30–38.

Railean, E. A. (2019). *Handbook of research on ecosystem-based theoretical models of learning and communication.* IGI Global. ISBN-13: 9781522578536

Renya, J. (2011). Digital teaching and learning ecosystem (DTLE): A theoretical approach for online learning environments. *In the proceedings of ascilite Hobart 2011.* Retrieved from https://www.ascilite.org.au/conferences/hobart11/downloads/papers/Reyna-concise.pdf.

Sundararajan, A. (2016).*The sharing economy: The end of employment and the rise of crowd-based capitalism.* MIT Press.

Voogt, J., & Akker, V. (2001). *Computer assisted learning. international encyclopedia for the social and behavioural sciences.*

Watwood, B., Jeff, N., & Deihl, W. (2009). Building from content to community: Thinking the transition to online teaching and learning *[ACTE White Paper].* Retrieved from https://www.researchgate.net/publication/280713047_Building_from_Content_to_Community_ReThinking_the_Transition_to_Online_Teaching_and_Learning.

# Part I
# Education Divide and Education Ecosystem: A Conceptual Perspective

# Chapter 2
# Education Divide

## Concepts and Dimensions

## 2.1 Introduction

This chapter is dedicated to explore the conceptual and practical dimensions of education divide. Education and its unfair distribution are the product of social factors, conventions, and regulations, which heavily determine the logic of distribution of education. To explore the concepts and dimensions of education divide, this chapter has been divided into the following six sections:

The chapter begins by exploring the concept of education as a social process (Sect. 2.2). Oxford dictionary defines education as systematic instructions disseminated to inculcate specialized academic knowledge and moral values to learners. Going beyond this definition, we identify education to be a holistic process, which has the ability to *improve multi-faceted credentials* among the learner (improved capability to learn and internalize), by virtue of which he/she can be a *responsible and able citizen* (ability to exploit given opportunity structure (Narayan and Petesch 2007) and contribute toward satisfying societal needs). Since this definition of education mirrors an approach toward holistic development of learners, an immense socio-economic-psychological difference therefore exists between the ones privileged to possess such education and the ones devoid of the privilege.

Section 2.3 deals with unequal prevalence of education in society from a sociological perspective. The theoretical possibilities of education are undeniably a crucial field of investigation. However, our research emphasizes on education in terms of its applicability and attempts to demonstrate how education, being embedded in social fabric, is governed by social norms, regulations, and logic of distribution. Being governed by social conventions, distribution of education to a great extent is guided by the dictates of social hierarchy (Francisco and Jeremie 2014). If we look into history, then we can trace multiple instances where education was only reserved for the upper strata of society, making it a weapon necessarily benefitting the social elites. With the passage of time, the world has witnessed several efforts dedicated to achieve democratic distribution of education (Ejike 2013; Winthrop and Matsui 2013). However, in spite of several initiatives undertaken for the cause of

© The Author(s), under exclusive license to Springer Nature Singapore Pte Ltd. 2021
S. Bandyopadhyay et al., *Bridging the Education Divide Using Social Technologies*,
https://doi.org/10.1007/978-981-33-6738-8_2

disseminating education along democratic lines, education divide, characterized by the ones having education and the ones devoid of it, continue to be an acute problem of contemporary society (Miller and Brown 2011).

In Sect. 2.4, the chapter explores the concept of education divide and characterizes the same in terms of *access, capability* and *opportunity divide*. This implies that education divide not only exists in terms of access to education. The monstrosity of the divide also gets manifested in terms of the lack of quality education, which disallows nurturing the capability of learners on a desired level. Moreover, lack of quality education creates an opportunity divide, which denies the ones on the disadvantageous side the ability to explore pronounced and enhanced opportunities (Barton et al. 2016; Park 2007). The characterizations of the education divide along the mentioned lines stem from our conceptualization of education in terms of its applicability and ability in preparing the learner in accordance to twenty-first-century socio-economic needs.

After exploring the concept of education divide, Sect. 2.5 proceeds to shed light on the policy-level initiatives undertaken globally to resolve the issues emanating because of the existing divide. The multiple policies undertaken to bridge education divide have diverse focus. While some have emphasized on the aspect of equal distribution of education by enabling access to education to all, others have attempted in going beyond access to impart quality education to learners, which will nurture their capability to perform better in contemporary market. Apart from these, policy-level initiatives have also been undertaken to impart education, which will enable the learners to exploit the opportunity structure by virtue of the knowledge acquired through education.

However, in spite of several policy-level initiatives undertaken along diverse lines to mitigate education divide, education divide is still a problem that haunts contemporary society (National Education Policy 2020). In Sect. 2.6, the chapter critically evaluates the outcomes of existing schemes and traces their inadequacy to their sporadic nature and lack of an ecosystemic perspective to educational processes.

While the implications of this education divide manifests along multifarious ways, in the following section we will initiate our discussion with what we mean by education as a social process and how education being a social process contributes in its unequal prevalence in society.

## 2.2  Education as a Social Process

Auerbach (2016) rightly asserts that any attempt dedicated to understand educational process must reflect its socially embedded nature and long-term influence on societal and economic formation. Conventional education comprising of standardized curriculum, which are the products of societal decisions, have so far and is still shaping and transforming individuals. While historically, attainment of education was decided by traditional social stratification, in the industrial society educational attainment got directly linked with economic affordability. In pre-industrial society, the privileged group, for whom education was exclusively reserved, primarily resorted to education to maintain and sustain their social power position. However, in the Industrial Age, attainment of education, being directly related to employment probabilities, have made education an investment choice, where people primarily invest in the hope of getting better employment opportunities.

The shift in the motivation of education attainment, marked by the advent and prosper of industrialization, reflects Gary Becker's conceptualization of how human skills and knowledge in a capitalist society is premised upon economic returns to education (Becker 1993). Such return is calculated on the basis of the impact quality education is expected to create on employment possibilities, which drive individuals to invest in themselves. The decision to become educated becomes merely a type of investment decision and an exercise of free choice. This often benefits the economically enriched groups in pursuit of education. Education being an investment choice can only be availed by a group of people, who can afford quality education to improve upon their already enriched socio-economic position. In pre-industrial era, education attainment was decided by social stratification, norms, and regulations, where individual's ascriptive traits served as qualifying criterion in receiving education; and, in industrial era, economic affordability gained primary position in the attainment of education (Auerbach 2016).

In contemporary period, several initiatives have been undertaken to extend education to the ones who were deprived of it due to social conventions and restrictions. However, quality education, which can mitigate economic and social divides among the have-s and have-nots, is still unaffordable to a large majority of marginalized segments across the world. By making education an investment choice, contemporary society has reduced education to a commodity, which can only be availed by the privileged sections of society (Park 2007). In contemporary society, there is no formal social mandate of restricting education of the underprivileged segments. However similar to traditional societies, quality education still remains exclusive to the privileged segment of the society. Education divide therefore still exists in an intensified state in the contemporary world. The reason for the education divide to sustain and retain its omnipresence can be traced back to education as a social process. Social norms and conventions, heavily determining educational attainment and application, have since time immemorial retained the status of education as an exclusive factor, reserved for the social elites, although its mode of operation has varied with time. In the following section, we will provide a brief glimpse of the unequal prevalence of education in society, which is a direct product of education being a social process, before delving into detail the nature and implications of education divide.

## 2.3    Education and Its Unequal Prevalence

Discriminatory social processes guiding the production and distribution logic of education is the driving factor behind the unequal prevalence of education in society. Social norms and regulations, since time immemorial, have made education an exclusive force. Even in contemporary times, although several efforts have been undertaken to educate the marginalized, education still remains a prospect, whose fruits are primarily realized by individuals of established backgrounds. This educational inequality runs in a vicious cycle, where it is not only induced by but also accelerates social and economic polarization. The advent and proliferation of industrial world has started treating individuals as human capital, where education serves to be the attribute ensuring the effectivity of each human capital in the arena of employment possibilities. As a result, the dominant group, by virtue of their social and economic footing, can acquire education and retain the same by virtue of acquired education.

This creates an education divide, where, as Mithaug (1996) identified, the right to education gets exercised as "freedom as power," as opposed to "freedom as right." "Freedom as power" gets reflected in a scenario, where the dominant group by virtue of their power position encroaches upon other's freedom. The freedom the dominant group exercise is therefore restrictive of the freedom of common mass. When education becomes "freedom as power," individual freeness collides with social freeness, instead of getting harmonized, thereby diverting equal opportunity (Park 2007). As opposed to "freedom as power," "freedom as right" considers every member of society as deserving a fair chance in the pursuit of personally desirable ends in life. Premised on "fair" rule, education from the perspective of "freedom as right" retains every individual's right to quality education, irrespective of socio-economic background. However, in the era of heightened educational consumerism, the right to education as "freedom as power" gains precedence in comparison to education as "freedom as right." Education from the perspective of "freedom as power" restricts the chances and opportunities of students from poor families (Patterson 1978). This marks a shift toward market ideology, which serves to stratify social classes through schooling, where schools reputed to disseminate quality education primarily admit students from affluent backgrounds (SNU 2003). The resultant divide that gets created is not justified by virtue of social conventions. In modern society, the discrepancy of educational attainment is sanctified by two myths: myth of liberal individualism (Bird 1999) and meritocracy myth (McNamee and Miller 2004).

Liberal individualism is imbibed with the philosophy that individual pursuit of profit can lead to collective profit of society (Bird 1999). This serves to justify the privileged groups' dominance over effective resources, which are mandatory to sustain the attribute of self-prosper. This in turn helps the privileged group to exercise their "freedom as power" to establish control over important resources, thereby denying the marginalized adequate possibilities to collect the fruits from those resources. This proves that the ideology of liberal individualism dedicated to maximize collective profit of society in reality attempts to do so only for a particular privileged section of society. In actuality, liberal individualism, giving primary emphasis to individual profit maximization, begets segregation, where the gap between the have-s and have-nots escalate in monstrous intensity.

Another myth which serves to sanctify the unequal distribution of resources in a capitalist industrialized world is the myth of meritocracy. Myth of meritocracy upholds the belief that social resources are distributed in society according to merits (McNamee and Miller 2004). This justifies the elites' access and indiscriminate usage of social resources, because the popular perception beholds that members of the dominant group are more meritorious. The truth behind this perception is that the marginalized group is never exposed to a supportive environment, by virtue of which they can explore and capitalize on their merit to derive self-benefit. In contemporary capitalist society, socio-economic and psychological factors indirectly serve to be hindering factors in the marginalized group's pursuit of education. Denying the marginalized the privilege of quality education, contemporary society inevitably ends up privileging the dominant group by recreating the myth of meritocracy.

Excessive amount of consumerism in education further intensifies the unequal distribution of education by reserving quality education only for the dominant, socio-economically affluent group (Levett 2003). Amidst such a scenario, education gets reduced to a commodity, schools get treated as suppliers and parents and students as customers. Driven by market ideology, public intervention gets replaced by private entrepreneurs with a profit-maximizing objective (Park 2007). Privatization of education leads to rapid degradation of public aided schools, which are the major affordable channels of disseminating education to the marginalized. This points to an important revelation: segregation between socio-economic classes both leads to and originates from education divide (Smith and Noble 1996).

Park (2007) conceptualizes education divide by analyzing the case of Specialized High Schools (SHs) in South Korea that provides an excellent example of how consumerism affects equal distribution of education. In Korea, SHs successful outcome in securing college admission (Jung 2007; Kwon 2006) led to drastic popularization of SHs among Korean students and parents. Marked as centers of excellence, SHs only admit students from affluent backgrounds. Deemed as schools disseminating quality education and help securing positions in reputed colleges, inability of the Korean common mass to admit their children in SHs due to the issue of socio-economic affordability creates a divide among Korean population. In the world of achievement, where the credibility of human capital gets judged by an individual's social, moral, intellectual, and economic credentials, possession of holistic and quality education immediately serves as a favorable criterion. People in possession of quality education therefore have better prospects to flourish in the arena of employability, in turn having better socio-economic credentials in comparison to the ones devoid of it. This proves that education inequality in Korea not just originates from socio-economic segregation but also paves the path for renewed socio-economic polarization, thereby making it a vicious cycle. While so far, we have discussed the reasons behind the existence of education divide, in the following sections we will take up in detail the conceptualization and implications of education divide.

## 2.4   Exploring Education Divide

Education divide, characterized by one having education and the one devoid of it, does not originate from and lead to solely economic discrepancy. We define education as a holistic process, which has the ability to *improve multi-faceted credentials* among the learner (improved capability to learn and internalize), by virtue of which he/she can be a *responsible and able citizen* (ability to exploit given opportunity structure and contribute toward satisfying societal needs). Therefore, an unequal distribution of such education will not only economically disempower the ones devoid of it, but will also restrict their social participation from multiple angles.

Lack of education not only creates socio-economic segregation but also psychologically demotivates members in pursuit of better opportunity scopes, which force them into sustained marginalization. Holistic disempowerment, which is caused due to education divide, makes it a crucial concern that has to be immediately addressed. Overcoming education divide does not simply call for attempts dedicated to provide access to education to the ones devoid of it. However, education divide can only be effectively mitigated when the marginalized group not only gets access to education, but also derive the capability to exploit acquired education in pursuit of generating better opportunity prospects. Only then will mitigation of education divide create a scenario, where the *have-nots* will derive an avenue to overcome their socio-economic-psychological marginalization on a holistic scale.

The issues of education divide and the urgency to overcome the same was so acute that equal distribution of quality education got recognized as an international agenda during the articulation of Sustainable Development Goals (SDGs). UNESCO has taken several efforts to extend education to the marginalized sectors, by virtue of which the underprivileged members can get the provision to widen their opportunity scopes. In both primary and secondary education, attempts have been taken to extend the applicability of education in the domain of workforce development. To boost the sector of higher education, UNESCO has provided considerable funding to improve the quality of higher education in different underdeveloped/developing nations. The motive was to holistically mitigate education divide, where instead of providing standardized education, UNESCO made provisions to deliver holistic higher education to the marginalized, which can have immediate effect in enhancing socio-economic credentials of learners (UNESCO 2018). However, in spite of such attention and international commitments, mitigation of education divide on a holistic scale still remains a far-fetched dream in contemporary society.

The reasons for the mass-scale unrealized outcome can be traced to the fact that although significant attention has been paid to provide access to education to the ones devoid of it, nurturing the capability of learners alongside so that they derive the credential to exploit acquired education to generate self-benefit, has been a widely neglected arena. Lack of capability of learners sustains the education divide, where access to education alone cannot solve the issue at stake. The way we define education on a holistic sense, education divide is characterized not just due to access divide, but also due to capability and opportunity divide, which restricts the learners to derive the credentials required to be a responsible and able citizen. Following we will explore education divide as an amalgamation of *access, capability* and *opportunity divides.*

### 2.4.1  Access Divide

Conventional attempts undertaken to shed light on the issue of education divide have primarily focused on the lack of access to educational resources. These efforts are premised on the conceptualization that education divide sustains because access to education is ununiformly distributed across society. As a result, the prospective solution to the pressing problem of educational inequality from such a viewpoint is to extend access to education to the marginalized groups.

Going by this logic, several nations have witnessed efforts, where access to education has been extended to one and all in order to address the issue of educational inequality. The Indian government's Right to Education Act was undertaken in 2009 to make education a fundamental right for 6–14-year olds and mandated reservation for students coming from economically weaker sections in education institutions (Chandra 2017). Similarly, in India, School Education for All (Rashtriya Madhyamik Shiksha Abhiyan) was initiated in 2009 to make education available and accessible for the age group of 14–15 years. Similar to the initiatives undertaken in India, in Cambodia, Educational Sector Support Project was launched in 2005 with the aim to expand educational facilities in poor areas (World Bank 2012).

The above-mentioned initiatives undertaken in India, Cambodia, and some other countries, and multiple other efforts undertaken across the world primarily attempted in mitigating education divide by providing improved access to education. The hypothesis was that improved access will satiate the educational demands of the marginalized, thereby helping them in securing lucrative opportunity scopes for themselves. Although the intentions of these initiatives were noble, it needs to be remembered that access alone is not sufficient in overcoming the education divide faced by the marginalized group. Even if the underprivileged are granted access to educational resources, they do not possess the capability to exploit access to educational resources to nurture their self-credentials and in turn pronounce their opportunity prospects. This proves that access divide, although features to be significant in the context of education divide, is not the only determining factor for education divide. Education divide persists beyond access divide, to the capability and opportunity divide, which bars the learners in becoming a responsible and able citizen by virtue of acquired education.

### 2.4.2  Capability Divide

Amartya Sen has rightly articulated the importance of cultivating capability set among target group in order to achieve holistic development (Sen 1988, 2003).

As narrated in Stanford Encyclopedia of Philosophy, "The capability approach is a theoretical framework that entails two core normative claims: first, the claim that the freedom to achieve well-being is of primary moral importance, and second, that freedom to achieve well-being is to be understood in terms of people's capabilities, that is, their real opportunities to do and be what they have reason to value." The main essence of capability approach rests in its attempt to provide unconventional parameters to evaluate social change in terms of the richness of human life resulting from it. Capability approach sees human lives as sets of "doings and beings" (functionings), and relates the evaluation of quality of life to the assessment of the quality to function (Sen 1988). Functionings are defined as the achievements of a person, where any functioning reflects part of the state of that person. Capability, reflecting various combinations of functionings a person can achieve, is a derived notion, getting manifested in a person's freedom to choose between different ways of living. Capability Approach, in considering people as active agents, rather than passive, formulates the claim that the functionings are constitutive of a person's being and evaluation of a person's well-being has to take into consideration a detailed assessment of the constituent elements.

Lack of capability, designating multi-faceted impoverishment of human life, is an important product of education divide. As discussed already, education divide is not simply derivative of lack of access to education. Even with adequate access, learners may not develop the desired capability required for human functioning through disseminated education, thereby sustaining education divide. Acquiring capability through education means possessing operating abilities to process and apply acquired education. Therefore, an enhanced capability gets reflected in a learner's ability to initiate independent thinking, logical reasoning and informed actions, which endows in the learner the credibility to translate their capability in pursuit of expanding opportunity prospects.

Often it is seen that, in spite of providing access to education, disseminated education remains ineffective in nurturing capability of learners, thereby sustaining the education divide. Amidst such a scenario, several attempts providing supplementary education have been initiated to nurture individual capability of learners through education. A classic example of this phenomenon is the shadow education practiced in Japan and Korea (Mori and Baker 2010). Given the ineffectiveness of public education system, there has been a rapid upsurge of supplementary private tuitions in Japan, Korea, and many other countries to disseminate education among learners, which instead of prescribing standardized curriculum, is dedicated to nurture capability of learners through personalized attention. Private supplementary educational efforts are emerging worldwide to compensate for the ineffectiveness of conventional education, which provided access to educational resources to the marginalized to some extent. However, majority of these initiatives remain incapacitated in nurturing self-credentials of learners (Sarangapani 2009).

In this context, it needs to be iterated that mitigation of access and capability divide, although necessary, is not a sufficient condition to mitigate education divide on a holistic level. Learners can develop individual capability by virtue of acquired education, but may not possess the ability to negotiate with their social surrounding to expand their opportunity scopes (Narayan and Petesch 2007; Park 2007). In that case, enhancement of capability remains confined to individual level, without getting expanded to yield benefit on social level. This highlights the importance of mitigating *opportunity divide* as also a precursory measure, similar to the mitigation of access and capability divide, in the process of addressing education divide on a holistic level. Education divide can be truly addressed only if the learners develop the capability and in turn derive the ability to nurture their self-credentials in pursuit of expanding and exploiting their opportunity scopes.

### 2.4.3  Opportunity Divide

Standardized curriculum-based education becomes ineffective in creating a positive impact in enhancing opportunity scopes of learners from all socio-economic backgrounds. As a result, despite a rise in global literacy rate, such growth is not coupled by increased livelihood opportunities (HBS 2014). This automatically creates a divide between the ones in possession of *effective* education and subsequently belonging to a better socio-economic status and the ones devoid of *effective* education, thereby having degrading his/her socio-economic scopes. The divide originates because of absence of suitable opportunities to learners, where learners can apply acquired education in pursuit of pronouncing socio-economic prospects. This proves that acquiring education is not the final step in the process of holistically mitigating education divide. Education divide can only be truly mitigated, when learners, by virtue of acquired education, derive the capability to exploit available opportunities to improve the conditions of their social and material well-being by virtue of which he/she can be a *responsible and able citizen*.

Cloward and Ohlin (1960) defines *opportunity structure* as the opportunities available to people in a given society, which are shaped by respective social organization and structure of that entity. As studied by Narayan and Petesch (2007), opportunities for disadvantaged people to realize own capabilities and interests is only possible when their access to information, socio-political inclusion or participation, accountability and capacity for local organization is guaranteed within their geographical location. Moreover, these four areas are influenced by societal values, norms, rights, rules, and other institutional arrangements. However, the disadvantaged individuals, in contrast to those in the upper strata of the society find themselves to be excluded from these resources and also away from the essential networks, connections, and information. Further, individuals, irrespective of their marginalized situation, should be able to exploit own agency which implies own ability to act individually or collectively to further own interests. Unfortunately, with scarce resources and capabilities, poor people are greatly constrained from having individual or collective choices (Narayan and Petesch 2007). Individuals from lower socio-economic background, having access to limited resources, find it is difficult to explore opportunities that are aligned with the twenty-first-century global market needs. Moreover, they are unable to take advantage of existing opportunity structure and cultivate agency to effectively utilize the already available resources for the purpose of achieving holistic development.

Bridging opportunity divide can be achieved through linking education with employable credentials, where curriculum is formulated and students are prepared in accordance to the needs of workforce demand structure. The linkage of education to workforce preparation is crucial in the process of mitigating extant opportunity and, consequently, education divide. An eradication of the same can be attained by facilitating greater transparency about desired capabilities (Barton et al. 2016). This requires transforming traditional education and pathways to help students achieve market-relevant post-secondary credentials. An increased high-school graduation rate, characterized by standardized curriculum, while important, is a hollow victory unless it is coupled with additional post-secondary education and training deemed necessary by contemporary market logic. This calls for bringing education out of the clutches of traditional pathways and replacing it by work-based learning experiences for young people, coupled with career awareness, exposure, and immersion experiences.

This calls for an education system, where students will advance based on demonstrated skills and knowledge. The advancement, instead of being teacher-centric and routine-driven, will be done on individual rate, where the learners will receive customized support to ensure they are able to reach mastery (Barton et al. 2016). Only amidst such a scenario, the learners, along with getting quality education, can also develop the skills to exploit acquired knowledge to improve their socio-economic performance. This can effectively lead to mitigation of opportunity divide and, consequently education divide, where equal distribution of quality and *effective* education will lead to holistic and collective development of socio-economic conditions.

## 2.5  Attempts to Bridge Education Divide: The Global Policy Frameworks

### 2.5.1  Education as a Right-Based Approach

Education, both as a right and as a means to achieve other human rights aims toward enhancing one's sense of freedom, promoting personal development, and strengthening sense of self-respect. It is seen as an essential element to attain poverty alleviation. However, enrolment of students to schools alone does not solve the growing problems of poverty and the gross inequality and injustice that exists on a global scale (Ortiz et al. 2012). The purpose of education is to enable individuals to participate effectively in society to promote harmony, equality, and tolerance (MHRD 2019). Keeping in mind the goals of education, in 1948, education was formally recognized as a human right by Universal Declaration of Human Rights and later recognized by UNESCO. Rights-based approach to education focuses on ensuring that every child has access to quality education that promotes an individuals' sense of dignity and personal development. As a human right, the focus of the formal institutional bodies was to bridge education divide by disseminating free, compulsory primary education to all children, development of secondary education system, accessibility of quality education to all children, equitable access to higher education and a provision for basic education for individuals who have not completed primary education. Thus, the right to education encompasses access to educational resources, elimination of discrimination at all levels of the educational system, to set minimum standards and to improve quality (UNICEF and UNESCO 2007). In addition, education is necessary for the fulfillment of any other civil, political, economic, or social right. In this context, right to education gets viewed as "freedom as right" as opposed to "freedom as power." Thus, the recurrent themes to right-based education is: access to education for all; education for children with disabilities; minority rights issues; and, protection from abuse at school (Lundy et al. 2017).

Right to education is not limited to providing or receiving quality education alone, it also encompasses provision of preparing students of any age group with appropriate learning skills, knowledge, and expertise. As the Committee on Economic, Social and Cultural Rights observes in the opening lines of its General Comment No. 13, "… education is the primary vehicle by which economically and socially marginalized adults and children can lift themselves out of poverty and obtain the means to participate fully in their communities." According to the Committee, "education in all its forms and at all levels shall exhibit the following interrelated and essential features: (a) availability; (b) accessibility; (c) acceptability; and (d) adaptability" (United Nations 1989).

Additional to these factors, the right-based approach of education also looks into the fact that students do not lose their rights after their school hours. This is according to the Committee on the Rights of the Child. The education rights protect a child from enjoying her/his civil rights to freedom of conscience and privacy as well as protection from abuse, neglect and cruel, inhuman and degrading treatment, including corporal punishment (MacDonald 2012).

To realize the education rights for children throughout the world, the United Nations has developed Millennium Development Goals (MDGs) in 2000, which focused on various aspects of human development besides education. Among these goals, the most relevant goal on education is goal 2: "Achieve universal primary education by 2015." The failure of MDGs to achieve holistic development urged UN to undertake Sustainable Development Goals (SDGs), which got internationally acknowledged as new targets for 2030. In the revised developmental plan, measures to ensure inclusive and equitable quality education and promote lifelong learning opportunities for all occupied a prominent status and got formalized as Goal 4 of the SDGs. Apart from the policy-level initiatives undertaken by international bodies like UN, several national governments and NGOs equally contributed to the vision of equitable distribution of education. While the operational scopes of these initiatives ranged from national, regional to local level, their motives mostly converged in achieving wider impact through effective and democratic dissemination of quality education (MHRD 2019).

Despite such initiatives on a global scale, the implementation has been limited to only few developed countries with 77 million children still not enrolled in school (UNO 2015). Unfortunately, one can never universalize standards or benchmarks of achieving access to education owing to varying contexts. For example, in some regions, girls feel deprived of getting access to education, let alone quality education, owing to impending problems of poverty and gender discriminations. Poverty is a key factor impeding school enrolment, primary and secondary school completion, and learning outcomes. Moreover, owing to poverty and marginalization, children from ethnic minority and indigenous communities consistently under-achieve. These were problems regarding poor access to education in some countries, whereas problems of quality education are still pertinent. Most attempts are focused on increasing access to students all across nations; various international organizations are working toward getting children into schools. Unfortunately, the problem is not only of access but also of ensuring quality learning in schools or educational institutions. To ensure quality education, it is actually important to evaluate the experiences a child gathers when in schools, the skills and knowledge sets they imbibe. Unfortunately, the quality of skills and knowledge that the children from impoverished backgrounds take away from the schools are of extremely poor quality. The failure of such schooling to fulfill human rights is illustrated by national test data from a number of countries including Bangladesh, Brazil, Ghana, Pakistan, Philippines, and Zambia. As mentioned earlier, focus has always been on student enrolment resulting in neglect of attention on attendance, completion, and attainment, or to the processes through which those outcomes can be achieved (UNICEF and UNESCO 2007).

As mentioned in the previous section, the barriers of access to quality education vary with different socio-economic-political situations of each country. Problems pertaining to underdeveloped or low-economic countries are high cost of quality education despite the provision for free primary education (WEF 2000). The cost of quality education varies with each country and there is no standard or uniform amount for the cost of education, making it difficult for the poverty-stricken countries to afford (GPE 2012). Children from these low-economic nations often fail to afford the costs of quality education (e.g., school fees, uniforms, resources, etc.), owing to additional costs incurred because of loss of family income due to child's absence from domestic duties.

Other barriers to quality education include early marriage for girls, violence, physical harms exhibited on students in underdeveloped nations of the world. UNICEF reports that 11 percent of girls are married before the age of 15. There are a large proportion of children who receive education in languages that are unknown to them (Save the Children 2015). Children with disabilities also face significant barriers to the realization of their rights throughout the world. All these problems are heightened by poverty that results in deplorable living conditions. Finally, an in-depth investigation reveals how fear of violence and physical harm impedes children from accessing their education rights. According to the study of UNESCO (2015a), 50% of the total out-of-school children in the world belongs from conflict-ridden areas; many face violence in schools.

Right of children with regard to their life and education can be successfully protected by ensuring and promoting child centric and child-friendly learning environment. Apart from focusing on improving learning environments, it becomes equally important to take into consideration what a child's perspective is (Lundy et al. 2017). In this context, it has been observed that, what happens in schools is seldom examined through the human rights lens, since the notion of rights in education is new. Keeping in mind the need to consider a child's perspective, a particular study has been conducted where 2500 children from 71 different countries have said that more funding from the government is required to access educational resources (Lundy et al. 2017). For children in some regions (Eastern Europe and Latin America and the Caribbean), education was among their top priorities, but for others it was not. In Asia–Pacific, the priority was to find a safe place where the children can play. Schools act as spaces where a child's right gets guaranteed, where she/he is able to attain knowledge with respect, where parents too find a place for respect. Therefore, it becomes imperative to secure schools to be a "rightful" place for children, peers, and their parents (Lundy et al. 2017).

### 2.5.2 "Education for All" Movement

In the context of human rights development, the Universal Declaration of Human Rights promoted *education for all* and *inclusive education* in 1948, which is "crucial to tackling global poverty, improving health…and enabling people to play a full, active part in their communities." Inclusive education is a statement of everyone's fundamental right to access education and not be excluded. Unfortunately, there are many groups of people who do not access this right. "Everyone has the right to education which is free, at least in the elementary and fundamental stages. Elementary education shall be compulsory." Yet "for 72 million children and 774 million adults, that right is violated every day" (Stubbs 2008). The marginalized section who are kept aside from the dominant education systems worldwide are the most vulnerable ones; they live in poverty, in remote rural environments or in conflict-prone areas.

To eradicate the persistent issue of educational inequality, *Education for All* (EFA) *Movement* was launched in 1990 as a global process led by UNESCO in partnership with other UN agencies, with a "World Declaration on Education for All," followed by an international "Framework for Action" in 2000 (WEF 2000). Annual "Education for All Global Monitoring Reports" provides data that are intended to inform and motivate stakeholders in pursuit of several goals related to equitable distribution of education (UNESCO 2015b). UNICEF and UNESCO (2007) produced a new framework document entitled "A Human Rights-Based Approach to Education for All" premised on three key rights pertaining to education, namely, the right to education access, the right to quality education, and the right to respect in the learning environment. As a follow up, activities along a dual axis happened, involving agreement of a Declaration and proposition of a draft Framework for Action at Incheon, South Korea, in May 2015. A consensus was reached between both UN agencies and participating states to unanimously move toward "inclusive and equitable quality education and lifelong learning for all" by 2030.

Following the adoption of EFA in 1990, more than 150 governments adopted the World Declaration on Education for All, an international initiative, at Jomtien, Thailand to increase efforts toward delivering the right to education to "every citizen in every society." Ten years later at the World Education Forum in Dakar 2000, Senegal, this commitment was reaffirmed and 164 governments pledged to achieve this Education For All (EFA) movement (a global commitment to provide basic quality education to all children, youth, and adults). Six goals were identified to be met by 2015. The Dakar Framework for Action mandated UNESCO to coordinate Governments, development agencies, civil society, and the private sectors, in cooperation with the four other conveners of the Dakar Forum (UNDP, UNFPA, UNICEF, and the World Bank) to achieve these six goals by working together. These six goals are aligned with the Millennium Development Goals formed in September 2000. As the leading agency, UNESCO focused its activities on five key areas: policy dialogue, monitoring, advocacy, mobilization of funding and capital, and capacity development (WEF 2000).

These six goals of EFA can be summarized as follows:

(a) Focusing on early childhood education, especially for the most disadvantaged and vulnerable children.
(b) Attempting to achieve universal free, quality, and compulsory primary education for all children, with a special focus on reaching out to girl children, children of marginalized communities, and those belonging to ethnic minorities.
(c) Ensuring learning and life skills of all young people and adults through equitable access to various skill generating programs.
(d) Attempting to achieve 50% increase in levels of adult women literacy by 2015 by implementing equitable access to basic primary education.
(e) Promoting equality in education attainment along gender lines at primary and secondary level by emphasizing on the equal right of female learners to access quality basic education.
(f) Focusing on improving every strand of the quality of education, to recognize their excellence and measurable learning outcomes for all, specifically in the avenues of literacy, numeracy, and essential life skills.

Efforts were made to integrate the activities of raising community awareness, coordinating community services, teacher/parent training, and adapting curriculum and low-cost teaching materials. The curriculum, textbooks, and learning materials need to be appropriate for all students; including all kinds of students within the education system. These teaching–learning materials must cater to all marginalized children irrespective of their socio-economic and cultural backgrounds.

After exploring the concept, goals, and dimensions of *education for all and inclusive education*, let us mention some policies and activities undertaken globally following the EFA guidelines:

*Philippines* is a country having experiences of colonialism characterized by income inequalities and a heterogeneous population comprising of multilingual and multi-ethnic communities. The study of "Education for All Global Monitoring Report" in 2015 reveals how Philippines successfully raised its adult literacy rate by 50%. (Roche 2016). The National Programme Support for Basic Education (NPSBE) played a crucial role in implementing the government's Basic Education Reform Agenda (BESRA) over a six-year period (2006–2012). The objective of this project was promotion of the processes of decentralization and rationalization of the basic education system. These processes were responsible toward enhancing equity, quality, governance, and financing of services in the nation (World Bank 2014).

*South Africa* too, having its own history of colonialism and apartheid, adopted the EFA goals and initiated various programs such as the Adult Education and Training (AET) in 2010. South Africa started providing a year of free pre-primary schooling and enrolment rate of students reached an impressive heights: it rose from 21% in 1999 to 77% in 2012. In Burundi, Ethiopia, Ghana, Kenya, and U.R. Tanzania, school fees have been abolished. Kenya claims to have achieved heightened levels in literacy along with empowering teachers and communities, ultimately resulting in improvement in students' learning achievements. In terms of bridging the gender gaps in education systems, Burkina Faso and Ethiopia has been partially successful in closing the gender gaps. Tajikistan used TV and radio campaigns to promote girls' education. Since 2005, the Forum for African Women Educationalists has catered to more than 6600 teachers in 38 countries within sub-Saharan Africa. In Swaziland, the percentage of children with sole use of textbooks rose from 74 to 99%. In Tanzania, primary teachers adapted teaching practices to diverse classroom needs (UNESCO 2012).

An investment of $35 million to administer a nationwide campaign enabled Nepal to witness an increased literacy rate by 2011. Nepal reduced the ratio of pupils per trained teacher from 260:1 in 1999 to 28:1 in 2013. In order to have a continued understanding regarding literacy rates, the Literacy Assessment and Monitoring Program (LAMP) emerged with the intention to measure literacy rates of five countries, including Jordan and Mongolia (Roche 2016).

Adopting the EFA goals, *Mexico* has made school participation of children aged 4–5 years mandatory. The enrolment ratio too has increased to a 101% (Roche 2016). "*Prospera Programme*," Mexico's biggest anti-poverty strategy, focused on giving advantage to country's poorest families with good education and health facilities. Prospera has increased school attendance by 20% among girls and 10% among boys, and has significantly improved child health. Mexico developed learning materials in 45 languages to help marginalized groups. *Nicaragua* and *Brazil* also implemented such programs and helped close gaps between rich and poor.

In *Cameroon*, farmers learned how literacy skills could help market participation. *Afghanistan* tripled the number of female teachers. Indonesia has established early childhood care and education (ECCE) centers in 65% of its villages where qualification of teachers are given umpteen importance (Roche 2016). "*Bantuan Operasional Sekolah*" is a program which aims to ensure that schools have sufficient funds to operate, reduce the education costs, and improve the administration structure in schools. The program covers approximately 43 million primary and secondary school students across Indonesia (Al-Samarrai 2015). In *Thailand*, extensive provision and awareness campaigns boosted ECCE attendance to 93%. *Jamaica* has designed a curriculum that is appropriately targeted to the progressive needs of five- and six-year olds. In *Bangladesh*, BRAC targets out-of-school children & prepares them for secondary education. Two out of three countries where lower secondary education was not compulsory in 2000 changed their legislation by 2012.

In India, EFA goals have been initiated in the forms of Right to Education Act (RTE) in 2009, which helped push student enrolments higher. Rural India saw improvement in nearly all aspects of school facilities and infrastructure between 2003 and 2010, including electrification and roads. Mid-day meals and school feeding programs in rural India have strongly increased girls' enrolment. India's RTE act improved the inclusion of children with disabilities. India's literacy program conducted assessments in 13 languages and more than 20 dialects (Chandra 2017; Jha, et al. 2013). In context to India, some of the initiatives that subscribe to Education for All are: *"Sarva Shikhshya Abhiyan"* (Education-for-all Movement), *"Beti Bachao Beti Padhao"* (Save the Girl, Educate the Girl), *"Saakshar Bharat Programme"* (India Literacy Mission).

In accordance with the EFA goals, India has come up with *"Sarva Shikshya Abhiyan"* (SSA) (Education-for-all Movement) that mandates children till age of 14 years to be part of free and compulsory primary education. SSA aims toward Universalization of Elementary Education (UEE) by taking forward an integrated approach, in partnership with the state. In an attempt to transform the scenario of elementary education of the country by 2010, SSA attempts in providing useful and quality elementary education to all children in the 6–14 years age group. Providing community-owned quality elementary education in mission mode and improving school performance can be identified as the primary motto of SSA. The welfarist intention of SSA also encompasses bridging of gender and social gaps (MHRD 2014).

To enable girl children with equal opportunity to access quality education, *"Beti Bachao Beti Padhao"* (Save the Girl, Educate the Girl) initiative has been launched in India. This policy-level initiative has enabled the country to positively transform the national scenario of primary education by increasing the net enrolment ratio of girl children. The elementary education has increased its budget to more than twofold, between 2007 to 2012. Student enrolment in rural parts of the country too has achieved new heights. Government policies in accordance with EFA have not only changed lives of children, but it has also altered adult lives through various lifelong learning training programs. Through institutions such as "National Institute of Open Schooling" and "Pratham Open School of Education", proposition for vocational and technical courses, certification for secondary and higher secondary education, as well as more specialized courses such as personality development and enhancement of soft skills has been introduced in the country. Women representing majority of illiterate adults have been incorporated in various nationwide government-sponsored literacy programs such as *"Saakshar Bharat Mission"* (India Literacy Mission*)*, which aims at empowering women and reach an 80% literacy rate (Nasreen and Bano 2016). Addressing gender gaps in education attainments in the country, India has, to some extent, successfully attained gender parity for primary and lower secondary school enrolment. Free textbook for girl students, bridging courses, back-to-school camps, add-on curriculum addressing social issues like gender, health, and violence and recruitment of female teachers can be identified as major factors contributing to such an achievement. The initiative has attempted in giving special emphasis on girl students belonging from marginalized backgrounds and remote areas (UNESCO 2015c). *"Saakshar Bharat Programme"* (India Literacy Mission) is premised on four broader objectives, namely, imparting functional literacy and numeracy to non-literates; acquiring equivalency to formal educational system; imparting need-specific skill development program; and promote a learning society by providing opportunities for continuing education (MHRD 2009). The primary objective of the program can be traced to its absolute dedication in imparting functional literacy to 70 million non-literate adults in the age group of 15 years and beyond (Chandra 2017).

Despite adopting these initiatives all across the world with regard to implementing the dream of EFA, EFA has not really succeeded in achieving all its goals by 2015. Based on the "Global Monitoring and Assessment Report of Education for All" in 2015, it was concluded that only one-third have achieved the six goals set. Only half the countries that signed up to the 2000 Education for All (EFA) agenda have achieved universal primary enrolment. "Despite not meeting the 2015 deadline, millions more children are in school than would have been had the trends of the 1990s persisted. However, the agenda is far from finished," said Irina Bokova, UNESCO's director general. She also said "We need to see specific, well-funded strategies that prioritize the poorest, especially girls, improve the quality of learning and reduce the literacy gap so that education becomes meaningful and universal." From 1990 to 2012, the student–teacher ratio decreased to some extent in more than 120 countries around the world. However, there was still shortage of trained teachers. "Trained teachers remain in short supply in one-third of countries: in several sub-Saharan countries, less than 50% are trained," the report said. As per the millennium development goals on education, students (both boys and girls) must complete elementary levels of education by 2015. However, after the MDGs became the dominant agenda throughout the world, too much focus on primary education adversely affected the "education for all" policy (Chonghaile 2015).

### 2.5.3 ICT and Education for All

Despite the above-mentioned efforts to achieve democratic distribution of quality education worldwide, there has been several gaps in terms of implementation of the policies. In that context, ICT in education has been propagated to facilitate interactive multi-dimensional education experiences in all parts of the world and also among all groups and categories of people. The purpose of ICT in education is to create borderless networks, facilitate innovative peer learning around the world and encourage learners to explore opportunities that are not limited within one's geographical boundaries. ICT has the potential to transform the traditional definition of classrooms by introducing learning which transcends boundaries, where a learner from any geographical area can connect with his/her teacher online. This brings in new options to deliver information, knowledge and provision for in-service teacher training and support. ICTs are thus increasingly seen as an integral part of modern education systems. In this context, policy-makers throughout the world are trying to make sure that ICTs are appropriately integrated in schools and in teaching pedagogies. ICT in education is also compelling the policy makers to rethink the skills and capabilities to be acquired by children to become active learners and workers in a knowledge society (UNESCO 2011).

This section of the chapter will now discuss several policy-level initiatives taken all over the world to propagate ICT in education, achieving education for all.

(a)  ASEAN ICT Masterplan 2020: The Association of South East Asian Nations (ASEAN) came up with the ASEAN ICT Masterplan in 2015 to thrust ASEAN toward a digitally enabled economy that is secure, sustainable, and transformative; and to enable an innovative, inclusive and integrated ASEAN Community. The masterplan includes initiatives toward mobilizing collaborative efforts between ICT and education sectors wherein learners are able to freely access ICT to enhance own learning. The objective of this policy was to advocate ICT education from an early age and to integrate ICT into planning, designing, and implementation of education curriculum, assessments, and teaching methodologies. Following the principles of "Education for All," ASEAN ICT Masterplan 2020 enriches the learning environment for students and equip them with the competencies needed to succeed in a knowledge economy (Huawei CSR 2017).

(b)  China's ICT Plan: In alignment with the education for all goals, China, like many other countries, have adopted a long-term ICT development plan, known as the State Informatization Development Strategy. This plan sets forth the nation's ICT goals for the next thirty years starting from year 2020. To achieve Education for all, this ICT for Education Policy aims at improvising the ICT infrastructure, deployment of free high-quality digital educational resources, and creation of online learning spaces. The primary objectives of this ICT for Education Plan by China are to bridge the gap between ICT adoption in urban and rural regions and also to promote education for all and lifelong learning in China. (Huawei CSR 2017).

(c)  The National Policy on Education in India, 1992 focused on the need to utilize potentials of education technologies in classrooms to improve quality of education. Under this policy statement, two schemes were adopted by the Government of India such as Computer Literacy and Studies in Schools (CLASS) and ICT@ Schools in 2004. The objective of the ICT Policy in School Education was to prepare the youth to compete in a future ready knowledge society. The ICT Policy in School Education aims to create an environment of collaboration, cooperation, and sharing by utilizing potentials of ICT in education. Such ICT-related policies promote universal, equitable, and free access to ICT enabled tools and resources to all students and teachers. The Policy focused on promoting development of localized quality content, resources, management, and networking of school administrators, teachers for the purpose of improved efficiencies in the schooling system (MHRD 2012).

(d) Singapore's ICT educational policy aims at building capacities of learners to harness economic competitiveness of the country, to promote lifelong learning and skill-based learning beyond schools to create better workforce. To execute this policy, three Master Plans (MP1, MP2, and MP3) were prepared by the government. MP1 focused toward equipping all teachers with necessary ICT skills that would help learners transport from an acquisition mode of learning to the kind of learning that leverages application, synthesis, and evaluation (UNESCO 2011).

(e) Uruguay came up with the ICT in education policy wherein the focus in to bring equity in knowledge access. The ICT in education policy aimed at providing all learners and teachers from public schools with universal and free access to computers. This would reduce the existing digital gap in the country. By ensuring equal access to information and communications to everyone in the country, this policy aims to promote social justice. This would facilitate development of new learning environments for a new generation of learners who are well equipped with ICT usage. In alignment with Education for All goals, ICT in Education Policy in Uruguay stimulates active participation of learners and teachers and increase awareness of the importance of lifelong learning (UNESCO 2011).

(f) Open Polytechnic in New Zealand: Open Polytechnic in New Zealand conducts vocational and skill-based training for adult learners by resorting to ICT as the disseminating medium. The institution attempts in disseminating technical and vocational training and higher professional and continuing education in distance mode and simultaneously conducts online learning courses for more than 31,000 students annually. The focus is on optimal utilization of technology in facilitating proactive learning processes. An impact analysis of the implementing architecture reveals the success of the system in promoting affordable, scalable, and accessible education to students. The findings also suggest the easy acceptance of online-only learning experiences by majority of the learners at Open Polytechnic. The proactive learning environment created by Open Polytechnic also enables the learners to participate in the blended learning environment by resorting to online and offline learning methods and materials (Latchem 2017).

(g) Teacher's Training using ICT: This project is run by the UNESCO-Asia–Pacific Programme of Educational Innovation for Development (APEID). It aims at improving the capabilities of teachers/facilitators by facilitating them with ICTs as pedagogical tools and to incorporate interactivity in teaching processes. These training happened through digital technology. The objective was thus to promote e-lesson plans and education software in regular classroom teaching. This program also propagated regional online teacher resource base and offline network of teacher-training institutions to share teacher-developed education courseware and innovative practices (UNESCO 2004).

(h) ICT Application for Non-formal Education (NFE) Programmes: The project ICT Application for Non-formal Education (NFE) Programmes attempts in

improving quality of life by eradicating poverty among marginalized rural population. The program attempts to reach its objectives by enabling the target group
with easy and enhanced access to virtual need-specific education programs.
Developed by the UNESCO Bangkok-based Asia–Pacific Programme of Education for All (APPEAL), this program comes with a bi-fold objective: firstly, it
explores the potential of ICT in facilitating optimal utilization and delivery of
existing resources, coupled with developing new resources to improve extant
quality of education and to enable learners equal access to Community Learning
Centres (CLCs). Secondly, to explore innovative ways on how ICT can be
deployed to improve non-formal education to attain the ultimate objective
of empowering individual learners and facilitating community development
(UNESCO 2004).

To summarize, these initiatives adopted by most nations aim toward increasing
access to ICT enabled educational resources owing to its capability to reach out to
maximum people. Most country-related policies point toward increasing access to
digital technology and Internet connectivity in remote regions so that the gap between
digital access in rural and urban areas can be bridged. Moreover, some of these ICT in
education Policies guarantees not only access but also dissemination of educational
content among all kinds of learners.

## 2.5.4  Vision of Education 2030: Transforming Lives Through Education

UNESCO organized the World Education Forum (WEF) 2015 in Incheon, Republic
of Korea where the primary objective was to address the existing problems that were
mentioned in the Global Monitoring Reports (GMR), published in the previous years.
Over 1600 participants from 160 countries participated in the WEF, 2015. Critiquing
the GMR, the participant countries and agencies together set out a refined vision
for education for the next fifteen years, which is called the Incheon Declaration
for Education 2030. As a follow up to the EFA Goals and MDGs, the Education
2030 aims toward establishing equitable distribution of education throughout all
nations. It addresses problems with regard to all kinds of exclusion, marginalization,
disparities, and inequalities in access, participation and learning outcomes. Among
the Sustainable Development Goals (SDG) adopted in Education 2030 formulation,
the SDG 4 assures "Ensuring inclusive and equitable quality education and promoting
lifelong learning opportunities for all" (UNESCO 2016).

Addressing the global and national education challenges, Education 2030 entails
a "humanistic vision of education and development that are based on human rights
and dignity; social justice; inclusion; protection; cultural, linguistic and ethnic diversity; and shared responsibility and accountability" (UNESCO 2016). These goals of
education promote the same to be a fundamental human right which is essential for

peace, tolerance, human ulfilment, and sustainable development. This scope of education addresses the existing education divide in terms of the capability and opportunity divides prevailing in all nations. These agendas of Education 2030 harnesses equity, inclusion, quality, improved learning outcomes within the lifelong learning approach so that everyone can harness own capabilities and ultimately avail opportunities for themselves.

The quality education mentioned in the agenda is understood as the kind of education that fosters creativity, knowledge and acquisition of literacy, numeracy and analytical skills among students (OECD 2018). Moreover, to achieve quality education and improve learning outcomes, it becomes important to ensure motivated, qualified, and well-trained teachers in all schools. As mentioned in SDG 4, access to lifelong learning becomes important and as a result what becomes equally important is the increased access to quality technical, vocational training, and higher education and research.

Directing more toward lifelong learning, discussions on acquiring twenty-first-century skills becomes significant here. To harness opportunities, students must acquire the appropriate skills which does not comprise of the conventional approaches to education delivery (Marisi 2019). These skills must include components of developing digital literacy, flexibility, and collaborative problem solving among learners. Aiming toward harnessing capabilities and opportunities, the Education 2030 espouses training opportunities for the out-of-school children and adolescents all across the nations. Formal curriculum must encompass these skills so that students not only masters the subject matter but also grasps the breadth of skills simultaneously (Winthrop et al. 2016). To ensure this access to skills among all students, role of technology becomes crucial. As digital connectivity becomes a ubiquitous component in today's world with libraries getting digitized and course materials becoming available through one's smartphones, systemic transformation of traditional learning environment into a technology-enabled learning environment becomes necessary. Thus, the agenda of Education 2030 is to give equal focus to science, technology, and innovation.

Realizing the role of education to be the main driver of development and the key to transform lives, Education 2030 goals thus had a single renewed education agenda which is holistic, ambitious, inclusive, and aspirational (UNESCO 2015d). Education 2030 additionally gives importance to the role of civil societies, private sectors in observing change in quality and access to education among all. This gives rise to the need to create and sustain an *education ecosystem* that nurtures an inclusive and equitable learning environment for all, adapting to the needs of the society at large.

## 2.6    Limitations of Existing Initiatives to Bridge the Divide

The Global Education Monitoring (GEM) Reports 2017–18 and 2018–19 evaluates yearly activities or initiatives taken up by governments all across developing and underdeveloped nations with regard to improvement in quality of education (Global Education Monitoring Report n.d.). According to these recent Reports, 264 million school-aged children are out of schools and the reasons behind such an outcome even after formulation of the Education 2030 agenda is because of the pertaining problems with regard to poverty, location of residence, gender-based inequalities, lack of trained teachers and poor education facilities. These recent GEM Reports have shown sub-Saharan African regions to be worst affected regions with regard to poor levels of education. Moreover, enrollment in skill-based education lags behind substantially, resulting in compromising economic growth, prosperity, and social well-being (Lueddeke 2019).

United Nations (2019) released Sustainable Development Goals (SDG) Report 2019 wherein status of achieving each of the 17 SDGs has been mentioned. Reporting on the status of achieving the SDG4 which is that of "ensuring inclusive and equitable quality education," the Report says that Sub-Saharan Africa and parts of Central and Southern Asia have the highest disparities in educational opportunities and outcomes. Students there are not entirely prepared for the complex global economy (Asian Centre for Human Rights 2003). Despite adoption of several initiatives toward bridging divides in education and witnessing improvement in quality of education, a huge number of children and adolescents from elementary and secondary school levels are lagging behind with regard to their proficiencies in reading and mathematics. More than 55 percent of the children not only need basic access to education but also quality education where they can be proficient in reading, writing, mathematics, and acquiring necessary skills. Skill-based education is important here as it helps students to compete in a global marketplace and thus address the problem of capability and opportunity divide.

Despite the goals and initiatives undertaken with regard to equitable distribution of education, many of the countries are yet to achieve their respective goals of attaining quality and access to education among the youths or adult learners especially. There has been not much improvement in inclusion of out-of-school children. More than 262 million children and adolescents (6–17 years old) were still out of school in 2017 (United Nations 2019). That represented nearly one-fifth of the global population in that age group. Despite the renewed focus in observing gender equality in terms of access to quality of education, girls from Central Asia, Northern Africa and Western Asia, and sub-Saharan Africa still face disparities in access. Despite the promise to increase number of trained teachers in classrooms, the underdeveloped and developing nations still have low percentages of trained teachers in all levels of education. The refined goal of education 2030 has its focus on lifelong learning, skill development. Unfortunately, within the four years from 2015 to 2019, there has been stark decline in adult literacy rates (United Nations 2019).

One of the country representatives for Europe and North America for SD Education 2030 Steering Committee, Mr. Walter Hirche said that nations all across the world are far away from reaching the education goals and targets. He suggests that more investment must be made on teacher's training as the poor quality of teaching is the most alarming cause in the declining status of education across the world (UNESCO 2020a). Furthermore, the Sustainable Development Goals-Education 2030 Steering Committee had published statements in January 2020 to celebrate the World Education Day (UNESCO 2020b). By way of addressing the crisis of education in all developing and underdeveloped nations, the Committee explored the problem of linearity. Most nations focus on improving the quality of education by increasing access to education through enrollments, by investing on quality teachers, teaching–learning aids and mostly focusing on improving school-based learning. However, quality cannot be improved by concentrating on these aspects alone. The associated components that form a learner's environment such as his/her cultural and psychological make up, political influence, available policies, and most importantly a conducive socio-economic environment influences one's learning outcome. Thus, the problems of education need to be looked at from a multi-dimensional perspective that influence learners' learning environment.

## 2.7 Conclusion

To summarize, it can be stated that right-based approach to education and policy formulations in that direction is necessary, but not sufficient to bridge education divide. Despite various attempts to strengthen education systems, majority of developing and less developed countries are still engulfed within the rigid, mechanical, discriminatory, inaccessible, and unattractive learning environments. Problems are more pronounced in underdeveloped nations, where lack of safety, hygiene and privacy, non-involvement of families and communities in learning process, unsupported teachers and schools and non-utilization of local resources worsen the education divide. This crisis in education is also because of the millions of learners being "left behind" owing to situations of conflict, protracted crisis, inequalities, etc. The education scenario across the world is not quite positive because governments, civil societies, or private entrepreneurs have not done enough to tackle inequalities, including gender disparities. Schools or learning institutions are not efficient enough when it comes to addressing the problems faced by the underdeveloped and developing nations with regard to improving quality of education and the overall learning environment.

Most of the development interventions for the underprivileged communities have been dominated by Government agencies and a handful of bilateral and multilateral institutions that defined the problems and implemented a narrow set of solutions. Instead, we would do better to think of development as an ecosystem: a complex system that has many entry points to stimulate organic growth. With democratization of science & technology and increase in global connectivity, a whole array of crowd-based development agents characterized by mobile phones and networked computers acting as online learning platforms have emerge, giving way to the possibility of utilizing these tools to address problems of education divide (Dehgan 2012). With the advent of twenty-first century, new technology gets integrated, new pedagogical models and curriculum gets designed. New technologies have capacities to support teachers and ensure flexible learning pathways.

Keeping this perspective in mind, we advocate for an ecosystemic approach to analyze extant education divide and to propose a social technology-driven framework that uses internet-enabled communications, platforms, and tools (Chui et al. 2012) to address this problem. In the field of education, Cremin (1976) applied the concept of ecology creating "configurations of education"; focusing on the need to interact, collaborate, and survive with various components. Education, being a social process, is embedded in the dynamics of social fabric. Thus, education is not an isolating factor and has to be taken into consideration the ecosystem and inter-related aspects crucial to education acquisition and dissemination. Thus, an ecosystemic approach to education takes into account the negotiations and interactions between different social, economic, political, and socio-psychological factors in the process of educational dissemination. In the following chapter, we will explore the dimensions of education ecosystem and trace a comprehensive evolution of the education ecosystem over time to arrive at the dynamics of modern education ecosystem and the pattern of negotiations governing it. In the said context, education divide will persist if different actors and influencers within an education ecosystem are not well-connected and not well-harmonized. This makes it crucial to nurture the collaborations within an education ecosystem effectively, which only bears the prospect in mitigating education divide on a holistic scale.

# References

Al-Samarrai, S. (2015). *Improving education through the Indonesian school operational assistance program (BOS) (English)*. Jakarta, Indonesia: World Bank Group. Available at: https://documents.worldbank.org/curated/en/525301468183561575/Improving-education-through-the-Indonesian-school-operational-assistance-program-BOS.

Asian Centre for Human Rights. (2003). *The Status of Children in India: An alternate report to the United Nations Committee on the Rights of the Child on India's first periodic report (CRC/C/93/Add.5)*. Retrieved from https://resourcecentre.savethechildren.net/sites/default/files/documents/2175.pdf.

Auerbach, P. (2016). *Education as a social process*. London: Palgrave Macmillan. https://doi.org/10.1007/978-1-137-56396-5_8.

Barton, D., Horvath, D., & Kipping, M. (2016). *Re-imagining capitalism*. United Kingdom: Oxford University Press.

Becker, G. (1993). *Human capital: A theoretical and empirical analysis, with special reference to education*. University of Chicago Press.

Bird, C. (1999). *The myth of liberal individualism*. Cambridge: Cambridge University Press.

Chandra, R. (2017). School readiness in India perspective, initiatives, practice and approaches. *Journal of Indian Education, XLII*. Retrieved from https://www.researchgate.net/publication/325806255_School_Readiness_in_India_Perspective_Initiatives_Practice_and_Approaches.

Chonghaile, N. C. (2015). *Education for All scheme has failed to meet targets, says Unesco.* Retrieved from https://www.theguardian.com/global-development/2015/apr/09/education-for-all-scheme-failed-meet-targets-unesco.

Chui, M. et al. (2012). *The Social Economy: Unlocking Value and Productivity Through Social Technologies (McKinsey Global Institute Report).* Retrieved from https://www.mckinsey.com/industries/high-tech/our-insights/the-social-economy.

Cloward, R. A., & Ohlin, L. E. (1960). *Delinquency and opportunity: A theory of Delinquent gangs.* New York: Free Press.

Cremin, L. A. (1976). *Public education.* New York: Basic Books.

Dehgan, A. (2012). Creating the new development ecosystem. *Science, 336*(6087), 1397–1398. https://doi.org/10.1126/science.1224530.

Ejike, O. (2013). Attitude towards gender equality in South-eastern Nigerian culture: Impact of gender and level of education. *Gender & Behavior, 11*(2), 5579–5585.

Francisco, F., & Jeremie, G. (2014). The measurement of educational inequality: Achievement and opportunity. *World Bank Economic Review, 28*(2), 210–246. https://doi.org/10.1093/wber/lht004.

Global Education Monitoring Report. (n.d.). Retrieved from https://en.unesco.org/gem-report/all reports.

GPE, Global Partnership for Education. (2012). *Education costs per child.* Retrieved from https://www.globalpartnership.org/funding/education-costs-per-child.

HBS. (2014). *Bridge the gap: Rebuilding America's middle skills* (Report, Harvard Business School, Accenture, Burning Glass Technologies). Retrieved from https://www.hbs.edu/competitiveness/Documents/bridge-the-gap.pdf.

Huawei: CSR. (2017). *The role of ICT in realising education for all by 2030.* Retrieved from https://s3-ap-southeast-1.amazonaws.com/elevatelimited-com/wp-content/uploads/publication/ICT4SDG4-Final-Version.pdf.

Jha, J., Ghatak, N., Mahendiran, S., & Bakshi, S. (2013). *Implementing the right to education act 2009: The real challenges* (Centre for Budget and Policy Studies, Bangalore). Retrieved from https://cbps.in/wp-content/uploads/RTE-Discussion-Paper.pdf.

Jung, J. S. (2007). *More than a half of the six specialized high school graduates in Seoul entered the SKY.* Seoul, Korea: Chosun Daily News.

Kwon, R. M. (2006). *90% of specialized high-school graduates admitted to top universities.* Herald Media. Seoul, Korea: Herald Media Inc. Retrieved from https://www.heraldbiz.com/site/data/html_dir/2006/06/07/200606070329.asp.

Latchem, C. (2017). *Using ICTs and blended learning in transforming technical and vocational education and training.* UNESCO, France and Commonwealth of Learning (COL), Canada. ISBN: 978-92-3-100212-0, 978-1-894975-85-8.

Levett, R. (2003). *A better choice of choice: Quality of life, consumption and economic growth.* London: Fabian society.

Lueddeke, R. L. (2019). *Survival: One health, one planet, one future.* New York: Routledge.

Lundy, L., Orr, K., & Shier, H. (2017). Children's education rights global perspectives. In *Handbook of children's rights: Global and multidisciplinary perspectives* (pp. 364–380). Abingdon: Routledge. Available at: https://www.researchgate.net/publication/312033111_Children's_Education_Rights_Global_Pespectives.

MacDonald, V. A. (2012). *Children's rights in education: Applying a rights based approach to education a resource guide and activity toolkit.* New York: UNICEF. Retrieved from https://www.unicef.ca/sites/default/files/imce_uploads/UTILITY%20NAV/TEACHERS/DOCS/GC/Childrens_Rights_in_Education.pdf.

Marisi, R. (2019). Developing the students' thinking and learning skills in the instrumental lesson. In *Handbook of research on ecosystem-based theoretical models of learning and communication.* IGI Global. ISBN-13: 9781522578536.

McNamee, S. J., & Miller, R. K. (2004). The meritocracy myth. *Sociation Today, 2* (1). Retrieved from https://www.ncsociology.org/sociationtoday/v21/merit.html.

Miller, R., & Brown, C. G. (2011). *The persistence of educational inequality.* Retrieved from https://www.americanprogress.org/issues/education-k-12/news/2011/12/02/10805/the-persistence-of-educational-inequality/.

Mithaug, D. E. (1996). *Equal opportunity theory.* Thousand Oaks, CA: Sage Publications.

MHRD. (2009). *National education policy.* Retrieved from https://mhrd.gov.in/sites/upload_files/mhrd/files/upload_document/SaaksharBharat_Decmber.pdf.

MHRD. (2012). *National policy on information and communication technology (ICT) in school education.* Retrieved from https://mhrd.gov.in/sites/upload_files/mhrd/files/upload_document/revised_policy%20document20ofICT.pdf.

MHRD. (2014). *Education for all: Towards quality and equity India.* Retrieved from https://mhrd.gov.in/sites/upload_files/mhrd/files/upload_document/EFA-Review-Report-final.pdf.

MHRD. (2019). *Draft national education policy.* Retrieved from https://www.mhrd.gov.in/sites/upload_files/mhrd/files/Draft_NEP_2019_EN_Revised.pdf.

Mori, I., & Baker, D. (2010). The origin of universal shadow education: What the supplemental education phenomenon tells us about the postmodern institution of education. *Asian Pacific Education Review, 11,* 36–48. https://doi.org/10.1007/s12564-009-9057-5.

Narayan, D., & Petesch, P. (2007). *Moving out of poverty: cross-disciplinary perspectives on mobility.* Retrieved from https://documents.worldbank.org/curated/en/869851468339560298/Moving-out-of-poverty-cross-disciplinary-perspectives-on-mobility.

Nasreen, N., & Bano, T. (2016). Global objectives of quality education—Possibilities and challenges. *IOSR Journal of Humanities and Social Science (IOSR-JHSS), 21*(2), 16–24. Retrieved from https://www.iosrjournals.org/iosr-jhss/papers/Vol.%2021%20Issue2/Version-4/D021241624.pdf.

National Education Policy. (2020). *Leave no child behind, bridge digital divide.* Retrieved from https://www.thehindu.com/news/national/nep-focus-leave-no-child-behind-bridge-digital-divide/article32225887.ece#!

OECD. (2018). *The future of education and skills.* Retrieved from https://www.oecd.org/education/2030/E2030%20Position%20Paper%20(05.04.2018).pdf.

Ortiz, I., Daniels, M. L., & Engilbertsdóttir, E. (2012). *Child poverty and inequality: New perspectives.* New York: UNICEF.

Park, H. Y. (2007). Emerging consumerism and the accelerated 'Education divide': The case of specialized high schools in South Korea. *Journal of Critical Education Policy Studies, 5* (2). Available at: https://eric.ed.gov/?id=EJ837401.

Patterson, O. (1978). Inequality, freedom, and the equal opportunity doctrine. In W. Feinberg (Ed.), *Equality and social policy* (pp. 15–41). Urbana, IL: University of Chicago Press.

Roche, S. (2016). Education for all: Exploring the principle and process of inclusive education. *International Review of Education, 62,* 131–137. https://doi.org/10.1007/s11159-016-9556-7.

Sarangapani, P. (2009). Quality, feasibility and desirability of low-cost private schooling. *Economic and Political Weekly, 44*(43), 67–69.

Save the Children. (2015). *The hidden workforce: A study on child labour in the garment industry in Delhi* (Working Papers id: 7090, eSocialSciences). Available at: https://ideas.repec.org/p/ess/wpaper/id7090.html.

Sen, A. (1988). Capability and well-being. *Oxford scholarship online.* https://doi.org/10.1093/0198287976.003.0005.

Sen, A. (2003). *Development as capability expansion.* In: Fukuda-Parr S, et al.*Readings in human development.* New Delhi and New York: Oxford University Press.

Smith, T., & Noble, M. (1996). *Education divides: Poverty and schooling in the 1990's.* Oxford: Blackwell Publishing.

SNU. (2003). *2003 Year Student's Report.* Seoul, Korea: Seoul National University Press.

Stubbs, S. (2008). *Inclusive education: Where there are few resources.* The Atlas Alliance. Retrieved from https://www.eenet.org.uk/resources/docs/IE%20few%20resources%202008.pdf.

UNESCO. (2004). *Harnessing technologies towards quality education for all in Asia and the pacific.* Bangkok: UNESCO. Retrieved from https://repo.mercubuana-yogya.ac.id/onnopurbo/library/library-ref-eng/ref-eng-3/application/education/unesco/ICT_Brochure2004.pdf.

UNESCO. (2011). *Transforming education: The power of ICT policies.* France. Retrieved from https://www.unesco.org/new/fileadmin/MULTIMEDIA/FIELD/Dakar/pdf/Transforming%20Education%20the%20Power%20of%20ICT%20Policies.pdf.

UNESCO. (2012). *Education for global monitoring report: Expanding equitable early childhood care and education is an urgent need.* Retrieved from https://en.unesco.org/gem-report/sites/gem-report/files/216038E.pdf.

UNESCO. (2015a). *Adolescents twice as likely to be out of school as children of primary school age, say UNESCO and UNICEF.* Retrieved from https://en.unesco.org/news/adolescents-twice-likely-be-out-school-children-primary-school-age-say-unesco-and-unicef.

UNESCO. (2015b). *Global education monitoring report.* Retrieved from https://en.unesco.org/gem-report/about.

UNESCO. (2015c). *Education for All 2000–2015: India is first in the race to reduce out of school children.* New Delhi. Retrieved from https://mhrd.gov.in/sites/upload_files/mhrd/files/document-reports/PPT_GMR_2015.pdf.

UNESCO. (2015d). *Education 2030 Framework for Action to be formally adopted and launched.* Retrieved from https://en.unesco.org/news/education-2030-framework-action-be-formally-adopted-and-launched.

UNESCO. (2016). *Education 2030: Incheon declaration and framework for action: For the implementation of sustainable development goal 4.* Retrieved from https://uis.unesco.org/sites/default/files/documents/education-2030-incheon-framework-for-action-implementation-of-sdg4-2016-en_2.pdf.

UNESCO. (2018). *UNESCO study report on financing higher education in Arab States. UNESCO regional Bureau for education in the Arab States: Beirut.* Retrieved from https://en.unesco.org/sites/default/files/financing.pdf.

UNESCO. (2020a). *Education needs patience not quick success.* Retrieved from https://www.sdg4education2030.org/education-needs-patience-not-quick-successes-24-january-2020.

UNESCO. (2020b). *SDG 2030 steering committee statement for a sustainable future invest in education.* Retrieved from https://www.sdg4education2030.org/sites/default/files/202001/International%20Education%20Day%20Steering%20Committee%20Statement%20EN_0.pdf.

UNICEF & UNESCO. (2007). *A human rights based approach to education for all: A framework for the realization of children's right to education and rights within education.* New York: UNICEF. Retrieved from https://www.unicef.org/publications/files/A_Human_Rights_Based_Approach_to_Education_for_All.pdf.

United Nations. (1989). *Convention on the rights of the child. Audio visual library of international law.* Retrieved from https://legal.un.org/avl/ha/crc/crc.html.

United Nations. (2019). *The sustainable development goals 2019.* New York: United Nations.

UNO. (2015). Millenium development goals report. Retrieved from https://www.un.org/millenniumgoals/2015_MDG_Report/pdf/MDG%202015%20rev%20(July%201).pdf.

WEF. (2000). *The Dakar framework for action; Education for all: Meeting for our collective commitments.* France: UNESCO. Retrieved from https://sustainabledevelopment.un.org/content/documents/1681Dakar%20Framework%20for%20Action.pdf.

Winthrop, R., & Matsui, E. (2013). *A new agenda for education in fragile states.* Working Paper: Center for Universal Education at Brookings. Available at: https://www.brookings.edu/wp-content/uploads/2016/06/08-education-agenda-fragile-states-winthrop.pdf.

Winthrop, R, Williams, P.T., & McGivney, E. (2016). *Skills in the digital age-how should education systems evolve?.* Retrieved from https://www.brookings.edu/research/skills-in-the-digital-age-how-should-education-systems-evolve/.

World Bank. (2012). *Cambodia—education sector support project (English).* Washington, DC: World Bank. Available at: https://documents.worldbank.org/curated/en/405811468214829113/Cambodia-Education-Sector-Support-Project.

World Bank. (2014). *Philippines: National program support for basic education.* Available at: https://projects-beta.worldbank.org/en/results/2014/04/10/philippines-national-program-support-for-basic-education.

# Chapter 3
# Education Ecosystem

## A Chronological Perspective

## 3.1 Introduction

*Ecosystem*, as a terminology mainly used in the fields of ecological sciences, is understood as systemic communities of living organisms which interacts and connects with the non-living elements in the environment through various nutrient cycles and energy flows; creating a complex network between organisms and their environments (Chapin et al. 2000). Thus, within the purview of ecological studies, the basic definition of ecosystem, as articulated by Sir Arthur Tansley in 1935, has been defined as an assemblage of the biotic or living organism in association with abiotic or non-living chemical and physical parts of the environment that affect living organisms in a specific geographical context. Therefore, the main components of the concept are its *abiotic* and *biotic* features and the interactions between them in a specific *context* (Real and Brown 1991). Organisms can be considered as individuals or as communities. *Ecosystems* create a complex network of interdependence between the biotic and abiotic components.

Giving a multidisciplinary approach in recent times, the concept of ecosystem has incorporated humans both as external and internal agents that are reciprocally affected by other components of ecosystems (McDonnell and Pickett 1993). Thus, the concept of ecosystem is used metaphorically in various disciplines where the concept is often attributed with connectedness, equilibrium, resistance or resilience, diversity, and adaptability. For example, socio-ecological models were developed to study the dynamic interrelations among various personal and environmental factors to understand different social or economic systems (Bronfenbrenner 1979, 1989). Social ecology pays explicit attention to the social, institutional, and cultural contexts of people-environment relations. In the domain of health research, a socio-ecological perspective on health emphasizes both individual and contextual systems (e.g., personal attributes in the context of physical and socio-cultural environment) and their interdependence at multiple levels that includes: individuals, groups, and organizations (McLaren and Hawe 2005).

© The Author(s), under exclusive license to Springer Nature Singapore Pte Ltd. 2021
S. Bandyopadhyay et al., *Bridging the Education Divide Using Social Technologies*,
https://doi.org/10.1007/978-981-33-6738-8_3

The concept of ecosystem in the field of education was first introduced by Cremin (1976), who iterated the need to create "configurations of education," focusing on the urgency to interact, collaborate and survive with various components. In the domain of education, ecosystems are understood as the network of biotic actors and the abiotic or non-living elements that are essential for quality teaching and learning. These actors include learners, parents, family, peer group, edupreneurs, government agencies, religious bodies, content developers, institutional bodies, educational associations, and curriculum developers who form the *biotic components* of an education ecosystem. An education ecosystem, just like the concept of ecosystem, also comprises of the non-living or *abiotic components* which includes all available material means such as books and other form of teaching-learning materials and tools, buildings, classrooms, assessment tools, etc., that are needed to disseminate education. These abiotic components have the capability to directly influence the nature of interactions among the biotic actors; thus, creating a network of interacting entities. Apart from the biotic and abiotic components, education ecosystem is shaped by a set of external influencers: social, economic, political, and socio-psychological context. These external influencers heavily determine the performance of an education ecosystem in inculcating effective and quality learning in a specific geographic context. This will be discussed in detail in Sect. 3.2, where we will be defining and conceptualizing *education ecosystem* in greater detail.

The interactive premise of education ecosystem therefore makes it an effective lens to analyze the production and distribution logic of education, instead of education system, which attempts to view the process in a linear fashion from the perspective of one-way dissemination of knowledge from teachers to learners. Demystifying education from an ecosystemic perspective thereby helps in understanding the interactions and exchange between different biotic and abiotic components within an education ecosystem embedded in a specific geographical context, determined by its social-political-psychological-economic structure. This viewpoint also indicates that the education ecosystem has not been stagnant through the ages. Tracing the historical evolution of education ecosystem reveals how it has changed with the change in time, along with social, psychological, economic, and political settings. This chapter attempts to explore the nature and change of education ecosystem through the passage of time in Sect. 3.3.

The chronological evolution starts with hunting gathering societies, where the motivation to learn mostly emanated from mankind's hunger to know more and the process of learning was mostly informal. The external factors had minimal influence on education. Hunting gathering societies made way for ancient society, the era which witnessed a prospered civilization marked by the advent of private property and social stratification. While hierarchy based on ascriptive traits slowly marked its emergence during this time, it is in the medieval ages that social stratification got more formalized. Marked by conquests, invasions, and intense desire to dominate, civilizations prospered in the medieval ages. It is also during this period that formal schools made its emergence. Education mostly remained a privilege of the ruling elites. However, invention of printing press during the latter half of medieval ages can be marked as an event rapidly altering the pattern of education dissemination.

The relatively unrestricted circulation of information and ideas following the discovery of printing press created the provision for democratic distribution of education, thereby breaking elite's monopoly over education. While the invention of printing press can be identified as revolutionary in the process of education dissemination, it could not extend education to all social groups overnight. It is in the modern industrial age that attainment of education got directly related to professional achievement. The promise of economic return infused in education compelled every social group in this age to acquire education in order to secure employment possibilities. Schools and academic institutions followed a factory model of education, attempting to shape learners in a way, which will be beneficial in furthering the industrial logic (Sleeter 2015). The influence of the external factors got pronounced during this era, where social, economic, political, infrastructural, and socio-psychological parameters significantly shaped the attainment of education.

The chapter discusses the limitations of modern education ecosystem in Sect. 3.4 by drawing upon the interaction pattern prevalent in the education ecosystem of modern society. While this era nurtured the interaction between different biotic and abiotic agents of the education ecosystem in a way which is most suited to further the socio-economic and political motives of modern society, it heavily fell short in meeting the emerging demands of twenty-first century. The skills, which have socio-economic value in the twenty-first-century setting, are mostly intangible in nature, and therefore difficult to master through traditional means. Social and emotional intelligence, creativity, and our abilities to innovate, cooperate and co-create as well as other critical skills of the future feature to be essential requirements guaranteeing improved socio-economic performance in twenty-first century setting (National Research Council 2011). In order to make learners' capable to fulfill the requirements of twenty-first century market, it is mandatory to impart among learners innovative skills by establishing purposive collaborations between different agents within an education ecosystem. The conventional educational dissemination process, as prevalent in modern society, falls short in meeting these criteria. The chapter concludes with a critical concern—the need to reorient the operational dynamics of education ecosystem of modern society and how to optimally use the connecting spirit of contemporary digital technologies in the process of reorientation.

## 3.2 Defining Education Ecosystem and Its Significance

In the field of education, Cremin (1976) applied the concept of ecology creating "configurations of education"; focusing on the need to interact, collaborate, and survive with various entities. In the domain of education, ecosystems are understood as the network of living (biotic) and the non-living (abiotic) entities that are essential for quality teaching and learning (Renya 2011). These living entities or actors include learners, parents, family, peer group, edupreneurs, government agencies, religious bodies, content developers, institutional bodies, education associations, and curriculum developers who form the immediate biotic entities of an education ecosystem. An education ecosystem emanating from the generalized concept of ecosystem also nurtures the non-living (abiotic) entities which includes all available material means such as school infrastructure including both physical and IT infrastructures, teaching-learning materials, assessment tools, etc. (Fig. 3.1).

An education ecosystem is dependent on the mutual and reciprocal relationships and interconnectedness between biotic and abiotic entities that are influenced by the changing social, economic, political, and socio-psychological environment at large. Hence, apart from the biotic and abiotic components, education ecosystem is shaped by a set of external factors that act as *influencers*, which can be categorized under *four* dimensions: *social, economic, political*, and *socio-psychological*. This is shown in Fig. 3.1. These external influencers set the context and heavily determine the performance of an education ecosystem in inculcating effective and quality learning.

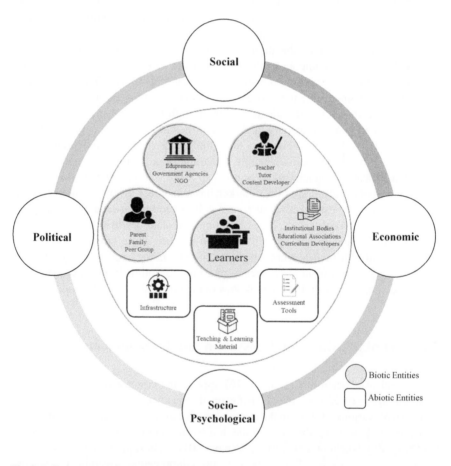

**Fig. 3.1** Components of education ecosystem

These external influencers in a geographical context determine whether the interaction of biotic and abiotic components will yield positive outcome in imparting quality education.

*The Social Factors* take into account social intricacies, norms, and regulations, which impact acquiring of education. For example, in the rural context of India, historically and till now the social context, to a large extent, has barred girls from getting access to higher education (Balatchandirane 2007).

*The Economic Factors* take a dual role in influencing education ecosystem. Firstly, access to quality education is expensive and very few can afford it. For example, educational disparity gets reflected in the Indian scenario due to the difference in education disseminated in high-cost private schools as compared to those of low-end government schools. While the private schools can be compared to the best educational institutions across the globe, they are expensive and only caters to learners from elite backgrounds. On the other end of the spectrum lies the low-end Government-aided public rural schools, where although education is affordable but the quality gets immensely compromised (Dey and Bandyopadhyay 2018). Secondly, education has always had an indirect yet very crucial relation with the market, which is heavily shaped by economic forces. Education only becomes effective if it can secure economic stability to the learner amidst a competitive market. At the same time, the demand of a particular economy also shapes the way education is perceived and imparted in a particular context.

*The Political Factors* take into account the political setup, the ideology of the ruling apparatus in influencing education ecosystem. For example, in Hitler's Germany, we can see how the Nazi body shaped education curriculum in a way to practice unquestionable obedience among the learners. Another example is the crisis in Syria. Since the beginning of the Syrian civil war in Syria in 2011, over half of its population has been displaced. One in four schools has been damaged, destroyed, or are being used as temporary shelters, leaving an estimated 2.08 million children and youth in Syria out of school (Kolstad 2018). The political parameter also includes the commitment of Government and other organizations in framing/implementing policies to disseminate education on a democratic level. If their commitments are not aligned to dissemination of universal and quality education, then education in itself can serve to be discriminatory force.

Finally, *Socio-Psychological*[1] *Factors* stem from individual motivation shaped by social factors, which heavily determine desire to learn and acquire education. For example, in underdeveloped nations, the financially insecure status of underprivileged communities has blurred their vision regarding the effectivity of education. Their hunger has made them in dire need of money, where the parents have no motivation to send their children to school (Chabba 2013). Rather, engaging the children in menial work at an early age seems practical from their context.

---

[1] Socio-psychological factors are personality traits and desires of an individual, shaped by the interaction between social (family, society, religion) and psychological factors (feelings, thoughts, beliefs).

We will discuss the above-mentioned ecosystemic entities (both living and non-living) and influence of external factors on them in greater details in subsequent sections. Keeping in mind the dynamic nature of an education ecosystem, it becomes essential to contextually observe and maintain the relation between different biotic and abiotic entities. Ultimately, to create an effective ecosystem, educational resources need to seamlessly work together within an interconnected network. For example, teachers interact with curriculum developers and content providers, who, in turn, moderate an abiotic component, i.e., teaching-learning materials. At the same time, it is not just the interaction of abiotic and biotic elements, rather their *configuration*, influenced by external influencers, that marks the fate of an education process. This ecosystemic perspective to education is in direct contrast to the conventional narrative of education, which views education as a teacher-centric, linear process of knowledge dissemination from teachers to students in a centralized fashion. This ecosystemic perspective views education as a collaborative process, characterized by mutual interdependence and interconnections between different biotic and abiotic elements that has the capability in disseminating quality education by encouraging dialogue and interactions among relevant entities involved in the education process.

Ideally, an effective education ecosystem must be based on purposive collaboration between different actors with external influencers, so that the effective learning can be imparted by negotiating with the hindrances and prospects laid by external factors. However, historically we have seen disruptions and breakdowns of the traditional education systems, giving rise to newer systems that are better aligned to its context and conditions. This dynamicity of educational ecosystem makes it crucial to intently study the alterations in education ecosystem over time. In the following section, we will provide an in-depth analysis of the way education ecosystem evolved with time, denoting the evolution of the interactions between biotic, abiotic, and external factors within an education ecosystem.

## 3.3   Evolution of Education Ecosystem: A Chronological Perspective

In order to understand the current functioning of the education ecosystems all across developed and developing nations, it is important to trace the evolution of educational ecosystems over time. This section explores education ecosystem as prevalent in hunting-gathering societies, ancient societies, medieval age, and modern age. A diachronic study of education ecosystem reveals how the dynamic nature of education ecosystem and the replacement of one ecosystem with another is a product of the changing social structures.

### 3.3.1 Education Ecosystem in Hunting Gathering Society

Hunting gathering societies are the most primitive and simplest form of societies (Nolan and Lenski 2008). The societal living was mostly communitarian in nature with a nomadic way of life. Hunting gathering societies represent a mode of subsistence dependent on exploitation of natural resources to sustain life and livelihood prospects. People in such societies resorted to the usage of crude tools like stone axes, spears and knives to hunt animals. Once the natural resources of a particular place exhausted, the members of these societies moved to other places. Without the basis of permanent settlement, these people were not interested in the accumulation of wealth.

Education in these societies was mostly practical, helping younger members to acquire skills required to sustain their way of living. The young were taught to manipulate tools, how to hunt and gather, how to fish, how to build huts, so on and so forth. Because of the absence of occupational specialization, children in these societies had to learn and adapt to their ways and cultural traditions (Gray 2011). The hunter gatherer children had to learn an enormous amount to become effective adults. Instead of being labor intensive, the hunting gathering way of life was knowledge and skill intensive in nature (Gray 2009). Instead of adults dictating the learning of things, children in hunting gathering societies were free to explore at all times. This was the product of the value system of their parents, who instead of valuing obedience, had a strong preference for cultivating children's wilfulness and independence. This was reflective of the non-hierarchical nature of those societies. Decisions in these societies were made on collective basis, through debate and discussion among members, instead of chiefs or "big men" imposing their will on the commoners (Lee 1990).

The social structure of hunting gathering societies requires assertiveness, creativity and individual judgment (DeVore et al. 1968). To adapt themselves to such a social structure, children acquired the skills of their culture and consolidated their knowledge through collective participation. During this time, formal and universal language was yet to make its widespread presence. Learning took place in natural settings and in informal ways, without the presence of dedicated infrastructure for the purpose. In the absence of structured teaching-learning material, knowledge was mostly disseminated via signs, symbols, gestures, paintings, and images. These signs, symbols, and gestures mainly comprised of teaching-learning materials in hunting gathering societies (Robinson 2009).

The education ecosystem of hunting gathering societies mainly comprised of learners, parents, family, and peer group among biotic components, teaching-learning materials in the form of cave painting, signs and symbols among the abiotic elements, where the social setup and social psychology served as the external enablers influencing the interaction between biotic and abiotic factors. Following, we will try to explain in brief the different biotic and abiotic components of the education ecosystem in hunting gathering societies and how the external social set up and social psychology influenced the interactions between the two.

The characteristics of biotic components of the education ecosystem in hunting gathering societies are as follows:

- *Learners*: Learners acquired knowledge mostly from hereditary and communitarian sources. Instead of following a standardized curriculum, learners acquired knowledge by playing freely and in interaction with the natural environment.
- *Parents, Family, and Peer Group*: In hunting gathering societies, there were seldom clear distinction between teachers and family members. It is the family members, including parents and peer group, who in this era were responsible toward accrediting within learners knowledge pertaining to social roles, responsibilities and awareness. Learning during that time occurred in absence of structured curriculum and was primarily driven by mankind's hunger to explore the world around and its surroundings.

The abiotic component is:

- *Teaching-Learning Materials*: There was no structured curriculum guiding teaching-learning materials in this time. As mentioned earlier, learning took place in natural settings and in informal ways, where in the absence of formal curriculum, knowledge was mostly disseminated via signs, symbols, gestures, paintings, and images. These signs, symbols and gestures mainly comprised of teaching-learning materials in hunting gathering societies. There were no fixed entities, who created these signs, symbols and images. Every member of the hunting gathering social setup were allowed to create such visual and imagery teaching-learning materials, which were in turn reflective of both individual and collective knowledge.

The external influencers impacting the learning entities can be elaborated as follows:

- *Social Factors*: There were no structured social norms and regulations guiding the interaction between biotic and abiotic factors of the education ecosystem during this time. Social structure, giving priority to assertiveness, creativity, and individual judgment, was conducive in ushering a learning environment, where learners were free to learn by exploring and interacting with their immediate natural environment (DeVore et al. 1968).
- *Socio-Psychological Factors*: In hunting gathering societies, two socio-psychological factors primarily motivated the learners: firstly, a fear for existence and secondly, the desire to explore immediate surroundings. The aspect of learning or acquiring of knowledge in hunting gathering societies was primarily triggered by these two factors. Learners acquired knowledge primarily to secure their existence in an uncertain and unknown surrounding. Secondly, in order to sustain their existence, they were inspired to explore their surroundings, so that they can have a peaceful existence by knowing the operational dynamics of nature. It is the socio-psychological parameters that primarily inspired the learning process and its nature in hunting gathering societies.

### 3.3.2 Education Ecosystem in Ancient Society

Traces of civilization of ancient society can be found in ancient Egypt, Persia, India, and in few other places. Hierarchy made its emergence in this era. Societal openness and lack of hierarchical structures in the hunting gathering societies soon got replaced with societal discrimination in the Ancient Society. Hierarchy based on birth started making its sway, where people with higher ascriptive traits started gaining privilege in different social domains. In ancient Egypt, we can see the prevalence of a caste-based social structure (University College London 2000). Flourishing around the fertile river bank of Nile, Egyptian civilization can often be identified as *the gift of the Nile*. The silt accumulated in the river bank gave Egyptian population enough prospects for agriculture. The fertile river valley of Nile and its ability in generating enough surplus crops marked the advent and ascent of Egyptian civilization, its social and cultural development (Wilkinson 2010). While during this era, Egyptians resorted to crude tools to cultivate crops, it is only with the passage of time and with the advent of improved tools, agriculture became the primary subsistence of the Egyptian people.

Contemporaneous with the Egyptian civilization, we can also trace flourishing of civilization in ancient India, which later became historically popular as the Indus Valley civilization. The civilization mainly flourished in what is today known as Pakistan and North-Western India and made its mark in history for its urban planning, baked brick houses, elaborate drainage, and water supply (Stein 2010). However, persistent drought led to migration of Indus Valley population from large urban centers to surrounding villages (Petraglia and Allchin 2007). During this time, migration of Indo-Aryan tribes from northwestern parts into Punjab can also be witnessed. Between the end of the Indus valley civilization and the emergence of second urbanization in Northern parts of India marked the advent of Vedic period, which was primarily characterized by the composition of the Vedas (Flood 1996). These Vedas or large collection of hymns bore an inseparable amalgamation of the religious culture of the Indo-Aryan tribes blended with preexisting religious cultures of the subcontinent, often said to have inspired the foundation of Hinduism. This was the period when caste systems were prevalent, giving rise to hierarchical system. Priests, warriors and free peasants were categorized one below the other within the highly complex hierarchical system of caste. Indigenous people were, however, excluded from the caste hierarchy, considering them to be occupationally impure.

Civilization in ancient Persia was marked by Achaemenids dynasty, established by Cyrus the Great (Briant 2002). Ranging from Balkans and Eastern Europe in the West to the Indus Valley in the East, Persian empire was larger than any other empire in ancient history. The vastness of the Persian empire can be rightly identified through the diversity the empire embraced. Comprising of people belonging from different origins and faiths, the Persian empire established its sway by virtue of its centralized, bureaucratic administration, commendable infrastructure such as road systems and a postal system, maintenance of one identity through the usage of one official language across its territories, and the development of civil services and an army (Holland 2007).

Having narrated in brief the societal structures of ancient civilizations that prospered across the world by citing some examples of ancient Egypt, India and Persia, we will now attempt in illustrating the education ecosystem, its nature and pattern of interactions in alliance to respective social settings existing during this Ancient Period. If we take into consideration the Egyptian context, then we can see that hierarchy prevalent in Egyptian society primarily shaped the acquisition and distribution of education. Similarly, in India and Persia, education became the weapon of the privileged group, shaped and in turn shaping the people belonging to the higher stratum of society. Unlike hunting gathering societies, where education was open to all and learning took place by virtue of exploring natural surroundings, in ancient society, democratic distribution of education got restricted (Gray 2008).

Being dominated by the powerful few, it is these people who designed the content of education, in accordance to what was considered important by the privileged group. If we take the instance of ancient Egypt, then we can see that education incorporated learning of professional activities, reading, and writing of hieroglyphics, mathematics and geometry (LEPOLE n.d.). Education in alliance to the Egyptian social structure was conformist and totalitarian in nature with the use of corporal punishment. While in hunting gathering societies, learning was initiated to cultivate willfulness and independence among learners, education in ancient societies primarily attempted in cultivating among learners' obedience and unquestionable reverence toward authoritative figures. In Egypt, only the sons of priests, architects, doctors and scribes were identified to have the potential ascriptive background to learn hieroglyphics (Wilkinson 2010), while higher education was only reserved for priests and religious elites.

The importance of religion in the paradigm of education can also be traced in ancient India. Religion formed the basis of caste system in India, and in turn also dictated the logic of distribution of education. The caste system of ancient India was a rigid one, comprised of "*chaturvarna*" or four groups: Brahmins (teachers and priests), Kshatriya (warrior), Vaishya (merchants), and Sudra (workers). It is only the Brahmins who had access to education in ancient Indian society (Stein 2010). Often Brahmin priests served as teachers in ancient Indian society, who taught the learners sacred religious texts. Only learners belonging from upper caste backgrounds were granted the permission to acquire education. Higher education in ancient Indian society was based on sacred religious texts, written in Sanskrit, which included literature, grammar, law, astronomy, medicine, and mathematics. Girls, considered as lesser beings, were also barred from attaining education in ancient Indian society. Religious institutions served as infrastructural spaces, where learners acquired education from religious gurus. The absolute authority of the religious teachers in ancient India shaped the system of education (Atlekar 1944).

The military and bureaucratic base of ancient Persian society made education a domain of state regulation. The pattern of education was mainly practical and moral in nature, disseminating bureaucratic skills among learners. Members belonging from higher ascriptive backgrounds, who were considered to be eligible in controlling state affairs, were mainly allowed to acquire education. Zoroastrianism (Religion Facts 2005), pre-Islamic religion dominated Persian faith. Territorial expansion of ancient Persian society was triggered by establishment of the said religion all across the world (Holland 2007). The religion is based on the idea of good over evil. While the victory of good over evil formed the base of education in the then Persian society, its practical nature is triggered by the desire to implement the mentioned victory. It is from the dualism of good and evil that Persian education acquired its moral nature.

Forming the above-mentioned discussion as the base, we will now proceed on to conceptualize the different biotic, abiotic, and external enabling factors of the education ecosystem in ancient society. The education ecosystem of ancient society comprised of learners, parents, family, and peer group, teachers and religious bodies as biotic components, infrastructure, and teaching-learning materials as abiotic components, where social and socio-psychological dimensions acted as external enablers in facilitating interaction between the biotic and abiotic components. Following, we will try to explain in brief the different biotic and abiotic components of the education ecosystem in ancient societies and how the external enablers influenced the interactions between the two.

The characteristics of biotic components of education ecosystem in ancient society are:

- *Learners*: Learners during this age mainly belonged from established social backgrounds, possessing ascriptive traits which are considered to be of high and esteemed social value. Acquiring education even in this age was determined by individual passion to know. However, the process of knowing, unlike in hunting-gathering societies, was not left on the learners. Rather, the contents to be learnt were determined by teachers, mostly from religious backgrounds.
- *Family, Parents, and Peer Group*: Similar to hunting-gathering societies, parents, family, and peer group, even in ancient society, retained their role in educating learners in the domain of building traditional family skills informally through socialization. However, it needs to be remembered that emergence of religious authorities as formal teachers during this age limited the role of family, parents, and peer group in educating the learners solely along informal ways.
- *Teachers*: This age saw the emergence of religious authorities as teachers. The pope of the church in Christian dominated areas, Brahmins in Hindu dominated regions, and prophets in Islamic areas acquired the role of teachers. Their pious and noble character, deemed of high value by the then societal structure sanctioned their absolute authority in educating learners. During Vedic age, teachers created their own learning space where learners resided with the teacher (the *guru*) to acquire uncontaminated and uninterrupted learning. Pupils were encouraged to stay with the *guru* because the religious prescriptions advocated that continuous and direct contact with a teacher of noble and pious character naturally produces greater effect on the minds of the students (Atlekar 1944).
- *Religious Bodies*: The religious bodies like the church and the temple acquired utmost importance in ancient societies, not only in determining religious aspects, but also affairs of state. By virtue of their omnipotent status, the religious bodies

were often guiding authorities in determining the nature of education to be disseminated, the appropriate content of education, and also in determining the potential teachers and learners, who can be appropriate disseminator and receptor of education, respectively. Often, we can find instances where education in ancient societies primarily received their funding from these religious bodies, thereby sanctioning the utmost importance of these bodies in the field of education (Joshi and Gupta 2017). While religious bodies in this age meddled with the process of education dissemination, education was still not institutionalized in ancient society. It was mainly disseminated on individual basis, premised on the personal relationship between the teacher and his subjects.

The abiotic components are:

- *Infrastructure*: Religious spaces, like the temple and church, served as infrastructural spaces to host educational activities in ancient societies. The sanctity of these spaces was in alliance to the nature of education disseminated during this era, which mainly attempted in cultivating pious and noble subjects.
- *Teaching-Learning Materials*: Religious texts served as teaching-learning materials in ancient societies. The morality infused in these texts served as the spirit under whose guidance learners acquired education.

The external influencers of the education ecosystem in ancient societies are:

- *Social Factors*: The social dynamics of ancient societies, unlike hunting-gathering ones, were not free and open. With the emergence of hierarchy, dissemination of education during this time served to reinforce social stratification. The instances of traces of early civilization in Egypt, India, and Persia points out how only a certain class of people, belonging from affluent social backgrounds, were granted the privilege to learn, where people from lower caste backgrounds and also females, considered as lesser beings were not considered to be worthy of attaining education.
- *Socio-Psychological Factors*: The socio-psychological make-up of individuals in ancient societies were mainly informed by some aspects such as the ability to become obedient, pious, and noble subjects and most importantly the urge to know more. While the first aspect affirmed learners' faith in an education system driven by religious personnel, the latter shaped the motivation of the learners of esteemed backgrounds to acquire knowledge. The way education acquisition and distribution in ancient society was shaped, it is clearly reflective of how social psychology acted as an enabler in realizing the learning process in the then society.

### 3.3.3  Education Ecosystem in Medieval Society

The medieval period in history, an age dominated by conquests and invasion driven by power hunger, saw the emergence and collapse of various empires. The Dark ages caused by Barbarian invasions led to the emergence of Carolingian period (also called as Carolingian Renaissance), with the Roman emperor Charlemagne as the ruler (Costambeys et al. 2011). This period saw nurturing and cultivation of literature, writing, arts, architecture, jurisprudence, and scriptural studies. This intellectual prosper led to the rebirth of education through reformation. Reformation happened in education leading to humanization of social relationships and respect for women (Cubberley 1920). Rebirth of education witnessed a transformation of Church's doctrine following rational philosophy. This age saw the emergence of biblically grounded systematic theology in education (Lillback 2016). The reformation in the field of education which happened during this time revised some elements of education in antiquity, where thirst for encyclopedic knowledge and personal development started gaining ground. This age saw the emergence of standardization of vocabulary to some extent, where Latin and Greek languages were mostly resorted to read all the manuscripts. The revised program in this time involved the study of body and mind, theoretical and practical knowledge, new skills and techniques, ancient languages, law and morality within schools and university parameters. It is in this age, with the advent of formal educational institutions on a wide scale that education first started getting institutionalized.

The reformed state marked the advent of humanism, where in the light of rational philosophy, man started gaining importance in terms of his self being, as opposed to divine essence. This philosophy radically altered social structure and consequently cast a major influence in reshaping art, architecture, education, politics, and other social domains. It is the invention of printing press during this time that gave further impetus to the social transformation that occurred following Reformation. The societal structure got permanently altered with the advent of printing press. The emergence of mechanical movable type printing introduced the era of mass communication, where unhindered circulation of information and ideas across the globe enabled the masses to enjoy the fruits of reformation. Popular awareness regarding the liberal tenets of reformation urged the masses to disregard unquestionable reverence toward dominant classes of society, which had by far been the norm. This subsequently threatened the power of political and religious authorities. Sharp increase in literacy broke the monopoly of literate elites on education, and the provision of mass-scale learning bolstered the emerging middle class. In this section, in the context of discussing education ecosystem, we have divided medieval age into two subdivisions—medieval society pre printing press invention and medieval society post printing press invention.

***Medieval Society Pre Printing Press Invention***: During this time, Jewish and Greco-Roman traditions prospered. These civilizations had a heavy intellectual base. History points out that Hebrew, Greek, and Roman languages had important contributions in the growth of global vocabulary and literary traditions (Bauer 2010).

Education in Jewish culture in the medieval ages was primarily the responsibility of family and involved reading, writing, and history of religion. Other than that, Mathematics, Astronomy, Hebrew literature, and Geography emerged as subjects which were taught to the pupils. While the introduction of these subjects happened within the confines of the educational curriculum, their contents were primarily dictated by sacred texts. This points out that in medieval ages, quite similar to that of ancient civilizations, religion retained its omnipotent status. Religion not only dictated the nature and pattern of education to be imparted, it also formed the basis of social stratification in medieval Jewish societies. Higher education was primarily disseminated by priests and scribes in the prophet's school. Dominance of religion in shaping education got reflected in the pattern of education disseminated in the Jewish societies of medieval age; teaching was based on cultivating discipline and unquestionable reverence toward religious authorities among learners, where through education learners were taught to believe in and effectively carry out religious rituals (Esposito 2014).

In the context of medieval Greece, Sparta emerged as an important city-state with a military base. The social structure of medieval Sparta shaped education accordingly, where the same was aimed to build brave, strong, and patriotic soldiers (Loizides 2012). Education in Sparta consisted of training for hunt, physical, and military services (Cubberley 1920). In order to make children physically strong, the pattern of education incorporated corporal treatments comprising of physical blows and suffering. Both girls and boys received similar education in Sparta, which prepared them for serving the community.

While Sparta can be recognized as the military base of medieval Greece, Athens was the intellectual hot-spot. It was the main educational, intellectual, and cultural center of medieval Greece. Athenian culture gave high emphasis on the study of arts and inculcated among pupils principles of both peace and warfare. It was aimed at cultivation of the students' physical, mental, and moral qualities. *A sound mind in a sound body* happens to be the motto of Athenian education, which gave equal emphasis to the study of both mind and body. The educational institutions of Athens mostly comprised of small private schools, where education was of high value. Although education in Athens was disseminated to inculcate among the learners a sense of order and beauty, it was not open to all. Social stratification prevalent in the then Athens heavily determined the acquisition of education (Davidson 1892). Although the son of a craftsman would learn to read, write, and count, it was the wealthier population who were only allowed to acquire complete education necessary to become real citizens. The pattern of education in Athens was driven to harmonize body and soul. Rituals, dance, singing, theater, games, and parades formed the basis of education.

While the Greeks developed civilization characterized by individual freedom and opportunity and a premium was placed on personal and political initiative, the Romans, unlike the Greeks, were practical, concrete, unimaginative, and executive people. The work of Rome was political, governmental, and legal, not artistic or intellectual like the Greeks. The Roman civilization established its prominence in medieval age under the rule of the Frankish king Charlemagne. A devout catholic, Charlemagne had a strong preference for military and religious education. Discipline, respect for power, and imitation were important part of education during the then Roman society (Cubberley 1920). Under the guidance of the monarch, monasteries in Roman society were encouraged to create schools for the Roman population.

It is during this time that education first got institutionalized. While in the earlier social phases, education dissemination was mostly individualized and restricted within the parameters of teachers' residence or religious spaces, in the medieval ages, involvement of monasteries in creating learning spaces or schools marked the advent of institutionalized education. However, institutionalized education did not necessarily made education an attribute of the masses. Social stratification, even in Roman societies, determined educational acquisition. Only people with valuable social and religious status were granted the permission to acquire education. Unlike Sparta, in Roman societies, girls were not allowed to acquire formal education. They were educated within families. In Roman society, pupils acquired professional skills in institutions known as guilds (Cubberley 1920). Family was responsible in inculcating domestic skills. Education, mostly moral, military, and religious in nature, comprised of physical training, song, music, good manners. The concept of honor was very important in Roman society. It is under the influence of such a social atmosphere, first European universities were developed, where the study of theology was formalized and authorized by both the Pope and King in unison.

Modern universities, like University of Bologna, University of Oxford, University of Naples Frederico II and many others trace their origins to medieval society. While these institutions in the medieval period operated under the guidance of Church and royal authorities, the creation of these spaces made way for the provision to detach education from religion and carry out educational dissemination in spaces, which are not meant for religious activities. Instead of being premised on individual relations between teachers and learners, education in the medieval ages with the creation of universities brought communities of teachers and learners in a single space for the purpose of learning. New teachers known as *sophists* came into the picture. The teachers and learners within the university parameter possessed in common a chapel, library, lecture rooms, and living rooms (Cubberley 1920).

The emergence of universities replaced the ancient method of individualized training in teachers' residences. With the emergence of universities, monasteries in Europe acquired the role to copy manuscripts, which often served as teaching-learning materials and copied manuscripts were made available in libraries for the students. University of Alexandria in Athens possessed the greatest library of manuscripts during this time (Webster 1913). Replacement of individualized training with universities saw the emergence of a defined curricula or course of study. Universities offered seven subjects: logic (thinking skills), Latin grammar, astronomy, geometry, rhetoric (how to write or speak to persuade), arithmetic, and music theory. These seven subjects were divided into the *trivium* and *quadrivium*. The easiest subjects were taught first: logic, grammar, and rhetoric. If the students passed in these subjects, they were allowed to continue the quadrivium—the remaining four subjects: advanced math, music, geometry, and astronomy. Eventually, universities added medical science, physics, moral philosophy, and metaphysics (cause and effect and defining the nature of things) (Cubberley 1920). This age saw the emergence of several university educated scholars who later made important contributions in the history of mankind.

Based on the above-mentioned discussion, we will now explain the different biotic, abiotic, and external enabling factors of the education ecosystem in medieval society. The education ecosystem of medieval society comprised of learners, parents, family, and peer group, teachers and religious bodies as biotic entities, infrastructure, and teaching-learning materials as abiotic entities, where social and socio-psychological factors acted as external enablers in facilitating interaction between the biotic and abiotic entities. Apart from being institutionalized, education ecosystem in the earlier phase of medieval society was quite similar to that of its former counterpart, as found in ancient society. Learners in medieval society, similar to that of ancient societies, were mainly coming from elite backgrounds. However, with the growing importance of power, conquests, and invasions, it became growingly important for the learners to establish themselves as brave and patriotic citizens and master physical training as a part of education. Thus, in medieval society, we can trace an emphasis on physical training included in the education curriculum. The role of parents, family, and peer group remained unchanged from ancient society, where these entities, even in medieval society, were entrusted in educating the learner along informal ways.

While in ancient society, the role of teachers, tutors, and content developers were entrusted to religious personnel, medieval period saw the emergence of secular entities called sophists, who ascended in the position of teachers to impart quality knowledge to learners. This does not mean that education got completely detached from religion during this phase. Religious institutions retained their influence as major funding bodies in the field of medieval education. However, religious authorities were supplemented by secular forces during this age, where several secular infrastructural spaces like universities and guilds came into emergence to host dissemination of professional skills to learners. However, in medieval era the funding to construct such infrastructural spaces primarily came from religious and royal authorities.

The social atmosphere of medieval society, marked by conquests and rebellion for territorial expansion, accordingly shaped the process of education. The urge for territorial expansion made education practical during this time. As a result, importance of physical training gained importance within the purview of education, where it was not only necessary for learners to become knowledgeable but also to possess courage and strength to defend one's knowledge and identity over others by force. This led to a social psychology, which can be identified as conducive in furthering the importance of practical education. While in hunting-gathering societies, fear of natural environment shaped the socio-psychological parameter of learners, in medieval period, fear of external invaders also triggered the learning process.

*Medieval Society Post Printing Press Invention*: The medieval society after the invention of printing press can be characterized as a social setup, marked by Reformation and its aftermath. The period following Reformation witnessed a scenario, where state gained precedence over individual. This age saw the emergence of popular assembly with an elective king and an independent developing system of law (MacCulloch 2005). Monasteries and churches were entrusted with the responsibility of restoring and prospering education. The universities, which got developed in the first phase of medieval age, got further developed during this time. With the development of universities as seat of rational learning began a period of world exploration and discovery, reawakening of the spirit of scientific inquiry and rise of democratic spirit (Cubberley 1920). This age thus can be identified as the era of important discovery; new trade route from Europe to India was discovered. This was a time when church started embracing new ideas, thereby showing greater tolerance.

It is during the fifteenth century that printing press got invented in Germany by Johannes Gutenberg, the German Goldsmith. 1450s saw the printing of Bible by Gutenberg. This 1300 page Bible is considered to be the second printed Bible, also referred to as the Gutenberg's Bible which was produced in 180 copies. With the passage of time, printing press, while made its emergence in Germany, gradually spread to the rest of Europe, doing justice to the proliferation of humanistic education (HISTORY 2018).

The invention of printing press, introducing the era of mass communication which not only contributed in producing teaching-learning materials in bulk, but altered the entire structure of society (Eisenstein 1980). The relatively unrestricted circulation of information and ideas following the advent of printing press broke the elite's monopoly on education and made the provision, where education could reach the mass. With the advent of printing press, the emergence of formal educational institutions scaled up. While schools were present in England and in the rest of Europe in ancient society, post printing press invention ushered the urge to establish schools in large numbers (Gillard 2018). It is a shift toward democratic distribution of education following the advent of printing press that marked the era of humanism, where man started gaining importance in terms of his self being, as opposed to divine essence.

The birth of printing press saw the advent of elementary and primary education all across Europe (Cubberley 1920). These schools taught in native language. Following the advent of printing press, the reformed social scenario gave a new emphasis to the development of secondary schools by supplying them with large amount of subject matter and a new motive. The new motive affirmed that education for children was intended for self-development, instead of being intended for the service of state or church. During this time, French society made its prominence, where French language got introduced in the mainstream educational curricula. The early traces of French society's love for equality got manifested in its religious fraternity during this time, where the same in Reims, located in the Grand East region of France, enabled boys from poor families to learn professional skills required to carry out successful trade (LEPOLE n.d.). Availability of teaching-learning materials in bulk during this phase successfully enabled education to break elite's monopoly over the same. The invention of printing press enabled pupils from not so affluent backgrounds to get the taste of education (Eisenstein 1980). However, it must be remembered that while this phase saw the democratic distribution of education to some extent, education was still largely dominated by religious fraternities, who were still prone to practice discrimination along ascriptive lines.

After giving a brief idea of the medieval societal set up post printing press invention, we will now proceed to explain the education ecosystem of this era. Different biotic, abiotic and external influencers of the education ecosystem of medieval society after the invention of printing press is narrated below:

The biotic entities of the education ecosystem during this era were:

- *Learners*: This phase saw a change in the learners' background. While in ancient and first half of medieval society, education was majorly restricted to the social elites, post printing press invention, availability of teaching materials in bulk led to a democratic distribution of education. In this phase, we can see the earliest instances of working-class group being granted the privilege to acquire education.
- *Parents, Family, and Peer Group*: With democratization of education process and establishment of formal education institutions after the invention of printing press, the role of peer group in the learning process became important. However, participation of parents and family was restricted in the domain of building traditional family skills and social skills among learners.
- *Teachers and Content Developers*: While religious authorities mainly served as teachers in this phase, we can also see traces of emergence of secular entities in the role of teacher. These entities were primarily hired by priests, popes, and other personnel of religious influence and were mainly paid by charitable institutions (Cubberley 1920).

Following the advent of printing press, mass-scale availability of teaching-learning materials saw the emergence of content developers, who mostly belonged from religious fraternities during this time. These entities primarily decided the contents, following which students were educated.

- *Religious and Independent Agencies*: Religious bodies retained their influence over education in this phase. However, the printing press, creating the provision for democratic distribution of education, somewhat reduced the omnipotence of these authorities in the field of education. Religious authorities, whose very ideology is stratificatory, gets negated with the vision of democratic distribution of education, where one and all, irrespective of their caste, religion, and background, was granted the privilege to acquire education. The spread of democratic education following reformation enabled the expansion of independent charity or public education institutions in England and in rest of Europe, where the premise of education for all was laid.

The abiotic components of the education ecosystem are:

- *Infrastructure*: This phase saw the emergence of several schools, which served as infrastructural spaces to disseminate education. Different parts of Europe also witnessed the emergence of charitable and low-cost schools during this time, which attempted in imparting affordable education to pupils from poor background.
- *Teaching-Learning Materials*: The advent of printing press created a direct impact on the teaching-learning materials during this time. Mass availability of teaching-learning materials enabled the mass to access these, thereby breaking the elite's monopoly over education

The external enabling factors of the education ecosystem are:

- *Social Factors*: The era of humanism influenced the social set up in a way, which subsequently became conducive in ushering an atmosphere, where democratic distribution of education can take place. The gradual importance of man in terms of his self being, as opposed to divine essence, contributed to some extent in nullifying the sanctity of ascriptive traits, thereby making every person worthy of acquiring education. Democratization of access to information and knowledge motivated men to identify themselves as worthy of attaining formal education, irrespective of his ascriptive traits.

- *Political Factors*: The age-old exploitation and discrimination that was practiced in the name of ascription was gradually getting questioned during this time. The age of humanism enabled men to counter the exploitation that had been normalized so far in the name of social status. Importance of man in terms of his self-being enabled them to demand certain rights by virtue of being man, even though he had unfavorable birth backgrounds. This created a political atmosphere during this time, which was conducive to the prosper of democratic distribution of education (Cubberley 1920).

### 3.3.4  Education Ecosystem in Modern Society

The rise of modern society started with industrialization and is marked by a decisive shift in socio-economic and political setting. From an economic standpoint, industries started to become the primary mode of production replacing agriculture, which happened to be the major means of sustenance in ancient and medieval age. The rapid boom of industries led to widespread migration from village to urban areas. Factories developed in numbers, where thousands of people left agriculture to seek employment as industrial workers. While occupation in ancient and medieval societies was primarily caste-based, emergence of industries paved the path for a social scenario, where people from all backgrounds can seek employment, irrespective of their ascriptive credentials. This does not mean that social stratification got eradicated in modern times. Rather, modern society, unlike its ancient and medieval counterpart, gave way for a new kind of stratification following economic lines. Along with the persistent caste-based distinctions in some geographical locations, modern society too witnessed class-based discriminations wherein individuals were discriminated on the basis of their financial status and not much on their ascriptive backgrounds (Cubberley 1920).

During this time, education emerged as that ladder which enabled individuals to secure upward mobility in the class ladder. The importance of achievement over ascription in modern society directly linked education with economic returns. In modern society, the primary motivation to learn got linked to securing better employment possibilities. It is only education that enabled individuals to secure better employment possibilities, thereby giving them the scope for upward mobility in the class ladder.

In this context, most notable model to depict the industrial paradigm of education is the Prussian model of education system that worked like a factory system (Marshall 1990). This model of education system realized in 1819 was based on the philosophy of controlling and dictating the minds of the learners. The Prussian model of education system comprised of schools like a factory, text books, and teachers operating around the authoritative principle. This model of education system dictated learners as to what to think, why to think, when to think, and duration of the thinking among students. This resulted in creation of a system that controls the minds of its future citizens (Lee 2014). The factory model of education is best suited to further the industrial logic of capital accumulation, which heavily shaped the social and economic conditions of industrial age. In order to sustain the industrial society through expansion of capital, the factory model of schooling was needed to produce "passive" and "productive" workforces; hence, in schools, learners were shaped according to the laid down specifications to meet the various demand of industrial society. The factory model of education attempted in cultivating "similar" entities, trained in standardized curriculum, thereby creating an obedient workforce. The inner life of the school, where the students were encouraged to practice unquestionable submission, thus became an anticipatory mirror, a perfect introduction to industrial society. The rapid development of institutions following industrialization served as appropriate spaces to host such educational activities.

Thus, the industrial paradigm of education follows a centralized bureaucratic model and administrative hierarchy of education, where the central education ministry holds the major decisions in creating a management body that takes care of monitoring and management of operative education systems. The central government is responsible toward controlling and standardizing the essential components of the existing education ecosystem such as students, teachers, funding, and facilities. The education ecosystem in the modern age is thus an assemblage of masses of students, teachers, and a centrally located school similar to a factory setup, resulting in an education ecosystem depending on factory pipeline system. Thus, the education ecosystem in this period primarily attempted in cultivating professional and cognitive abilities of learners through standardized curriculum, often depriving pupils of self-explorations, thereby degrading their courage to learn anything new (Luksha et al. 2017).

The Prussian Model too focused on building capacities of the teachers. The objective of such training was to force teachers to emphasize on cultivating the nature of a child rather than just focusing on the mind. Training of teachers was necessary, as it is useless to have the machinery without the skilled workman, or the well-trained workman without the suitable premises (Marshall 1990).

The basic characteristics of the Prussian education ecosystem were: free schooling for poor, professional teachers, standard salary for teachers, extended school year for adult learners, standard process of monitoring of students, and curriculum focusing on building national identity.

This Prussian education system that originated in the eighteenth century is still followed in most countries worldwide in this current age of twenty-first century. The basic characteristics of the Prussian model was instilling absolute obedience and uniformity within the students and ignoring the desires of the students within the framework of education. This changed paradigm of education in industrial era contradicts the philosophy of the hunter-gathering society where learning did not depend on memorization of lessons. The playful and explorative instincts of children get compromised in an education system characterized by repetition and memorization of lessons. This aspect has been beautifully captured by Toffler (1970) who decried the "Industrial Era School" in his book Future Shock:

> Mass education was the ingenious machine constructed by industrialism to produce the kind of adults it needed. The problem was inordinately complex. How to pre-adapt children for a new world – a world of repetitive indoor toil, smoke, noise, machines, crowded living conditions, collective discipline, a world in which time was to be regulated not by the cycle of sun and moon, but by the factory whistle and the clock.

The factory model of education systems introduced in the Western part of the world in the seventeenth and eighteenth centuries, finds a strong place in the developed and developing nations through the process of colonization. This model has primarily influenced the colonial countries such as Africa, Latin America, and India during their respective periods of colonialism. Frantz Fanon in his major works discusses the influence of this factory system of education on third world country education system, resulting in the "colonization of the mind." Fanon opposed the argument that the principles and philosophies propounded in the West is applicable in all parts of the world, making the norms of the West universalized (Fanon 1963). The colonizers most often tend to believe that they are helping the "colonized" in improving their lives and their environment. The colonizer thus creates a distorted image of the colonized. This uneven relationship and acceptance of the same started guiding and shaping the nature and process of education in colonized countries as a replication of the western form of education model (Shizha and Kariwo 2011).

Giving a brief idea of the way education is shaped in modern society, we will now proceed on to narrate the different biotic and abiotic entities along with the external influencers of the education ecosystem in modern society, which governs the interaction between biotic and abiotic factors of the education ecosystem (Fig. 3.2).

The characteristics and functions of the biotic components of the education ecosystem are:

- *Learners*: In the modern industrial era, learners from all backgrounds have provisions to learn. However, the nature of education they receive is dependent on their socio-economic status and particular geographical locations. Moreover, unlike ancient and medieval societies, modern society make educational attainment directly proportional with economic incentives. This motivates learners from all socio-economic backgrounds in modern age to acquire education in order to further their market prospects (Cubberley 1920).
- *Parents, Family, Peer Group*: Parents, family, and peer group accounts to be the most immediate factors of a learner's learning environment. In modern industrial society, these entities are mainly responsible in educating a learner in informal ways by virtue of socialization. In modern society, parents, family, and peer group form assistive components to a learner in the process of learning. However, non-uniform awareness and educational levels of these entities often creates differentiation in the assistance they provide. While learners having learned family and

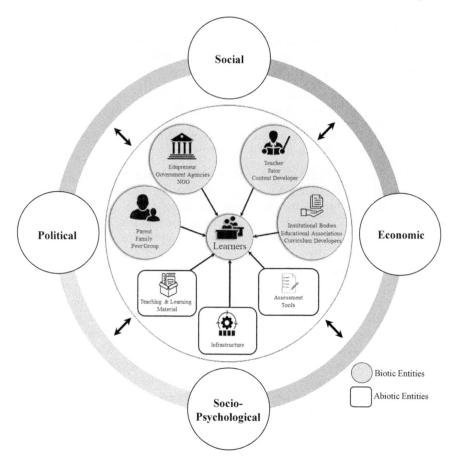

**Fig. 3.2** Education ecosystem in modern age

peer group shows better learning outcomes, the ones belonging from illiterate backgrounds consequently show deplorable learning outcome (Park 2007).

- *Teachers, Tutors, and Content Developers*: In this age, due to attempts toward secularization of education, religious personnel no longer served as the sole teachers. This age saw the emergence of teachers as professional entities, who were mainly appointed by the state or by private and non-governmental entities. Working in alliance with the private and government agencies, teachers, tutors and content developers not only shaped the nature of education to be disseminated, but were also responsible in practically disseminating the decided pattern of education among the learners. They were also responsible in administering the assessment tools, which will be most suitable to appropriately judge the learning outcome of a student. The resultant standardization of teaching process often restricted the freedom of teachers on how to teach. In the modern society, students were taught keeping in mind the national concerns. The importance of teachers in the modern education ecosystem makes attainment of quality education heavily reliant on the teachers' teaching pattern. Institutions with quality and accountable teachers therefore show an improved learning outcome of students in comparison to those institutions, which suffer from teacher absenteeism, low quality, and accountability (Dreze and Sen 2013).

- *Edupreneurs, Government Agencies, and NGO*: The importance of education in modern society not only made the same a state concern, but also attracted several private players or edupreneurs, who took an active role in this time to shape the nature of education in modern society through creation of profitable academic institutions. Along with private and public bodies, several non-governmental organizations during this time also contributed in devising strategies and practical pathways of disseminating education following a not-for-profit model. These entities were responsible in building infrastructures to host educational activities and administering appropriate teaching-learning materials which will shape learners to serve the logic of industrial expansion. These entities also shaped the assessment parameters, against which the learning outcomes of the learners will be measured. A critical investigation of practical operations highlights how the policies and strategies of these bodies directly contribute in unequal distribution of education in modern days. While private players often come up with equipped educational infrastructure, it is often expensive and unaffordable to the common mass. On the other hand, while government and non-governmental bodies make the provision for affordable education, quality often gets compromised in such a scenario (Kumar 2011).
- *Institutional Bodies, Educational Associations, and Curriculum Developers*: Due to the emergence of several educational institutions during this time, there was a need to manage these institutions from an administrative angle. Thus emerged institutional bodies, who were responsible to manage educational institutions from an administrative angle. Along with institutional bodies, educational associations emerged during this time who were mainly responsible to give a structured shape to education. These Educational Associations or commonly called Educational Boards, in alliance with curriculum developers shaped and formalized content of education to be disseminated to the learners. These three entities in amalgamation were responsible for formalizing and giving a structured shape to the pattern of education that a learner receives. These bodies directly interacted with Edupreneur, Government Agencies, and NGOs, where while the former helped the latter in devising strategies, policies, and practical pathways of disseminating education, the latter in turn directly influenced the standardized paradigm following which educational content and aspects were structured and formalized. It is the structuration and formalization of education done by Institutional Bodies, Educational Associations, and Curriculum Developers that directly guided the teaching ways of teachers and tutors. The content formulated by content developers was directly influenced by these bodies, following whose structuration guidelines, educational contents were created. Apart from influencing biotic elements, these bodies also influenced abiotic parameters, thereby

deciding infrastructural requirements and shaping teaching-learning materials and assessment parameters.

The abiotic elements of the education ecosystem are:

- *Infrastructure*: Partial detachment of education from religion in the modern industrial society saw the emergence of secular spaces to host educational activities. These infrastructures were the direct product of policies, strategies, and practical pathways undertaken by Edupreneur, Government Agencies, and NGOs in the process of education dissemination. However, some instances can be seen wherein religious-educational activities were disseminated in not-for-profit modes in several religious-educational hubs such as that of the Madrasas where pupils belonging from the Islamic religion enrolled themselves in these schools to get educated. Shaping a learner's tangible and intangible learning environment, infrastructural parameters are somewhat responsible in shaping the teaching parameters of teachers and tutors. For example, in modern industrial era, where students came in numbers, teaching was difficult in absence of proper infrastructure like classroom, blackboards, etc. However, practical operations often reflect how quality infrastructure in modern times is reserved for the privileged group of learners, where the learners coming from underprivileged backgrounds are often exposed to educational infrastructure, which are not well-equipped (Dey and Bandyopadhyay 2018). Schools as infrastructural spaces rose to utmost importance during this time, which majorly controlled the acquisition and distribution of educational resources. While low-cost public or government sponsored schools lacked both quality education and infrastructures, expensive private units established their influence as centers of excellence during this period. This automatically creates a socio-economic divide, where the marginalized are denied scopes to attain education and subsequently lack of quality education restricts their life and livelihood prospects (Musthafa and Stephen 2019).
- *Teaching-Learning Materials*: Teaching-learning materials of modern industrial age were primarily formulated by public and private entities, in alliance with institutional bodies, educational boards, and curriculum developers. The teaching-learning materials in the modern society were formulated in a way, which is most appropriate to further the logic of industrial expansion. Factory model of education system facilitated teaching-learning materials that are monotonous, un-updated, and non-critical in nature. The reason is the production of conformist variety of learners, focusing on securing similar kind of industry-related work during this age. However, with the advent of Information and Communication Technology during the Modern Age, curriculum developers started updating teaching-learning materials by making them digital, attractive, and interactive in nature, making learning enjoyable. However, this form of digital teaching-learning materials has limited access only among those who can afford high-cost quality education.
- *Assessment Tools*: In modern society, education being the key to achievement, was infused with the promise of economic return. Hence it was necessary to devise assessment tools, against which the learning outcome of a student can be measured in a standardized manner. Institutional Bodies, Educational Associations, and

Curriculum Developers directly impacted assessment tools, their nature and parameters against which the learner's credentials were to be assessed. The nature of assessment was shaped in a way to favor learners belonging from elite backgrounds. While privileged learners got fair chances in performing better, learners of underprivileged backgrounds, because of the lack of quality teachers, infrastructures, teaching-learning materials, and other educational resources possessed less chances of scoring high in conventional assessment parameters (Lee 2014).

The external enablers of the education ecosystem in modern society are:

- *Social Factors*: The social set up in modern industrial society saw a hierarchical social order following a class-based stratification logic based on the financial status of individuals. However, this does not imply that modern society saw complete eradication of discrimination along ascriptive lines. A critical investigation of modern education ecosystem reveals how in the context of certain underdeveloped nations, girls are often denied the access to education, which is considered as an attribute suitable and reserved for the superior gender (Balatchandirane 2007). Along with gender discrimination, traces of unequal distribution of education along racial lines can also be seen, where modern education ecosystem often bars learners from certain birth backgrounds into acquiring quality education (Islam 2018). The uniqueness of modern age can be traced to the emergence of a social structure, which identified education to be indispensable in the process of holistic socio-economic development of mankind. Education being directly associated with economic incentives created a social consciousness, which deemed education to be very important (Luksha et al. 2017). However, affordability of quality education being a major parameter, it is often seen that only the socially privileged group gained access to quality educational resources during this time. The marginalized sections, lacking access to quality education due to the issue of affordability, remained incapacitated in furthering their economic status by virtue of education. This age thus witnessed the convergence of social and economic status, where the socially impoverished remained economically impoverished in modern society in spite of several governmental policies undertaken to enable equitable distribution of education.
- *Economic Factors*: It is in the industrial age, where achievement got precedence over ascription, educational attainment got directly linked with economic returns. From an economic standpoint, schools of modern society became production spaces cultivating market consciousness among learners through a factory system of teaching and learning (Thompson 2019). In that context, only that education was considered relevant by the curriculum developers, which furthered the logic of capital accumulation through industrial expansion. As a result, access to quality education, which ensures economic return, became expensive and very few could afford it (Dey and Bandyopadhyay 2018).
- *Political Factors*: The political context in this age was primarily governed by ruling elites, where production and distribution logic of education was mostly centralized in the hands of the powerful few. However, the role of government in unequal distribution of education remains paradoxical (Flaten 2017). This age saw

the emergence of several policies in the formal civic domain to facilitate democratic distribution of education. However, while policies assured equal distribution
of education irrespective of an individual's caste, creed, and social background in
the formal level, its practical implementation is very much dependent on the operational dynamics prevalent in the immediate socio-political environment. Political
power concentrated in the hands of the few while saw the emergence of liberal
policies, the unequal distribution of power restricted practical translation of policies, thereby keeping the same restricted within the formal domain. Moreover,
consumerism in education driven by privatization made little provisions for the
marginalized to derive benefit out of policy formulations (Park 2007).

- *Socio-Psychological Factors*: While the social psychology in modern society
  nurtures individual motivation to learn in order to economically succeed, the
  shaping of psyche is done in accordance to the socio-economic positioning of
  individuals. Individuals of affluent backgrounds are motivated to learn advanced
  science, technology, and social sciences to broaden their intellectual horizon,
  whereas underprivileged groups are denied access to quality educational resources
  and possess low aspiration level. They also have poor social capital, where they
  do not have appropriate role models to motivate them into pursuing education on
  higher levels (Liu et al. 2019).

## 3.4   Limitations of Modern Education Ecosystem

The earlier section sheds light on the interaction between biotic, abiotic, and external
influencers as prevalent in the modern education ecosystem. An in-depth investigation reveals how the external surroundings positively contributed in establishing the
dominance of factory model of education all across the globe. The factory model
of education incorporating learners from all backgrounds led to huge increase in
school enrolments all across the world. Nations with both autocratic and democratic
mode of governance got attracted to the idea and practice of mass schooling. The
wave of mass schooling reached its zenith in the post World War II scenario, driven
by nationalism and the urgency to identify education as the fundamental right for
all children. However, schooling system as a genre attracts a multitude of critics
from different related domains. Time magazine on December 10, 2006 reported a
story on stagnancy in education stating that the conventional educational practice
has failed to change itself in alliance to the changing socio-political and economic
scenario. The article metaphorically argued that if Rip van Winkle suddenly woke up
after a century, he would notice drastic changes around him, with the sole exception
of school being a familiar sight. Although technological, infrastructural, and other
transformations in the surroundings will dazzle Winkle, it is the school, its unaltered
operations that will give him a familiar atmosphere. If we critically analyze then we
can rightly conclude that conventional education system, premised on the Prussian
model, have not matured at all with the passage of time (Sleeter 2015). It centers
around a physical infrastructure called school, which can be identified as a building

where learners regularly go, following a set pattern and for a stipulated period of time. The pattern of education disseminated and the ways of disseminating knowledge has mostly remained unaltered with the change in time. This stagnancy can also be explicitly noted in the anthem of mass schooling, where schools across the globe mostly follow a similar pattern in determining where, when, and how children learn.

Children across the globe go to schools in stipulated times, although the hours spent in school vary from one national context to the other. In schools, teachers guide children with the prescribed activities, where the latter are grouped by age and receive education based on the curriculum decided by concerned authorities, without incorporating inputs from students themselves. Observation, feedback, and peer discussion seldom feature to be evaluating parameters. A variety of subjects are taught to students during school hours. Students go through this teacher-centric learning pattern, with special emphasis given to academic subjects. This pattern of education requires the students to learn via repetition and memorization of facts, where the students' progress is ultimately tested following examinations administered by teachers. Excessively teacher-centric and centralized, factory model of education disallows learners to cultivate their agency (Luksha et al. 2017). Learners in this education model are imparted knowledge following a linear way of dissemination from teachers, where they are forced to be passive recipients in the learning process.

Many scholars have explicitly postulated the limitations of modern education ecosystem in terms of poor quality teaching equipment, old or un-updated text books, non-super visionary teachers, populated classrooms, absentee students, and rigid monitoring system (Pigaglio 2016; Bereday 1969; Coombs 1968). It is highly hierarchical focusing on discrimination between a high-talented from low-talented learners, outcasts from intellectual elites (Luksha et al. 2017). The learners from marginalized backgrounds lack quality teachers, adequate classrooms, and quality teaching-learning materials. The consequent disparity existing within an education ecosystem comprising of students, teachers, and materialistic possessions of teaching materials and the learning environment are the prime cause behind the emergent crisis of modern education systems throughout the world. The factory system of education characterized by hierarchical differentiations nurtures the "elitist" educational system; creating gaps within the mass. This attempts in creating education divide. While the discussion in the earlier sections of this chapter shows how education has been an exclusive force historically, reserved for the social elites, it is only in modern society that education got directly linked to securing economic incentives. It is true that education divide has existed since time immemorial, but the economic return to education, a feature of modern society, made the aspect of education divide a crucial concern, which is urgent to mitigate in order to ensure holistic development.

The only positive effect the modern education ecosystem has created is extending education formally to all groups of people. Such an educational extension is only limited to providing access to educational resources to the marginalized groups of people (World Bank 2012, 2014). The expected belief was that improved access will satiate the educational demands of the marginalized, thereby helping them in securing lucrative opportunity scopes for themselves. Although the intentions of these initiatives were noble, it needs to be remembered that access alone is not sufficient in improving the learning outcomes of the marginalized group. Even if the underprivileged are granted access to educational resources, they do not possess the capability to exploit access to educational resources to nurture their self-credential and in turn pronounce their opportunity prospects. The focus on providing access, without taking necessary initiatives to nurture capability and opportunity scopes of learners creates a scenario, which sustains and intensifies education divide in modern society.

Lack of capability, designating multi-faceted impoverishment of human life, is an eminent product of education divide. Education divide does not result solely due to lack of access to quality educational resources. In certain cases, it can be seen that while learners have adequate access to educational resources, they may not develop the desired capability required for human functioning through disseminated education, thereby sustaining education divide. Being capable refers to the learner's credential in possessing operating abilities to process and apply acquired education. This implies that an enhanced capability helps a learner to be independent in his/her ability to think, logically reason, and also be able to taken informed actions. This capability to critically think and understand would later help the learner exploit his/her opportunity prospects (Sen 1988, 2003). As shown in Chap. 1, education divide persists because of the simultaneous existence of access, capability, and opportunity divide prevalent among marginalized groups of people in modern society. It is the inability to cultivate holistic credentials among learners that mark the crisis of modern education ecosystem and subsequently paves the path for sustaining and intensifying education divide.

In cases, where provision for equal access to educational resources has been made, it is often seen that such initiatives are seldom practically translated in modern society. While modern society has witnessed the emergence of several policies to extend educational resources to all, marginalized groups of learners are still exposed to low quality biotic and abiotic educational conditions. The learning outcome of learners from marginalized backgrounds often get affected due to the lack of quality teacher, unfavorable family backgrounds, low quality teaching-learning materials and educational infrastructure, and so on. The first step toward mitigating education divide is to make provisions for improved biotic and abiotic educational facilities to all groups of learners. The emergence of digital technologies and the promise it offers can be identified as an aspect of utmost value in this context.

The emergence of digital technologies in the latter half of modern society has radically altered the socio-economic operations of contemporary times. The promise of digital technologies in altering conventional patterns of social operations has accredited the same with a revolutionary destiny, which has been gradually deployed in the field of education to bring redeeming transformations (Privateer 1999). Introduction of digital technologies in the field of education has witnessed a change in the content of teaching-learning materials in modern era. Supplementing teaching-learning materials with digital multimedia contents and audio-visual aids leads to formulation of contents which are attractive to students. Use of audio-visual materials has the capability to produce contents, which can be retained better by students.

Moreover, digital technologies also have the capacity to usher virtualized teaching and learning. As shown earlier, lack of quality teacher can be identified as one of the major reasons marking the crisis of modern education ecosystem. Digital technologies offer the promise of providing students with access to specialized instruction disseminated by teachers beyond local context. Finally, freed from physical restrictions, digital technologies have the potential to offer quality virtual teaching-learning to remotest corners of the modern world (Herselman et al. 2018). The above-stated attributes of digital technologies therefore offers promising prospects in improving biotic and abiotic conditions of modern education ecosystem. Because of the said potential, we will now attempt in investigating how digital technologies can be optimally used in the field of education to better the learning outcomes of learners in modern society, which can be identified as the first step toward mitigating education divide. This we will take up in detail in the following chapter.

## 3.5  Conclusion

The chapter discusses at length the conceptual and operative dimensions of education ecosystem. After defining and explaining the significance of education ecosystem, the chapter traces the evolution of education ecosystem over time. An in-depth analysis of the evolution of education ecosystem explains how the biotic, abiotic, and external influencing parameters of education ecosystem have changed historically. By tracing the historical evolution of education ecosystem, we have finally arrived at the interaction and operational patterns of modern education ecosystem. A critical investigation of modern education ecosystem has enabled us to identify the intrinsic limitations of the same in improving learning outcomes of students in a holistic scale. This urges us to explore the potential of digital technologies in the field of education.

With this concern in mind, we move onto Part II of our book *(Education Ecosystem in a Digitally Connected World: Bridging the Education Divide)*, where we have attempted in exploring how digital technologies can be exploited optimally in the process of mitigating extant education divide. In doing so we have attempted in tracing how Information and Communication Technologies (ICT) first got introduced in the field of education and the way it evolved to create an education ecosystem characterized by improved biotic and abiotic conditions. However, the chapter ends with the incapacitation of ICT measures in providing improved facilities to all groups of learners. Utilization of ICT in education has primarily been secured for the elitist group of learners. In cases where ICT has contributed in improving biotic and abiotic educational components for the marginalized group, it has done so without optimally negotiating with the external influencers. This has contributed in marking the inadequacy of ICT measures in overcoming the issue of education divide.

This chapter also highlights that improving biotic and abiotic entities is necessary, but it is not a sufficient condition in mitigating education divide. It is only the establishment of improved biotic and abiotic facilities, by optimally negotiating with the external influencers that bears the prospect in mitigating education divide. While contemporary ICT efforts in education have managed to improve biotic and abiotic conditions, their negligence of the external influencers has limited their scope in securing desirable outcomes.

This paves the path for the next part, Part II of our book, where we have conceptually demystified the potential of new wave of ICT with the advent of social technology, comprising of social software and socially enabled applications. Here, we have explored how social technology is conducive in establishing purposive collaborations within biotic, abiotic, and external influencing factors within an education ecosystem. Finally, our part II ends with Chap. 6, where we have narrated our framework by integrating social technologies with education ecosystem, which bears promising prospects in mitigating education divide by establishing purposive collaborations between different biotic and abiotic factors, by adequately considering the external influencers within an education ecosystem.

# References

Atlekar, A. S. (1944). *Education in ancient India* (2nd ed.). Benaras: Nand Kishor and Bros. Educational Publishers.

Balatchandirane, G. (2007). *Gender discrimination in education and economic development: A study of Asia* (V.R.F. Series. No. 426). Institute of Developing Economies, Japan External trade Organization. Retrieved from https://www.ide.go.jp/library/English/Publish/Download/Vrf/pdf/426.pdf.

Bauer, S. W. (2010). *The history of the medieval world: From the conversion of Constantine to the first crusade* (1st ed.). W. W. Norton and Company. ISBN-13: 978-0393059755.

Bereday, G. Z. (1969). *Essays on world education: The crises of supply and demand*. New York: Oxford Central Bank of Nigeria.

Briant, P. (2002). *From Cyrus to Alexander: A history of the Persian Empire*. Pennsylvania: Eisenbrauns. ISBN 978-1575060316.

Bronfenbrenner, U. (1979). *The ecology of human development*. Cambridge, MA: Harvard University Press.

Bronfenbrenner, U. (1989). Ecological systems theory. In *Annals of child development*. London: Jessica Kingsley Publishers.

Chabba, A. (2013). Education inequality in India. *RESET. Digital for Good*. Retrieved from https://en.reset.org/blog/education-inequality-india.

Chapin, F. S., Zavaleta, E. S., Eviner, V. T., Naylor, R. L., Vitousek, P. M., Reynolds, H. L., et al. (2000). Consequences of changing biodiversity. *Nature, 405,* 234–242.

Coombs, P. H. (1968). The world educational crisis: A systems analysis. *The Educational Forum, 34*(1), 141–142. https://doi.org/10.1080/00131726909339817.

Costambeys, M., Matthew, I., & Simon, M. (2011). *The Carolingian world*. Cambridge University Press. ISBN 978-0521563666.

Cremin, L. A. (1976). *Public education*. New York: Basic Books.

Cubberley, E. (1920). *The history of education*. Houghton Mifflin Company.

Davidson, T. (1892). *Aristotle and ancient educational ideals*. New York: Charles Scribners Sons.

DeVore, I., Murdock, G. P., & Whiting, J. W. M. (1968). Discussions, part VII: Are the hunter-gatherers a cultural type? In R. Lee & I. DeVore (Eds.), *Man the hunter*. Chicago: Aldine.

Dey, P., & Bandyopadhyay, S. (2018). Blended learning to improve quality of primary education among underprivileged school children in India. *Education and Information Technologies*. https://doi.org/10.1007/s10639-018-9832-1.

Dreze, J., & Sen, A. (2013). *An uncertain glory: India and its contradictions* (Vol. 2013). Princeton University Press.

Eisenstein, E. (1980). *The printing press as an agent of change.* Cambridge University Press. ISBN-13: 978-0521299558.

Esposito, J. (2014). *The Oxford dictionary of Islam.* Oxford: Oxford University Press. https://doi.org/10.1093/acref/9780195125580.001.0001.

Fanon, F. (1963). *The wretched of the earth.* New York: Grove Weidenfeld.

Flaten, L. T. (2017). Spreading Hindutva through education: Still a priority of the BJP? *India Review, 16*(4), 377–400.

Flood, G. D. (1996). *An introduction to Hinduism.* Cambridge University Press. ISBN 978-0-521-43878-0.

Gillard, D. (2018). *Education in England: A history.* Retrieved from www.educationengland.org.uk/history.

Gray, P. (2008). *A brief history of education.* Retrieved from https://www.psychologytoday.com/blog/freedom-learn/200808/brief-history-education.

Gray, P. (2009). Play as a foundation for hunter-gatherer social existence. *American Journal of Play, 1,* 476–522.

Gray, P. (2011). The evolutionary biology of education: How our hunter-gatherer educative instincts could form the basis for education today. *Evolution: Education and Outreach, 4,* 28–40. https://doi.org/10.1007/s12052-010-0306-1.

Herselman, M., Botha, A., Mayindi, D., & Reid, E. (2018). Influences of the ecological systems theory influencing technological use in rural schools in South Africa: A case study. In *International Conference on Advances in Big Data, Computing and Data Communication Systems (icABCD),* Durban. https://doi.org/10.1109/ICABCD.2018.8465432.

HISTORY. (2018). *Printing press.* Retrieved from www.history.com/topics/inventions/printing-press.

Holland, T. (2007). *Persian fire: The first world empire and the battle for the west.* Anchor Publishing. ISBN-13: 978-0307279484.

Islam, M. (2018). *Combating racial discrimination in the United States.* Retrieved from https://thegeopolitics.com/racial-discrimination-in-the-united-states/.

Joshi, A., & Gupta, R. K. (2017). Elementary education in Bharat (that is India): Insights from a postcolonial ethnographic study of a Gurukul. *International Journal of Indian Culture and Business Management, 15*(1), 100–120.

Kolstad, K. (2018). *Accessing education in the midst of the Syria crisis.* Retrieved from https://www.nrc.no/news/2018/april/accessing-education-in-the-midst-of-the-syria-crisis/.

Kumar, S. S. V. (2011). *The education system in India.* Retrieved from https://www.gnu.org/education/edu-system-india.en.html#sasi.

Lee, R. B. (1990). Primitive communism and the origin of social inequality. In S. Upham (Ed.), *Evolution of political systems: Sociopolitics in small-scale sedentary societies* (pp. 225–246). ISBN: 0521382521

Lee, J. (2014). *The untold history of modern U.S. education: The founding fathers.* Retrieved from https://www.wakingtimes.com/2014/01/28/untold-history-modern-u-s-education-founding-fathers/.

LEPOLE. (n.d.). *The history of education.* Retrieved from https://lepole.education/en/pedagogical-culture/22-history-of-education.html.

Lillback, P. (2016). The reformation and education. *Tabletalk Magazine.* Retrieved from https://www.ligonier.org/learn/articles/reformation-education/.

Liu, T., Uchida, Y., & Norasakkunkit, V. (2019). Socio-economic marginalization and compliance motivation among students and freeters in Japan. *Frontiers in Psychology.* Retrieved from https://doi.org/10.3389/fpsyg.2019.00312.

Loizides, A. (2012). *The Spartan education.* Retrieved from https://www.ancient.eu/article/342/the-spartan-education/.

Luksha, P., Cubista, J., Laszlo, A., Popovich, M., & Nineko, I. (2017). *Educational ecosystems for societal transformation* (Global Education Futures Report).

MacCulloch, D. (2005). *The reformation: A history*. Penguin Books. ISBN-13: 978-0143035381.

Marshall, H. (1990). Beyond the workplace metaphor: The classroom as a learning setting. *Theory into Practice, 29*(2), 94–101. https://doi.org/10.1080/00405849009543438.

McDonnell, M. J., & Pickett, S. T. A. (1993). *Humans as components of ecosystems: The ecology of subtle human effects and populated areas*. New York: Springer-Verlag.

McLaren, L., & Hawe, P. (2005). Ecological perspectives in health research. *Journal of Epidemiology and Community Health, 59*(1), 6–14. https://doi.org/10.1136/jech.2003.018044.

Musthafa, M., & Stephen, R. (2019). Education of the marginalized; in the context of policy initiatives for universalization of elementary education. *International Journal of Research in Social Sciences, 9*(7). Retrieved from https://www.ijmra.us/project%20doc/2019/IJRSS_JULY2019/IJMRA-15949.pdf.

National Research Council. (2011). *Assessing 21st century skills: Summary of a workshop*. Washington, DC: The National Academies Press. https://doi.org/10.17226/13215.

Nolan, P., & Lenski, G. (2008). *Human societies: An introduction to macrosociology*. Routledge.

Park, H. Y. (2007). Emerging consumerism and the accelerated 'education divide': The case of specialized high schools in South Korea. *Journal of Critical Education Policy Studies, 5*(2).

Petraglia, M., & Allchin, B. (2007). *The evolution and history of human populations in South Asia: Inter-disciplinary studies in archaeology, biological anthropology, linguistics and genetics*. Springer Science & Business Media. ISBN 978-1-4020-5562-1.

Pigaglio, R. (2016). *Morocco's public education system sinks into crisis*. Retrieved from https://international.la-croix.com/news/moroccos-public-education-system-sinks-into-crisis/4398#.

Privateer, P. M. (1999). Academic technology and the future of higher education: Strategic paths taken and not taken. *The Journal of Higher Education, 70*(1), 60–79. Published by: Ohio State University Press. Retrieved from https://www.jstor.org/stable/2649118.

Real, L. A., & Brown, J. H. (1991). *Foundations of ecology: Classic papers with commentaries*. Chicago: University of Chicago Press.

Religion Facts. (2005). *Zoroastrianism*. Retrieved from https://www.religionfacts.com/zoroastrianism.

Renya, J. (2011). Digital teaching and learning ecosystem (DTLE): A theoretical approach for online learning environments. *Changing Demands, Changing Directions*. Retrieved from https://www.ascilite.org.au/conferences/hobart11/downloads/papers/Reyna-concise.pdf.

Robinson, A. (2009). *Writing and script: A very short introduction*. Oxford: Oxford University Press.

Sen, A. (1988). *Capability and well-being* (WIDER conference paper).

Sen, A. (2003). Development as capability expansion. In *Readings in human development*. New Delhi and New York: Oxford University Press.

Shizha, E., & Kariwo, M. T. (2011). Impact of colonialism on education. In *Education and development in Zimbabwe*. Sense Publishers. https://doi.org/10.1007/978-94-6091-606-9_2.

Sleeter, C. E. (2015). Multicultural education vs. factory model schooling. In *Multicultural education: A renewed paradigm of transformation and call to action*. San Francisco: Caddo Gap Press.

Stein, B. (2010). *A history of India*. Wiley.

Thompson, K. (2019). *Postmodernism and education*. Retrieved from https://revisesociology.com/2019/09/25/postmodernism-and-education.

Toffler, A. (1970). *Future shock*. USA: Random House Publisher.

University College London. (2000). *Egyptian chronology*. Retrieved from https://www.digitalegypt.ucl.ac.uk/chronology/index.html.

Webster, H. (1913). *Ancient history*. Boston: D.C. Heath and Co.

Wilkinson, T. (2010). *The rise and fall of ancient Egypt: The history of a civilisation from 3000 BC to Cleopatra*. Bloomsbury Publishing PLC. ISBN: 0747599491.

World Bank. (2012). *Cambodia—Education sector support project (English).* Washington, DC: World Bank. Retrieved from https://documents.worldbank.org/curated/en/405811468214829 113/Cambodia-Education-Sector-Support-Project.

World Bank. (2014). *Philippines: National program support for basic education.* Retrieved from https://projects-beta.worldbank.org/en/results/2014/04/10/philippines-national-program-sup port-for-basic-education.

# Part II
# Education Ecosystem in a Digitally Connected World: Bridging the Education Divide

# Chapter 4
# ICT in Education

## 4.1 Introduction

The use of computers as a teaching–learning tool is playing a vital role in supplementing and complementing education process all over the world. For the last 50 years, educators made use of computers in different ways to support and enhance teaching and learning (Molnar 1997). Consequently, the contemporary use of the term "E-learning" has different meanings in different contexts. In the school sector, "E-leaning" refers to the use of both software-based (where learners use specially designed learning software without connection to the Internet) and online learning (use of Internet in teaching–learning process), whereas in business, higher-education and training sectors, it refers primarily to a range of online practices "that uses the affordances of the Internet to deliver customized, often interactive, learning materials and programs" (Nicholson 2007). Proper use of computer in education offers the opportunity to enhance student learning, increase teacher productivity, and develop more effective schools (Charp 1988; Decuypere 2019).

There has been a three-stage evolution process in the utilization of computers as a useful tool in teaching–learning process. In the following section, we describe this as three generations of computer usage in teaching–learning process:

*First Generation*: Pre-Internet era, when computers were getting used in a stand-alone mode, i.e., a mode where a computer is running only local applications *alone* without accessing any network;

*Second Generation*: Internet era, when computer and communication got converged, giving rise to a digitally connected world through Internet;

*Third Generation*: Social Internet era, where *social technologies* facilitate anytime-anywhere social interactions using Internet-enabled mobile devices (Razzaque 2020). Social technology, in this context, is an umbrella term used to capture a wide variety of terminologies depicting internet-enabled platforms and tools, e.g., web 2.0, mobile 2.0, social media, social software, etc., which has the potential to establish *collaborative connectivity* among billions of individuals over the globe (Chui 2012).

In this chapter, we will focus on first and second generation only; we will explore the third generation in the next chapter.

In its first generation, deployment of ICT in the field of education primarily tried to supplement education process through computer-assisted learning (Voogt and Vanden 2001). In this phase, learning happened in either (i) face-to-face setting, where students received proprietary e-content through teachers in physical classrooms or, (ii) self-paced learning, where learners accessed pre-stored, proprietary learning content from computer, either at home or at school. This self-paced mode is also termed as asynchronous mode of learning, where learners learn from the digital content only and there is no direct scope to interact with the teacher during the learning process.

This phase saw the incorporation of computer as a subject as well as computer-aided learning in the teaching–learning process by institutional bodies, educational associations, and curriculum developers. Government and private agencies contributed in making computers a part of school infrastructure during this time. Deployment of ICT in the field of education during this phase radically altered the nature of teaching–learning materials (Akele 2013; Mooji 1999; Smeets and Mooji 2000). Teaching–learning material, which was so far of physical nature, got digitized during this time. This did not imply that digital teaching–learning materials had universal access. Only educational institutions with proper digital infrastructure or learners having access to computer as well as proprietary digital content at home could make use of such digital content. Thus, deployment of computer in learning process is not uniform across the world.

With pervasive use of Internet, we saw the emergence of second generation of ICT deployment in the field of education with widespread availability of online, non-proprietary/free digital content along with availability of online *virtual* teachers outside classroom (Dey and Bandypadhyay 2018). Internet-enabled e-learning in this phase got endowed with immense possibility to impact the education performance of learners, who were previously devoid of quality teachers and quality teaching–learning content. This helped in conducting online teaching–learning activities outside the four walls of classrooms, provided learner has access to internet-enabled computer and has capability to derive benefits from available online resources. During this phase, government and non-government agencies attempted in securing computers for students and teachers on an individual level (e.g., one-laptop-per-child movement: Kraemer et al. 2009) to improve their digital literacy, familiarity, and frequency of usage. This phase also witnessed the effort of institutional bodies and educational associations in formalizing certification from e-learning platforms and promoting e-distance learning in higher education. Along with that, the second generation of ICT in education also influenced assessment parameters, where computer-based personalized assessment started taking place.

The efforts of second generation, although can be sited as conducive in extending the provision of quality education, it did little to address the educational needs of underprivileged segments. The presence of computers or digital devices was mandatory in order for e-learning to flourish. But as the practical scenario highlights, only elite educational institutions and individuals, who possessed adequate resources to host e-learning activities, got the benefit of e-learning initiatives. Majority of common mass during this time still lacked access to internet-enabled personal digital devices, which heavily restricted their prospect to optimally exploit e-learning activities to enhance educational performance.

Moreover, in both first and second generation, learning with the help of ICT was not adequately learner-centric, thereby restricting learner's autonomous participation by disallowing them to go beyond access to digital content (Watwood et al. 2009; Wright et al. 2020). Thus, to make learning participatory and to have a democratic effect in the teaching–learning process, there emerged a third generation of ICT in the field of education. With the emergence of smart phones and a new wave of ICT, namely, social technology, comprising of socially enabled application and software (e.g., blogs, e-forum, social media), started the third generation, which attempted in deploying the spirit of ICT to conduct participatory and democratic teaching–learning activities. This phase attempted in securing co-construction of knowledge by establishing purposive collaborations between teachers, learners and other entities in the education ecosystem through social technology. Enabling one and all to contribute in the collaborative learning process, this phase saw the blurring of boundaries between teachers and learners, where anyone can be a virtual teacher / student in this cyberworld. This phase witnessed the emergence of a combination of formal and informal learning process, where provision was made for mobilizing crowd knowledge and expertise for content creation and knowledge dissemination, thereby promoting lifelong learning in the process. All these aspects of third generation will be taken up in Chap. 5.

We have reserved this chapter to discuss only about the first and second generation attempts of deploying ICT in education and the different efforts undertaken during these two phases to arrive at a discussion dedicated to explore the issue of education divide from an ecosystemic perspective. This chapter is divided into two sections:

- The first part traces an evolutionary journey of how ICT got deployed in the field of education. It bears an in-depth narrative of how computer assisted learning became vogue in the first generation, followed by internet enabled e-learning in second generation;
- The second section attempts in narrating education ecosystem in the information age, while demystifying the issue of education divide from an ecosystemic angle. This section highlights the importance of addressing the impact of external influencers of the education ecosystem in any attempt dedicated to address the issue of education divide.

## 4.2   ICT in Education: An Evolutionary Perspective

### 4.2.1   Generation 1: Computer Assisted Learning

The first phase of introducing ICT in the field of education started with *computer assisted learning*. During this phase, computers were used to deliver digital instructional content to learners. In this phase, computer assisted learning was either mediated by teachers in a face-to-face setting or it enabled self-paced learning among learners through the use of personal computers (Voogt and Vanden 2001). In self-paced learning mode, learners were allowed to interact with interactive multimedia learning materials stored in computers. Thus, in this mode, computer assisted learning helped to transform teaching–learning process, at least to some extent, from traditional teacher-centered delivery of content to learner-centered approach, trying to secure active participation of the learner through self-paced learning using pre-programmed digital teaching–learning materials. With Intelligent Tutoring Systems (ITS) coming in vogue, self-paced learning became more effective, since the emergent system, using techniques of artificial intelligence, got endowed with the potential to capture students' behaviors and knowledge to moderate the pace of learning (Woolf 2007). However, since number of learners possessing personal computers during that era was few, such computer assisted learning remained inaccessible to majority of the students devoid of access to necessary digital infrastructure. The computers to which the students had access during this time were mostly housed inside educational institutions.

Although some elite institutions during this time possessed the necessary infrastructure to conduct computer assisted learning, optimal usage of computers for the purpose of education was mostly limited (Voogt and Fisser 2015). Moreover, successful computer assisted learning in school was heavily reliant on teachers' digital expertise. This can be considered a hindering factor. Even though the motive of computer assisted learning can be traced to securing active participation of the learners in the education process, practical operations reveal how such a set up was inadequate in facilitating education along dialogic terms. While computer assisted learning encouraged interaction with students, only those interactions successfully materialized which were in accordance to the programmed environment. If the student's concept of the modeled interaction differed from the author of the program, the students could not ask questions unless those questions were already programmed in the environment. Moreover, the available digital contents are proprietary in nature, limiting the students' exposure to a wide variety of learning content. The above stated factors marked the inadequacy of computer assisted learning. While it supplied students with quality digital content, it majorly failed in reaching out to a larger group of students and in cases, where they could reach out, they remained incapacitated in securing active participation of the learners.

These inadequacies coupled with widespread applications of Internet triggered the beginning of 2nd generation of ICT in education, which is characterized by internet enabled e-learning (Anderson 2008).

## 4.2.2   Generation 2: Internet Enabled E-Learning

Internet-enabled e-learning environment or online learning can be divided into two categories: *synchronous* and *asynchronous* (Garrison 2011). *Asynchronous mode* promotes learning anytime, anywhere using digital content. People/organizations interested in imparting knowledge have the freedom to enrich the digital knowledge pool/platforms by providing various forms of e-content in the cyber-space (e.g., YouTube, Udemy, Khan Academy, etc.). Incorporation in the digital world immediately makes the study materials accessible to a wide spectrum of learners, either free or with a cost. With the advent of MOOCs[1] (Siemens 2013; Rai and Deng 2016), various asynchronous learning platforms were introduced that changed the entire learning landscape to a virtual one. Examples are edX, Courseera, Udacity, Furture-Learn, Udemy, etc. Although synchronous interaction may be possible in MOOCs using online chat and offline discussion forums, one-to-one personalized interaction with teacher is not possible due to high volume of students enrolled in a course. Also, there has been very little research on MOOCs at the primary or K-12 level in general.

Any asynchronous, self-paced e-learning assumes that the learner has individualized access to a computer with internet. Additionally, the learner has to be proficient in English due to poor availability of e-learning materials in regional languages. Hence, this mode is not always suitable for rural/underprivileged students of non-English speaking countries.

In *synchronous mode*, students and instructors are geographically separated but meet online at a scheduled time using video-conferencing tools in a virtual classroom. Lectures, discussions, and presentations occur at that specified hour in the virtual classroom. Online tutoring services are designed for learners of any age and any education level and they can avail this service from the comfort of their home, provided they have computer with internet connectivity.

In recent years, use of online learning platforms has increased to a great extent. A study conducted by Babson Survey Research Group found that "more than 6.3 million students in the United States took at least one online course in fall 2016, a 5.6% increase from the previous year" (Allen and Seaman 2015). Similarly, Bean (2019) has indicated that distance education has nearly tripled in community colleges of California over the last twelve years. To support these students, colleges have increased their online services including online tutoring (Bean 2019). All over the globe, several universities and institutions offer distance learning program through online tutoring in order to offer learning solutions to students, who have problems in receiving in-person campus assistance. Through online tutoring services, they can get the opportunity to interact with teachers online beyond the boundaries of the physical campus. The concept of Open University revolutionized the scope of the distance learning programs, which is a viable learning alternative to the traditional form of face-to-face institutional education. Many open universities all over the globe use online teaching as one component of their education process (Major 2015).

---

[1] A massive open online course (MOOC) is online course aimed at unlimited participation and open access via the web.

Several edupreneurs are offering online synchronous learning platform for privileged learners, such as—Chegg Tutors, Skooli, Wyzant, Tutor.com, SpecialEdTutoring.com (focusing on students with learning difficulties), etc. These synchronous e-learning initiatives connect students with online teachers of their choice. However, because of high expenses associated with these services, the question arises whether such methodologies of dissemination of knowledge can be used for disseminating education for underserved school children with limited economic backup.

When e-learning methods described above are being combined with traditional classroom methods, it can be termed as *Blended Learning*, which is a combination of face-to-face learning and e-learning. In "blended learning," the word *blended* signifies use of two or more distinct methods of learning. This may comprise of different degree of blending of physical classroom instructions/on-site teaching assistance along with online instructions/computer-based teaching–learning materials. Ultimate objective of this *blending* is to ensure learners' knowledge acquisition process to improve their learning potentials. As indicated by Dziuban et al. (2004), "Blended learning should be viewed as a pedagogical approach that combines the effectiveness and socialization opportunities of the classroom with the technologically enhanced active learning possibilities of the online environment, rather than a ratio of delivery modalities." Blended Learning Classrooms can be defined as a "flexible learning environments," where students learn via collaboration and communication both locally and globally, beyond the confines of the classrooms (Watson 2008). "The widespread adoption and availability of digital learning technologies has led to increased levels of integration of computer mediated instructional elements into the traditional F2F [face-to-face] learning experience" (Bonk and Charles 2006).

Smart-Class Solutions are examples of blended learning in classrooms, where the teacher uses face-to-face instructional methods in classroom with computer-based digital teaching–learning materials. A typical smart classroom has tools for (i) creating and delivering *smart content*; (ii) facilitating *smart interaction and engagement* with students; and, (iii) evaluating students' *smart assessment* methods (Saini and Goel 2019). There are several edupreneurs, who offer a range of expensive education services and products including multimedia contents and tools for smart-classes for high-cost private schools.

In the context of developing and underdeveloped nations, internet enabled e-learning offers scanty prospects in educating marginalized learners due to non-availability of digital resources (Internet and internet-enabled personal digital device) and lack of capability to exploit available e-learning facilities for generating prospects of self-betterment. In such cases, deploying internet to improve educational facilities must take into consideration social, economic, political, and other allied hindrances, which will secure optimal utilization of internet facilities. Appropriate consideration of external influencers of the education ecosystem has the potential in enhancing the capability of learners to exploit their knowledge resources in pursuit of opportunity scopes, thereby mitigating education divide.

While in the second generation, attempts were undertaken to improve the interactions between biotic and abiotic entities of an education ecosystem, the content-centric and teacher-centric learning process remained ineffective in addressing the demands of twenty-first century. Thus, a need was felt to establish digital connections between different entities in the education ecosystem in order to inculcate effective learning by virtue of purposive collaborations (Banerjee and Belson 2015). In order to make learners' capable to fulfill the requirements of twenty-first century market, it is mandatory to impart among learners innovative skills by establishing purposive collaborations between different agents within an education ecosystem. This paved the path for a scenario, where it became necessary to cultivate social and emotional intelligence, creativity, and our abilities to cooperate and co-create as well as other critical skills of the future in defining learners' successes in the context of twenty-first century. (National Research Council 2011). Thus, in order to make learning contextual to the requirements of contemporary socio-economic set up, a third generation of ICT emerged, which attempted in deploying the *social* spirit of social technology to enable collaborative learning by establishing purposive digital connections between different entities in the education ecosystem. We will discuss the issues pertaining to 3rd Generation in the next chapter.

In the next section, we will illustrate the education ecosystem in this digital age to show the interaction patterns between different biotic and abiotic entities in the context of external influencers and will take up in detail the ineffectiveness of extant ICT-initiatives in addressing the issue of education divide holistically.

## 4.3 Education Ecosystem in Information Age: Exploring Education Divide

As indicated in the previous section, rapid proliferation of information technologies paved the path for information age, in which digital technologies gradually started entering and altering the field of education. Both first and second generation of digitization in education brought technology in redefining the process of content creation and delivery; both these generations primarily witnessed creating, sharing and accessing instructional content in digital forms, including online courses, digital libraries, games, apps, etc. (Banerjee and Belson 2015). In other words, both these generations mainly attempted introduction of digital delivery of content in supplementing conventional educational patterns, as has been prevalent since industrial times. Thus, during this phase, it is only the abiotic elements of the education ecosystem, namely, infrastructure, teaching–learning materials and assessment tools, that got digitized. Additionally, in second generation, efforts were undertaken to improve educational practices by deploying the potential of internet in augmenting the infrastructure. Through internet-enabled infrastructure, e-learning activities, both in synchronous and asynchronous mode, started getting implanted to improve educational practices.

While the digitization mainly altered the abiotic components, both the biotic components and external influencers got consequently impacted by these changes in abiotic entities. At the same time, the dynamic interaction patterns between biotic, abiotic and external influencers in information age started determining the education ecosystem in this age, as illustrated in Fig. 4.1.

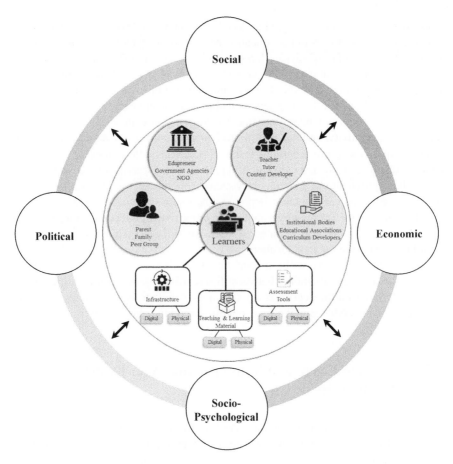

**Fig. 4.1** Education ecosystem in the information age

### 4.3.1   The Abiotic Entities

*Infrastructure*: Digitization of school infrastructure includes Internet connectivity with computers and accessories connected to Internet. In order to promote e-learning activities outside school, learners should have access to personalized computing devices along with Internet through public/private internet service providers at an affordable cost. Hence, access to digital infrastructure, whether institutional or individualized, depends on the contextual socio-economic condition: digital infrastructure is "going to be far more present in highly industrialized countries than in the less developed world; and far more present for middle-class households in developed countries than for poor households in those same countries" (Sassen 2002; Jensen 1998; Hoffman and Novak 1998).

The information age witnessed efforts by different private, public and non-governmental entities in implanting digital infrastructure in educational institutions

(Tomczyk and Oyelere 2019). For example, if we look into the Bolivian scenario, then we can see how the national government funded in providing majority of the Bolivian public schools with computers to be used by both teachers and students for the purpose of academic training. Similarly, several other nations like Brazil, Cuba, Scotland, and others witnessed policy formulations along the lines of supplementing educational institutions with necessary digital infrastructure appropriate to conduct teaching–learning activities through ICT. Infrastructure can be identified as a domain, which got directly affected with the introduction of digital technologies in the field of education. However, although prospects are laid across the globe to supplement educational institutions with digital infrastructure on a democratic level, a critical examination of the practical scenario reveals how only few institutions were endowed with the capacity to optimally utilize the implanted infrastructure.

Voogt and Vanden's (2001) study reveals that in spite of efforts taken to equip majority of public schools in the USA with digital infrastructure, the digital resources remained underutilized due to low levels of teacher inclination toward digital usage. This highlights that while digital technologies directly impacted an abiotic parameter of education ecosystem like infrastructure, such adoption also cast an indirect influence on biotic parameters. Shaping of abiotic entities by digital technologies can only yield desirable outcome, if the biotic entities are also improved in accordance, by keeping in mind the impact of external influencers of the education ecosystem, so that the undertaken efforts can contribute in successfully integrating ICT in teaching–learning practices. For example, one of the major factors ensuring optimal utilization of digital infrastructure in schools has to be coupled with organizing contextual digital literacy training for teachers, which will improve their digital expertise necessary to conduct teaching–learning activities through ICT. And these trainings have to be contextual, by keeping in mind the external influencers of the education ecosystem, namely, social, economic, political, and psychological dimensions, which form the immediate context of the teachers (Knowlton 2000; Bingimlas 2009).

***Teaching–Learning Materials***: Digital teaching–learning materials or digital content for teaching–learning is at the heart of both computer-assisted learning and e-learning initiatives. Introduction of digital technologies directly impacted teaching–learning materials in the education ecosystem of information age. The teaching–learning materials, which were so far available in physical form, got digitized during this era. Digitization of teaching–learning materials implied using multimodal communication tools (text-graphics-audio–video) to prepare the same. Digitization of teaching–learning materials cast a significant influence on the biotic factors of education ecosystem. Use of audio-visual aids can make teaching–learning materials not only more attractive and interesting but also more effective for students (Bindu 2016; Mayer 2002). However, learners face two problems with the availability of online digital content as teaching–learning materials: (i) Most of the digital content available is in English. Therefore, non-English speaking learners, especially in the context of developing and underdeveloped non-English speaking countries have difficulties in getting direct benefit from these materials and, (ii) proprietary digital TLM is expensive and not all learners can afford it. At the same time, although the availability of free digital content is increasing day by day, it is difficult for a learner to choose authentic and effective material from the vast pool of available materials. Coping with abundance of digital content is a challenge to both teachers and learners. As indicated by Simon (1971), "In an information-rich world, the wealth of information means a dearth of something else: a scarcity of whatever it is that information consumes. What information consumes is rather obvious: it consumes the attention of its recipients. Hence a wealth of information creates a poverty of attention and a need to allocate that attention efficiently among the overabundance of information sources that might consume it." Thus, the abundance of content in this context puts increasing pressure on learners' attention span, which is now a scarce resource (Davenport and Beck 2001). Hence, it is essential to find effective ways to deal with this in teaching–learning practice. In this context, Weller (2011) has raised two issues for further exploration: how can teachers take advantage of abundance in their own teaching practice, and how can teachers train learners to make use of it.

*Assessment Tools*: Introduction of ICT in the field of education witnessed a scenario, when in the information age, assessment tools started getting digitized (Gomersall 2005). Multiple ways came up to deploy digital tools in the process of assessment for learning. This age saw the emergence and proliferation of e-assessment parameters, where several schools, higher educational institutions, and professional associations resorted to the same to measure their students' skills and expertise (Rovai and Ponton 2008; Scheuermann and Julius 2008). Digitization of assessment process enabled preparation of a tailored feedback, interventions, or action plans in pursuit of improving learning and attainment of education.

In this Information age, sometimes different examination boards and academic organizations also conduct electronic examination to gauge students' performances. However, maintaining optimal security, availability of a large number of hardware necessary to conduct electronic examination on a large scale often pose as hindrances in the process of transition from physical paper-based examination to digital assessment.

While knowledge-based assessment of cognitive abilities such as reading, writing, mathematical ability, memorization of facts, etc., are tangibly understood by conventional assessment and evaluation through standardized and automated testing, the demanded skills in the twenty-first century are less tangible and therefore more challenging to access with e-assessment methods. Throughout the cycle of life-long learning, evaluations of several other skills, such as creativity, collaborative problem solving, social-emotional as well as other critical skills of the future, must be included in determining learners' success in the twenty-first century (National Research Council 2011; Darling-Hammond and Adamson 2014).

### 4.3.2  The Biotic Entities

*Learners*: The information age threw open a wide array of possibilities in front of the learners, which enabled them in utilizing the digital medium for educational pursuits (Luksha et al. 2017). Computer-assisted learning in the first generation and e-learning in the second generation accredited in the learners the autonomy to select from a wide variety of digital contents and online teachers to improve their educational practices. In synchronous mode of learning, there are several platforms supporting online tutoring services, where learners get a chance to meet expert tutors online to learn a subject at a scheduled time using video-conferencing tools in a virtual classroom set up. However, these synchronous e-learning initiatives are expensive and only a few can afford it all over the globe. In asynchronous mode of learning, there are several options to access online courses asynchronously. MOOC, for example, as open online resources of courses, allows learners to access variety of courses online in a self-paced mode or blended mode (Siemens 2013). However, it must be noted in this context that while the learners were given the opportunity to choose and navigate, the learning environment in which they operated was immensely passive and content-centric. Rai and Deng (2016) identified several issues leading to reduced effectiveness of online courses from learners' perspective. First of all, learners are increasingly becoming passive information viewers, focusing more on collecting materials rather than using it. Secondly, online courses do not provide any personal support; however, it has been observed that learners are motivated to learn when the teacher or facilitator is available for guidance. Thirdly, since learners are primarily self-selecting the courses, they are not sure what to learn and how much to learn at their level. Sometimes, they fail to evaluate the difficulty-level of these courses and they withdraw from the course abruptly. Other related problems are Internet connectivity issues, lack of availability of courses in different languages and the learning potential of learners, enabling them to self-select and self-study a subject. Several researchers have noted that online learning is not about quality learning content only, but increasingly "it is about the skilled facilitation of learning by faculty who understand how to interact with and engage students in this new learning landscape" (Watwood et al. 2009). Anderson (2008) noted: "Education, however, is not only about access to content. The greatest affordance of the Web for education use is the profound and multifaceted increase in communication and interaction capabilities."

At the same time, introduction of digital technologies in and outside classroom in no way attempted in making education inclusive. The socio-economic conventions still determine the quality of education a learner would receive by virtue of his socio-economic status. Digital technologies during this phase mostly have attempted in supplementing conventional educational practices through ICT, thereby remaining inadequate in addressing education divide. Affordability of technology poses a hindrance in the context of marginalized groups of developing nations (Tomczyk and Oyelere 2019). In cases where attempts have been made to deploy technology to supplement different abiotic educational entities (e.g., digitizing infrastructure or teaching–learning materials), the same has been done without adequately familiarizing the target group with the technical gadgets. Digital technologies, even in today's world, remain mostly alien to majority of the global population, mostly to the marginalized groups of developing nations. This unfamiliarity creates a double divide—between the ones privileged to acquire education and exploit digital technologies in the pursuit of education and the ones devoid of both. In a world, where digital technologies can offer immense prospects in transforming the dynamics of education ecosystem, the aspect of digital divide, featured by the lack of communication with the digitally connected world, further intensifies the extant education divide.

*Parents, Family, and Peer Group*: The role and participation of the parents in the education ecosystem remained the same as in modern industrial society, where digital technologies were not resorted to establish connections between parents and other agents in the education ecosystem. However, digital learning paved the path for a new kind of divide, where often children of educated and digitally literate parents started performing better through digital learning as compared to the ones devoid of such privilege, thereby sustaining education divide. Also, introduction of ICT in education requires possession of personal digital devices (e.g., desktop or laptop) to participate in out-of-classroom learning processes. This motivated financially affluent parents and family members of this age to procure computers for their children, so that they can utilize the same for educational pursuits. This also made it crucial for parents to possess digital expertise themselves, so that they can motivate their children to use the medium to attract educational benefits. Furthermore, use of internet in conducting teaching–learning activities created an environment, which supports improved peer group interaction (Foutsitzi and Caridakis 2019).

*Teachers, Tutors, Content Developers*: The introduction of digital technologies enabled the teachers and tutors to expand their horizon in the field of education. The information age granted the teachers the option to explore the possibilities to teach all across the world virtually and to explore a plethora of instructional content available in the digital medium. Teachers and tutors play a crucial role in successful integration of ICT in teaching–learning processes. They should not only know content but also the pedagogy to impart knowledge effectively by integrating technology (Zhao and Cziko 2001). While in the pre-information age, quality of learning was dependent on a teacher's teaching quality and accountability, in the information age, a teacher's digital expertise and inclination of digital usage contributed immensely in ensuring effective knowledge dissemination through ICT. Effective integration of ICT helps teachers to create enabling learning conditions for students (Lebow 1993; Jonassen and Reeves 1996). This makes it necessary to contextually train teachers on ICT usage, along with devising proper pedagogical strategies that will ensure effective teaching learning (Knowlton 2000; Bingimlas 2009). Content developers in information age started designing digital contents, which are suitable to get circulated via the digital medium. They resorted to audio-visual aids while creating educational contents, which made the same attractive to learners.

In the information age, different national governments adopted measures to train teachers on digital literacy, along with equipping educational institutions with digital infrastructures, to ensure optimal utilization of installed digital infrastructure in teaching–learning practices. For example, if we look into Bolivian context, then we can see how the nation attempted in incorporating teachers' digital literacy training in its project on conducting educational practices through ICT (Tomczyk and Oyelere 2019). Agency of Electronic Government and Information and Communication Technology of Bolivia (AGETIC), according to the data from the Ministry of Education indicates the distribution of more than 100 thousand computers to teachers of public schools under the "one computer one teacher" project in the year 2011. This initiative was undertaken to increase the digital literacy and awareness of teachers, who are considered to be crucial mediators in facilitating education along the lines of ICT in Bolivia. However, a critical investigation reveals the incapacitation of the measures in yielding desirable outcomes. The trainings' negligence on methodologies of pedagogical use remained ineffective in enhancing the Bolivian teachers' digital expertise and motivation of usage optimally, which subsequently hindered effective educational practices through ICT.

Similarly, Voogt and Vanden (2001) reveals that while in the US context, majority of public schools had adequate digital infrastructure through public initiatives, most of it remained underutilized due to low levels of teacher inclination toward digital usage. Only few teachers with a constructivist teaching approach resorted to ICT in the process of knowledge dissemination. This highlights the importance of teachers and their digital expertise and motivation of usage in the process of successfully integrating ICT in educational practices. Deplorable standards of the former immensely contribute in hindering the latter.

***Edupreneurs, Government Agencies, and NGOs***: Edupreneurs, Government Agencies, and NGOs act as enablers in supplementing educational institutions and individuals with e-learning infrastructure, tools, platforms, and services. Numerous ICT-initiatives and projects were initiated by national government of different countries, supported by the World Bank, the European Commission, the United Nations, and many other donors (Hawkins 2005). Policy makers all across the world aim at utilizing ICT in such a manner that it becomes an intrinsic requirement for creating effective education systems. The United Nations Millennium Declaration (UNMD 2000) contains a commitment to "ensure that benefits of new technologies, especially information and communication technologies ....are available to all." In the "Declaration of Principles" for the World Summit on the Information Society (WSIS 2003), goals were set for developing "a people-centered, inclusive and development-oriented Information Society, where everyone can create, access, utilize and share information and knowledge, enabling individuals, communities and peoples to achieve their full potential in promoting their sustainable development and improving their quality of life" (WSIS 2003).

In this context, governments in different nations have come up with modalities for designing and implementing plans and strategies that would likely produce the above-mentioned results. These policies have tried to focus on three pillars, namely, (i) access to ICT infrastructures and equipment, (ii) improving teacher capacities; and, (iii) monitoring and evaluation (UNESCO 2011). Focus has always been on those geographical regions having poor or little quality of education. This brings us to the goal of governments all across the world which is to reduce disparities and increase equity in education. This is done by deploying more financial and human resources and developing specially tailored programs to reach underserved areas and vulnerable groups. Based on the goals of SDG4, Governments have focused on three priorities of education that can be addressed by using ICT-based tools such as: inclusive and equitable education, quality education and lifelong learning. The SDG4 proposes use of ICT to support access to inclusive and equitable education that caters to the basic needs of students and the labor market, and also by ensuring individual opportunities throughout lifetime (Huawei: CSR 2017). Though ICTs have proved to be a potential medium in reaching out to the most unreachable groups, governments struggle to find out the ways and conditions in which quality education can be improved and costs of ICT-driven education systems can be reduced. However, countries worldwide have shown evidences where countries have wasted scarce resources on ICT hardware and on unsatisfactory training and software production without achieving targeted outcomes.

There are several examples, where we find how private entities attempted in supplementing educational institutions with digital infrastructure, crucial to carry out teaching–learning activities with the help of ICT. For example, if we look into the Korean context, then we can see how the specialized high schools in Korea funded by private educational players attempted in extending quality digital infrastructure to elite group of Korean students (Park 2007). The presence of digital infrastructure enabled the students of specialized high schools in Korea to use digital services for attracting educational benefits. Similarly, Cuban government provided majority of public primary, secondary, and pre-university education centers with personal computers, to be accessed by both teachers and students for academic training (Salazar 2017). In some context, it can also be seen how the maintenance aspect of the implanted digital infrastructure was entrusted on the non-governmental bodies. For example in Bolivia, Agency of Electronic Government and Information and Communication Technology of Bolivia (AGETIC), according to the data from the Ministry of Education, distributed more than 100,000 computers to teachers of public schools in the year 2011, whose maintenance responsibility was in turn entrusted on non-governmental organizations operative in Bolivia (Tomczyk and Oyelere 2019).

E-learning is transforming educational practices all over the globe, and, as a consequence, the e-learning industry is expanding rapidly with its vast array of offerings to business organizations, government bodies, and individuals (Docebo 2016). The global e-learning market was worth an impressive $107 billion in 2015. Today, e-learning market size surpassed USD 200 billion in 2019 and is anticipated to grow at over 8% CAGR between 2020 and 2026 (Pappas 2019). One of the reasons for this increasing growth is the demand from developing countries. E-Learning provides access to world-class educational resources, which may not be available to the learners in developing countries (Pappas 2019). For example, according to Technopak's analysis, India's digital learning market was at US$ 2bn in 2016, growing at a CAGR of 30% and is expected to reach US$ 5.7bn by 2020 (Technopak 2016). Unfortunately, in consonant with the elitist bias in our education system in India, these initiatives are primarily urban-focused. In spite of some Government initiatives, the rural populations are still far away to enjoy the benefits of these e-learning initiatives. Moreover, majority of e-learning initiatives, both Government and private, are focusing on either higher education or professional education with little emphasis given on school education.

**Institutional Bodies, Educational associations, and Curriculum Developers**: To improve ICT adoption in academic institutions, institutional bodies, educational associations, and curriculum developers have incorporated study of computers in the curriculum on one hand, and promoted use of digital technologies to disseminate education on the other. Institutional bodies under ministry of education are entrusted with the responsibility to oversee that the implanted digital infrastructure in school is getting optimally utilized to conduct teaching–learning activities. Educational Associations in the information age started devising practical pathways to formalize the use of ICT in educational practices. This age has witnessed the formalization of certification from e-learning platforms and promoting e-distance learning in higher education. Furthermore, the curriculum developers have made it absolutely crucial to incorporate digital literacy programs in the curriculum to enhance digital expertise and motivation for digital usage of both teachers and learners.

### 4.3.3  The External Influencers

*Economic*: The potential of ICT to promote economic growth is a well-accepted phenomenon, but this is not a universal truth. It has been observed that rich industrialized countries and several countries in transition have profited from the information age and attained high economic growth. However, the impact of ICT on economic growth is not so prominent in developing countries, and even less in underdeveloped countries (Bon 2007). There are three reasons behind this: (i) lack of accessibility of digital devices and infrastructure (internet and digital services) at an affordable price; (ii) lack of capability (both individual capability and organizational capability) to use digital devices, platforms and applications; and, (iii) lack of opportunity to exploit the acquired *digital* capability to generate economic benefits.

The same observation is true in the domain of ICT-enabled education. Rich industrialized countries are economically much better equipped to reap the benefits of ICT-driven education as compared to developing and underdeveloped countries. Even within a country, the variability of economic conditions favors richer population in urban areas to get the benefits, both in terms of accessibility and affordability of ICT-mediated education. Hence, alternative learning spaces facilitated by digital technologies have still not made their way into the mainstream on a mass scale level. This makes affording alternative education premised on digital technologies a hindering factor in many parts of the globe, especially in developing context. This creates a vicious cycle: unaffordability of quality education creates low economic return from education for the economically weak sections, who are seldom motivated to acquire education and pronounce their opportunity prospects by virtue of acquired education. Education and training increase individual cognitive capacity and, as a result, augment productivity, which leads to increased individual earnings. However, the economic divide is one of the factors that inhibit learners to access ICT-enabled quality education at an affordable cost.

*Social*: Sassen (2002) argued that electronic space (or, digital space) is embedded within social space and, hence, digitization is not a purely technological event. Thus "electronic space is inflected by the values, cultures, power systems, and institutional orders within which it is embedded." This would result in "variable outcomes of these technologies for different social orders." This variability in outcome in a social context can be estimated in terms of E-readiness, which is a measure indicating the ability of an entity to leverage ICT for a designated purpose (GhoshRoy and Parijat 2017). A Harvard University research project on the "Readiness of the Networked World" proposed a framework for developing countries to evaluate their e-readiness. Readiness in this context is defined as "the degree to which a community is prepared to participate in the Networked World, which is gauged by assessing a community's relative advancement in the areas that are most critical for ICT adoption and the most important applications of ICTs" (Dada 2006; CID 2006). Poor e-readiness results in poor ICT adoption capability, which creates digital exclusion, and, as a consequence, a newer form of social stratification. In the context of education, ICTs cannot play a vital role unless they are adopted by different groups within society (Ziemba 2013). The process of ICT adoption has to be holistic in the sense that not only the Institutions should be in a position to absorb ICT-driven initiatives, ICT adoption within households is also important to make e-learning initiatives a success (Ziemba 2016). Unequal and unsuccessful adoption by different groups of people would result in both digital as well as social exclusion. For example, factors identified as influential to the adoption and usage of e-learning includes not only the institutional infrastructure but also staff attitudes and skills and perceived student expectations (King and Boyatt 2015). Often people belonging to the lower stratum of the society failed to benefit from digital learning due to lack of access to digital resources and consequent alienation from the digital medium, which hindered their capacity to optimally utilize the same. In fact, it is the prevalent social convention that makes digital technologies an elite medium, suitable to get utilized by the privileged few. The influence these social factors cast on educational attainment proves that improving the interactions between biotic and abiotic entities using ICT is not sufficient in improving learning outcome of learners. An attempt to mitigate education divide must take into account the social factors responsible toward smoother adoption of ICT within the social system.

   *Socio-Psychological*: The vision of a connected world has made emergent digital technologies part and parcel of everyday life in the information age. This has created a *socio-psychological* context, which is marked by the desire of individuals to access digital medium in everyday life. Amidst such a scenario, a divide is created in the domain of e-education between the learners having access as well as awareness regarding the e-learning tools and platforms and the ones devoid of the same. The importance of the digital medium during this time rose to such an extent that the ones unaware of it were often identified as unfit in participating in the socio-economic affairs of the emergent market dominated by such technical aspects. This digital ignorance of a learner creates an alienation from learners who are digitally knowl-edgeable. This affects the motivation of learners to acquire education using e-learning practices. Quality education, as we have already seen, has been exclusively a priv-ilege reserved for the elites. While contemporary society has witnessed the emer-gence of several attempts to extend educational services to all, research shows that learners, who have been deprived of education for long, are often not motivated to acquire education by availing the additional opportunities. Dembo and Seli (2004) rightly show that students fail to benefit from academic support services and courses because of the following reasons: "(a) students believe they can't change, (b) they don't want to change, (c) they don't know what to change, or (d) they don't know how to change." These reasons result in a low motivational level, which disallow the learners to exploit additional opportunities in pursuit of acquiring education, thereby sustaining education divide.

*Political*: Achieving Sustainable Development Goal 4, which is "Ensure inclusive and equitable quality education and promote lifelong learning opportunities for all," is one of the most important and challenging tasks in international development. The global scenario has witnessed the emergence of several policies in different countries to integrate ICT on a mass scale level to ensure "equitable quality education." However, the operative political scenario of a country, ridden with exploitation and concentration of power in the hands of the few have seldom witnessed successful grass-root permeation of undertaken policies in the formal level. Often it is seen that learners from established background are given the opportunity to expand their knowledge base by benefitting from digital learning, where marginalized learners often lack access and are unable to participate in the digital forum and get benefit from the same. As stated by Wales et al. (2016), "Whether countries are run on the basis of patronage networks, whether politicians have short or long time horizons, and the relative power of different groups will all affect whether a government invests in education, how it undertakes reforms, and how effectively policies are designed and implemented. Understanding the political structures and incentives underlying education systems should therefore be a priority."

De La, Croix and Doepke (2009) has indicated that the share of public and private schools in a region and the representation of a social class in the political power affect the quality of public-school education. When the ruling political party is pro-poor because of higher representation of the poor in the party, the public schools attract more financial support to improve quality of public education. However, if the ruling political party is reluctant toward subsidizing quality education for the poor, expensive private education will grow, thus degrading the quality of public education (Das 2019).

## 4.4  Conclusion

The discussions in the chapter highlight that only when coherent interactions are maintained between biotic, abiotic, and external influencers within an education ecosystem, prospects of mitigating education divide can be created on a holistic scale. In this context, initiatives toward solely enriching biotic and abiotic entities, which different national governments tried to implement through ICT, remain inadequate in achieving desirable impact. Thus, initiatives undertaken both in the first and second generation of ICT usage in the field of education to impact the biotic and abiotic entities of an education ecosystem create further education divide due to the negligence of external influencers' impact in the said process.

In order to establish a coherent interaction pattern between biotic, abiotic, and external enablers, it is important for ICT-initiatives to transcend from providing digital instructional content to establishing effective digital connections among the three entities of the education ecosystem (Watwood et al. 2009). Although ICT measures have attempted in making sporadic interactions between the teaching–learning community, it immensely falls short in establishing purposive collaborations between biotic, abiotic entities, and external influencers of an education ecosystem. Thus, a need has emerged to implement the *social* spirit of social technology for the purpose of conducting effective teaching–learning activities through establishing *collaborative connections* between the biotic, abiotic entities, and external influencers of the education ecosystem. We have reserved in Chap. 5 to explore the potential of social technology in facilitating effective teaching–learning process.

However, it needs to be remembered that the collaborative spirit of social technology alone cannot mitigate education divide, if it is not getting mediated by a digital platform hosting different educational entities. The digital platform, apart from integrating different biotic and abiotic entities of education ecosystem, must also trigger collaboration by keeping in mind the specificities of external influencers of the education ecosystem. This highlights the need for a social technology-enabled framework, which would be capable of positively contributing toward effective mitigation of education divide on a holistic scale. The operational and functional intricacies of a social technology-enabled framework infused with the capacity to eradicate education divide has been dealt detail in Chap. 6.

# References

Akele, F. E. (2013). Information and Communication Technology as Teaching and Learning Space for Teachers of English Language in Schools. *Journal of Emerging Trends in Educational Research and Policy Studies, 5*(1).

Allen, I. E., & Seaman, J. (2015). *Grade level: Tracking online education in the United States.* Babson Survey Research Group and Quahog Research Group, LLC. Available at: http://www.onlinelearningsurvey.com/reports/gradelevel.pdf.

Anderson, T. (2008). *Theory and practice of online education* (2nd ed). ISBN 9781897425084.

Banerjee, P., & Belson, G. (2015). *Digital education 2.0. From content to connections.* Deloitte Review.

Bean, M. V. (2019). *Effective practices for online tutoring. Position paper.* The Academic Senate for California Community Colleges. Retrieved from https://files.eric.ed.gov/fulltext/ED601995.pdf.

Bindu, C. N. (2016). Impact of ICT on teaching and learning: A literature review. *International Journal of Management and Commerce Innovations, 4*(1), 24–31. ISSN 2348-7585

Bingimlas, K. A. (2009). Barriers to the successful integration of ICT in teaching and learning environments: A review of the literature. *Eurasia Journal of Mathematics, Science & Technology Education, 5*(3).

Bon, A. (2007). Can the Internet in tertiary education in Africa contribute to social and economic development? *International Journal of Education and Development using Information and Communication Technology (IJEDICT), 3*(3). Retrieved from https://www.researchgate.net/publication/255649262_Can_the_internet_in_tertiary_education_in_Africa_contribute_to_social_and_economic_development.

Bonk, C., & Charles, R. G. (2006). *The handbook of blended learning: Global perspectives.* Local Designs: Wiley.

Charp, S. (1988). Computer use in education. Trends, challenges and opportunities. Children in the information age. *Pergamon.* https://doi.org/10.1016/B978-0-08-036464-3.50012-0.

Chui, M. et al., (2012). *The social economy: Unlocking value and productivity through social technologies* (McKinsey Global Institute Report). Retrieved from https://www.mckinsey.com/industries/high-tech/our-insights/the-social-economy.

CID. (2006). *Readiness for the networked world—A guide for developing countries.* Retrieved from https://www.readinessguide.coms.

Dada, D. (2006). E-Readiness for developing countries: Moving the focus from the environment to the users. *Electronic Journal of Information Systems in Developing Countries, 27*(6), 1–14. https://doi.org/10.1002/j.1681-4835.2006.tb00183.x.

Darling-Hammond, L., & Adamson, F. (2014). *Beyond the bubble test: How performance assessments support 21st century learning.* Publisher: Jossey-Bass. ISBN-10: 1118456181

Das, A. (2019). Education and its Politicisation: With Indian Examples. Retrieved from https://www.researchgate.net/publication/330141893_education_and_its_politicisation_with_indian_examples.

Davenport, T. H. & Beck, J. C. (2001). *The attention economy: understanding the new currency of business.* Harvard Business School Press. ISBN 1-57851-441-X

De La Croix, D., & Doepke, M. (2009). To segregate or to integrate: Education politics and democracy. *The Review of Economic Studies, 76*(2), 597–628. Retrieved from https://www.jstor.org/stable/40247615.

Decuypere, M. (2019). Open education platforms: Theoretical ideas, digital operations and the figure of the open learner. *European Educational Research Journal, 18*(4), 439–460. https://doi.org/10.1177/1474904118814141.

Dembo, M., & Seli, H. (2004). Students. Resistance to change in learning strategies courses. *Journal of Developmental Education, 27*(3).

Dey, P., & Bandyopadhyay, S. (2018). Blended learning to improve quality of primary education among underprivileged school children in India. *Education and Information Technologies,* Springer. https://doi.org/10.1007/s10639-018-9832-1.

Docebo. (2016). *Elearning market trends and forecast 2017–2021.* Retrieved from https://eclass.teicrete.gr/modules/document/file.php/TP271/Additional%20material/docebo-elearning-trends-report-2017.pdf.

Dziuban, C., Hartman, J., & Moskal, P. (2004). Promising practices in online learning: Blended learning—The convergence of online and face-to-face education. *Blended learning, EDUCAUSE Review.* Retrieved from https://files.eric.ed.gov/fulltext/ED509636.pdf.

Foutsitzi, S., & Caridakis, G. (2019). ICT in education: Benefits, challenges and new directions. In*The Proceedings of 10th International Conference on Information, Intelligence, Systems and Applications (IISA),* PATRAS, Greece. https://doi.org/10.1109/IISA.2019.8900666.

Garrison, D. R. (2011). *E-learning in the 21st century: A framework for research and practice.* New York: Taylor & Francis. ISBN. 0-203-83876-9

GhoshRoy, S., & Parijat, U. (2017). Does e-readiness of citizens ensure better adoption of government's digital initiatives? A case based study. *Journal of Enterprise Information Management, 30*(1), 65–81. https://doi.org/10.1108/JEIM-01-2016-0001.

Gomersall, B. (2005). *Practical implementation of e-testing on a large scale, and implications for future e-assessment and e-learning* Shipley, West Yorkshire, UK. Retrieved from https://web.archive.org/web/20120505111916/http://www.btl.com/community/papers/.

Hawkins, R. (2005). *Enhancing research and education connectivity in Africa—The findings of the African Tertiary Institution Connectivity Study (ATICS) and Lessons for the Future of Campus Networks,* World Bank, Washington. Retrieved from: https://www.oecd.org/dataoecd/49/48/357 65204.pdf.

Hoffman, D. L., & Novak, T. P. (1998). Bridging the Racial Divide on the Internet. *Science,* *280*(5362), 390–391. https://doi.org/10.1126/science.280.5362.390.

Huawei: CSR. (2017). *The role of ICT in realising education for all by 2030* [Report]. Retrieved from https://s3-ap-southeast-1.amazonaws.com/elevatelimited-com/wp-content/uploads/public ation/ICT4SDG4-Final-Version.pdf.

Jensen, M. (1998). *Internet connectivity in Africa* [Report]. Available at: https://demiurge.wn.apc. org/africa/.

Jonassen, D., & Reeves, T. (1996). Learning with technology: Using computers as cognitive tools. *Handbook of research educational on educational communications and technology.* New York: Macmillan.

King, E., & Boyatt, R. (2015). Exploring factors that influence adoption of e-learning within higher education. *British Journal of Educational Technology, 46*(6), 1272–1280. https://doi.org/10.1111/ bjet.12195.

Knowlton, D. S. (2000). A theoretical framework for the online classroom: A defence and delineation of a Student-centered pedagogy. *New Directions for Teaching and Learning, 2000*(84), 5–14.

Kraemer, K. L., Dedrick, J., & Sharma, P. (2009). One laptop per child: Vision vs. reality. *Communications of the ACM, 52*(6), 66–73. https://doi.org/10.1145/1516046.1516063.

Lebow, D. (1993). Constructivist values for instructional systems design: Five principles toward a new mindset. Educational Technology. *Research and Development, 11*(3), 4–16.

Luksha, P., Cubista, J., Laszlo, A., Popovich, M., & Nineko, I. (2017). Educational ecosystems for societal transformation. Global education futures report. Retrieved from https://www.futurewor lds.eu/w/1/c/c2/GEF_Vision_Educational_Ecosystems_for_Societal_Transformation.pdf.

Major, C. H. (2015). *Teaching online: A guide to theory, research, and practice.* Johns Hopkins University Press. Available at https://jhupbooks.press.jhu.edu/title/teaching-online.

Mayer, R. E. (2002). Multimedia learning. *Psychology of learning and motivation, 41*, 85– 139. Retrieved from https://pdfs.semanticscholar.org/7a68/c08e7a8a44f242567e6257f0d67f58 b5b152.pdf.

Molnar, A. (1997). Computers in education: a brief history. *Technological Horizons in Education, 24*(11).

Mooji, T. (1999). Guidelines to Pedagogical Use of ICT in Education. In *The Proceedings of 8th Conference of the European Association for Research on Learning and Instruction (EARLI).* Goteborg, Sweden.

National Research Council. (2011). *Assessing 21st century skills: Summary of a workshop.* Washington, DC: The National Academies Press. https://doi.org/10.17226/13215.

Nicholson, P. (2007). *A history of E-learning.* Springer, Dordrecht: Computers and Education.

Pappas, C. (2019). Online learning statistics, Top 20 eLearning Statistics For 2019. Retrieved from https://elearningindustry.com/top-elearning-statistics-2019.

Park, H. Y. (2007). Emerging consumerism and the accelerated 'education divide': The case of specialized high schools in South Korea. *Journal of Critical Education Policy Studies, 5*(2).

Rai, L., & Deng, C. (2016). Influencing factors of success and failure in MOOC and general analysis of learner behaviour. *International Journal of Information and Education Technology, 6*(4).

Razzaque, A. (2020). M-Learning improves knowledge sharing over e-Learning platforms to build higher education students' social capital. *SAGE Open.* https://doi.org/10.1177/215824402092 6575.

Rovai, A., & Ponton, M. B. (2008). *Distance learning in higher education: A programmatic approach to planning, design, instruction, evaluation, and accreditation.* Teachers College Press. ISBN 978-0-8077-4878-7.

Saini, M. K., & Goel, N. (2019). How smart are smart classrooms? A review of smart classroom technologies. *ACM Computing Surveys, 52*(6). https://doi.org/10.1145/3365757.

Salazar, J. A. (2017). Educacion y TICs: aprender disfrutando. *CUBAHORA.* Retrieved from https:// www.cubahora.cu/sociedad/educacion-y-tics-aprender-disfrutando.

Sassen, S. (2002). Towards a sociology of information technology. *Current Sociology, 50*(3), 365– 388.

Scheuermann, F., & Julius, B. (2008). *The transition to computer-based assessment–new approaches to skills assessment and implications for large-scale testing.* Luxembourg, Luxembourg. Retrieved from https://web.archive.org/web/20091229150729/http://crell.jrc.it/RP/reporttransition.pdf.

Siemens, G. (2013). Massive open online courses: Innovation in education. *Open educational resources: Innovation, research and practice.* Vancouver: Commonwealth of Learning and Athabasca University.

Simon, H. A. (1971). *Designing organizations for an information-rich world.* Baltimore, MD: The Johns Hopkins Press. Retrieved from digitalcollections.library.cmu.edu.

Smeets, E., & Mooji, T. (2000). The impact of ICT on the teacher. In *The Proceedings of European Conference on Educational Research,* Edinburgh, Scotland. Retrieved from https://hdl.handle.net/2066/212197.

Technopak. (2016). *Whitepaper on digital learning market in India. Technopak & Simplilearn.* Retrieved from https://www.technopak.com/Files/Whitepaper-on-Digital-Learning-Market-in-India.pdf.

Tomczyk, Ł., & Oyelere, S. S. (2019). *ICT for learning and inclusion in Latin America and Europe.* Cracow: Pedagogical University of Cracow. https://doi.org/10.24917/9788395373732.

UNESCO. (2011). *Transforming education: The power of ICT policies. France.* Retrieved from https://www.unesco.org/new/fileadmin/MULTIMEDIA/FIELD/Dakar/pdf/Transforming%20Education%20the%20Power%20of%20ICT%20Policies.pdf.

UNMD. (2000). *United Nations Millenium Declaration,* General Assembly resolution 55/2. United Nations, New York.

Voogt, J., & Fisser, P. (2015). Computer assisted instruction. In *International encyclopedia for the social and behavioural science* (2nd ed). https://doi.org/10.1016/B978-0-08-097086-8.92027-0.

Voogt, J., & Vanden, A. (2001). Computer assisted learning. *International Encyclopedia for the Social and Behavioural Sciences.* https://doi.org/10.1016/B0-08-043076-7/01625-9.

Wales, J., Magee, A., & Nicolai, S. (2016). How does political context shape education reforms and their success? Lessons from the Development Progress project. *Overseas Development Institute.* Retrieved from https://www.odi.org/sites/odi.org.uk/files/resource-documents/10808.pdf.

Watson, J. (2008). Blended learning: The convergence of online and face-to-face education. Promising Practices in Online Learning. *North American Council for Online Learning.* Retrieved from https://files.eric.ed.gov/fulltext/ED509636.pdf.

Watwood, B., Nugent, J., & Deihl, W. (2009). *Building from content to community: [Re]Thinking the transition to online teaching and learning,* ACTE White Paper. Retrieved from https://www.researchgate.net/publication/280713047_Building_from_Content_to_Community_ReThinking_the_Transition_to_Online_Teaching_and_Learning.

Weller, M. (2011). A pedagogy of abundance. *Spanish Journal of Pedagogy, 249,* 223–236.

Woolf, B. P. (2007). Building intelligent interactive tutors: Student-centered strategies for revolutionizing e-learning. *Morgan Kaufmann.* https://doi.org/10.1016/B978-0-12-373594-2.X0001-9.

Wright, N., Miller, E., Dawes, L., et al. (2020). Beyond 'chalk and talk': Educator perspectives on design immersion programs for rural and regional schools. *International Journal of Technology and Design Education, 30,* 35–65. https://doi.org/10.1007/s10798-018-9487-7.

WSIS. (2003). *Declaration of Principles. Building the information society: A global challenge in the new Millennium.* United Nations, New York.

Zhao, Y., & Cziko, G. A. (2001). Teacher adoption of technology: A perceptual control theory perspective. *Journal of Technology and Teacher Education, 9*(1), 5–30.

Ziemba, E. (2013). The holistic and systems approach to a sustainable information society. *Journal of Computer Information Systems, 54*(1), 106–116.

Ziemba, E. (2016). *Towards a sustainable information society: People, business and public administration perspectives.* Newcastle upon Tyne: Cambridge Scholars Publishing.

# Chapter 5
# Emergence of Social Technologies

## *Social* Meets *E-Learning*

## 5.1 Introduction

This chapter attempts to show how the characteristics of contemporary digital technology have significantly contributed in making learning a social process. We will demonstrate the potential of this technology to trigger a transition from twentieth-century conceptualization of learning as a centralized, teacher-centric, pipelined process to twenty-first-century conceptualization of learning as a decentralized, student-centric process. We have reserved the term "*social technology*" to refer to this contemporary digital technology, which happens to be a new wave of ICT. While we will provide formal definitions to justify the terminology usage, social technology in this context is an umbrella term used to capture a wide variety of terminologies depicting internet-enabled communications, platforms, and tools, e.g., web 2.0, mobile 2.0, social media, social software, etc., which has the potential to establish *collaborative connectivity* among billions of individuals over the globe.

The inclusive spirit of social technologies and socially enabled platforms, enabling collaboration and connections among appropriate entities and facilitating effective networking between and across social groups, give a new dimension to the practice of teaching-learning process. Contemporary social technology not only supports teachers and students to create and exchange educational resources and learning artifacts[1] within Institutional framework, its potential to foster informal communication also enables learners to use social technology and socially enabled platforms to encourage informal learning outside classroom.

---

[1] A *learning artifact* (or *educational artifact*) "is an object created by students during the course of instruction. Under the constructionist theory of educational psychology, the concept of making knowledge visible is a central component. The creation of learning artifacts is a technique used to allow students to display their knowledge in a public forum (usually the classroom)."—Wikipedia.

© The Author(s), under exclusive license to Springer Nature Singapore Pte Ltd. 2021    101
S. Bandyopadhyay et al., *Bridging the Education Divide Using Social Technologies*,
https://doi.org/10.1007/978-981-33-6738-8_5

The ability of social technology to facilitate effective collaboration has made *sharing* the premise of contemporary social and economic transactions. The emergence of sharing economy in the twenty-first century, guided by the principal of using social technology to foster effective collaboration, has significantly altered extant and traditional economic practices. This emergent economy identifies every human entity as potential producer/consumer of knowledge, therefore an able contributor to the collaborative socio-economic framework. It is the connecting spirit of contemporary social technologies that have paved the path for optimal capturing and application of crowd knowledge to generate socio-economic benefits, which has a long-term implication in realizing twenty-first-century education process.

The chapter is divided into two main sections: the first part, after providing definitions of social technology and its associated components, attempts at characterizing the same to arrive at the prospects it has to offer in both economic and social domain. The latter section discusses practical instances of utilizing social technologies and socially enabled platforms as a mean to facilitate teaching and learning practices. The practical evidences placed amidst theoretical characterization of social technologies will enable the readers to appreciate the possibility of contemporary digital technologies in creating personalized and socially situated forms of learning, where learners can actively participate in the teaching-learning process. In this context, in order to appreciate the usefulness and impact of social technology on education, we have evaluated the extant approaches from four angles, as suggested by Roblyer (2005): (1) examining the effectiveness of social technology to improve teaching-learning process; (2) examining the impact of social technology to achieve important societal goals (e.g., equitable education/education-for-all); (3) investigating the negative side effects of social technology on learners and formulate strategies to make the impact more positive; and, (4) highlighting problems regarding implementation of social technology in education and suggesting mechanisms for better implementation strategies.

## 5.2  Social Technology: A Conceptual Perspective

We have entered into a new era of *networked world*. In today's world, technology has enabled us to interact, innovate and share knowledge in ways, which were previously unthinkable. We call this the Networked Society (Castells 2004), enabled by internet-enabled communications, platforms and tools, that include regular personal computers, embedded computers, and mobile personal devices (Cell-phones, PDAs, Tablets), connected together using computer networking technologies. We call them *social technology,* an umbrella term used to capture a wide variety of terminologies depicting internet-enabled communications, platforms, and tools, e.g., web 2.0, mobile 2.0, social media, social software, etc., which has the potential to establish *collaborative connectivity* among billions of individuals over the globe. Social media (e.g., wiki, blogs, social networking sites like Facebook, twitter, Instagram, etc.) are one of the significant socially enabled applications powered by social technology.

This digital revolution is giving rise to a new economy –that can be termed as "digital network economy" (Brousseau and Nicolas 2007). When two persons connect, their lives change. With everything connected our world changes.

The term *social technologies* refer to "tools and practices that constitute our increased capacity for personal communication, production, publication, distribution and sharing." (Hagen and Robertson 2010). Social technologies can be characterized by "greater social participation in mediated contexts" (Boyd 2007). The *social* nature of social technologies has enabled us to shift the control of technology away from organizations and companies (Battarbee 2003). As narrated by Shirky (2008): "The ease with which we can now connect, communicate, produce, share, replicate, locate and distribute information has had, and continues to have, a profound impact on our social, cultural and technological practices." Some of these impacts can be exemplified as follows:

- Billions of people now use social media for communicating, learning, marketing, shopping, and decision making. Internet-based social media sites enable us to create and consume multi-modal user-generated contents; facilitate us to stay connected with friends, family, colleagues, customers, or clients. Social networking can have a social purpose, a business purpose, or both, through sites such as Facebook, Twitter, LinkedIn, and Instagram, among others. Social networking has become a significant base for the marketing and advertising sectors, seeking to engage customers. Increasing use of social media platforms including social networking sites, blogs, video sharing sites, etc., now allows consumers to seamlessly share their consumption behaviors online. Such *socially shared consumption* (Kunst and Ravi 2014) can range from electronic word-of-mouth to formal online reviews as well as automated product mentions facilitated by social media applications.
- The rapid development of social technology has enabled the development of what we call the new *platform economy* (Parker et al. 2016, 2017), an emerging economic arrangement, which brings together strangers in one forum and fosters effective exchange of goods and services among them (e.g., Airbnb, Lyft, LendingClub, etc.). In this digitally driven platform economy, consumers and service providers form a collaborative network using the platform. Platform is the foundation of the entire ecosystem, providing a space for the exchange of information, trading, logistics, and other facilities to consumers and service providers. They perform various economic activities on the platform including information exchange, demand matching, payment and receipt and delivery of goods. The participants of the platform economy interact and cooperate with each other, which enables them to create greater value (Lehdonvirta et al. 2019).
- The notion of platform economy, being a digital facilitator in economic and social transaction, is premised on the ideological and operative dynamics of sharing/collaborative economy (Sundararajan 2016). This nascent form of economic arrangement encourages shared creation, production, distribution, trade and consumption of goods, services and ideas by *crowd* (e.g., YouTube, Airbnb, Etsy, bla-bla-car, etc.), and hence termed as *crowd-based capitalism* (Sundararajan

2016). This attempt to build an integrated economy through effective sharing of goods (both informational goods and physical goods) and services is premised on the motivational and philosophical foundation of "sharism." The collaborative culture cultivated by sharing economy has enabled billions of people across the globe to get connected and actively participate in the process of achieving social development and developing collective capacities to solve social atrocities (Tapscott and Williams 2006).

- The notion of *crowd collaboration* in a business context is an extension of what is known as outsourcing: operationalizing some of the internal business functions using external business entities. However, instead of an organized business body with a centralized governing apparatus, crowd collaboration has a decentralized premise and relies on free individual agents (the *crowd*) to collaborate to perform a given operation or to find solution for a given problem using social technologies (Tapscott and Williams 2006). This kind of outsourcing is also referred to as *crowd-sourcing* (Horton and Chilton 2010). These crowd-based operations may be incentivized by monetary or equivalent reward, though it is not always mandatory.
- Benkler and Nissenbaum (2006) uses the term 'networked information economy' and "commons-based peer production" to describe a "system of production, distribution, and consumption of information goods characterized by decentralized individual action carried out through widely distributed, non-market means that do not depend on market strategies." The examples of such collaborative efforts are creation of free and open-source software and Wikipedia.

For the first time in history, social technology-enabled tools and socially enabled applications and platform democratize the mechanism for self-expressions at a global scale. At the same time, these tools and applications enable billions of people to connect and cooperate with others on a global scale. Shirky (2008) argues that with the advent of these online social tools, virtual groups can be formed anytime-anywhere, without any restriction of time, space, and cost. These virtual communities have enabled formation of new kind of organization and governance, making them more efficient by reducing the costs of communication, collaboration, and coordination. This enabled the citizens over the globe to leverage existing social capital and also to create new forms of social and human capital.

As narrated by Tapscott (2014), "The Age of Networked Intelligence is an age of promise.... It is not simply about the networking of technology but about the networking of humans through technology. It is not an age of smart machines but of humans who, through networks, can combine their intelligence, knowledge, and creativity for breakthroughs in the creation of wealth and social development. It is an age of vast new promise and unimaginable opportunity."

## 5.2.1  Defining Social Technology

Historically, the term "Social technology" has two meanings (Li and Bernoff 2011): a term related to "social engineering," a concept developed in the nineteenth century (Pelikan 2003; North and Wallis 1994; Schotter 1981), and a term to depict "internet-enabled *social software*," a concept that evolved in the early twenty-first century (Andersen 2011; Derksen et al. 2012; Chui et al. 2012).

As the conceptualization of social technologies varies from "social engineering" to "social software," for our purpose, we will be focusing on the second depiction of "Social Technology" and try to derive the meaning of social technologies in terms of "digital technologies used by people to interact socially and together to create, enhance, and exchange content" (Andersen 2011; Derksen et al. 2012; Chui et al. 2012). Social technologies are defined as any digital technology used for social purposes or on a social basis, and includes social hardware (traditional communication tools, e.g., PC or smart mobile devices), social software (operating platforms, e.g., web 2.0 or mobile 2.0), and socially enabled applications (tools and services, e.g., social media) (Alberghini et al. 2010).

Chui et al. (2012) defines social technologies as digital technologies that people use to interact with each other socially to create, enhance, and exchange content. The following three characteristics distinguish social technologies from other technologies:

- Social technology is a derivative of information technology;
- Social technology provides rights to communicate with anyone and create and/or modify content in a distributed fashion;
- Social technology provides distributed access to communication tools and digital content.

## 5.2.2  Components of Social Technologies

As indicated earlier, social technology in our context is an umbrella term used to capture a wide variety of terminologies depicting internet-enabled communications, platforms and tools, e.g., web 2.0, mobile 2.0, social media tools, social software, etc., which has the potential to establish *collaborative connectivity* among billions of individuals over the globe. In the following sub-sections, we will illustrate these components of social technology.

### Web 2.0: From Mass Communication to Communication by the Masses

As per World Wide Web Consortium (W3C), "The World Wide Web is the universe of network-accessible information, an embodiment of human knowledge." Web 1.0 was the first generation of it, facilitating static web presence of several companies, e-commerce, and information repositories. Generally, websites in the web 1.0 era are known as *Read-Only Web*, since they are engineered, designed, developed, and maintained by professional web developers or content experts and users can only view them, without any provision to contribute in them.

Web 2.0, also termed as "Read-Write Web," Participative (or Participatory) web (Blank and Reisdorf 2012) or Social Web is the second generation of World Wide Web that enables and encourages users' contributions and interactions. Web 2.0 technologies allows for many common web applications such as social networking, blogs, wikis, and many other tools for real-time collaboration (Zyl 2009). O'Reilly (2005) originally coined the term web 2.0 to differentiate the dynamic, collaborative, and interactive features of web 2.0 from the static, non-interactive features of web 1.0. Web 2.0 has shifted the directionality of the flow of content over the internet from a purely producer-centered model to a more multi-directional model enabling participation of any individual and generation of online content by the masses (Kim et al. 2009).

Thus, web 2.0 has opened opportunities for participation by ordinary users in content generation. Any user can produce and consume contents over the internet using any application on web 2.0 platform, be it user-generated videos on YouTube or product reviews in Amazon or status updates on Facebook, etc. Blank and Reisdorf (2012) describes web 2.0 as an "antithesis of the mass society model (Rosenberg and White 1957) of mass media that has dominated Western societies for the past 150 years." The production and distribution of content by mass media requires large amounts of investment which is available only to large organizations such as radio and television networks, newspapers, book publishers, etc. With the emergence of web 2.0 platform, we notice a huge shift from a "mass society model" to a personalized production and distribution model (Benkler and Nissenbaum 2006).

According to Blank and Reisdorf (2012), success of web 2.0 depends on two primary features. First, the "network effects," which indicates that the value of product or service increases with increasing number of users. On the Internet, network effects are easier to achieve, since users' participation can grow very easily on web 2.0 platform. For example, value of video sharing platform like Youtube or social networking site like Facebook is high because of the network effects that have facilitated the user-growth. The second feature of web 2.0 is the "platform" itself that create simple, reliable environments where users can participate and interact. Examples of web 2.0 enabled platforms include social networking sites (e.g., Facebook), video sharing sites (e.g., YouTube), hosted services, blogs, wikis, collaborative consumption platforms (e.g., Airbnb, Lyft, etc.), etc. The two components are intimately linked: the platform provides the structure that helps network effect to emerge, provided large numbers of users believe that the platform is valuable. Based on this analysis, Blank and Reisdorf (2012) defines web 2.0 as: "Using the Internet to provide platforms through which network effects can emerge."

### Mobile 2.0: The Social Web Meets Mobility

Web 2.0 is primarily a collection of browser-based Internet technologies that enables anyone with a computer and internet connection to participate in any web 2.0 platforms. Mobile 2.0 is a successor to web 2.0, leveraging the strength and capabilities of web 2.0-supported applications and extending them to the mobile platform, making them more powerful and usable through Mobile Apps. Mobile web 2.0 or simply mobile 2.0 is used to improve and enrich mobile computing, enabling users to access the advanced features of the web anytime, anywhere, on the go using Mobile Apps.

The way people interact with mobile phones and the way they conduct their daily lives are changing. Users are exposed to services that just a few years ago could not have been imagined to exist via a mobile phone (Boyera 2007). They include web applications including social media services that integrate GPS, camera, Maps, mobile wallet, and the list continues. In today's world, mobile devices act as complex carriers for receiving and providing multi-modal information, and, at the same time, as platforms for novel services. The mobile applications are also generating newer possibilities that enable the mobile devices to act as a powerful interface to communicate with the external world through ubiquitous access to the Internet.

In the near future, we may assume that the web 2.0 services will mainly be accessed from mobile devices. One obvious reason for using mobile web is that users can access web 2.0 and related internet-enabled services anywhere, anytime, on the go with an internet-connected smartphone. Smartphones enable us not only to get access to Internet on the go, but also to combine functions of the device (e.g., GPS, camera, etc.) with the capabilities of the Internet. Many mobile apps draw information from the web or run almost entirely from the web. At the same time, mobile web use the context-aware services that probe the location, state of user (walking/sitting), availability of user (from calendar), weather, etc., to personalize the service provisioning.

### Socially Enabled Applications: Social Media

Traditionally, Internet, in the age of web 1.0, used to be content provider only and users were passive consumers of those contents. Increasingly, consumers are utilizing applications on web 2.0 enabled platforms, e.g., social networking, blogs, wikis, etc., to interact by producing and consuming content. These socially enabled applications on web 2.0 platform can be described as *social media*, which can now significantly impact the dynamics of interactions within informal social groups and formal organizations. These applications, such as blogs (e.g., bloggers), video sharing (e.g., YouTube), presentation sharing (e.g., SlideShare), social networking (e.g., Facebook, LinkedIn), instant messaging (e.g., Skype), and groupware (e.g., Google Docs), facilitate active participation of users, thereby promoting a more socially connected digital platform (Anderson 2007). According to Kietzmann et al. (2011), "Social media employ mobile and web-based technologies to create highly interactive platforms via which individuals and communities share, co-create, discuss, and modify user-generated content."

There is a general agreement of what digital tools may be *classified* under social media, but there is no single definition of social media, especially across disciplines (Carr and Hayes 2015). Social media have often been conceptualized techno-centrically, considered to be synonymous with web 2.0 (O'Reilly 2005). Additionally, most of the time, the term "social media" and "social networking sites (SNS)" are used interchangeably. Though SNSs (e.g., Facebook, Twitter, etc.)—by their nature—are typically social media tools, not all social media are inherently social networking sites (Carr and Hayes 2015).

Some existing definitions focus on the nature of message exchange pattern in social media. For example, Russo et al. (2008) defined social media as, "those that facilitate online communication, networking, and/or collaboration" (p. 22). Lewis (2010) described "social media" as a "label for digital technologies that allow people to connect, interact, produce and share content" (p. 2). However, according to Carr and Hayes (2015), "these definitions are problematic in that they could easily be applied to other communication technologies such as email, missing the unique technological and social affordances that distinguish social media."

We will follow the definition by Carr and Hayes (2015), who defines social media as: "Social media are *Internet-based channels* that allow users to *opportunistically interact and selectively self-present*, either in *real-time or asynchronously*, with both *broad and narrow audiences* who derive *value from user-generated content* and the *perception of interaction* with others." The clarifications of the terms used in the definition are given below (based on Carr and Hayes (2015):

*Internet-Based*: Social media are a set of online tools operating on Internet. Web 2.0 may be sufficient but not necessary for developing social media tools.

*Opportunistically Interact and Selectively Self-Present (also Known as Channel dis-entrainment)*: In a face-to-face communication, both the participating agents in the communication dyad need to present simultaneously. However, in social media, user participates as and when he or she is willing to do that (Walther 1996).

*Either in Real-Time or asynchronously*: Although social media support real-time chat functionalities (synchronous communication), social media predominantly provide asynchronous communication tools that do not require simultaneous presence of interacting participants, making temporal commitments discretionary; user can participate whenever he/she wants to participate in social media channel (Walther 1995, 1996).

*Broad and Narrow Audiences (also Termed as Mass-Personal Communication)*: Mass-personal communication refers to situations when "mass communication channels are used for interpersonal communications, interpersonal channels are used for mass communication, and when individuals simultaneously engage in mass and interpersonal communication" (O'Sullivan and Carr 2018). Social Networking sites, for examples, (e.g., Facebook, Twitter, etc.) are ideal venues to explore mass-personal communication, where users are allowed to broadcast messages to a mass audience, or, multicast message to a group of audience, or unicast message to a single audience; on the other hand, receivers may reply either interpersonally to the individual or group or through a mass message of their own (Walther et al. 2010).

*User-generated Value*: According to Carr and Hayes (2015), "the value (i.e., benefit or enjoyment) of using social media is derived from the contributions from or interactions with other users rather than content generated by organization or individual hosting the medium." The value of the social medium may be different from its content, generated by an individual user/organization. For example, a broadcast message on a product or service may be promoted in a social media channel by an organization, but individuals may derive greater utility and value not from the message itself but from the user-generated comments about that message. Their perception about the product or service may be less influenced by the organization-generated message but more by the peer feedback (Walther et al. 2010).

*Perception of Interaction with Others*: With the proliferation of digital agents, algorithms, and other Artificial Intelligence-based mechanistic features operate online, it is possible that users *perceive* an interactive element while operating on a social media channel, even if that interaction is not with other human users. In other words, a social media channel provides a sense of interactive engagement with others, even when the interaction is not with human users. Additionally, geocentric services like Foursquare (a local search-and-discovery mobile app) and Tinder (a location-based social search mobile app) may "allow an individual to perceive herself or himself as interacting with others in a specific location (e.g., airport terminal, city park) even without message exchange—merely acknowledging the presence of others may facilitate perceptions of interaction" (Lindqvist et al. 2011).

Apart from these key terminologies used in defining social media, Vuori (2011) characterizes and categorizes social media applications from the perspective of 5C: *communication, collaboration, connecting, completing, and combining* (5C), as illustrated below:

*Communication*: Social media tools provide opportunities to publish contents, express opinions, and create influence through sharing content and/or opinion. Communication is executed through blogs and microblogs (e.g., Twitter), media sharing systems (e.g., Youtube, SlideShare, etc.), instant messaging (e.g. WhatsApp), etc.

*Collaboration*: Social media enables users to create and edit content collectively without location and time constraints. Wikis (e.g., Wikipedia) are examples of social media applications supporting collaborative creation and updation of contents.

*Connecting:* Social networking sites enable users to form online virtual communities by connecting people with similar interests and creating communities around these interests.

*Completing*: Social media tools are used to augment content or connect content with other content. Examples are: Pinterest, Google Reader, and Digg.

*Combining:* Combined social media sites are typically called as mash-ups, meaning "a coherent combination of pre-existing web services that allow a certain user within a platform to use another application, in a specific window, without the need to get out of the initial website" (Bonson and Flores 2011). Google Maps, for example, allows users to pinpoint geographically the locations of hotels and restaurants, and so on.

However, these characteristics of Social media in form of the 5C's are non-exclusive and only suggestive. There are social media tools that support two or more functionalities. For example, Facebook and Twitter can embed videos and photographs from another location on the Web; similarly, wikis can provide RSS feeds to keep up with updates on a certain article (Vuori 2011).

These components of social technologies that are most commonly utilized by users or participants in form of social media tools, web 2.0 applications and the smartphone enabled mobile 2.0 brings us to the discussion on the indispensability of platforms or platform organizations. The subsequent sections will elaborate the importance of platform organizations and their inherent component of collaboration and sharism, facilitating users to connect and collaborate with one another effortlessly.

### 5.2.3  Platform Organization and Sharing Economy

Twentieth century gave rise to large scale business organizations that follow a pipeline model of supply chain, controlling a linear series of activities mostly within their own companies. Thus, the flow of *value* in the traditional *pipeline* business model is linear from a producer to a consumer. "Pipeline businesses create value by controlling a linear series of activities—the classic value-chain model. Inputs at one end of the chain (say, materials from suppliers) undergo a series of steps that transform them into an output that's worth more" (Alstyne et al. 2016, p. 4). In this centralized, organization-centric pipeline configuration, the distance between consumer and producer is large and linear, and the consumers have no control on the resources invested in production of goods and services and their distribution.

With the advent of social technologies, this linear structure and producer-consumer relationship got disrupted with the emergence of a new economic organization, called the **Platform Organization**. A *platform* presents the digital infrastructure and rules for a marketplace that connects producers and consumers. Examples are: Uber, Airbnb, Amazon, YouTube, and similar companies that disrupted the markets. The main asset of a platform is its network of producers and consumers. In contrast to pipeline strategies, "*resource orchestration* is more important than *resource control*, and facilitating interactions and managing relationships have a higher priority than internal optimization" (Alstyne et al. 2016; Parker et al. 2016, 2017). In this digitally driven platform organizations, consumers and producers (of goods or service) form a collaborative network using the platform. Platform is the foundation of the entire ecosystem, providing a space for the exchange of information, trading, logistics, and other facilities to consumers and producers. A large number of consumers and producers constitute the major players of the platform organization. The participants of the platform interact and cooperate with each other, which enables to create greater value. Here, the production process is decentralized and it is consumer-centric; rather, it blurs the difference between producers and consumers, creating a new term called *prosumers.* Additionally, the resources are coordinated outside the boundary of platform organization and the value is created outside the platform organization. For example, Google owns *YouTube platform* but the products (the video content of YouTube) are not generated by YouTube but by its users. And, those YouTube users can play the role of both producer and consumer of content. Similarly, the platform Airbnb does not own a single hotel, but the users of this platform can play the role of both producer and consumer of temporary living spaces available on rent (like a hotel space).

Thus, Platform businesses create an ecosystem comprising of four components:

- *Owners* of the platform (controller and arbiter e.g., Uber owns Uber Platform but not the cars)
- *Providers* who serve as the platforms' interface (e.g., mobile device running Uber Apps)
- *Producers* who create their offerings (e.g., Car with drivers in Uber)
- *Consumers* who use those offerings (e.g., the passengers who hire the car as and when needed).

This notion of platform organization also brings about the concept of sharing/collaborative economy, which includes shared creation, production, distribution, trade and consumption of goods, services and ideas by different people and organizations via digital platform (Gerwe and Silva 2020). The motivation and philosophy behind the collaborative building of value that results from sharing goods and services is termed "sharism." Sharing economy may be defined as "any marketplace that brings together distributed networks of individuals to share or exchange otherwise underutilised assets" (Koopman et al. 2015, p. 4). Extant Research on the Sharing Economy (SE) has posited that SE-based ventures had four commonalities between them: (1) focus on resource sharing: both tangible (e.g., physical resource) and non-tangible (e.g., knowledge resource); (2) belief in the commons, (3) trust between strangers, and (4) critical mass (Botsman and Rogers 2010). Through the use of social technologies, especially mobile apps and web 2.0, researchers believe that it has ushered a new era of ***crowd-based capitalism*** that could enable anyone to enter the mainstream economic activities by collaborating their efforts (Sundararajan 2016). Wikipedia is an example where people collaborate to create content and information giving rise to open source movement. There is a strong historical and global connection between the emergence of peer-to-peer platforms and a widespread feeling that the new technology-enabled practices empower people (Benkler and Nissenbaum 2006).

Instead of relying on extant market agents to facilitate purposive exchange, contemporary sharing economy premises itself on peer-to-peer relationships and the potential of the same to trigger effective collaborations along socio-economic axis. A *peer-to-peer marketplace* is defined as a connecting digital platform, linking people with the need for a particular product/service with those in possession of the desired product/service, which are lying unutilized for the moment. It is sharing economy that happens to be the theoretical umbrella, based on which the P2P marketplaces are designed. Premised on the ideals of sharing economy, P2P marketplaces attempt to prevent mis-utilization or over-utilization of resources by triggering effective collaborations between otherwise unrelated agents. Optimum usage of resources guaranteed by collaborative consumption and re-usability of extant resources has enabled P2P marketplaces to occupy noteworthy position in contemporary economy, which has in turn triggered the shift toward globalization and democratization of information. The intention in this context is to create a connected generation, who, by virtue of effective collaboration, is endowed with the capacity to disrupt extant socio-economic functioning in unimaginable ways. Today's world is increasingly witnessing successful business models in different fields, which are premised on the ideal of collaborative consumption facilitated by P2P marketplace. AirBnb in hospitality and Lyft in transportation serve to be perfect examples giving practical shape to the theoretical possibilities of sharing economy and drastically transforming the way industries conventionally operate (Sundararajan 2016). At the same time, it opens up the opportunity for an individual to get engaged in part-time/freelancing activities. Rise of *gig-economy* is one of the key characteristics of sharing economy principles that gives rise to contract works and individual entrepreneurship (Sundararajan 2016). A service provider in a sharing economy platform is indeed an independent entrepreneur, offering his/her unused asset using any peer-to-peer marketplace. For example, any individual can offer his/her service as a part-time driver in any ride-sharing platform (e.g., lyft or BlaBlaCar) and earn some money.

In the next chapter (Chap. 6), we will show how platform organization can be created using this concept of sharing economy in the domain of education, thus enabling a transition from twentieth-century conceptualization of learning as a centralized, teacher-centric, pipelined process to twenty-first-century conceptualization of learning as a decentralized, student-centric process supported by digital platform enabling collaboration and connections among appropriate entities. However, before going into that, we will discuss in the next section the contemporary initiatives to use social technologies and socially enabled platforms in teaching-learning process and will evaluate their effectiveness.

## 5.3   Impact of Social Technologies on Teaching and Learning: Contemporary Initiatives

### 5.3.1   Introduction

The participatory and collaborative spirit of social technology-driven tools and platforms has a strong similarity with socio-cultural accounts of learner-centric, decentralized, twenty-first-century education system "where knowledge is constructed actively by learners with the support of communal social settings" (Selwyn 2015). These digital social platforms encourage personalized and socially situated forms of learning, with learners actively participating in the process of co-construction of online knowledge (Lameras et al. 2009). At the same time, these technology-supported networks of learners and teachers have the possibilities to realize teaching and learning as a social process through collective participation. For these reasons, these technology-driven initiatives create a great enthusiasm among some educators and educationalists, who have started believing this as "the future of education" using a new set of terminology as "school 2.0," "education 2.0," and "learning 2.0" (Hargadon 2008; Selwyn 2015).

Social technology-enabled tools and platforms are now playing an increasingly vital role not only in formal education in schools and colleges but also in informal learning including lifelong learning (Greenhow and Askari 2017; Rehm et al.

2019). Some platforms are specially designed for education purpose (e.g., Edmodo, Coursera, etc.); some are dedicated to the advancement of professional/research activities (e.g., LinkedIn, ResearchGate, academia.edu, etc.); whereas, some other social media platforms are designed for social interactions and content sharing for entertainment purposes (e.g., Facebook, Twitter, YouTube, etc.). These varied platforms are progressively getting used for both in-school and out-of-school learning, focusing on academic and non-academic variety of learning (Greenhow et al. 2014; Manca and Ranieri 2016; Rodríguez-Hoyos et al. 2015). Teachers are also using social media for professional development, student engagement, engaging with peer group and experts globally for sharing and discussing learning contents, etc. (Carpenter and Krutka 2014; Macià and Garcia 2017; Sauers and Richardson 2015; Ito et al. 2013).

However, it is to be remembered that teaching and learning is a social process and application and adoption of technology in education needs to be viewed from a socio-technical perspective. A socio-technical perspective studies interactions between "technologies that people construct and use in collaboration" (Lamb and Davidson 2002). In other words, in a socio-technical network in the domain of education, the dynamic interrelationship between humans (educators, students, administrators), structures (learning groups, educator groups, institutions, policies), and technology (e.g., social media) should be taken into consideration in order to successfully implement any educational technology (Mlitwa 2007). Hence, educational application of the social technology is rather "more complex, constrained and compromised than prevailing descriptions of 'education 2.0' and 'school 2.0' would suggest" (Selwyn 2015).

In order to appreciate the usefulness and impact of any technology on education process, Roblyer (2005) suggested that there should be four kinds of impact studies that need to be carried out: (1) studies that establish the effectiveness of technology to improve teaching-learning process; (2) studies that examine impact of technology to achieve important societal goals (e.g., equitable education/education-for-all); (3) studies that investigate the negative side effects and formulate strategies to make their impact more positive (Raza et al. 2019); and, (4) studies that highlight problems with implementation of technology in education and suggest mechanisms for better implementation strategies.

***Studies to Establish the Effectiveness of Technology***: Whenever an impact-creating technology positively disrupts our socio-economic landscape (e.g., positive impact of social technologies and digital social platforms in business), educational technology professionals often assume, even in the absence of proper impact study, that the benefits of these technologies are equally valid or applicable in the domain of education (Roblyer 2005). There is a significant body of research, highlighting the positive impact of social technologies and socially enabled platforms not only in our everyday lives and livelihood, but also on K–12 and higher education (Greenhow and Askari 2017; Rehm et al. 2019). However, very few studies have attempted to measure technology's effectiveness at improving student learning outcomes in and outside classrooms (Greenhow and Askari 2015, 2017). We will discuss this in details in Sect. 5.3.2.

***Studies to Examine Impact of Technology on Important Societal Goals***: It is important to examine whether or not the anticipated benefits expected out of applications of social technology in education is evenly distributed among students, teachers, and other stakeholders irrespective of their demographic variability. For example, are underserved students benefiting as much from access to social media as compared to their privileged counterparts (Greenhow et al. 2019)? We need to examine impact of education technology on equity and access in order to ascertain that, it is not widening the Digital Divide, which, in turn, may increase the education divide further. Very few studies have examined the benefit of social technology in education from the perspective of underserved communities, looking at differences among learners or teachers, or differential access to technology (Greenhow and Askari 2017). For example, to promote social media integration in teaching practices, it is important to provide access to computer and Internet at home as well as increased opportunities for professional development (Kale and Goh 2014). We will discuss this in detail in Sect. 5.3.3.

***Studies to Investigate the Negative Side Effects of Technology***: Roblyer (2005) argued that we need to have some form of socio-psychological theories that can help predict negative side effects of proposed technology and tune the use of technology in order to make its impact more positive. As an example, it is important to examine whether integration of mobile technologies in-school life promotes cheating during examination, and, if so, what should schools do to implement them differently (Roblyer 2005). Similarly, access to internet may expose young students to unwanted and harmful contents. At the same time, it may distract students toward online entertainment (e.g., games and video-based amusement) and unproductive socialization using social networking sites (e.g., Facebook). If so, what should be the policy decisions to avoid those issues? We will discuss this in details in Sect. 5.3.4.

***Studies to Examine Effective Implementation Strategies***: Most of the ICT implementation initiatives in the context of development are exogenous in nature. They mainly attempt in externally imposing their welfare initiatives without giving attention to the technology adoption capabilities of individual actors of the targeted community. This approach assumes that development can be achieved through acquisition and implementation of technology alone (Mansell 2010). This approach results in implementation failures of ICT-interventions, since they fail to recognize the importance of the context and of users' capabilities (Giolo 2012). The endogenous approach, on the other hand, attempts in undertaking developmental initiatives by taking into account the target group's culture and contexts. These approaches are premised on the conceptualization that the impact of ICT usages "are caused not by the technology, but by the new forms of informational behaviour they facilitate." (Mansell 2010). The endogenous model thus focuses more directly on resources, aspirations, and capabilities of users in the context of development. In our context, implementation studies should attempt to explain how, why, and for whom the technological approach works well in given situations (Roblyer 2005). For example, Callaghan and Bower (2012) studied the effectiveness of social networking sites on students in a 10th-grade commerce classes in Australia to find out improvement in students' analytical skills along with improvement in digital literacy and level of motivation. They found that the effectiveness of social media usage depends on how the teachers are implementing the guidelines and mediating the learning process over usual socialization on the platform. Hence, an effective implementation strategy must consider the wider social, economic, political, and cultural contexts of the societal act of learning. We will discuss this in details in Sect. 5.3.5.

## 5.3.2 Effectiveness of Social Technology-Enabled Tools and Platforms in Education

Social technology-enabled platforms including social media has percolated extensively among the general public at large. Millions are participating on Facebook, YouTube, Pinterest, Twitter, and so on, producing and consuming contents in various forms and modalities. However, the nature of participation and digital social behavior of each individual are widely different and depends on numerous factors such as demographic profiles, attitude and inclination toward online media, peer group profile, and so on. To understand social media adoption, Forrester Research has developed a *Social Technographics Ladder* to benchmark social media users by their level of participation in social media. This survey-based benchmarking method takes into account current social technology-based platforms including social networking sites (Li and Bernoff 2011). Online users are categorized in a ladder-like structure into seven categories:

From top to bottom on the ladder, the categories are:

*Creators*: As the name suggests, they are the creators of online contents of different forms and modalities that other people consume. They are the backbone of social media because they provide the motivation for others to participate in online platforms.

*Conversationalists*: This group drives the conversation in online social sphere. Instead of creating new content, they share and spread contents available online.

*Critics*: This group comments on social media posts, gives feedback, and reviews available contents with their own opinions and judgments. They sometimes serve as moderators to ensure the usefulness of the online content.

*Collectors*: This group of people aggregates good content on the Internet. They play a more passive role in the process since they collate contents but do not actively interact with it.

*Joiners*: The joiners maintain a social profile on different social networking sites but rarely participate.

*Spectators*: As the name suggests, these people consume contents from online platform without disclosing their identities as far as possible. Both Joiners and Spectators are playing a passive role in social platforms.

*Inactives*: These people neither create nor consume social content of any kind. However, this number is shrinking fast.

It is true that some people belong to multiple groups in different contexts. Creators can also be conversationalists as well as collectors. However, people who are passive users need external support and motivation to participate as active users in online platforms. As one might expect, user typologies created in Social Technographics Model can vary from country to country. Also, engagement profiles are related to age, gender, and socio-economic conditions. Although the number of inactive users is reducing day by day, still the majority of participants in social platforms are mostly passive users (Li and Bernoff 2011).

Hence, in the context of learners and teachers using social media for educational purpose, the participation and engagement profile would vary extensively, as per the above description. In the next section, we will describe the possible role learners and teachers play in this context.

### From Learners' Perspective

**Learners as Passive Recipients**: One of the primary uses of social technology-enabled platforms is to create information and knowledge repositories of user-generated content. These *digital social repositories* are hosted and maintained not only by formal platforms like Wikipedia or YouTube, but also by numerous individuals and organizations in the form of blogs, discussion forums, specialized knowledge, and information aggregation platforms (e.g., portals related to advisory services related to health, agricultural, and so on), etc. They can be called *social repositories,* since anyone from the *social crowd* can be the contributors to those repositories. Apart from that, social networking sites like Facebook, Instgram, etc., are also allowing users to fetch and exchange content in an informal way. Thus, learners can instantly search and access the most relevant information and knowledge from these repositories of content available online (OECD 2018a). Several studies claim that social networking sites also create new perspectives in the process of acquiring knowledge (Wodzicki et al. 2012; Manasijevic et al. 2016).

Hence, from a learner's perspective, a primary and useful way to use social media is to consume contents from digital social repositories as passive *Spectators*. However, there are some negative implications of informal acquisition of information and knowledge from online sources. First, since these contents are user-generated (i.e., anyone can be a creator of content), the authenticity and quality of online contents are not always assured. So, it becomes the responsibility of learners to adjudge the authenticity of online sources to avoid getting misinformed (OECD 2018b). Hence, young learners need support from teachers/mentors to develop the skills needed to critically evaluate online information (Hatlevik and Hatlevik 2018). At the same time, there needs to be a crowd-based mechanism embedded in the platform itself to adjudge and moderate "bad" information including aggressive, sexual, or dangerous content.

**Learners as Participants**: Use of online social networks (e.g., Facebook) for entertainment purposes and to develop and maintain interpersonal relationships is well-established (Mcdool et al. 2016). In the context of learning, studies show that students also use social networks for exchanging views or ideas, asking and responding to questions within peer group, etc., (Tess 2013; Cooke 2017), thus influencing the learning process. Zachos et al. (2018) highlighted that the students' participation in social media such as Facebook, Classroom 2.0, Quora and Ning.com can help them to discuss lessons covered in classroom, share materials, form study groups, etc. Through these social interactions, students build their knowledge of interest as well as maintaining their social connections. Researchers also agree that online socialization improves social capital of learners (Mcdool et al. 2016; Wood et al. 2016), which in turn have a positive influence not only on learners' knowledge acquisition process, but also on expanding their networks that would help them to develop their professional careers. However, use of social networks not always creates a uniform impact on education process of learners. As mentioned earlier, it depends on students' social technographic profile including their interest, motivation, learning culture at school and family, etc.

*Learners as Actors*: The social tools and platforms facilitate learners to move beyond socialization and passive access of online resources by enabling them to create and share content. This will help learners to engage in collaborative knowledge building. Learners can, for example, use online video blogs to practice a language or use wiki for collaborative writing (Palaigeorgiou and Grammatikopoulou 2016).

Social media provides opportunities for students to share and document discussions, which will enable them to share knowledge, assess contributions of others in this discussion and get feedback from peers and teachers/mentors (Mondahl and Razmerita 2014). Wiki, for example, as a social tool, facilitates co-creation of knowledge through asynchronous exchange of views and ideas among peers (Cress and Kimmerle 2007). Blogs are useful tools used to create a forum for students to document their thought process and reflect on the views of others (Al-Fadda and Al-Yahya 2010). According to Geyer et al. (2008), "This contextual collaboration seamlessly integrates content sharing, communication channels and collaboration tools into a unified user experience that enables new levels of productivity." This will eventually promote learner agency, autonomy, and engagement through creation of a digital social learning space that is beyond physical, geographic, institutional, and organizational boundaries (McLoughlin and Lee 2010).

As discussed earlier, the social technographic profile of learners will determine the extent of active involvement of learners in social media; active participation as creators are still less common among learners in comparison with more passive activities, such as watching video clips. So, learners should be encouraged and motivated to get more involved in participatory activities (e.g., blogging, file-sharing, visiting chatrooms and spending time in a "goal-oriented" virtual world), which would, in turn, empower them to become independent thinkers (Middaugh et al. 2017). Thompson et al. (2014) have demonstrated that both social and cognitive components are equally important in learning process. Also, students should practice learning both autonomously and collaboratively. Here, teachers need to play the important role of encouraging students toward greater levels of contextual social interaction and teamwork in educational activities.

### From Teachers' Perspective

Social platforms including social media can be viewed from the teachers' perspective as an educational environment which is wealthier with instantaneous access to useful and relevant online resources than conventional educational settings. At the same time, social media help teachers to bring their students closer that would improve learners' educational experiences, reinforce students' motivation for learning, and will help them to expand the learning process beyond the restrictions of a conventional classroom. In addition, such a student-centered perspective can offer students an active role in the learning process, by producing a more flexible and creative learning environment (Martell 2015; Zachos et al. 2018).

From the perspective of teachers, studies have indicated that social media not only supports classroom learning (Greenhow and Askari 2017), but also facilitates a variety of networking activities across the school context, thus promoting informal learning to nurture learners' personal interests through extracurricular activities (Greenhow and Gleason 2012). At the same time, teachers are also using social media for professional development (Gao and Li 2017; Greenhalgh and Koehler 2017). Now, teachers can access resources from across the world; and, while doing so, they find new bases of professional community (Prestridge 2019). In the formal learning place inside classroom, teachers use social media to share learning materials and interact with students. Outside classrooms, teachers use social media to provide formal and informal guidance and facilitate group work through their peer networks (Brandon et al. (2019). Moreover, social media can enhance the spirit of technology-based assessment through tracking and monitoring of students' activities. For example, using social media applications such as wikis and blogs, it is possible to track the degrees of learners' contributions to educational activities. By combining learning, teaching, and assessments using social media tools, both teachers and learners can collaborate toward a more meaningful teaching-learning experience in and outside classroom.

However, *social technographic profile* (Li and Bernoff 2011) of teachers in general is different from that of adolescent learners. Hence, it is important to identify the readiness and proficiency of the teachers who is primarily responsible toward utilizing the potentials of social media in their classrooms. Since teachers are very much accustomed to traditional course-driven educational systems, they are sometimes hesitant to accept this new technology-driven educational system (Lemke and Coughlin 2009). Especially, teachers belonging to developing nations or nations that have been slow in adopting social/digital technologies are less likely to have proper training needed for social media integration. Moreover, teachers are not always in favor of using social media in educational procedures. For example, in a study conducted in Greece, it was found out that students are more amenable to the use of Facebook in education than their teachers, although they use it more for entertainment and socialization purpose (Tsoni et al. 2015). Similarly, in another study (Visagie and deVilliers 2010) conducted among teachers from five different countries (Canada, USA, South Africa, United Kingdom, and Australia), there were only a few who "would consider applying Facebook, as part of their teaching strategy." Hence, it is felt that the teachers should be encouraged to take advantage of the *social* nature of digital social platforms to improve communication and cooperation with their students in order to enhance students' participation in teaching-learning processes.

### 5.3.3 Impact of Social Technology-Enabled Tools and Platforms on Satisfying Societal Goals

With increased digitization of socio-economic as well as personal activities, the divide between those who are reaping the benefit of technological developments and those who are not is increasing. This *digital divide* or *digital exclusion* is one of the major reasons for social exclusion. Therefore, in a technology-driven society, bridging digital divide is a pre-condition for bridging education divide. Hence, the question we need to address in our context is: how can we promote digital inclusion of digitally excluded community, so that they can be a part of social technology-enabled education process.

As the digital world is expanding, the *digital access divide*—the gap between those who have Internet access and those who do not—is decreasing (OECD 2018b). This has become possible with wider penetration of smartphones, which is making the need for a costlier device like computer/laptop for internet access almost redundant. In fact, in rural areas of developing countries, there are people who have not seen a computer, but now they have a smartphone, using which they can access internet-enabled tools and platforms. In case of technology-driven education, digital access of a student is related to his/her economic, social, and cultural status. It has been observed that privileged students have access to uninterrupted Internet connectivity at home, which may not be true for underprivileged students. It is also country-specific. For example, in developed countries, over 98% of disadvantaged students had Internet access at home. However, these percentages were much lower for disadvantaged students in Turkey (50%), Mexico (45%), Jordan (40%), Chile (38%), and Costa Rica (38%) (OECD 2016).

However, getting access to digital technologies and platforms only does not ensure its usage because of prevailing inequalities in skills and usage patterns. We call it *digital capability divide*, which can be classified into four broad categories (OECD 2018b; Helsper et al. 2016):

a. Operational skills: skills needed to use computing devices (smartphone, tablet, computer) to access internet-enabled tools and platforms;
b. Information-navigation skills: cognitive skills needed to access digital contents (use of search-engine to find information) and ability to understand, verify and evaluate information;
c. Social skills: ability to be a part of virtual communities through online interactions, create online peer-groups for socialization and information exchange, and build digital social capital;
d. Creative skills: skills needed to create and share quality content online.

Usage patterns refer to the type of activities that people perform online (OECD 2018b) and it varies with socio-demographic variability, such as gender, age, education, and Internet experience. For example, younger people are more inclined to participate in social media for socialization purpose compared to older adults (VanDeursen and VanDijk 2014). Additionally, lack of motivation to use internet among underprivileged community appears to directly influence and enhance digital capability divide (VanDeursen and VanDijk 2015).

Digital skills and use of the Internet are related to students' economic, social, and cultural status. It has been observed that "Outside school, disadvantaged students tend to prefer using the Internet for chatting rather than sending emails. They are also less likely to use the Internet to read the news (55%) or to obtain practical information (56%) in comparison with advantaged students (60% and 74%, respectively)" (OECD 2017). Moreover, Helsper (2017) has indicated the need of support from family, friends, and teachers. A study conducted among students in the Netherlands observed that "those who are in most need of digital support (because they experience most problems online) seem to find it most difficult to get quality support, strengthening the digital divide among those who need help in using the Internet and those who do not" (Helsper and VanDeursen 2017).

Attempts toward bridging digital access and capability divide will give rise to a "third-level digital divide," focusing on inequalities in material benefits and outcomes out of Internet usage (VanDursen and Helsper 2015; OECD 2018b). The third-level digital divide "refers to the idea that equal access, skills and use may not necessarily result in equal offline outcomes." We call it *digital opportunity divide*. It concerns "disparities in the returns from Internet use within populations of users who exhibit broadly similar usage profiles and enjoy relatively autonomous and unfettered access to ICTs and the Internet infrastructure." As a result, individuals with higher social status can exploit the existing opportunity structure more effectively and meaningfully, and hence, can achieve more beneficial offline outcomes out of Internet use than their lower-status counterparts. This implies that, even if equal online access and skills is assured, students may have unequal opportunity scope derived out of internet usage. Disadvantaged students may not be aware of how to take advantage of technology resources (e.g., online courses, advisory services, or job searching platforms) to turn online prospects into offline opportunities.

Next chapter and Part III of this book in particular are devoted to systematically examine practical means of bridging education divide through digital inclusion using social technology-enabled platform. We will demonstrate that we need to look at this issue from an ecosystemic perspective and not only from a technology perspective.

### 5.3.4 Negative Side Effects of Social Technology-Enabled Tools and Platforms

The more time a learner spends online, the greater will be his/her risk to get exposed to online risks (OECD 2018b). Attempts to minimize online risks may reduce negative side effects of social technology-enabled platforms, but this will, in turn, limit learner's online opportunities and freedom. Online risks for a young learner can be roughly classified as: *content risks* (where a learner, intentionally or unintentionally, is recipient of inappropriate contents), *contact risks* (where a learner gets involved online with *risky* peer or personal communication), and *conduct risks* (where a learner intentionally gets involved with undesirable online activities (e.g., gambling) and contributes to creation of risky content or contact) (Hasebrink et al. 2008; Staksrud and Livingstone 2009).

*Content Risks*: As pointed out earlier, learners encounter with numerous amounts of content online in different forms and modalities. First of all, from the perspective of learning, these user-generated contents are usually not verified and the quality of content is not assured. This creates problem for a learner, if he/she is unable to critically evaluate online sources. Secondly, the digital medium contains varied forms of dangerous content, including pornographic and aggressive materials, which can influence learners in undesirable ways. With a target group comprising of children from 25 European countries, the EU Kids Online survey insightfully highlights that potentially harmful user-generated content online has been encountered by 21% of 11-16-year olds (OECD 2018b). This included hate messages (12%), self-harm sites (7%), pro-eating disorder sites (10%), suicide sites (5%), and drug taking sites (7%). Finally, the study points out how an alarming 14% of European children belonging to the age group of 9-16-year olds had encountered images in the digital forum infused with sexual content (Livingstone et al. 2011).

*Contact Risks*: The contemporary society has witnessed an increased usage of social networking sites by learners for the purpose of developing and maintaining interpersonal bonds (Mcdool et al. 2016). Although such an occurrence can be identified as a great opportunity for learners to form a virtual peer group, a critical analysis points out that learners tend to be less careful regarding selection of online *peer group* (Wood et al. 2016). Poor management of online privacy settings often compel learners to engage in unwanted virtual interactions, which subsequently enhance the possibility of mishaps, including sexual abuse and harassment, personal data misuse, and others (Lupton and Williamson 2017). To add further, virtual interactions occurring via social networking sites can have detrimental effect on a learner's wellbeing (Best et al. 2014). The quantitative form of interaction in social media (in the form of "likes," "favourites," or "retweets") can cause adolescents to be increasingly worried about those numbers they get on their posts, which creates a stressful mental condition. Another significant concern among parents and educators is cyberbullying.[2]

---

[2]Cyberbullying is defined as "an aggressive, intentional act carried out by a group or individual, *using electronic forms of contact,* repeatedly and over time against a victim who cannot easily defend him or herself" (Smith et al. 2008).

The means for cyberbullying are diversifying with the availability of newer digital social platforms and tools (Livingstone and Smith 2014).

*Conduct Risks:* Technological development has transformed internet into a virtual space, which not only enables children to access a vast multitude of resources available online, but also equips them in generating their own contents. This unrestricted authority granted to children to create and exchange content online can be detrimental, where learners themselves may get engaged in producing and distributing harmful contents which include hateful materials about other children, provoking racism, or distributing images with sexual content. Also, they may be actively involved in online gambling, hacking or cyberbullying or similar such tasks.

Apart from these three categories, Internet addiction is a growing problem among learners of all age groups. PISA (Programme for International Student Assessment) defines a term called "extreme Internet users" which describes a learner who spends more than 6 h online per day outside school. "Extreme Internet users" reported less life satisfaction and were more likely to be bullied at school (OECD 2017). "Extreme Internet users" performed worse across all subjects in the PISA test, even after accounting for differences in socio-economic backgrounds.

Use of social technology-enabled tools and platform in education is usually done in three ways for in-school and out-of-school learning (Greenhow et al. 2014; Manca and Ranieri 2013; Rodríguez-Hoyos et al. 2015):

(a) Using platforms that are specially designed for education purpose (e.g., Edmodo, Ning, and e-learning platforms like Coursera, Udemy, etc.);
(b) Using specialized platforms dedicated to support professional/research activities (e.g., LinkedIn, ResearchGate, academia.edu, etc.);
(c) Generic social media platforms, originally designed for social interactions and content sharing for entertainment purpose (e.g., Facebook, Twitter, YouTube, etc.)

Use of generic social media platforms in- and out-of-classroom by learners and teachers is unstructured and unsupervised, and, as a result, have all the negative side effects mentioned above. Dedicated and specialized platforms used for teaching-learning purpose are less risky on that account, but disallow users to access the vast possibilities and potentials of the open cyber-world. We will discuss this issue in the Sect. 5.3.5.

## 5.3.5 Effective Implementation Strategies to Promote Social Technology-Enabled Learning

"Computers have been oversold and underused, at least for now," claimed Cuban (2001) in his book "Oversold and Underused: Computers in the Classroom." Many proponents of school reform through new technologies used to believe that computers in the classroom can positively transform educational process. However, Cuban (2001) argued that when teachers are not becoming a part of implementation process that are trying to reshape schools and unless the process of computerization pays more attention to civic and social goals of schooling rather than technology, presence of computers alone cannot produce worthy outcome.

Today we are in the middle of a new wave of computerization in classroom and beyond-classroom, and this new wave is powered by social technologies and socially enabled applications. However, in order for technology to have a meaningful impact on education, we need to focus not on technology per se but on how the technology is getting implemented. According to Greenhow et al. (2019), "The answer to questions such as "How does technology X affect learning outcomes?" is always, "It depends" (Fishman and Dede 2016). It depends on how the learning environment is designed. It depends on the curriculum and activities designed to foster learning. It depends on the teacher, and on the students."

In this section, we will assess the implementation strategies of social technology-enabled tools and platforms in education to promote in-school and out-of-school learning in two domains of applications: (i) application of generic social media platforms originally designed for social interactions and content sharing for entertainment purpose (e.g., Facebook, Twitter, YouTube, etc.) and, (ii) application of integrated *digital learning platforms* that are specially designed for education purpose (e.g., Edmodo (n.d.), Ning (2018)), including Learning Management Systems with embedded *social* features and e-learning facilities (Garmendía and Cobos 2013; McIntosh 2018: for a comprehensive list of Learning Management and e-learning Tools and Platforms).

Uses of generic social media platforms like Facebook is quite common to support teaching-learning process and are considered effective in terms of openness, interactivity, and sociability. Studies show that students use Facebook primarily for socialization purpose; at the same time, it also supports informal learning activities (Cooke 2017), either directly or indirectly. However, extensive surveys to analyse impact or examining about their actual use are not very common; some researchers also questioned the academic use of generic social media platforms (Manca and Ranieri 2016; Zachos et al. 2018).

A study conducted with Italian academic staff (Manca and Ranieri 2016) has shown that social media use is still restricted in formal academic activities and teachers are not always interested to integrate these into teaching practices. Manca and Ranieri (2016) has found out several reasons for that, such as cultural resistance, pedagogical issues, or institutional constraints. Low level of faculty adoption in teaching practices has also been emphasized by Brown (2012). Also, there are socio-cultural factors (Manca and Ranieri 2013; Veletsianos et al. 2013), like, perceived loss of teachers' traditional roles, managing informal relationships with students on social media or the issue of privacy threats, that inhibits some groups of teachers from using social media.

The primary reason for non-adoption of generic social media in teaching-learning process can be traced to the popular perception that, social media is too uncertain and unstructured means to manage educational communication in institutional contexts. There is neither any standard guideline nor any structured implementation framework in order to assist teachers and students to use generic social media platforms in and out-of-classroom. In fact, prior to implementing a technology initiative, any organization needs to undertake strategic planning to realize its mission and to spell out what it desires to achieve through the use of the technology (McAfee 2009). However, use of generic social media in educational environment is still an individual's choice (of respective teachers and their students) and not guided by any institutional strategic framework.

On the other hand, there are integrated *digital learning platforms* that are specially designed for education purpose. According to Richard and Dede (2012), *digital learning platforms* can be defined as a networked environment supporting interactive interfaces for teachers and students. They usually have: (i) tools to be used by teachers for creating multimedia content, lessons and assignments, managing and evaluating students' activities; (ii) a real-time and teacher-directed interaction framework in and outside classroom. D*igital learning platforms* are derivatives of Learning Management Systems (LMS), created to support delivery of online courses and to manage and evaluate student engagement (Lochner et al. 2015). Now, social tools are also getting added to LMS to make it *social LMS* (Garmendía and Cobos 2013). Cuellar et al. (2011) have examined ways to combine social networking tools with LMS in order to obtain positive learning outcomes. Social networking tools are also getting integrated with e-learning environment to make e-learning more interactive and effective. (Mohamad 2018).

One advantage of using *social LMS* systems is that the teaching-learning activities are placed in a single virtual learning environment (VLE). When social media tools are used in isolation, student–teacher or student-student interactions and contributions are distributed over various un-connected or poorly organized places on the web (Bubaš et al. 2010). For example, interactions can happen over Twitter or Facebook or Whatsapp and collating and accessing those records of interactions are problematic. According to Marenzi et al. (2008), the content provided with the use of social media tools should be "integrated in a way that makes access to these distributed resources as easy as to learning materials in a conventional LMS." Hence, a single unified platform is a desirable solution.

Even then, there are implementation issues that need to be considered. Cultural factors with respect to the current collaborative atmosphere within an education institution should be assessed in order to support the way teachers and students communicate in that setting. Additionally, both teachers and students should know why the technology platform is being introduced and institutional support is very much needed to train, encourage and sustain the use of the technology throughout the entire period of its adoption.

## 5.4  Conclusion

The chapter highlights in detail the conceptual and operational dimensions of social technology. The collaborative spirit with which social technology is embedded has enabled digital technologies to transcend from providing instructional digital content to establishing purposive digital connections among diverse social agents. This attribute has made application of social technology a crucial step in the field of education. The collaborative spirit of social technology has the ability to transform education from teacher-centric, centralized and individualistic to learner-centric, decentralized, collaborative and connection driven. This marks the importance of social technologies in facilitating education through the creation of teaching-learning communities. However, it needs to be asked at this juncture, that while application of social technology in the field of education is crucial in making education process connection driven, is it sufficient in mitigating extant education divide with the help of established connections.

It is indeed true that application of social technology in the field of education leads to the creation of teaching-learning community, integrated with the virtue of purposive collaborations. The importance of such community formation rests in its ability to co-construct knowledge by establishing purposive collaborations between teachers, learners, and other agents involved in the process of educational dissemination. However, while application of social technology is mandatory in the process of effective community formation in the field of education, it is not sufficient in sustaining purposive interactions among diverse agents. Application of social technology although has the prospect of connecting physically scattered people, it cannot ascertain who will be part of the community, how the community will be cultivated and who will moderate the collaborations taking place in the community. Therefore, in order to cultivate an effective teaching-learning community, we need to create an integrated platform, which will be infused with the collaborative potential of social technology. Making platform organization as its premise, this integrated platform will create the path for a crowd-based socio-economic arrangement, where different active agents can facilitate transaction of knowledge and other resources anytime-anywhere, using digital platforms, to fulfill different goals. This integrated platform will deploy the potential of social technology in establishing purposive collaborations among different agents involved in the education process, moderate their knowledge exchange, thereby helping in cultivating an effective teaching-learning community.

It needs to be iterated at this juncture that while creation of an integrated platform can ensure effective community formation between different agents involved in the education process, such a creation does not automatically translate into being conducive in eradicating extant education divide. Creation of an integrated platform can lead to community formation based on common interest or shared knowledge acquisition quest, but it is not sufficient in democratic distribution of knowledge. For example, such a platform can lead to the formation of a subject-oriented community, like a physics forum, but it cannot ensure participation of the marginalized students in the said community. This highlights that while creation of an integrated platform is crucial for effective community formation, it can only make a desired impact in mitigating education divide if the platform is created by adequately negotiating with the external influencers of an education ecosystem. This marks the urgency for creating an integrated platform by taking into consideration external influencers, like social, economic, political, and socio-psychological dimensions, which will be conducive in community formation effective to mitigate extant education divide (Morell et al.

2020). This paves the path for our next chapter where we will take up in detail this aspect. The next chapter is dedicated to spell out our framework in creating an integrated digital platform, by optimally negotiating with external influencers, which will pave the path for community formation among diverse agents involved in the education process and in turn create promising prospects for mitigating education divide with the support of facilitated collaborations among the community members.

# References

Alberghini, E., et al. (2010). Implementing knowledge management through IT opportunities: definition of a theoretical model based on tools and processes classification. In *Proceedings of the 2nd European conference on intellectual capital*. Lisbon, Portugal.

Al-Fadda, H., & Al-Yahya, M. (2010). Using web blogs as a tool to encourage pre-class reading, postclass reflections and collaboration in higher education. *US-China Education Review, 7*(7), 100–106.

Alstyne, M. W., Parker, G., & Choudary, S. P. (2016). Pipelines, platforms, and the new rules of strategy. *Harvard Business Review, 94*, 16.

Andersen, K. N. (2011). Social technologies and health care: Public sector receding, patients at the steering wheel? In *the Conference proceedings Social Technologies 11: ICT for Social transformations*.

Anderson, P. (2007). *What is Web 2.0? Ideas, technologies and implications for education* (JISC Reports). Retrieved from http://www.jisc.ac.uk/media/documents/techwatch/tsw0701b.pdf.

Battarbee, K. Co-experience: the social user experience. *Proc. CHI 2003*.

Benkler, Y., & Nissenbaum, H. (2006). Commons-based peer production and virtue. *Journal of Political Philosophy, 14*, 394–419.

Best, P., Manktelow, R., & Taylor, B. (2014). Online communication, social media and adolescent wellbeing: A systematic narrative review. *Children and Youth Services Review, 41*, 27–36. https://doi.org/10.1016/j.childyouth.2014.03.001.

Blank, G., & Reisdorf, B. (2012). The Participatory Web. *Information Communication and Society, 15*(4), 537–554. https://doi.org/10.1080/1369118x.2012.665935.

Bonson, E., & Flores, F. (2011). Social media and corporate dialogue: the response of the global financial institutions. *Online Information Review, 35*(1), 34–49.

Botsman, R., & Rogers, R. (2010). *What's mine is yours: The rise of collaborative consumption*. New York: HarperCollins.

Boyd, D. (2007). Social network sites: Public, private, or what? Retrieved from www.danah.org/papers/KnowledgeTree.pdf.

Boyera, S. (2007). Opportunities and challenges of web technologies on mobile platform. In *Proceedings of datamatix gitex conference, Dubai, UAE*. Retrieved from http://www.w3.org/2007/08/sb_gitex/all.html.

Brandon, D. L., et al. (2019). Welcome to Cloud2Class: social media in education. *Teachers College Record, 121*(14).

Brousseau, E., & Nicolas, C. (2007). *Internet and digital economics: Principles*. Methods and Applications: Cambridge University Press.

Brown, S. A. (2012). Seeing Web 2.0 in context: A study of academic perceptions. *The Internet and Higher Education, 15*(1), 50–57.

Bubaš, G., Ćorić, A., & Orehovački, T. (2010). The evaluation of the use of online community tool Ning for support of student interaction and learning. In *Proceedings of the 21st central European conference on information and intelligent systems* (pp. 171–178). Varaždin: Croatia.

Callaghan, N., & Bower, M. (2012). Learning through social networking sites: the critical role of the teacher. *Educational Media International, 49*(1), 1–17.

Carpenter, J. P., & Krutka, D. G. (2014). How and why educators use Twitter: A survey of the field. *Journal of Research on Technology in Education, 46*(4), 414–434.

Carr, C. T., & Hayes, R. A. (2015). Social media: Defining, developing, and divining. *Atlantic Journal of Communication, 23*(1). https://doi.org/10.1080/15456870.2015.972282.

Castells, M. (2004). *The network society: a cross-cultural perspective.* Edward Elgar Publication.

Chui, M., et al. (2012). *The social economy: Unlocking value and productivity through social technologies* (McKinsey Global Institute Report). Retrieved from https://www.mckinsey.com/industries/high-tech/our-insights/the-social-economy.

Cooke, S. (2017). Social teaching: Student perspectives on the inclusion of social media in higher education. *Education and Information Technologies, 22,* 255–269. https://doi.org/10.1007/s10639-015-9444-y.

Cress, U., & Kimmerle, J. (2007). A systemic and cognitive view on collaborative knowledge building with wikis. *International Journal of Computer-Supported Collaborative Learning,* 3(2), 105–122. Springer: New York.

Cuban, L. (2001). *Oversold and underused: Computers in the classroom.* Cambridge, MA: Harvard University Press.

Cuellar, P. M., Delgado, M., & Pegalajar, C. M. (2011). Improving learning management through semantic web and social networks. *Expert Systems with Applications, 38,* 4181–4189.

Derksen, M., et al. (2012). Social technologies: Cross-disciplinary reflections on technologies in and from the social sciences. *Theory Psychology, 22*(2), 139–147.

Edmodo. (n.d.). Retrieved from https://go.edmodo.com/schools/.

Fishman, B., & Dede, C. (2016). Teaching and technology: New tools for new times. In D. Gitomer & C. Bell (Eds.), *Handbook of research on teaching* (5th ed., pp. 1269–1334). Washington, DC: American Educational Research Association.

Gao, F., & Li, L. (2017). Examining a one-hour synchronous chat in a microblogging-based professional development community. *British Journal of Educational Technology, 48*(2), 332–347.

Garmendía, A., & Cobos, R. (2013). Towards the extension of a LMS with social media services. In Y. Luo (Ed.), *Cooperative design, visualization, and engineering (CDVE 2013)* (Vol. 8091)., Lecture notes in computer science Berlin, Heidelberg: Springer.

Gerwe, O., & Silva, R. (2020). Clarifying the sharing economy: Conceptualization, typology, antecedents, and effects. *Academy of Management Perspectives, 34*(1). https://doi.org/10.5465/amp.2017.0010.

Geyer, W., SilvaFilho, R. S., Brownholtz, B., & Redmiles, D. F. (2008). The trade-offs of blending synchronous and asynchronous communication services to support contextual collaboration. *Journal of Universal Computer Science, 14*(1), 4–26.

Giolo, F. (2012). Why is information system design interested in ethnography? Sketches of an ongoing story. In G. Viscusi, G. M. Campagnolo & Y. Curzi (Eds.), Phenomenology, organizational politics, and IT design. *The social study of information systems* (pp. 1–30). Hershey, Pennsylvania: IGI Global.

Greenhalgh, S. P., & Koehler, M. J. (2017). 28 days later: Twitter hashtags as "just in time" teacher professional development. *TechTrends, 61*(3), 273–281.

Greenhow, C., & Askari, E. (2015). Learning and teaching with social network sites: A decade of research in K-12 related education. *Education and Information Technologies, 22,* 623–645. https://doi.org/10.1007/s10639-015-9446-9.

Greenhow, C., & Askari, E. (2017). Learning and teaching with social network sites: A decade of research in K- 12 related education. *Education and Information Technologies, 22*(2), 623–645.

Greenhow, C., & Gleason, B. (2012). Twitteracy: Tweeting as a new literacy practice. *The Educational Forum, 76,* 463–477.

Greenhow, C., Gleason, B., & Li, J. (2014). Psychological, social, and educational dynamics of adolescents' online social networking. *Media Education, 5*(2), 115–130.

Greenhow, C., Cho, V., Dennen, V., & Fishman, B. (2019). Education and social media: Research directions to guide a growing field. *Teachers College Record, 121*(14). https://www.tcrecord.org ID Number: 23039.

Hagen, P. & Robertson, T. (2010). Social technologies: Challenges and opportunities for participation. *ACM International Conference Proceeding Series*, 31–40. https://doi.org/10.1145/1900441. 1900447.

Hargadon, S. (2008). *Web 2.0 is the future of learning*. Retrieved from http://www.stevehargadon. com/2008/03/web-20-is-future-of-education.html.

Hasebrink, U., Livingstone, S., & Haddon, L. (2008). Comparing children's online opportunities and risks across Europe: Cross-national comparisons for EU Kids Online. London: EU Kids Online. Retrieved from http://eprints.lse.ac.uk/id/eprint/21656.

Hatlevik, I., & Hatlevik, O. (2018). Students' evaluation of digital information: The role teachers play and factors that influence variability in teacher behavior. *Computers in Human Behavior, 83*, 56–83. https://doi.org/10.1016/j.chb.2018.01.022.

Helsper, E. (2017). A socio-digital ecology approach to understanding digital inequalities among young people. *Journal of Children and Media, 11*(2), 256–260. https://doi.org/10.1080/17482798. 2017.1306370.

Helsper, E., & VanDeursen, A. (2017). Do the rich get digitally richer? Quantity and quality of support for digital engagement. *Information, Communication & Society, 20*(5), 700–714. https:// doi.org/10.1080/1369118x.2016.1203454.

Helsper, E., VanDeursen, A., & Eynon, R. (2016). Measuring types of internet use, from digital skills to tangible outcomes. Retrieved from http://www.lse.ac.uk/media@lse/research/Research-Projects/DiSTO/Pdf/DiSTO-MTIUF.pdf.

Horton, J. J., & Chilton, L. B. (2010). The labor economics of paid crowdsourcing. In *Proceedings of the 11th ACM conference on electronic commerce*, June 2010, 209–218. https://doi.org/10. 1145/1807342.1807376.

Ito, M., Gutiérrez, K., Livingstone, S., Penuel, B., Rhodes, J., Salen, K., & Watkins, S. C., et al. (2013). Connected learning: An agenda for research and design. *Irvine, CA: Digital Media and Learning Research Hub*. Retrieved from: https://dmlhub.net/publications/connected-learning-age nda-for-research-and-design/index.html.

Kale, U., & Goh, D. (2014). Teaching style, ICT experience and teachers' attitudes toward teaching with Web 2.0. *Education and Information Technologies, 19*(1), 41–60.

Kietzmann, J. H., Hermkens, K., McCarthy, I. P., & Silvestre, B. S. (2011). Social media? Get serious! Understanding the functional building blocks of social media. *Business Horizons, 54*(3), 241–251. https://doi.org/10.1016/j.bushor.2011.01.005.

Kim, D. J., Hall, S. P., & Gates, T. (2009). Global diffusion of the Internet XV: Web 2.0 technologies, principles, and applications: A conceptual framework from technology push and demand pull perspective. *Communications of the Association for Information Systems, 24*, 657–672.

Koopman, C., Mitchell, M., & Thierer, A. (2015). The sharing economy and consumer protection regulation: The case for policy change. *The Journal of Business, Entrepreneurship & the Law, 8*(2), 530.

Kunst, K., & Ravi, V. (2014). Towards a theory of socially shared consumption: literature review, taxonomy, and research Agenda. In *Proceedings of the 22nd European conference on information systems*. Retrieved from https://pdfs.semanticscholar.org/b722/b0ed3cce8093514c8b7946478d3 bdbbf71c8.pdf.

Lamb, R. & Davidson, E. (2002). Social scientists: managing identity in socio-technical networks. In *Proceedings of the 35th annual hawaii international conference on system sciences*, Big Island, HI, USA. https://doi.org/10.1109/hicss.2002.994034.

Lameras, P., Paraskakis, I. & Levy, P. (2009). Using social software for teaching and learning in higher education. In Hatzipanagos. S. & Warburton, S. (Eds.), *Handbook of research on social software and developing community ontologies* (pp. 269–284). Hershey PA: IGI Publishing.

Lehdonvirta, V., Kässi, O., Hjorth, I., Barnard, H., & Graham, M. (2019). The Global platform economy: A new offshoring institution enabling emerging-economy microproviders. *Journal of Management, 45*(2), 567–599. https://doi.org/10.1177/0149206318786781.

Lemke, C., & Coughlin, E. (2009). The change agents. *Educational Leadership, 67*(1), 54–59.

Lewis, B. K. (2010). Social media and strategic communication: Attitudes and perceptions among college students. *Public Relations Journal, 4*(3), 1–23.

Li, C., & Bernoff, J. (2011). *Groundswell, expanded and revised edition: Winning in a world transformed by social technologies.* Harvard Business School Press Books. ISBN: 978–1-4221-2500-7.

Lindqvist, J., Cranshaw, J., Wiese, J., Hong, J., & Zimmerman, J. (2011). I'm the mayor of my house: Examining why people use foursquare-a social-driven location sharing application. In *Proceedings of SIGCHI conference on human factors in computing systems, Vancouver, BC, Canada.* https://doi.org/10.1145/1978942.1979295.

Livingstone, S. et al. (2011). *Risks and safety on the internet: the perspective of European children: full findings and policy implications from the EU Kids Online survey of 9–16 year olds and their parents in 25 countries EU Kids* (Online Network). Retrieved from http://eprints.lse.ac.uk/33731.

Livingstone, S., & Smith, P. (2014). Annual research review: harms experienced by child users of online and mobile technologies: the nature, prevalence and management of sexual and aggressive risks in the digital age. *Journal of Child Psychology and Psychiatry, 55*(6), 635–654. https://doi.org/10.1111/jcpp.12197.

Lochner, B., Conrad, R., & Graham, E. (2015). Secondary teachers' concerns in adopting learning management systems: A U.S. Perspective. *TechTrends, 59*(5), 62–71.

Lupton, D., & Williamson, B. (2017). The datafied child: The dataveillance of children and implications for their rights. *New Media & Society, 19*(5), 780–794. https://doi.org/10.1177/146144 4816686328.

Macià, M., & Garcia, I. (2017). Properties of teacher networks in Twitter: Are they related to community-based peer production? *The International Review of Research in Open and Distributed Learning, 18*(1). https://doi.org/10.19173/irrodl.v18i1.2644.

Manasijevic, D., Zivkovic, D., Arsic, S., & Milosevic, I. (2016). Exploring students' purposes of usage and educational usage of Facebook. *Computers in Human Behavior, 60,* 441–450. https://doi.org/10.1016/j.chb.2016.02.087.

Manca, S., & Ranieri, M. (2013). Is it a tool suitable for learning? A critical review of the literature on Facebook as a technology-enhanced learning environment. *Journal of Computer-Assisted Learning, 29*(6), 487–504.

Manca, S., & Ranieri, M. (2016). Facebook and the others. Potentials and obstacles of Social Media for teaching in higher education. *Computers & Education, 95,* 216–230. https://doi.org/10.1016/j.compedu.2016.01.012.

Mansell, R. (2010). *Power and interests in developing knowledge societies: Exogenous and endogenous discourses in contention.* IKM Working Paper No. 11, 2010.p. 7. Available at: http://wiki.ikmemergent.net/files/IKM_Working_Paper-11-Robin_Mansell-July2010-final-pdf.pdf.

Marenzi, I., Demidova, E., & Nejdl, W. (2008). *LearnWeb 2.0. Integrating social software for lifelong learning.* Retrieved from https://www.semanticscholar.org/paper/LearnWeb-2.0.-Int egrating-Social-Software-for-Marenzi-Demidova/b1db0a2bba9e08bb257ece3d543c82b7b2f5 0543.

Martell, C. (2015). Age of creative insecurity: Student-centered learning: Historical Paper 7. *Journal of Education for Library and Information Science, 56*(1). Retrieved from https://eric.ed.gov/?id= EJ1073577.

McAfee, A. (2009). *Enterprise 2.0: New collaborative tools for your organization's toughest challenges.* Boston, Massachusetts: Harvard Business Press.

Mcdool, E., et al. (2016). Social media use and children's Wellbeing. Discussion Paper Series, Institute of Labor Economics. Available at: http://www.iza.org.

McIntosh, D. (2018). *Vendors of learning management and elearning products* (Report, Trimeritus eLearning Solutions Inc, March 2018). Retrieved from https://teachonline.ca/sites/default/files/pdfs/vendors_of_elearning_products_march2018.pdf.

McLoughlin, C., & Lee, M. J. W. (2010). Personalised and self regulated learning in the Web 2.0 era: International exemplars of innovative pedagogy using social software. *Australasian Journal of Educational Technology, 26*(1), 28–43. https://doi.org/10.14742/ajet.1100.

Middaugh, E., Clark, L., & Ballard, P. (2017). Digital media, participatory politics, and positive youth development. *Pediatrics, 140*(2), S127–S131. https://doi.org/10.1542/peds.2016-1758q.

Mlitwa, N. (2007). Technology for teaching and learning in higher education contexts: Activity theory and actor network theory analytical perspectives. *International Journal of Education and Development using ICT, 3*(4), 54–70. Retrieved from https://www.learntechlib.org/p/42219/.

Mohamad, R. (2018). The effectiveness of social networking applications in e-learning. *Advances in Intelligent and Soft Computing book series (AINSC), 109*. https://doi.org/10.1007/978-3-642-24772-9_12.

Mondahl, M., & Razmerita, L. (2014). Social media, collaboration and social learning—a Case-study of Foreign language learning. *The Electronic Journal of e-Learning, 12*(4), 339–352. Retrieved from: https://files.eric.ed.gov/fulltext/EJ1035665.pdf.

Morell, F. M., Espelt, R., & Cano, M.R. (2020). Sustainable Platform economy: Connections with the sustainable development goals. *Sustainability 2020, 12(18),* 7640. https://doi.org/10.3390/su12187640.

Ning. (2018). Retrieved from https://www.ning.com/blog/2018/01/ning-education-social-media-today.html.

North, D., & Wallis, J. (1994). Integrating institutional change and technological change in economic history: A transaction cost approach. *Journal of Institutional and Theoretical Economics, 150,* 609–624.

O'Reilly, T. (2005). What is web 2.0? design patterns and business models for the next generation of software. *International Journal of Digital Economics, 65,* 17–37.

O'Sullivan, P. B., & Carr, C. T. (2018). Mass-personal communication: A model bridging the mass-interpersonal divide. *New Media & Society, 20*(3), 1161–1180. https://doi.org/10.1177/146144 4816686104.

OECD. (2016). *Are there differences in how advantaged and disadvantaged students use the Internet.* PISA in Focus, No. 64. Paris: OECD Publishing. https://doi.org/10.1787/888933253149.

OECD. (2017). *PISA 2015 results (Volume III): Students' Well-Being, PISA.* Paris: OECD Publishing. https://doi.org/10.1787/9789264273856-en.

OECD. (2018a). *Writing in a changing world.* Trends Shaping Education Spotlights, No. 16. Available at: http://www.oecd.org/education/ceri/Spotlight-16-Writing-in-a-Changing-world.pdf.

OECD. (2018b). *New technologies and 21st century children: Recent trends and outcomes.* OECD Education Working Paper No. 179. EDU/WKP(2018)15. Available at: https://one.oecd.org/document/EDU/WKP(2018)15/en/pdf.

Palaigeorgiou, G., & Grammatikopoulou, A. (2016). Benefits, barriers and prerequisites for Web 2.0 learning activities in the classroom. *Interactive Technology and Smart Education, 13*(1), 2–18. https://doi.org/10.1108/itse-09-2015-0028.

Parker, G., Alstyne, M. V., & Choudary, S. (2016). *Platform revolution: How networked markets are transforming the economy, and how to make them work for you.* WW Norton: New York, USA.

Parker, G., Van, Alstyne, M.V., & Jiang, X. (2017). Platform ecosystems: How developers invert the Firm. *MIS Quarterly, 41*(1), 255–266.

Pelikan, P. (2003). Bringing institutions into evolutionary economics: another view with links to changes in physical and social technologies. *Journal of Evolutionary Economy., 13,* 237–258.

Prestridge, S. (2019). Categorising teachers' use of social media for their professional learning: A self-generating professional learning paradigm. *Computers & Education (Elsevier), 129,* 143–158. https://doi.org/10.1016/j.compedu.2018.11.003.

Raza, M. Y., Khan, A. N., Khan, N. A., & Bano, N. (2019). Dark side of social media and academic performance of public sector schools students: Role of parental school support. The *Journal of Public Affairs*. https://doi.org/10.1002/pa.2058.

Rehm, M., Manca, S., Brandon, D. L., & Greenhow, C. (2019). Beyond disciplinary boundaries: Mapping educational science in the discourse on social media. *Teachers College Record, 121*(14).

Richard, J., & Dede, C. (2012). *Digital teaching platforms: Customizing classroom learning for each student*. New York: Teachers College Press.

Roblyer, M. D. (2005). Educational technology research that makes a difference: series introduction. *Contemporary Issues in Technology and Teacher Education, 5*(2). Retrieved from http://www.citejournal.org/vol5/iss2/seminal/article1.cfm.

Rodríguez-Hoyos, C., Haya Salmón, I., & Fernández-Díaz, E. (2015). Research on SNS and education: The state of the art and its challenges. *Australasian Journal of Educational Technology, 31*(1), 100–111. https://doi.org/10.14742/ajet.995.

Rosenberg, B., & White, D. M. (1957). *Mass culture: The popular arts in America*. Glencoe: Free Press.

Russo, A., Watkins, J., Kelly, L., & Chan, S. (2008). Participatory communication with social media. *Curator: The Museum Journal, 51*, 21–31. https://doi.org/10.1111/j.2151-6952.2008.tb00292.x.

Sauers, N. J., & Richardson, J. W. (2015). Leading by following: An analysis of how K–12 school leaders use Twitter. *NASSP Bulletin, 99*(2), 127–146.

Schotter, A. (1981). *The economic theory of social institutions*. Cambridge: Cambridge University Press.

Selwyn, N. (2015). Challenging educational expectations of the social web: A web 2.0 far? *Nordic Journal of Digital Literacy, 2015*(4), 72–84.

Shirky, C (2008). *Here comes everybody*: Penguin Press.

Smith, P., et al. (2008). Cyberbullying: Its nature and impact in secondary school pupils. *Journal of Child Psychology and Psychiatry, 49*(4), 376–385. https://doi.org/10.1111/j.1469-7610.2007.01846.x.

Staksrud, E., & Livingstone, S. (2009). Children and online risk: powerless victims or resourceful participants? *Information, communication and society, 12*(3), 364–387. https://doi.org/10.1080/13691180802635455.

Sundararajan, A. (2016). *The sharing economy—The end of employment and the rise of crowd-based captitalism*. Cambridge: MIT press.

Tapscott, D. (2014). *The digital economy*. McGraw-Hill. https://b-ok.asia/book/2481587/0e33f1?regionChanged.

Tapscott, D. & Williams, A. D. (2006). *Wikinomics: How mass collaboration changes everything*. Portfolio.

Tess, P. A. (2013). The role of social media in higher education classes (real and virtual)-A literature review. *Computers in Human Behavior, 29*(5), A60–A68. https://doi.org/10.1016/j.chb.2012.12.032.

Thompson, C., Gray, K., & Kim, H. (2014). How social are social media technologies (SMTs)? A linguistic analysis of university students' experiences of using SMTs for learning. *Internet and Higher Education, 21*, 31–40. https://doi.org/10.1016/j.iheduc.2013.12.001.

Tsoni, R., Sypsas, A., & Pange, J. (2015). Students' perspectives about the educational dimension of the social network Facebook. In *Proceedings of the 8th international conference in open & distance learning*, Athens, Greece.

VanDeursen, A., & Helsper, E. (2015). The third-level digital divide: Who benefits most from being online? *Communication and information technologies annual, 10*, 29–52. https://doi.org/10.1108/s2050-206020150000010002.

VanDeursen, A., & VanDijk, J. (2014). The digital divide shifts to differences in usage. *New Media and Society, 16*(3), 507–526. https://doi.org/10.1177/1461444813487959.

VanDeursen, A., & VanDijk, J. (2015). Toward a multifaceted model of internet access for understanding digital divides: An empirical investigation. *The Information Society, 31*(5), 379–391. https://doi.org/10.1080/01972243.2015.1069770.

Veletsianos, G., Kimmons, R., & French, K. (2013). Instructor experiences with a social networking site in a higher education setting: expectations, frustrations, appropriation, and compartmentalization. *Educational Technology Research and Development, 61*(2), 255–278. https://doi.org/10.1007/s11423-012-9284-z.

Visagie, S., & deVilliers, C. (2010). The consideration of Facebook as an academic tool by ICT lecturers across five countries. In *Proceedings of the SACLA conference (SACLA2010)*. South Africa, Pretoria: University of Pretoria.

Vuori, V. (2011). *Social media changing the competitive intelligence process: Elicitation of employees' competitive knowledge* (Doctoral Thesis). Retrieved from https://www.researchgate.net/publication/309637579_Social_media_changing_the_competitive_intelligence_process_E licitation_of_employees'_competitive_knowledge.

Walther, J. B. (1995). Relational aspects of computer-mediated communication: Experimental observations over time. *Organizational Science, 6*, 186–203. https://doi.org/10.1287/orsc.6.2.186.

Walther, J. B. (1996). Computer-mediated communication: Impersonal, interpersonal, and hyperpersonal interaction. *Communication Research, 23*, 3–43. https://doi.org/10.1177/009365096023001001.

Walther, J. B., Carr, C. T., Choi, S., DeAndrea, D., Kim, J., Tong, S., & Heide, V. D. B. (2010). Interaction of interpersonal, peer, and media influence sources online: A research agenda for technology convergence. In Z. Papacharissi, Z. (Ed.), *The networked self* (pp. 17–38). Routledge: New York, NY.

Wodzicki, K., Schwämmlein, E., & Moskaliuk, J. (2012). Actually, I wanted to learn: Study related knowledge exchange on social networking sites. *Internet and Higher Education, 15*(1), 9–14. https://doi.org/10.1016/j.iheduc.2011.05.008.

Wood, M., Bukowski, W., & Lis, E. (2016). The digital self: How social media serves as a setting that shapes youth's emotional experiences. *Adolescent Research Review, 1*(2), 163–173. https://doi.org/10.1007/s40894-015-0014-8.

Zachos, G., et al. (2018). Social media use in higher education: A review. *Science Education, 8*(4), 194. https://doi.org/10.3390/educsci8040194.

Zyl, A. S. V. (2009). The impact of social networking 2.0 on organisations. *The Electronic Library, 27*(6), 906–918. https://doi.org/10.1108/02640470911004020.

# Chapter 6
# A Digital Framework Toward Bridging Education Divide Using Social Technology

## 6.1 Introduction

Contemporary technological development, leading to the enhanced proliferation of mobile devices, web technologies, social networks, broadband connectivity, and cloud services has successfully paved the path for easy exchange of information, ideas, and resources across the globe. Today's society can be rightly identified as a "digitally-connected global society," which enables each and every individual to be a potential contributor in the process of building a better community. The connecting spirit of digital technologies is suited to effectively trigger collaboration for a social mission, enable people to participate in local governance, and facilitate easy exchange of knowledge and expertise, thereby casting a positive influence in the process of community development. In this chapter, we propose to study the connection and collaboration among various entities that enables formation of virtual communities to bridge the existing education divide. Formation of these virtual communities has the most positive effect on social capital when they can increase network density and facilitate the spread of knowledge and information.

In the last chapter, we have discussed how social technologies and socially enabled applications have given rise to the concept of platform economy, which is a crowd-based, socioeconomic arrangement where different active agents can transact anytime-anywhere, using digital platforms, to fulfil different transaction goals. For example, it can create a new form of market where strangers exchange goods and services effortlessly using digital platforms, owned by respective vendors (e.g. Airbnb, Kickstarter, Lyft, etc.). The principles of platform economy are in close alliance to the concept of sharing/collaborative economy. Sharing economy, premised on collaborative consumption, advocates for a way of economic operation, which is based on effective exchange. In such an economy, production, distribution, and consumption of goods, services, and ideas take place by virtue of sharing resources by otherwise unrelated agents (Sundararajan 2016).

This conceptualization has blurred the distinction between:

S. Bandyopadhyay et al., *Bridging the Education Divide Using Social Technologies*,
https://doi.org/10.1007/978-981-33-6738-8_6

133

- *Producer-Consumer*: It encourages the notion of prosumerism,[1] where consumers can produce or participate in the production process, enabling collaborative creation of value (Paltrinieri and Piergiorgio 2013).
- *Marketplace and Traditional Company*: As a consequence of prosumerism, the concept of peer-to-peer marketplace emerges, which connects people requiring a product or a service (consumer) with people who can offer it (producer). Sundararajan (2016) describes this as "crowd-based capitalism—a new way of organizing economic activity that may supplant the traditional corporate-centered model." For example, *BlaBlaCar* is a car-pooling marketplace that connects drivers and passengers willing to travel together between cities in Europe, thus challenging the entire rail infrastructure in Europe.
- *Professional-Amateur*: In platform-based economy, since creation of products or services is no longer controlled by centralized corporate entities, the products and services can come through mobilization of crowd-based resources, where the *creators* may not be professional in true sense of the term. For example, a host in Airbnb is not a professional hotelier.

Thus, one can say that platform-based transaction among multiple active agents is based on the principle of *personalisation, collaboration,* and *informalisation* of transaction processes.

This concept of social technology-driven digital platform can also be applied to create a learning space, satisfying twenty-first century learning needs that are based on similar premise of *personalisation, collaboration,* and *informalisation* of learning process (Redecker and Punie 2013). In this chapter, we propose a learning platform in order to make a transition from content-centric, teacher-centric, and centralized learning process of the industrial age to a connection-centric, learner-centric, and decentralized learning process of the *socio-digital* age (driven by social technologies and socially enabled applications).

Before discussing a social technology-based digital learning framework that attempts to bridge inequalities and disconnections in the learning process, let us first focus on a social learning theory, called "Connected Learning" on which our digital framework is based. Connected learning is based on the premise that learning and development are embedded within social relationships and cultural contexts (Penuel et al. 2016). It puts emphasis on learning practices that are beyond formal education and focuses on informal learning as well, mediated by learner's socio-economic-cultural-political context (Braun 2019). Connected learning is learning that is interest-driven, supported by peers and mentors, and connected to academic, economic, and civic opportunities.

In this chapter, after tracing the root of connected learning in the historical context of different theories of social learning, we have described the conceptualization and design principles of connected learning framework in Sect. 6.2. Subsequently, in Sect. 6.3, we have proposed a digital framework toward creating an online connected

---

[1] *Prosumerism* is a trend in the information age that encourages consumers to become producers of products and services, disregarding the "factory-based" or "Institutional based" centralized model of production process.

learning environment and analysed the proposed framework from the perspective of education ecosystem in the socio-digital age (i.e. a digital age driven by social technologies and socially enabled applications). Subsequently, based on this framework, we have architected a digital platform with an objective to bridge extant education divide (Sect. 6.4). Since the proposed platform is driven by internet and internet-enabled devices, implementation and successful operationalization of this platform for underprivileged community is fully dependent on (i) accessibility of internet and internet-enabled devices; (ii) users' capability to effectively use technology; and, (iii) applicability of internet and internet-enabled devices, as perceived not only by learners, but also by other connected agents, specifically in the context of underprivileged community. We have discussed all these issues in Sect. 6.5 with a concluding proposal to mitigate these operational challenges through the involvement of transition intermediaries.

## 6.2  The Conceptual Foundation: *Connected Learning Theory*

### 6.2.1  *The Need*

The traditional, teacher-centric model of classroom teaching, where "one teacher in one classroom teaches one subject at a time to one class," has been criticized by several researchers in multiple disciplines for a long time (Kumpulainen and Sefton-Green 2014; Facer 2011). This model considers students as an individual having "knowledge hole," to be filled up with knowledge and information by teacher, who is the main character in a teaching-learning process (Nugroho 2017). Classroom teachings are not customized to satisfy individual needs; and the learning process is administered using disconnected subjects across disconnected periods at schools. Several researchers have pointed out that rigidity in curricula, syllabus-driven textbooks, a chalk-and-talk and monologue teaching methods, although necessary to some extent, are not sufficient to develop personalized and participatory learning practices that are needed to cultivate innovative and creative spirit among learners (Mehan 1979; Kumpulainen and Lipponen 2013; Kumpulainen and Sefton-Green 2014).

The complexities of twenty-first century society demand a new kind of educational arrangement that is capable of responding to students' holistic learning needs. This new educational arrangement should promote a student-centric learning environment to suit student's needs and learning styles. Teachers should take the role as facilitators, who treat students as subjects rather than object and help students to participate in leaning activities as active agents so that they can develop themselves holistically. Twenty-first century learning needs include abilities to think critically, act analytically, communicate with others digitally to participate and collaborate beyond time and space for learning through knowledge co-creation (Trilling and Fadel 2009).

This is possible by purposive integration of social technologies and socially enabled applications with learning environment within and beyond classroom, enabling social connection and knowledge co-creation.

However, availability of digital and mobile technologies within and outside classroom alone is not sufficient to ensure their meaningful integration with learning process. It requires a technology-driven pedagogical innovation and transformation, so that learning can be socially embedded, interest-driven, and oriented toward educational opportunity (Ito et al. 2013). In this context, we will discuss the theory of **connected learning**, which forms the basis of a social technology-driven learning framework, needed to expand the virtual connections between learners and different biotic and abiotic agents within a learner's socio-economic-cultural-political context. Such connected learning framework is designed to stress the value of learner's agency and autonomy and to break boundaries between formal and informal learning in the pursuit of holistic development with relevant resources and tools (Ito et al. 2013; Kumpulainen and Sefton-Green 2014).

## 6.2.2   The Background

Connected learning is based on the premise that *learning is a social process* and developments are embedded within social relationships and cultural contexts (Penuel et al. 2016). It puts emphasis on learning practices that are beyond formal education and focuses on informal learning as well, mediated by learner's socio-economic-cultural-political context (Vygotsky 1978).

The notion of *social learning* formed the foundation of learning process even in hunting gathering societies (as discussed in Chap. 3.3.1). However, the formal pedagogical theory behind the concept of learning as a social process was primarily initiated by Lev Vygotsky.

**Social Constructivism**: Constructivism is a learning theory whose core principle is: learners actively create or 'construct' their own knowledge and meaning from their experiences (Fosnot 1996). The two streams of thoughts in this domain are known as: cognitive *constructivism* and *social constructivism*. While cognitive constructivists focus on the inner psychological and mental processes, social constructivism focuses on co-construction of knowledge through social interaction (Vygotsky 1978). Vygotsky rejected the assumption made by cognitive theorists that it was possible to separate learning from its social context. He argued that all cognitive functions have a deep relationship with social interactions and social context and that learning is not simple assimilation and accommodation of new knowledge by learners; it is the process by which "learners were integrated into a knowledge community."

Vygotsky's sociocultural theory of human learning describes a framework where social interaction plays a primary role in the development of cognition. It views learning as a two-stage process: first, at a social level, a learning process starts with interaction with others; and then, at an individual level, the learning experience is integrated into the individual's mental structure (Vygotsky 1978). Vygotsky also theorizes a concept of "zone of proximal development" (ZPD). It depicts the difference between a child's individual capabilities (to be developed by *self*) and potential capabilities (to be acquired under adult guidance or in collaboration with "more capable peers") (Vygotsky 1978). Thus, Collaborative learning forms the basis for knowledge and skills acquisition, facilitating intentional learning (Briner 1999).

Since Vygotsky's work, several researchers have investigated the role of community and social interaction as part of the learning process. Some of those theories related to connected learning is given below:

**Social Learning Theory**: The social learning theory (Bandura 1977) considers the role of personal cognitive capability as well as the environment, thus combining both cognitive psychology and behaviorism. Bandura (1977) states: "Learning would be exceedingly laborious, not to mention hazardous, if people had to rely solely on the effects of their own actions to inform them what to do. Fortunately, most human behaviour is learned observationally through modelling: from observing others, one forms an idea of how new behaviours are performed, and on later occasions this coded information serves as a guide for action." His theory assumes that people can learn by observing other people, which is known as observational learning (Simsek 2012). Bandura's theory is related to the theories of Vygotsky, which also emphasize the central role of social learning. However, Bandura's theory is based on cognitive development through observational learning (observing the behaviors of the other under certain environmental conditions), whereas Vygotsky's theory is based on cognitive development through interactions and guided learning from "more capable peers."

**Community of Practice (CoP)**: Wenger (1998) introduces the notion of *community of practice* to depict learning as a social activity. Communities of practice (CoP) are defined as "groups of people who share a concern or a passion for something they do and who interacts regularly to learn how to do it better" (Wenger 1998). In this context, the primary intention is to facilitate social participation in a way that it effectively inculcates knowledge to learners. This helps individuals to actively participate in the formation of learning communities and in turn create one's identity through such communitarian participation (Wenger et al. 2002). The definition of community of practice becomes crucial at this juncture. Defined as a group of people collaborating over a specific practice and creating his/her identity by virtue of shared communitarian experience, community of practice can be identified as a positive catalyst in ushering a collaborative learning space, enabling learners to learn and modify their actions by interacting with other communitarian members (Basak et al. 2017).

**Connectivism**: Connectivism is *a network-driven social learning framework* that attempts to theorize learning in a digitally connected world through the formation of networks or connections (Siemens 2005). According to Stephen Downes: "...knowledge is distributed across a network of connections, and therefore learning consists of the ability to construct and traverse those networks" (Downes 2007). In todays' world, social technologies and socially enabled applications have empowered people to produce and consume knowledge and information across cyberspace. Connectivism emphasizes how these technologies contribute to new avenues of learning.

It assumes that "learning does not simply happen within an individual, but within and across the networks." The difference of connectivism as a learning theory from other approaches is the assumption that: "learning (defined as actionable knowledge) can reside outside of ourselves (within an organization or a database), is focused on connecting specialized information sets, and the connections that enable us to learn more are more important than our current state of knowing" (Siemens 2005).

Connectivism as a theory of learning in a digitally connected world has been criticized by several researchers (Verhagen 2006). Connectivism says that learning is the process of creating connections using technology and that learning can occur within a network structure. However, the concepts of *learning* and *knowledge* need to be differentiated in this context; knowledge can be found in network (technology), but it will be interpreted differently by learners during the process of learning (based on individual's knowledge acquisition and processing capabilities). Moreover, connectivism treats "technology" as a "culture-free black box" with a premise that social technologies enable learning (Smidt et al. 2017). However, the formation, distribution, acquisition, and use of "content" (knowledge) from the network are important to support the process of learning (Bell 2011). Connectivism principles primarily assume self-regulated learning; however, learners' context of learning strongly influences the scope of self-regulated learning (Pintrich and deGroot 1990). Connectivism largely treats technology as a tool independent from its context and its users.

In subsequent sections, we will introduce and discuss different dimensions of **connected learning** in details, since it would form the conceptual foundation of our digital platform, designed toward bridging education divide using social technologies and socially enabled applications.

### 6.2.3   Connected Learning

Based on the foundation of social constructivism, community of practice and connectivism and modelled using contemporary digital age learning, **Connected Learning** is a formal, pedagogical articulation of a collaborative, networked learning process. Connected learning is a learning theory situated in the digital age that exploits the ubiquitous affordance of social technologies to cater to the twenty-first century learning needs (Kumpulainen and Sefton-Green 2014). Connected learning attempts to create a community-driven, collaborative learning network that not only improves individual learning outcomes but also seeks to support communities and collective capacities to integrate learning with opportunity (Ito et al. 2020). Connected Learning is a shift from passive assimilation of knowledge and information to participatory learning. Learning happens best when learners co-construct knowledge through social interactions with their peers, mentors, and teachers, enabling them to create as well as consume knowledge.

Connected learning is learning that is "interest-driven, supported by peers and mentors, and connected to academic, economic, and civic opportunities" (Wortman and Mizuko 2019). Today's social technologies and socially enabled applications allow anytime-anywhere access to information and knowledge, thus providing the opportunity to learners to satisfy specialized learning need and pursue interest-driven learning. The connected learning framework empowers learners to pursue a personal interest-driven learning with the support from teachers, peers, caring adults, experts from communities. This framework, with multi-layered connectivity with different agents, helps learners to boost their bridging social capital, which, in turn, help learners to link this interest-driven learning to academic accomplishment, career achievement, or civic engagement. Here, learning and cultivation of knowledge are associated not only with formal connections with in-school teachers, tutors, or the curriculum, but with informal connections with everyone participating in the network. In this framework, a learner is also seen as a knowledgeable participant, a meaningful contributor in the network (Grech 2019; Kumpulainen and Sefton-Green 2014; Holland et al. 1998; Wenger et al. 2002). While connected learning is applicable to learners of all ages (Thigpen and Steffen 2020), the framework at its initial stage dealt with young adults and adolescents only.

In earlier chapters, education ecosystem has been depicted as a network of biotic and abiotic entities, whose dynamic interactions are contextualized by four influencers, viz. economic, social, political, and socio-psychological. Conventional educational reform initiatives mostly focused either on how technology has been deployed or on the way institutional changes have evolved. Marking a departure from conventional approach, connected learning attempts in understanding the dynamics of social change via networks of agents: an approach that aligns with the proposed ecosystemic perspective.

A connected learning platform is open and scalable, allowing learning to happen across diverse sites of learning—homes, schools, physical and virtual communities, and informal learning institutions. Thus, it allows combining a centralized, institution-based learning framework with a more decentralized, informal network-based learning framework (Quigley et al. 2019).

## 6.2.4  Design Principles of Connected Learning Platform

Connected learning platform design neither rely on digital technology alone nor on social process. Rather, it requires a socio-technical approach to system design (Baxter and Sommerville 2011). It considers human, social, and organizational factors, as well as technical factors in system design that would support developing interests, relationships, skills, and a sense of purpose (Ito et al. 2020). The core design principles (Ito et al. 2013) are listed below:

**Interest-Powered**: In a connected learning framework, a learner is able to nurture his/her interest either through self-learning or mentored learning. Researchers have shown that interest- and passion-driven learning help learners to achieve higher order learning outcomes (Zamora 2017).

**Production-Centered**: Connected learning framework encourages learners to actively produce, create, experiment, and design knowledge artifacts[2] (Newman and Conrad 1999), which is supported through giving online access to digital tools and circulating it via virtual social connections for wider benefits.

**Peer-Supported**: Connected learning framework demonstrates a "socially meaningful and knowledge-rich ecology of ongoing participation, self-expression and recognition" (Garcia 2014). In their everyday engagement with peers and friends using virtual social connections, learners exchange, contribute and share knowledge and information with peers, making learning meaningful, relevant, and resilient.

**Shared Purpose**: The connected learning framework identifies specific supports and outcomes of learning that are embedded in joint activity and shared purpose. Formation of interest- and purpose-specific virtual communities using social technologies and socially enabled application allows learners to share interests with mentors, teachers, and their peers and contribute to a common purpose. It also encourages cross-generational and cross-cultural learning, centered around common goals and interests.

**Academically Oriented**: Connected learning recognizes that "learners flourish and realize their potential when they can connect their interests and social engagement to academic studies, civic engagement, and career opportunity" (Ito et al. 2013). Hence, within a connected learning framework, formal academic teachings within classroom must integrate the socially and culturally meaningful contexts and link them with available opportunity structure. This would enable them to realize their true potential and move toward prosperous economic life.

**Openly Networked**: Connected learning environments allow learners to learn, both formally and informally, in multiple settings, be it in school, home, or community. Online digital platforms within a connected learning framework can make learning resources abundant, accessible, and visible across all learner settings (Ito et al. 2013).

### 6.2.5  Connected Learning and Educational Equity

Connected learning is a student-centric learning theory, which argues that *network of relationships* among learners and other agents, and a *learning environment* that satisfies learners' personal interests and needs, are critical to realize an effective learning process. The equity agenda is at the core of this democratic framework (Ito et al. 2020). As indicated in Chap. 2, researchers have shown that formalized, institutionalized education creates education divide in the form of access divide, capability divide, and opportunity divide. In contrast, Ito et al. (2013) point to the

---

[2]Knowledge Artifacts (KA) are "objects that convey and hold usable representation of knowledge" (Holsapple and Joshi 2001). KAs are carriers of knowledge that supports its sharing, and also contribute to the evolution of the community by supporting its natural learning processes (Salazar-Torres et al. 2008) (e.g. contents of a blog, a video created on YouTube, contribution in a discussion forum, etc.).

possibilities for connected learning platforms to reach the underprivileged communities more effectively, since learners may join diverse communities of interest online and access information and knowledge from anywhere, so long as they are connected to the Internet.

However, it has also been seen that socio-economically privileged learners have more access to technology-enhanced connected learning environments at higher rates (Carfagna 2014; Rafalow 2020; Reich and Mizuko 2017). For example, availability of out-of-school learning opportunities is more pronounced for economically and socially privileged learners, which can contribute to inequity (Duncan and Murnane 2011), and new learning technologies could intensify these inequities. Hence, in order to use connected learning framework to bridge the extant education divide, the design principles should have a stronger consideration for less resourced learners. In the following sections, we will first discuss a framework toward creating an online connected learning environment. Subsequently, based on the proposed framework, we will show how to architect a digital platform that attempts to bridge the education divide.

## 6.3   A Framework Toward Creating an Online Connected Learning Environment

### 6.3.1   The Connected Learning Environment: A Conceptual Framework

Despite changing patterns of demands in the global labor market and the need to incorporate new learning skills, educational ecosystems all across nations continue to follow the traditional "factory model" form of learning (Luksha et al. 2017). As Toffler (1970) describes, the industrial paradigm of education follows a centralized bureaucratic model and administrative hierarchy of education. The traditional education ecosystem of today is thus an assemblage of masses of students, teachers and a centrally located school similar to a factory setup, resulting in an education ecosystem depending on factory pipeline system.

The proposed Connected Learning framework is a transition from this content-centric, teacher-centric, and centralized education ecosystem of the industrial age to a connection-centric, learner-centric, and decentralized education ecosystem of the socio-digital age (driven by social technologies and socially enabled applications). It puts digital platform at the core of the framework (Fig. 6.1), connected to other socially enabled digital platforms and services. These socially enabled platforms and services include: generic and purpose-specific social media including social networking sites (e.g. Facebook, Academia.edu), online knowledge sharing platforms (e.g. Wikipedia, YouTube), e-learning sites (Udemy, Coursera), peer-to-peer marketplace (e.g. Amazon, Airbnb), and so on, as explained in Sect. 5.3.

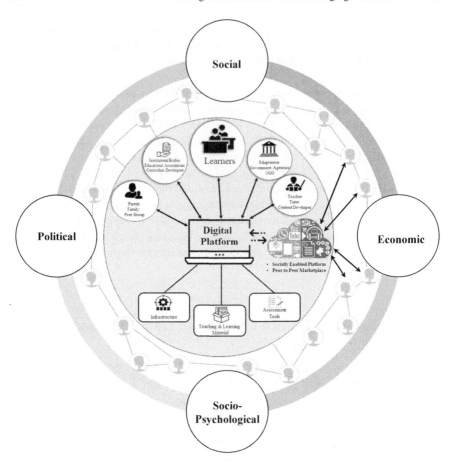

**Fig. 6.1** A social technology-driven connected learning framework: an ecosystemic perspective

All biotic and abiotic components are connected to this digital platform. This *digital core* does not rule out the possibilities of physical interactions between different entities as and when needed. In fact, some form of blending of digital and physical is needed not only to match in-school and out-of-school learning, but also to engage underprivileged community members into this platform, as will be illustrated in the next section.

The entire system is embedded in a crowd-based environment, creating equal opportunities for everyone connected to the system. The role of *crowd capital* in the education ecosystem, powered by social technologies, is a significant departure from earlier ecosystem, enabling a transition from *content* to *connection*.

Crowd capital can be identified as a knowledge resource, produced by the crowd and integrated by a digital platform through its use of crowd capability. Crowd capability is defined by the "structure, content, and process by which a platform engages with the dispersed knowledge of the *crowd*" (Prpic and Shukla 2013).

From our research perspective, crowd capital can serve as the key resource triggering the process of connected learning. Contemporary society has witnessed an increasing importance of crowd capital as a potential resource endowed with the capacity to usher positive change. The proponent of the IS-mediated phenomenon of peer production, Benkler and Nissenbaum (2006) rightly states: "Commons-based peer production is a socioeconomic system of production that is emerging in the digitally networked environment. Facilitated by the technical infrastructure of the Internet, the hallmark of this socio-technical system is collaboration among large groups of individuals who cooperate effectively to provide information, knowledge or cultural goods without relying on either market pricing or managerial hierarchies to coordinate their common enterprise" (Benkler and Nissenbaum 2006).

Several cyber knowledge resources, like Wikipedia and YouTube, have successfully utilized the crowd knowledge available in the digital forum. Several e-learning platforms act as linking forums, connecting people in need of specific knowledge resources to domain experts virtually. Our research is premised on the concept of dispersed knowledge, originally developed by F.A. Hayek in the noteworthy work, "The Use of Knowledge in Society," where he described dispersed knowledge as a "body of very important but unorganized knowledge... the knowledge of the particular circumstances of time and place" (Hayek 1945).

The proposed framework is infused with an ideology to augment the traditional brick and motor structure of education dissemination as followed conventionally. Redesigning the traditional learning space into a social technology-enabled shared learning space entails shifting to virtual classrooms, which facilitate learning anytime, anywhere, without the presence of physical infrastructure. If we look into contemporary digitized era, then we can see how with the rapid penetration of smartphones, the mobile devices often act as learning devices to the users. People informally learn from the knowledge available digitally from several online knowledge sources, for example Wikipedia, which is a crowd-based repository of knowledge. The collaborative learning space created by social technologies and socially enabled platforms has enabled one and all to contribute in the collective knowledge pool, where anyone can be disseminators of knowledge as well as learners in the process. Such an environment questions the monopoly of teachers, where crowd knowledge also acts as the source of knowledge. The way digitization has altered the learning process has enabled public and private players to embrace digital technologies more in order to mitigate extant education divide. However, such endorsements have to be coupled by contextual digital literacy training, so that the target group, apart from gaining access, also develops the credentials to exploit digital services in pursuit of learning.

## 6.3.2 Redefining the Configurations and Interactions of Biotic Entities

As depicted in Fig. 6.1, all biotic and abiotic components are connected to the digital platform and are influenced under four dimensions. The changing roles of biotic components in the context of the proposed framework are given below:

**Learners**: OECD (2018) has come up with a Learning Framework 2030 keeping in mind the disruptive changes in education ecosystems globally. The focus is on creating students or learners who will possess own agencies; moving toward creating "Future-ready students." These learners need to exercise their agencies in their own learning sphere throughout life; giving way to lifelong learning. Agency refers to the ability to undertake informed actions and actively participate in the affairs of the world and develop better abilities to influence immediate conditions and circumstances. The proposed connected learning framework focuses on creating autonomous learners who are capable of reacting and energising own power and creativity (Corson 1980). According to Christensen et al. (2008), future learning environment must be learner-centric because students have different types of intelligence, they do not learn the same way. To serve all learners effectively, learning should be both personalized and customized. The changing need of twenty-first century learning is based on personalization, collaboration, and informalization (informal learning) (Redecker and Punie 2013). A learner-centered education ecosystem is premised on personalization, collaboration, and informalization of skill-based learning, with special emphasis on lifelong learning mediated through ICT. Simultaneously, technological development coupled with structural alterations in the global labor markets has made generic and transversal skills important in the context of contemporary socioeconomic setup. Acquisition of these skills enables a learner to participate in the lifelong learning process, who by virtue of the same is expected to develop a flexible response to change. Possession of these skills also enables the learners to develop survival attributes to compete and fair in collaborative learning and working environments (Redecker and Punie 2013).

**Parents, Family, and Peer Group**: Parents, family, and peer group accounts to be the most immediate factors of a learner's learning environment. Collaboration, as the other component of twenty-first century learning needs, is not associated with classroom learning alone; it encompasses informal learning through virtual peer grouping and mentor-supported network where knowledge and skills can be acquired by building virtual learning communities (Basak et al. 2017). These "crowd-based" virtual communities can comprise of people from any sociocultural or age groups (Bardhan et al. 2014). Social technologies in this context play vital role in fostering virtual collaborative learning spaces. Collaborative learning gives way to informalization as the final characteristic of maintaining and fostering future of learning. Spaces for collaboration have been a necessary condition for innovation (Hannon et al. 2011).

**Teachers, Tutors, and Content Developers**: Apart from in-school teachers and home tutors, Connected Learning paradigm saw the emergence of out-of-school virtual (online) teachers and content developers, who are mainly self-appointed and operate either as volunteers or receive their wages from the learning platform. Those virtual teachers are subject matter experts, but may not be professional/Institutional teachers and the teaching method may be synchronous, asynchronous, or blended (Chap. 4). There are numerous *formal* e-learning sites (e.g. Udemy, Khan Academy, Coursera, etc.), and *informal* blogs, discussion forums and video tutorials (in YouTube, for example), promoting interactive digital learning environment, where numerous known/unknown experts form the *online teaching community*. This learning environment makes excellent use of technology, for instance interactive whiteboards, visualizers, and so on, and can create stimulating and engaging learning experience for learners.

**Edupreneurs, Government Agencies, and NGO**: Institutionalization of education in contemporary society is controlled by both Government, and private players or for-profit edupreneurs, who take an active role to shape the nature of education dissemination in modern society. Along with private and public bodies, several non-profit, non-governmental organizations also contribute in devising strategies and practical pathways of disseminating education for the underprivileged section of the community. These entities not only guide the teachers and content developers in shaping the content of education to be disseminated, they are also responsible in building infrastructures to host educational activities and devising appropriate teaching-learning materials. In the era of Connected Learning, these entities will act as social technology-driven *Platform Provider* to implement the connected learning framework and to mobilize other biotic and abiotic entities/crowd resources to create a decentralized, digital platform-oriented learning environment. As indicated in previous chapter, *"resource orchestration"* in this distributed digital platform is more important than *'resource control'* (as practised in centralized and Institutionalized education system), and facilitating interactions and managing relationships have a higher priority than internal optimization" (Alstyne and Parker 2017; Cui et al. 2017; Parker et al. 2016; Parker et al. 2017). Additionally, for underprivileged community members with little knowledge on digital usage, these entities also serve as intermediaries that positively influence the technology diffusion processes by linking actors and activities, and their related skills and resources to create momentum for a socio-technical system change (Kivimaa et al. 2019). This will be discussed in details in Sect. 6.5.

**Institutional Bodies, Educational Associations, and Curriculum Developers**: Structuration and formalization of today's education at different levels are done by Institutional Bodies, Educational Associations and Curriculum Developers that directly guide the method of teaching and curriculum development to operationalize the Institution-driven education processes. The content formulated by content developers is directly influenced by these structuration guidelines. However, Connected Learning Framework creates a personalised learning environment that supports and motivates each student to nurture his or her passions, make connections between different learning experiences and opportunities, and design their own learning projects and processes in collaboration with peer group and mentors through social connection in a virtual environment. Thus, structuration and formalization of learning process, as followed in today's conventional education system, become less important in this framework. Sometimes, the digital platform plays the role of Educational Associations and Curriculum Developers (e.g. Coursera); but, this framework puts equal emphasis on informal, out-of-school learning as well and rely more on social connections than centralized entities.

### 6.3.3   Redefining the Configurations and Interactions of Abiotic Entities

The changing roles of abiotic components in the context of the proposed framework are given below:

**Infrastructure**: Social technology-driven connected learning platform reduces the time and cost intrinsic to setting up and maintenance of *physical infrastructure*. Moreover, the dependence on physical infrastructures (like brick-and-mortar schools and colleges) and local amenities (e.g. road, electricity, etc.) for their effective functioning can be evaded to a great extent with the help of social technology aided learning. In this learning framework, learning is not limited to formal institutionalized spaces for learning; it is not bound by age too. School students be it children or adults can be part of the learning process which may not be confined to the boundaries of a school or institution. Personalized learning space in this technology-driven framework can only be created through internet-enabled mobile devices, which would help learners to communicate, interact, and share information with the world outside. Mobile based learning which includes both synchronous and asynchronous modes of learning have been successful in reaching out to students of different age groups. UNESCO recognizes future mobile devices to be digital, easily portable, usually owned and controlled by an individual rather than an institution, able to access the internet and other networks. Thus, learning infrastructure in this context consists of (i) internet-enabled digital platform at the back-end, and (ii) internet-enabled mobile devices including any portable, connected technology, such as basic mobile phones, e-readers, smartphones, laptops, and tablet computers at the user-end.

**Teaching-Learning Materials**: Teaching-learning materials in contemporary education system are primarily formulated by public and private entities, following a prescribed standardized curriculum structure, specified by institutional bodies, educational boards, and curriculum developers. However, in connected learning framework, where learning is interest-driven and socially mediated, teaching-learning-materials are generated spontaneously by the *crowd* of experts. As indicated earlier, there are numerous *formal* e-learning sites (e.g. Udemy, Khan academy, Coursera, etc.), and *informal* blogs, discussion forums and video tutorials (in YouTube, for example), that provide digital learning content, where numerous known/unknown experts design and deliver digital content, keeping in mind the interest of the learning communities.

**Assessment tools**: In modern society, education is considered to be the key to achievement and is infused with the promise of economic return. Hence it was necessary to devise assessment tools, against which the learning outcome of a student can be measured in a standardized format by Institutional bodies and educational associations. While conventional assessment pattern is tuned to measure knowledge-based cognitive abilities like reading, mathematical ability, writing, memorization of facts, etc., the same is not fit to assess the intangible skills of twenty-first century. The altered setup of twenty-first century makes it crucial to assess a learner's ability by measuring his/her social and emotional intelligence, creativity, the ability to cooperate, co-create and innovate other related skills. In order to ensure improved socioeconomic performance in the twenty-first century, possession of the above-mentioned skills is deemed necessary in the changed context (National Research Council 2011; Darling-Hammond and Adamson 2014). In a distributed, online learning environment, assessment and evaluation of learners are challenging tasks, and there should be opportunities for student self- and peer assessment. Several independent Online Virtual Assessment Platforms are also coming up to assess students' knowledge and skills across various dimensions.

### 6.3.4  Interactions with External Influencers

The proposed Connected Learning Framework influences as well as gets influenced by four external influencers, namely, social, economic, political, and socio-psychological within the education ecosystem (Fig. 6.1).

The collaborative potential of social technology enables the learners to become more *social* by virtually connecting them to the global opportunity structure, thereby allowing them to expand beyond their immediate local context. The collaborative learning spaces, offered by social technologies, help the learners in both intra and inter community networking, thereby having positive influence in enhancing both bridging and bonding social capital. This bridging and bonding social capital not only facilitate collaborative learning, but also has a positive influence in enhancing awareness regarding outside world, including career and other livelihood opportunities.

The interaction between the proposed framework and the extant *economic* environment is bi-fold. From the learners' perspective, the collaborative learning space offered by this framework has a positive impact in reducing the learners' opportunity divide through bridging market separation (Singh et al. 2015) by virtually connecting them to global opportunity structure. Moreover, by virtually connecting learners with the global pool of teachers and other agents, social technology-driven connected learning framework is not only cost-effective in terms of infrastructural requirement but also beneficial in facilitating quality learning.

Virtual and personalized learning space created by this framework also has the potential to facilitate learning that overcomes the hindrances posed by *political* turmoil in a particular context. The virtual connectivity it offers ushers in a collaborative learning space, unperturbed by the hindering factors of the immediate local context. If we take into account Syria's instance as an example, then we can see that the loss of education resultant because of the political turmoil of the nation can, to some extent, be evaded through this learning framework. In spite of random shutting down of schools, the Syrian children can still have prospects to learn, if digital services are available and used purposively for creating a personal learning environment. However, given the issue of political unrest, there is always a doubt as to whether the concerned authorities are benevolent enough to make digital services available to its citizens. In addition to this, widespread acceptance of this framework requires support from policy makers and expert thinkers. At the same time, there has to be a conscious strategy to integrate in-school and out-of-school learning using connected learning framework.

Finally, the proposed framework, through the formation of virtual communities, exposes the learners to the outside world, which, in turn, nurtures their motivation level in pursuit of education and boosts their *socio-psychological* well-being. The collaborative learning space, enabling one and all to contribute in the education process, has a positive impact in motivating learners in the pursuit of interest-driven learning.

## 6.4  Architecting a Digital Platform to Bridge Education Divide

In this section, we present an architecture of a digital platform that uses social technologies and socially enabled applications to realize proposed Connected Learning Framework. The suggested platform aims to digitally bridge education divide, by connecting underprivileged learners with relevant agents and opportunities online. In Part III of this book, we will demonstrate how this platform, which realizes an ICT-enabled "capability framework," can create a "personal learning environment (Attwell 2007)," embedded in a collaborative learning space, which, in turn, enables the learners to interact, collaborate, and participate to transform the way they live, learn, and work. The idea of a Personal Learning Environment (PLE) in this context recognizes that learning is an ongoing and continuous process (not restricted in classroom alone) and is driven by the interest and passion of an individual. PLE supports learning from multiple providers in different contexts and situations (Attwell 2007).

The proposed digital platform based on Connected Learning Framework aims to create a personalised learning environment around the learner, embedded in a collaborative learning space, that integrates a range of learning resources (Fig. 6.2), supporting the following activities:

*Self-paced Individual Learning*: This refers to *online asynchronous learning* where individuals use online tutorial, courseware, discussion forum, blogs or any other digital multimedia materials, which may not be explicitly designed for educational purpose, such as accessing knowledge and information sharing sites like YouTube.

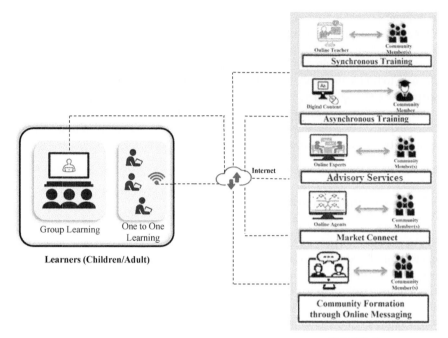

**Fig. 6.2**   The functional architecture of our platform

*Assisted Learning*: This refers to **online synchronous learning** (through embedded video-conferencing tools), conducted by means of structured learning paths that can be implemented in two different ways:

- Interact online with teachers and experts in the domain of study, either free or fee-based, who can guide the learners with varying degree of teaching support;
- Interact online with mentors/councelors, who can guide the learner what to study, why to study, how to study and from where to study in the online learning space;
- In case of skill-based training, the learners also interact with market agents, who would support the learners to utilize their skills after completion of training, thus providing a linkage to the market and helping the learners to discover newer market opportunities.

*Collaborative Learning Through Community of Practice*: Community of Practice (introduced in Sect. 6.2.2) refers to a group of people who share specific practice-related knowledge among communitarian members. Collaborations among the members of community of practice, or practitioners in other words, results in collective learning, which makes community of practice a collaborative learning space. An online community of practice can act as a facilitator to create knowledge repository, initiate discussion forums, provide access to experts, and promote relevant exchange over synchronous and asynchronous mode of operations. Only such an optimal facilitation through creation of practice-oriented community bears the potential in simultaneously cultivating social capital and bridging capability divide of communitarian members through the creation of collaborative learning spaces. This interpersonal communitarian bond will not only facilitate peer-to-peer learning but also help to bridge the opportunity divide for participants to improve their economic performance through linkage with appropriate agents. Created through a network of interrelationships among all those participating in the process (e.g. learners, teachers, tutors, experts, etc.), these interrelationships are intrinsic to collaboration within a community pursuing a common learning goal.

## 6.5   Some Implementation Challenges for the Underprivileged Community

Since the proposed platform is driven by internet and internet-enabled devices, implementation and successful operationalization of this platform for underprivileged community is fully dependent on (i) accessibility of internet and internet-enabled devices; (ii) users' capability to effectively use the technology; and, (iii) applicability of internet and internet-enabled devices, as perceived not only by learners, but also by other connected agents, specifically in the context of underprivileged community.

### 6.5.1   Accessibility of Internet and Internet-Enabled Devices

While internet and smartphone penetration are rapidly increasing, there are still over three billion people who don't have access to the Internet (ITU 2019). Nearly 60 percent of the world's population is already online. However, although the coverage gap (those who do not live within the footprint of a mobile broadband network) is as low as 9% (ITU 2019), still over 40 percent of the world's total population remains unconnected to the internet. At the same time, percentage of people accessing Internet also varies across socioeconomic profiles. In developed countries, most people are online, with close to 87% of individuals using the Internet. In the least developed countries (LDCs), on the other hand, only 19% of individuals are online in 2019 (ITU 2019). This divide is also prevalent within countries as well, where the poor, elderly, and rural people are less likely to be connected. Women also have less access than men, especially in low-income countries (Pisa and John 2019).

Similar disparity exists in case of accessibility to internet-enabled mobile devices (smartphones, tablets), and, growth in mobile technology varies widely across and within nations. People in advanced economies are more likely to have smartphones and are more likely to use the internet and social media than people in emerging economies. In a survey conducted by Pew Research Center (Taylor and Laura 2019), it has been found out that, "a median of 76% across 18 advanced economies surveyed have smartphones, compared with a median of only 45% in emerging economies." In some countries like South Korea, Israel, and The Netherlands, smartphone penetration is more than 90%; whereas countries like Poland, Russia, and Greece have only around 60% penetration. The smartphone usage rate also varies substantially in emerging economies, ranging from 60% in South Africa and Brazil to 40% in Indonesia, Kenya, and Nigeria (Taylor and Laura 2019).

However, the proliferation of mobile technologies is growing rapidly around the globe. The number of active mobile broadband subscriptions continues to grow strongly, with an 18.4% per year (ITU 2019). For example, as on 2020, Internet users in India are 50% of its population with a yearly growth rate of 23%. Currently, internet is predominantly accessed via smartphones (91%) in India. While overall mobile phone users in India is 78%, smartphone users have increased to 67% in 2020, although not all smartphone users are accessing Internet (Kemp 2020).

## 6.5.2  Users' Capability

There are several government and private initiatives all over the globe to increase Internet accessibility for the underprivileged community, making available cheap smartphones and affordable Internet connectivity (Pisa and John 2019). However, improved accessibility will not always ensure improved usability of any system; users' capability needs to be cultivated so that they can use smartphone and internet effectively to satisfy their needs.

For example, in the context of ICT-based personalized education, two most popular models for mobile learning in schools are one-to-one (1:1) programmes and Bring Your Own Device (BYOD) initiatives. In the former, all students are given individual devices free of cost. On the other hand, in Bring Your Own Device (BYOD) initiatives, learners bring their own devices with schools supplying or subsidizing devices for students who cannot afford them. The 1:1 programme is more common in lower economic countries, while the BYOD strategy is usually implemented in developed nations (UNESCO 2013).

These initiatives, in order to do justice to the EFA goals and Education 2030 goals, are dedicated to equip every learner with complete access to mobile devices. Recent technological development, leading to widespread availability of affordable mobile devices, has given further impetus in realizing the vision of these initiatives (UNESCO, 2013). One Laptop per Child (OLPC) programme can be rightly identified as one of the major initiatives attempting to give a practical shape to this 1:1 model of learning. Dedicated to address the educational needs of marginalized learners of developing countries, OLPC was primarily conceived with the vision for equitable and inclusive education dissemination. However, the initiative attracted heavy criticism from researchers and domain experts, arguing that the initiative with its "utopian" vision of education overlooks complex social problems that can pose a serious hindrance in the process of educating marginalized learners with the help of technology. Affording the expensive infrastructural cost associated to such a model and the reliance it takes on the ministry level to ensure effective roll-out can be identified as major barriers hindering successful realization of the 1:1 model of learning. Moreover, a critical evaluation reveals how some of the 1:1 initiatives have excessively focused on technology at the cost of neglecting the importance to train teachers and students regarding the designed architecture, which subsequently have hampered optimal utilization of the model by the members of education community. The above-stated reasons majorly hindered the initiatives to achieve widespread impact, thereby iterating the fact that "*although access is important, it is not sufficient*" (Valiente 2010) as a noteworthy reminder. In spite of the criticisms, OLPC was to some extent successful in doing justice to its premise, the 1:1 model of learning. Latin America to some extent successfully applied this model to address its deplorable conditions of education (Lugo and Schurmann 2012). Although the entire globe has reached a universal consensus regarding the potential of the 1:1 model, researchers are yet to come with appropriate operational dynamics, which will equip the initiatives to create widespread impact.

Majority of the underprivileged population in developing countries does not have the capability to use smartphone and internet effectively to satisfy their need. There are several reasons for this. One of the primary reasons is, non-availability of local content. Most of the content available online are in English, and hence may not be comprehendible to underprivileged community members having low literacy rate. The vast majority of the population simply do not know what information is available, where to find it, and how to use it. The usage pattern also varies across gender as well as socioeconomic and educational profile. So, enhancing users' capability to help them in using the system is not limited to offering a digital literacy training or a training on the proposed digital platform. Facilitating knowledge and information exchange among marginalized groups is a complex process and requires contextual application of ICT to address users' needs and concerns.

In the context of improving rural education in developing countries, mere applications of education technology-related tools and practices will not improve learning experiences and outcomes of rural children (Kalolo 2018). The design challenge is therefore about finding ways to appropriately integrate digital technologies in education systems that would help both teachers and learners to accept and adopt the digital technologies as new methods of learning systems. Researchers have conceptualized the concept of digital maturity both in the context of individual and organization (Vardisio and Patricia 2015). In order to improve digital maturity of underprivileged population, the following three dimensions need to be taken into account:

- E-awareness: the aptitude to understand the opportunities of digital technology.
- Digital literacy: competencies to use digital technologies to fulfil personal and professional objectives.
- Informational literacy: the ability to retrieve, understand, and interpret information coming from digital sources.

Thus, the concept and consequent design and development efforts need to be tuned according to the learning context and capabilities of underprivileged learners.

In our framework, the role of *mentors/teachers* and *peer* group will play a very important role in nurturing users' capability. Through a wide range of studies and analyses, Raposa et al. (2016) have demonstrated the importance of mentorship and social relationships to cultivate shared interests and skills. They have also demonstrated the effectiveness of "natural" mentors in a connected learning platform, as compared to formal or "assigned" mentoring, especially in the context of marginalized and vulnerable youth (Raposa et al. 2016; Schwartz and Jean 2016).

### 6.5.3   Perceived Applicability of Internet and Internet-Enabled Applications

Even if smartphone with Internet connectivity is available to an underprivileged user, who may also be capable of using it, will that ensure effective usage of smartphone and Internet? There is always a cost-factor involved with this usage, even if it is subsidized. So, what are the benefits an underprivileged user will get against this financial investment, other than some entertainment and socialization using Facebook, for example? So, in our context, users need to be properly motivated, highlighting the demonstrated benefits of proposed connected learning platform. Digital inclusion must be linked with socioeconomic inclusion of underprivileged community so as to motivate users to practice digital means. Digital connectivity must be able to link an underprivileged user with larger opportunity structure encompassing connections and practices that help young people find their way to success in the wider world, which includes academic, career, civic, and political opportunities (Ito 2020). As the United Kingdom Cabinet office recognized in 2004: "Digital inclusion is not about computers, the internet or even technology, it is about using technology as a channel to improve skills, to enhance quality of life, to drive education, and to promote economic well-being across all elements of society. Digital inclusion is really about *social* inclusion, and because of this, the potential for technology to radically improve society and the way we live our lives should not be underestimated" (Cabinet Office 2004). Muir (2004) argued that other than promoting access and imparting basic digital training, the importance of community connections using digital media needs to be emphasized.

There is vast potential to use ICT to build social capital and contribute to community development and formation. However, it is largely untapped and unrecognized in many areas. The power of social technologies to establish virtual connectivity and enhance bonding and bridging social capital among underprivileged users help them to establish linkages to various form of resources that enhance economic and social development. The issues of trust and sustainability are central to this development. The findings of recent researches insightfully highlight the effectivity of internet in facilitating voluntary participation and creation of social networks among rural communities, thereby positively influencing the social capital of rural members. In this context, it needs to be remembered that internet usage is not limited to securing participation in local organizations and expansion of social networks. In order to achieve wider impact through ICT, technology must be resorted to acquire new knowledge about local activities and dynamics (Barbara 2015; Pénard and Poussin 2010). An in-depth investigation reveals that learning improvement among learners occur, when they seek out to different people and web resources for information, advice, ideas and solutions, instead of relying on a single community or known group of people (Hopkins and Thomas 2004).

## 6.6   Conclusion

In this chapter, we have proposed a social technology-driven connected learning framework and outlined an architecture of a digital platform to realize the proposed framework using social technology and socially enabled applications. The analysis of the proposed framework from an ecosystemic perspective reveals that the proposed digital platform is not only a technological artifact[3] (Verbeek and Pieter 2012) but also a socio-technical artifact[4] (Vermaas et al. 2010; Silver and Markus 2013), working in a social context, and entails the engagement of many social actors. Here, the technology at its core is enabling a network of biotic and abiotic components, promoting their dynamic interactions in the context of socio-economic-cultural-political context (Fig. 6.1).

The introduction of socio-technological innovations in society to solve social problems require a deep transition from older system to a new technology-mediated system and it entails simultaneous development (co-evolution) of technologies, service operations, and people's practices and mindsets (Kivimaa et al. 2019; Geels 2002). In our context, it is a transition from a face-to-face, centralized, teacher-and content-centric learning environment to a virtual, decentralized, connection-centric, collaborative, and personalized digital learning environment. These *socio-technical transitions* take care of changes in user practices and formal and informal institutional structures (including sociocultural, economic, regulatory, etc.) so that technology can be smoothly integrated with the extant social system (Markand et al. 2012). The concept of sociotechnical transition stresses the interdependence of technological, social, cultural, and political dimensions, as well as the mutual adjustment of these dimensions (Smith et al. 2010).

Hence, in order to manage a socio-technical transition for underprivileged community involving multiple agents, *transition intermediaries* play an important role to speed up transitions. In our context, transition intermediaries can be defined as actors that positively influence transition processes by linking actors and activities, and their

---

[3]"**Technological artifacts** are in general characterized narrowly as material objects made by (human) agents as means to achieve practical ends. Moreover, following Aristotle, **technological artifacts** are as kinds not seen as natural objects: **artifacts** do not exist by nature but are the products of art".

[4]Socio-technical artifacts are product or process artifacts with which humans must interact in the context of a social system to provide their utilities.

related skills and resources, with existing regimes in order to create momentum for socio-technical system change (Kivimaa et al. 2019). An intermediary facilitates and enables use of the digital platform, as well as takes an active role with the aim of empowering disadvantaged groups.

In order to do justice to the motto of digital inclusion, several commentators have emphasized the role of "trusted intermediaries" that help in triggering the process of digital inclusion. As a solution, researchers have advocated the usefulness of third sector organizations,[5] which "can play a crucial role in encouraging and supporting take-up" of digital technologies (Richardson and Angela 2013).

In Part III of our book, one of our objectives will be to demonstrate how this socio-technical transition can be managed through a transition intermediation process so that we can attempt to bridge education divide using social technology-enabled connected learning platform. We will show our implementation experience in rural India in a pilot scale. In order to integrate the technology with users' context and accelerate the process of technology adoption, *transition intermediaries* at different levels and different capacities were employed. First of all, the social entrepreneurs, during the process of implementing and operationalizing the platform, have acted as a transition intermediary to manage the transition from a traditional learning space to a decentralized, internet-enabled virtual learning space. Local coordinators and local NGOs also have played a crucial role in motivating and sustaining motivations of the user community. Online teachers and more knowledgeable peer and mentors as intermediaries have also guided the users in online forums as and when needed. We will discuss all these issues including our implementation experience in next chapters through empirical studies in the context of rural India.

# References

Alstyne, M. V., & Parker, G. G. (2017). Platform business: From resources to relationships. *GfK Marketing Intelligence Review, 9*(1), 25–29. https://doi.org/10.1515/gfkmir-2017-0004.

Attwell, G. (2007). The personal learning environments-The future of eLearning?. *eLearning Papers, 2*(1). Retrieved from https://www.researchgate.net/publication/228350341_Personal_Learning_Environments-the_future_of_eLearning.

Bandura, A. (1977). *Social learning theory.* New York: General Learning Press.

Barbara, B. (2015). Does the Internet matter for strong ties? Bonding social capital, Internet use, and age-based inequality. *International Review of Sociology, 25*(3).

Bardhan, A., Dey, P., & Bandyopadhyay, S. (2014). Connecting generations: Creation of web based virtual communities for imparting formal and informal education to the underprivileged children by elderly. In *the proceedings of the International Federation on Ageing (IFA)'s 12th Global Conference on Ageing*, Hyderabad, India.

Basak. J., Bandyopadhyay. S., Bhaumik. P., & Roy. S. (2017). Cultivating Online Communities of Practice as Rural Knowledge Management Strategy in India. In *Proceedings of the 18th European Conference on Knowledge Management (ECKM 2017)*, Barcelona, Spain.

---

[5]Third sector organizations is a term used to describe "a range of organisations that are neither public sector nor private sector. It includes: voluntary organisations. community organisations. registered charities" (Richardson and Angela 2013).

Baxter, G., & Sommerville, I. (2011). Socio-technical systems: From design methods to systems engineering. *Interact. Computing, 23*(1).

Bell, F. (2011). Connectivism: Its place in Theory-informed research and innovation in technology-enabled learning. *International Review of Research in Open and Distance Learning, 12*(3).

Benkler, Y., & Nissenbaum, H. (2006). Commons-based peer production and virtue. *Journal of Political Philosophy, 14*(4), 394–419. https://doi.org/10.1111/j.1467-9760.2006.00235.x.

Braun. L.W. (2019). *Connect to connected learning: Trainers show how small and rural communities can adopt CL principles.* American Libraries Magazine. Retrieved from https://americanlibrari esmagazine.org/2019/05/01/connect-connected-learning-library-programming/.

Briner, M. (1999). *Learning theories.* Denver: University of Colorado.

Cabinet Office. (2004). *Enabling a digitally United Kingdom: A framework for action.* Retrieved from http://www.cabinetoffice.gov.uk/publications/reports/digital/digitalframe.pdf.

Carfagna, L. (2014). *Beyond learning-as-usual: Connected learning among open learners.* Irvine, CA: Digital Media and Learning Research Hub.

Christensen, C. M., et al. (2008). *Disrupting class: How disruptive innovation will change the way the world learns.* New York: McGraw Hill.

Corson, D. J. (1980). Chomsky on education. *Australian Journal of Education, 24*(2), 164–185. https://doi.org/10.1177/000494418002400205.

Cui, M., Pan, S. L., Newell, S., & Cui, L. (2017). Strategy, resource orchestration and e-commerce enabled social innovation in rural China. *Journal of Strategic Information Systems, 26*(1), 3–21.

Darling-Hammond, L., & Adamson, F. (2014). *Beyond the bubble test: How performance assessments support 21st Century Learning.* Publisher: Jossey-Bass; ISBN-10: 1118456181.

Downes, S. (2007). *What Connectivism Is.* University of Manitoba. Retrieved from http://ltc.uma nitoba.ca/moodle/mod/forum/discuss.php?d=12.

Duncan, G. J., & Richard, J. M. (2011). *Whither opportunity?: Rising inequality, schools, and children's life chances.* New York: Russell Sage.

Facer, K. (2011). *Learning futures: Education, technology and social change.* London: Routledge.

Fosnot, C. T. (1996). Constructivism: A psychological theory of learning. In C. T. Fosnot (Ed.), *Constructivism: Theory, Perspectives and Practice* (pp. 8–33). New York: Teachers College Press.

Garcia, A. et al. (2014). *Teaching in the connected learning classroom.* Irvine, CA: Digital Media and Learning Research Hub. Retrieved from https://dmlhub.net/publications/teaching-connected-learning-classroom/index.html.

Geels, F. (2002). Technological transitions as evolutionary reconfiguration processes: A multi-level perspective and a case-study. *Research Policy, 31*, 1257–1274.

Grech, S. (2019). *Connected learning in the higher education of Refugees: A critical report.* Malta: Commonwealth Centre for Connected Learning. Retrieved from: https://connectedlearning4ref ugees.org/wp-content/uploads/2019/12/Connected-Learning-in-the-Higher-Education-of-Ref ugees-A-Critical-Report.pdf.

Hannon, V., Patton, A., & Temperley, J. (2011). *Developing an innovation ecosystem for education.* CISCO. Retrieved from https://www.globalcitizenleaders.com/wp-content/…/Innovation-Educat-CISCO.pdf.

Hayek, F. A. (1945). The use of knowledge in society. *The American Economic Review, 35*(4), 519–530.

Holland, D., Lachicotte, W., Skinner, D., & Cain, C. (1998). *Identity and agency in cultural worlds.* Cambridge, MA: Harvard University Press.

Holsapple, C. W., & Joshi, K. D. (2001). Organizational knowledge resources. *Decision Support Systems, 31*(1), 39–54.

Hopkins, L., & Thomas, J. (2004). *e-social capital: Building community through electronic networks.* Institute for Social Research, Swinburne University. Retrieved from www.sisr.net/wir edhighrise/papers/ buildcommunity.pdf.

Ito, M. et al. (2013). *Connected learning: An agenda for research and design.* Digital Media and Learning Research Hub, Irvine, CA, USA. ISBN 9780988725508. Retrieved from https://dml hub.net/publications/connected-learning-agenda-for-research-and-design/index.html.

Ito, M. et al. (2020). *The Connected Learning Research Network: Reflections on a Decade of Engaged Scholarship.* Irvine, CA: Connected Learning Alliance. Retrieved from https://clalliance.org/publications/.

ITU. (2019). *Measuring digital development: Facts and figures 2019.* International Telecommunication Union (ITU): Telecommunication Development Bureau.

Kalolo, J.F. (2018). Digital revolution and its impact on education systems in developing countries. *Educ Inf Technol.* https://doi.org/10.1007/s10639-018-9778-3.

Kemp, S. (2020). *Digital India 2020.* Retrieved from https://datareportal.com/reports/digital-2020-india.

Kivimaa, P., Boon, W., Hyysalo, S., & Klerkx, L. (2019). Towards a typology of intermediaries in sustainability transitions: A systematic review and a research agenda. *Research Policy, Elsevier, 48*(4), 1062–1075.

Kumpulainen, K., & Lipponen, L. (2013). Crossing boundaries in dialogic learning: A chronotopic analysis of learners' agency work. In *Interplays between dialogical learning and dialogical self,* (pp. 193–217). Charlotte, NC: Information Age Publishing.

Kumpulainen, K., & Sefton-Green, J. (2014). What is connected learning and how to research it? *International journal of learning and media, 4*(2), 7–18.

Lugo, M.T. & Schurmann, S. (2012). *Turning on mobile learning in Latin America: Illustrative initiatives and policy implications.* Paris, UNESCO. Available at http://unesdoc.unesco.org/images/0021/002160/216080E.pdf.

Luksha, P., Cubista, J., Laszlo, A., Popovich, M., & Nineko, I. (2017). *Educational Ecosystems for Societal Transformation.* Global Education Futures Report.

Markard, J., Raven, R., & Truffer, B. (2012). Sustainability transitions: An emerging field of research and its prospects. *Research Policy, 41,* 955–967.

Mehan, H. (1979). *Learning lessons: Social organization in the classroom.* Cambridge, MA: Harvard University Press.

Muir, K. (2004). *Connecting communities with CTLCs: From the digital divide to social inclusion.* Sydney: The Smith Family. Retrieved from http://library.bsl.org.au/jspui/bitstream/1/609/1/Connecting%20communities%20with%20CTLCs.pdf.

National Research Council. (2011). *Assessing 21st century skills: Summary of a Workshop.* Washington, DC: The National Academies Press. https://doi.org/10.17226/13215.

Newman, B., & Conrad, K.W. (1999). *A framework for characterizing knowledge management methods, practices and technologies* (the knowledge management forum). Retrieved from www.km-forum.org.

Nugroho, A. (2017). Contemporary teaching and learning. *Reform, 53.* University of Muhammadiyah Malang. Retrieved from research-gate.net/publication/334760794_contemporary_teaching_and_learning.

OECD. (2018). The future of education and skills Education 2030. Retrieved from https://www.oecd.org/education/2030/E2030%20Position%20Paper%20(05.04.2018).pdf.

Paltrinieri, R., & Piergiorgio, D. E. (2013). Processes of inclusion and exclusion in the sphere of prosumerism. *Future Internet, 5,* 21–33. https://doi.org/10.3390/fi5010021.

Parker, G., Alstyne, M. V., & Choudary, S. (2016). *Platform revolution: How networked markets are transforming the economy, and how to make them work for you.* WW Norton: New York, USA.

Parker, G., Van Alstyne, M. V., & Jiang, X. (2017). Platform Ecosystems: How developers invert the firm. *MIS Quarterly, 41*(1), 255–266.

Pénard, T., & Poussin, N. (2010). Internet use and social capital: The strength of virtual ties. *Journal of Economic Issues, 44*(3), 569–595.

Penuel, W. R., Daniela, D., Katie, V. H., & Ben, K. (2016). A social practice theory of learning and becoming across contexts and time. *Frontline Learning Research, 4*(4), 30–38.

Prpic, J., & Shukla, P. (2013). The theory of crowd capital. In *Proceedings of the 46th Annual Hawaii International Conference on Systems Sciences.* Washington, DC: IEEE Computer Society.

Pintrich, P. R., & deGroot, E. V. (1990). Motivational and self-regulated learning components of classroom academic performance. *Journal of Educational Psychology, 82*(1), 33–40.

Pisa, M., & John, P. (2019). *governing big tech's pursuit of the next billion users.* [CGD Policy Paper. Washington, DC: Center for Global Development]. Retrieved from https://www.cgdev. org/publication/governing-big-techs-pursuit-next-billion-users.

Quigley, C. F., Herro, D., Shekell, C., Heidi C., & Jacques, L. (2019). Connected learning in STEAM classrooms: Opportunities for engaging youth in science and math classrooms. *International Journal of Science and Mathematics Education.* https://doi.org/10.1007/s10763-019-10034-z.

Rafalow, M. H. (2020). *Digital divisions: How schools create inequality in the tech era.* Chicago, IL: University of Chicago Press.

Raposa, E. B., Jean, E. R., & Carla, H. (2016). The impact of youth risk on mentoring relationship quality: Do mentor characteristics matter? *American Journal of Community Psychology, 57*(3–4), 320–329.

Redecker, C., & Punie, Y. (2013). The future of learning 2025: Developing a vision for change. *Future Learning, 2*(3), 17. https://doi.org/10.7564/13-fule12.

Reich, J., & Mizuko, I. (2017). *From good intentions to real outcomes: Equity by design in learning technologies.* Irvine, CA: Digital Media and Learning Research Hub.

Richardson, R., & Angela, A. (2013). *The role of social intermediaries in digital inclusion: The case of social housing.* [Research Report RR2013/10]. Centre for Urban & Regional Development Studies (CURDS), Newcastle University. Retrieved from https://www.ncl.ac.uk/media/wwwncl acuk/curds/files/digital-inclusion.pdf.

Salazar-Torres, G., Colombo, E., Da Silva, F. S. C., Noriega, C. A., & Bandini, S. (2008). Design issues for knowledge artifacts. *Knowledge-Based Systems, 21*(8), 856–867. https://doi.org/10. 1016/j.knosys.2008.03.058.

Schwartz, S. E. O., & Jean, E. R. (2016). From treatment to empowerment: New approaches to youth mentoring. *American Journal of Community Psychology, 58*(1–2), 150–157.

Siemens, G. (2005). Connectivism: A learning theory for the digital age. *International Journal of Instructional Technology and Distance Learning, 2*(1). Retrieved from http://www.elearnspace. org/Articles/connectivism.htm.

Silver, M. S., & Markus, M. L. (2013). Conceptualizing the socio technical (ST) artifact. *Systems, Signs & Actions, 7,* 82–89.

Simsek, E. (2012). *Social learning.* Boston, MA: Springer. Retrieved from https://link.springer. com/referenceworkentry/10.1007%2F978-1-4419-1428-6_374.

Singh, R., Agarwal, S., & Modi, P. (2015). Market separations for BOP producers: The case of market development for the chanderi cluster weavers in India. *International Journal of Rural Management, 11*(2), 175–193.

Smidt, H., Matsu, T., & Kaveh, A. (2017). The future of social learning: A novel approach to connectivism. In The *proceedings of the 50th Hawaii International Conference on System Sciences.* https://doi.org/10.24251/hicss.2017.256.

Smith, A., Voss, J., & Grin, J. (2010). Innovation studies and sustainability transitions: The allure of the multi-level perspective and its challenge. *Research Policy, 39*(4), 435–448.

Sundararajan, A. (2016). *The sharing economy: The end of employment and the rise of crowd-based capitalism.* MIT Press.

Taylor, K. & Laura, S. (2019). *Smartphone ownership is growing rapidly around the world, but not always equally.* Pew Research Center. Retrieved from www.pewresearch.org.

Thigpen, L. L., & Steffen, T. (2020). *Connected learning: How adults with limited formal education learn.* Volume 44 of American Society of Missiology Monograph Series. ISBN: 1532679378.

Toffler, A. (1970). *Future shock.* New York: Random House.

Trilling, B., & Fadel, C. (2009). *21st century skills: Learning for life in our times.* San Francisco: Jossey Bass.

UNESCO. (2013). *The future of mobile learning: Implications for Policy makers and planners.* Retrieved from https://unesdoc.unesco.org/ark:/48223/pf0000219637.

Vardisio, R., & Patricia, C. (2015). Digital maturity: What is and how to build it. *In the proceedings of international conference the future of education* (5th edition), Florence, Italy. Retrieved from https://www.researchgate.net/publication/303683893_Digital_maturity_what_is_and_how_to_build_it.

Valiente, O. (2010). *1–1 in Education: Current practice, international comparative research evidence and policy implications* [OECD Education Working Papers, No. 44]. Paris: OECD Publishing. https://doi.org/10.1787/5kmjzwfl9vr2-en.

Verbeek, P., & Pieter, E.V. (2012). *Technological artifacts: A companion to the philosophy of technology.* Wiley-Blackwell.

Verhagen, P. (2006). *Connectivism: A new learning theory.* Retrieved from http://www.scribd.com/88324962/Connectivism-a-New-Learning-Theory.

Vermaas, P., Peter, K., Ibo, V.P., & Maarten, F. (2010). *A philosophy of technology: From technical artefacts to sociotechnical systems.* Morgan & Claypool.

Vygotsky, L. S. (1978). *Mind in society: The development of higher mental processes.* Cambridge, MA: Harvard University Press.

Wenger, E. (1998). *Communities of practice: Learning, meaning, and identity.* Cambridge: Cambridge University Press.

Wenger, E., McDermott, R., & Snyder, W.M. (2002). *Cultivating communities of practice.* Harvard Business Press.

Wortman, A., & Mizuko, Ito. (2019). Connected learning. *The International Encyclopedia of Media Literacy.* https://doi.org/10.1002/9781118978238.ieml0037.

Zamora, M. (2017). MOOCs and Their Afterlives: Experiments in Scale and Access in Higher Education. *Reimagining Learning in CLMOOC.* University of Chicago Press.

# Part III
# Exploring Impact of Social Technologies on Education Ecosystem: Some Empirical Studies in Rural India

# Chapter 7
# Exploring Rural–Urban Education Divide in India

## 7.1 Introduction

This chapter attempts to explore the education divide that exists between rural and urban India. In this context, it is crucial to reiterate that education divide, referring to the divide between one having quality education and the one devoid of it, forms the base of our research; and, marginalization of rural learners of India and not the intrinsic rurality has urged us to consider the same as our research context. The rural communities in developing nations like India form the practical context of our theorization, where we have attempted in implementing our blended learning platform in the Indian rural context. In this regard, it is important to clarify that rural sector in developing countries like India, where majority of the population belongs to underprivileged category, can be rightly justified as a marginalized space. The social exclusion, which Indian rural sectors suffer from puts them in the disadvantageous side of education divide, where the existing education ecosystem falls short in addressing the issues faced by Indian rural learners. Hence, the stringent and hierarchical dichotomy between rural and urban does not inform the base of our research; rather, the way we have categorized the territorial spaces (urban/rural), primarily in the context of developing nations, is in terms of the privileges (or lack of them) they experience, where the rural sphere undeniably account to be marginalized spaces. We can find several instances and academic works which have explicitly characterized rurality in terms of its marginalization (Heidi and Lou 2009; Chandra 2014). We will attempt in demystifying the intrinsic discrepancies between rural and urban India in terms of quality educational resources and how it subsequently creates education divide between the two territorial spaces.

Education systems in India are suffering from discriminatory teaching–learning practices leading to unequal learning outcome levels. Socioeconomic stratification in India gives rise to disparate access to quality education in the country, where the richest 5% in urban locales can afford to spend 29 times more on education than most rural households can afford to spend on the same (Chakravarty 2018). This brings us to the rising distinctions between Government-funded, free public schooling and private-funded, high fee-paying urban private schooling in the country, where imparting quality education is mostly restricted to those high-cost, high-end urban private schools (FICCI 2014). In this context, Jimenez and Lockheed (1995) studied the increasing performance levels among students enrolled in private schools that are located in urban areas (ASER 2019). These students have shown better cognitive abilities than those in public schools in rural areas. Free government (public) schools and government aided schools in rural areas are witness to continuous decline in academic performances of students. Some of the reasons behind such poor performances can be cited as the non-availability of well-trained teachers, regular absenteeism of teachers, poor quality of teaching materials and lack of supervision (Kumar and Rustagi 2010). Additionally, these rural schools are still engulfed within rigid curriculum, unattractive learning environments, lack of safety, hygiene and privacy, non-involvement of families and peer groups in learning process, unsupported teachers and schools and non-utilization of local resources. These discussions on varied forms of education systems in the country bring us to the existing divide created between students based on geographical location and socioeconomic backgrounds. However, this divide can be better understood or explored from the three variants of education divides (as mentioned in Chap. 2) such as that of access divide, capability divide, and opportunity divide.

Section 7.2 of this chapter will delve deeper into these three variants of divides still existing in the context of rural India. Owing to several education reform movements including the "Education for All" Movement, there has been significant educational expansion in India with regard to physical infrastructure of schools and enrolment of students, both at the primary and secondary levels of education in India. Unfortunately, the student dropout rates at rural areas continue to be high at 57%. Indian education system has improved with regard to facilitation of infrastructures in schools. However, this has not led to improvement in student learning outcome levels at both elementary and secondary schools. Annual Status of Education Report (ASER 2014) validates the above statement by showing deterioration in terms of reading, arithmetic and writing among learners in their elementary school levels. Finally, the problems of opportunity related divides in the Indian education systems are created as a result of the lack of skill-based learning.

Section 7.3 illustrates the rural disadvantages, causing rural–urban education divide. Despite improvement of infrastructures in rural schools by the government, quality of learning in rural areas is declining. In this section, the reasons will be traced from an ecosystemic perspective by analysing the impact of four external influencers (e.g. social, political, economic, and socio-psychological) in rural context that are affecting the biotic and abiotic components, making their interactions ineffective. This section is followed by Sect. 7.4, describing the number of ICT-driven initiatives undertaken by both the central and state governments and private agents to disseminate quality education to all and to bridge rural–urban education divide using ICT. After elaborating such initiatives, we explore the limitations of these initiatives in Sect. 7.5 and suggest possible remedial actions to address those limitations.

## 7.2   Rural–Urban Education Divide

### 7.2.1   Access Divide

The access to education is not limited to access to school only in terms of school enrolment; from an ecosystemic perspective, access to education includes access to appropriate biotic and abiotic components of learning in the remote rural regions of the country. So, with reference to the biotic entities, access divide includes disparities in access to good quality teachers, supportive parents, family and peer groups, interested edupreneurs and efficient government administration. Similarly, with reference to the abiotic entities, access divide includes disparities in access to quality school infrastructure, attractive teaching–learning materials, effective assessment tools, and, above all, access to a favorable learning environment.

Remote rural schools of India are marked by non-availability of properly trained teachers who are unable to incorporate attractive teaching methods in classrooms (Dreze and Sen 2013). This is in contrast to the high-cost private schools in the urban locales comprising of quality teachers who are well trained in effective teaching methods including use of quality digital content. Along with teachers, other biotic entities such as parents and peer groups in rural areas too exhibit low levels of motivation to support the learners in terms of providing conducive learning environment at home. Moreover, good quality urban private schools are not accessible to rural parents, both physically (because of distance) and economically. Government administration, despite adoption of several education-based policies and reforms in the remote rural locales, has been unable to ensure access to quality education in government-sponsored schools (Singhal 2019). The reasons behind such problems of access to the biotic components of learning in rural areas can better be understood from the perspectives of the four external influencers of the learning ecosystem in the context of rural India, which will be elaborated in Sect. 7.3.

The problems of access divide can be further explicated by exploring lack of access to the *abiotic components* of learning which includes availability of proper teaching–learning materials and tools, school infrastructure including buildings, classrooms, and digital infrastructures such as computer, Internet connectivity, etc., and also proper assessment tools that are needed to evaluate learners' capability and potential in today's context. Madangopal and Madangopal (2018) studies several deficiencies in terms of classroom sizes, availability of electricity, hardware conditions, digital content, and ICT skills in rural public schools.

To improve learning outcome levels and overall quality of education among learners of all age groups, it becomes imperative to introduce ICT in education in schools. However, lack of appropriate infrastructure for enabling the use of ICT for school education in rural India is a serious bottleneck with most rural public schools having poor computer resources. Although there is an increase in internet penetration in rural India, its usage and proper utilization is still limited in remote areas as compared to that in the urban areas. Despite availability of computers in most rural public schools, utilization of the same is a questionable affair, resulting in a large proportion of computers that are in non-workable conditions (NIEPA 2018). As a result, access to digital education in rural schools is not guaranteed in comparison to its abundance in urban private schools. Additionally, despite introduction of ICT in rural public schools, learners are unable to learn the usage of computers and Internet appropriately owing to the disparate student to computer ratio in the school computer labs. Although the best student to computer ratio is 2:1, most public schools have a ratio of 50:1; and, in some remote rural public or low-cost private schools, it is as low as 135:1. Moreover, only few computers have internet connectivity and students are prohibited from using the Internet (Naik et al. 2019).

Apart from better access to ICTs in private schools in urban locales, there is a huge gap in the kind of curriculum followed in these schools in comparison to the public and low-cost private schools in rural areas. Students from high-cost privatized schools in urban areas not only get acquainted with subject-specific curriculum but also get opportunities to be involved in sports, co-curricular activities, and competitions in order to ensure holistic growth which is rare among low-cost private aided or government schools in remote locales of the country (Sreekanthachari and Nagaraja 2013).

These problems of access to abiotic components of learning such as lack of proper digital infrastructures, poor road ways, absence of appropriate teaching–learning materials, curriculum, etc. has been addressed by the government in the past in form of adoption of several policies. These policies include *Sarva Shiksha Abhiyan (SSA), National Mid-Day Meal scheme, Computer Literacy and Studies in Schools (CLASS)* project, *Rashtriya Madhyamik Shiksha Abhiyan (RMSA), "Smart Schools"* Project, *E-Basta,* and many others. We will discuss these policies in subsequent sections. Most of these policies aimed at increasing access to digital education as well as better-quality teachers and teaching–learning materials among the students in remote rural regions of India. However, despite adoption of such policies, access divide still exists between rural–urban education systems in the country.

### 7.2.2 Capability Divide

Bridging access divide is a necessary pre-condition to bridge education divide; however, access divide alone is not responsible for the prevalent education divide. We have introduced the notion of capability divide in Chap. 2 (Sect. 2.4.2), where we have mentioned the importance of cultivating capability sets among target group in order to achieve holistic development (Sen 1988, 2003). Lack of capability, designating multi-faceted impoverishment of human life, is an important reason for education divide. Even with adequate access, learners may not develop the desired capability required for human functioning through disseminated education, thereby sustaining education divide. Acquiring capability through education means possessing operating abilities to process and apply acquired education toward a desirable outcome.

Education in India, especially in rural India has always been characterized by teaching methods that predominantly include mindless rote learning without comprehension and endless repetition of various mathematical tables (Dreze and Sen 2013). Teaching methods rarely focus on improving one's capabilities and are mostly teacher-centric and repetitive. As a result, a significant portion of the student population in primary schools of rural India remains incompetent in simple reading, writing ability and the ability to do simple arithmetic (ASER 2014). Annual Status of Education Report (ASER) studies quality of learning through measuring child's ability to read, write, and do arithmetic. Unfortunately, ASER (2014) shows no improvement in these three skills among students from public or low-cost private schools in rural regions in the last nine years. Since 2005 there has been a decline in the number of students who can read a class 2 level text by almost 15%. Similarly, there too has been a reduction in the number of students in class 8, who are able to solve simple divisions in arithmetic. In contrast, the quality of learning in urban private schools has improved with regard to both curriculum and competency building of students. High-cost private schools in urban locales significantly outperform their rural public school counterparts (Chudgar and Quin 2012).

Non-availability of quality teachers, deplorable condition of teaching–learning materials, irregularity in teacher attendance, and lack of student-centric learning in remote rural schools are some of the most obvious causes behind such disparity. As a result, the focus of Indian Government is now on improving the learning outcomes at all levels among the learners irrespective of their weak socioeconomic backgrounds (GOI 2013). However, as pointed out by Dreze and Sen 2013), the teaching pedagogy and curriculum followed in rural public schools do not cater to or support the varying characteristics and needs of learners. Their capabilities are not properly harnessed owing to the limitations in the teaching–learning methods followed in rural schools. These limitations have led to increasing dissatisfaction with the quality of public schooling and have given rise to calls for increasing involvement of the private sector in education. Despite the rise of low-cost private schools with high teacher accountability in many remote rural areas, the issue of quality education still gets neglected, as these schools concentrate more on profits rather than on enhancing quality learning (Nambissan 2014).

In midst of the social changes brought about by twenty-first century, the objective of education and learning has shifted more into competency building, critical and creative thinking, collaboration, enhancement of life skills, etc., with a strong focus on integrating ICT with teaching–learning practice. These new forms of knowledge and skills require certain tools and skills that were previously not known to any educational institutions. However, the budgetary constraints together with absence of skills and attitudes to implement these changes have left rural public schools with a deficiency of professional innovation and expansion (Fox and McDermott 2015). On the other hand, the urban schools are quickly adopting to the changing scenario of education and learning by focusing on learner-centric curriculum, computer education, co-curricular activities, competitions, skill building etc., making learners capable and harness one's potential according to twenty-first century learning needs (Sreekanthachari and Nagaraja 2013).

Students will need to apply higher order thinking and cognitive skills to real world, real-life, and real time tasks (Crockett et al. 2011). The world is now going through a terrible learning crisis revolving around the uncertainty about the kinds of skills the jobs of future would require. As a result, students and teachers need to be prepared focusing more on reading and writing skills, the ability to interpret information, form opinions, be creative, enhance communication skills, communicate well, collaborate, and be resilient. The World Bank's vision is toward a teaching–learning process for all children and youth, that would help them to acquire the skills they need to be productive, fulfilled, and involved (World Bank 2019).

In order to imbibe the updated twenty-first century skills, knowledge and information, learners need to be familiarised with the cyber-world. ICT in education and training becomes important in this modern industrial age wherein learners (of any age group) are able to utilize appropriate cyber resources by themselves and upgrade themselves in accordance with the changing global scenario. However, the rural mass lacks proper training in availing the appropriate content available on Internet. The vast majority of the rural population simply do not know what information is available, where to find it and how to use it (Sein 2011). Moreover, public schools, despite presence of digital infrastructures fail to integrate ICT in education owing to the following causes:

(i)   Teachers' proficiency in integration of ICT in existing curriculum: Teachers are neither proficient nor willing to modify traditional educational practices with ICT tools and platforms. In this context, incorporating training for ICT use in teaching pedagogy would be more beneficial than training teachers to use ICT tools per se. (Madangopal and Madangopal 2018).

(ii)  Resistance to technology: Resistance toward usage and utilization of digital technology by the teachers and learners of all ages from rural areas restrains digital inclusion in remote rural India. From the perspective of teachers, this resistance is not only related to fear of learning a new skill, but also a result of the apprehension toward changing role of teachers from being a store-house of knowledge (as perceived by the learners) to the manager of the teaching–learning process (Satveer 2017).

This discussion on lack of capabilities among the disadvantaged sections of society also brings us to the further discussion on the lack of appropriate opportunities available in the rural regions. The next section of the chapter will discuss the problems related to existing opportunity divides between metropolitan cities and remote rural regions.

### 7.2.3   Opportunity Divide

Bridging access divide and capability divide are necessary pre-conditions but not sufficient to bridge education divide holistically. We have introduced the notion of opportunity divide in Chap. 2 (Sect. 2.4.3), where it has been indicated that acquiring education is not the final step in the process of holistically mitigating education divide. Education divide can only be truly mitigated when learners, by virtue of acquired education derive the capability to exploit available opportunities to improve the conditions of their social and material well-being. The opportunity divide creates a divide between the ones in possession of *effective* education, competencies and appropriate skills and subsequently belonging to a better socioeconomic status and the ones devoid of the same, thereby having poor socioeconomic scopes.

As mentioned in the above two sections, several agencies both governmental and private, are working toward bridging education divide in terms of bridging access and capability divides. However, it is to be noted that the learners, after becoming capable in certain knowledge and skills, need to add value to their acquired knowledge and skills by utilizing them to exploit wider opportunity scopes. As pointed out by Narayan and Petesch (2007), individuals from disadvantaged sections of society lack required resources to exploit one's capabilities and interests which are in abundance among students from better socioeconomic backgrounds. Unfortunately, with scarce resources and capabilities, marginalized people are greatly constrained from having individual or collective choices (Narayan and Petesch 2007). This ultimately creates divide in terms of opportunities between those who can avail appropriate opportunities and those who cannot.

In India, the unorganized work force belonging from the rural regions often face limitations in achieving certain skills that are appropriate for the twenty-first century global work demands (World Economic Forum (2016). To enhance their skills, especially the skills of rural young adults, Indian education system has traditionally focused on adult literacy, vocational training and continuing education courses. There are initiatives like *Skill India* or the *National Skills Development Mission* of India, where the Government has focused on sensitizing the rural youth in skill building within the domain of agriculture, health, home sciences, technology, business, and commerce. Further, in alignment with the SDG4 renewed goals of focusing on Lifelong learning of adults, Indian Government has developed its Lifelong Education and Awareness Program (LEAP) comprising of adult literacy, competency trainings and skill based vocational trainings.

However, implementation of these plans faces several hindrances in rural context, thus creating a divide between rural and urban learners. Hasaba (2013) noted several challenges in the context of rural adult literacy education programs: "These included a lack of adequate resources for things such as scholastic materials; lack of enough trained teachers; lack of classrooms; learners needing to walk long distances to class; paucity of employment prospects upon completion of the programmes; no remuneration for instructors; missing of classes during rainy seasons (Uganda and Vietnam); no opportunity for further training, absenteeism and the programme not addressing the learners' problems."

McCannon (1983) points out that many significant barriers faced by rural adults regarding pursuing adult learning after completion of formal schooling. The foremost barriers are: distance, lack of prior educational attainment, non-availability of counselling services, lack of family support and financial assistance. Cross and McCartan

(1984) calls these barriers to be *situational barriers*, *institutional barriers,* and *dispositional barriers* (Dixson and Bairamova 2019). Situational barriers are understood as the kind of barrier wherein an individual is bound by responsibilities on job or at home and as a result are not getting sufficient time to participate in trainings. Institutional barriers are those kinds of barriers that discourages working adults from taking part in any training-related activities. Their odd working hours, household responsibilities refrain them from participating in any kind of educational program at an older age. Often class schedules do not match with the interested adult learners' time or sometime expensive course fee make them turn away from the trainings. Dispositional barriers restrain prospective adult learners from participating in any vocational or skill-based activities owing to others' negative attitudes or perceptions about the learner. Many a times the older citizens refrain from learning anything new at a ripe age because of their low esteem. Adults with poor educational background have low confidence in their ability to learn, as a result they too refrain from getting trained from experts.

The discrepancy in distribution of educational resources between rural and urban India points out that rural learner not only lack quality education due to scanty access to educational resources and inadequate capabilities, but there also exist an opportunity divide between rural and urban learners that affects market performance of rural learners at the end of their formal education. Urban learners, equipped with better biotic and abiotic educational resources and operative in a scenario where the external influencers positively contribute in their knowledge acquisition process, are endowed with better market prospects as compared to their rural counterpart. Urban learners have better access to and better knowledge regarding market dynamics, where they can encash their acquired knowledge and skills in pursuit of profitable returns. The *market separation* faced by rural community in general thereby places them in the disadvantageous side of opportunity divide (Bandyopadhyay et al. 2020). Bartels (1968) conceptualizes *market separation* in terms of four components—spatial separation, financial separation, temporal separation, and informational separation. *Spatial separations* mark the territorial or geographical distances that exist between the producer of a commodity or service and the consumer. *Financial separation* can mean either a consumers' inability to purchase any product/services or the producers' lack of access to capital or both. *Temporal separation* implies the difference that exists between the time when a specific product has been consumed and the time when it was produced. Informational separation means the asymmetry that lies between a producer and customer in the market in terms of information. In the context of opportunity divide between rural and urban learners, we can see that all the four mentioned components work for urban learners in a more conducive way. The urban learners are spatially and temporally closer to market, which enables them to derive a better perspective on market operations and in turn orient their knowledge and skills accordingly to secure better employment opportunities. Similarly, they have better financial and information resources compared to their rural counterparts, which together contribute in placing urban learners on the advantageous side of the opportunity divide. The rural learners, because of their socioeconomic status and geographical positioning, are distant from market sites spatially, temporally, informationally, and financially. This contributes in restricting their opportunity scopes, where, due to the above-stated factors, they are unable to derive a fair understanding of market requirements and in turn fall short in tuning their knowledge and skills in accordance to market requirements.

## 7.3   Exploring Rural Disadvantages

Despite several developmental efforts in Indian villages, individuals face persistent problems along social, economic, socio-psychological, and political lines within specific rural context. These four external influencers influence interactions between biotic and abiotic entities in the education ecosystem. This section will now discuss the disadvantages faced by the rural learners in accordance to the four external influencers of an education ecosystem and how these disadvantages ultimately result in the extant education divides along the lines of access, capability, and opportunity divide.

### 7.3.1   Social Factors

Social conventions, norms, regulations, customs shape individual's mental makeup and how he/she conceives the happenings of the society. These social conventions, norms, etc., are specific to particular context, often leveraging and sometimes restricting occurrence of any activity by the social actors. The following social factors are responsible toward creating the disadvantages in remote rural areas, which further enhances education divide:

*Social Discrimination*: Indian society has been traditionally hierarchical in nature. The caste system practiced by the Indian society did not allow social mobility across certain groups. These discriminations were further sanctified and naturalized through religious mandates. Dalits (who are at the lowermost in the caste hierarchy) are the worst affected from the age-old practice of caste discriminations followed by the tribal population who are kept outside the hierarchical structure of the caste system (Kurian 2007).

Indian education system (both formal and non-formal) witnesses various forms of discrimination and violence exhibited among students from lower socioeconomic backgrounds. These discriminations can be categorized into: (i) discrimination in terms of access to education, (ii) discrimination within classrooms, (iii) discrimination with regard to access to appropriate life opportunities through education and skill development. Some examples of these caste based discriminations include children from lower caste (Dalits in many cases) sitting at the back of the classroom, not being allowed to use school facilities or equipment that are otherwise accessible by students from other superior caste groups. Moreover, these learners from backward caste groups are highly ignored by the education system by not giving them adequate attention in learning and skill development (CSEI 2015).

Social discriminations include differentiations in terms of one's religion, ethnicity, language, belief and most importantly according to one's caste and class lines. Rural India, belonging to the disadvantageous side of social discriminations, witness unequal preferences in terms of experiencing access, capability, and opportunity divides. Parents, being a biotic entity within an education ecosystem abide by these differentiations by enrolling their children in schools that cater to a particular community or caste or specific religion. Thus, discriminations are reflected in one's school enrolment preferences. These varied categorizations of schools in terms of caste, class, religion forces parents to send their children to specific category of schools in accordance to their respective caste-class-religious affiliations. Thus, school enrolment rates vary profoundly based on one's affiliation with specific religious and caste communities.

Apart from religious or caste-based differentiations prevalent in rural school setting, there are community-specific exclusivity attached with enrolment of students in schools. There are certain communities where there is no tradition of sending children to schools and very little peer pressure existing in those communities (Wazir 2002). Several public schools located in the central parts of India have witnessed lower percentage of students who were affiliated with Islamic and Dalit communities. The reason behind their lesser number is the presence of children from Hindu communities in the same schools, making these community-based differentiations in terms of caste and religious lines a huge problem with regards to access to education (Borooah and Iyer 2007).

Apart from the influence of social discriminations on preferences of schools, it has been observed that children, based on one's caste or religious affiliations, are physically punished by the school teachers (PROBE 1999). This humiliation does not create an environment conducive to learning and thereby alienating students. These atrocities are mostly prevalent in low-cost private and public schools that are dispersed across the villages of India.

Thus, to summarize, in the rural education landscape, the access, capability, and opportunity divides are more pronounced among certain groups of students (both children and adults) as a result of the age-old traditions of discriminating individuals based on her/his affiliations within certain community, characterized by particular religion or caste group.

***Gender Discrimination***: The denial of access to education and training to girls in rural India creates inequalities between men and women in society. In Asia, the relative deprivation of women with respect to men is much higher as compared to the other regions of the world. Along with low proportion of females with respect to males, their survival rates too are much lower than males (Sen 1990). Girls from lower socioeconomic backgrounds are denied access to education, discouraging them from going to schools. The drop-out rates in primary schools is much higher among the girls than that of the boys. Whereas, for the rural adults, the illiteracy rate is much higher among the women than that among the men. After completing elementary levels of education, girl students are often pushed into assisting with household chores or taking care of the family or getting married early. As a result, they choose to drop out from secondary schools (Taneja 2018). "It is girls, and marginalised groups such as the very poor and the disabled, who are often left behind. While girls attend primary school in roughly equal numbers to boys, the gap widens as they get older and more are forced to drop out to help with work at home or get married" (Williams 2013). Poorer families located in the remote rural fringes of the country find it economically not beneficial to send girls to schools and also to spend money on their uniform, textbooks, and other stationaries, as the parents feel the return on investment behind sending girls to schools is much lesser (Balatchandirane 2007). It is a common belief among the rural parents that boys or sons will take care of them in their old age whereas girls, who will eventually be married off, will not take care of them in their old age, resulting in preference of sons over daughters to send to schools. This leads to the argument of "son-preferences" in several communities where more boys than girls are sent to schools by parents in several disadvantaged rural locations. Thus, to summarize, rural schools have seen gender biasness in school enrolment where boys are more likely to be enrolled in schools than the girls.

With regard to discriminations between female and male adult learners or producers in rural areas, researchers have pointed out how restrictions are placed on their mobility, their freedom to use the income they earn, their autonomy to purchase assets and sell their products, their rights to take decisions about the family and so on (Kumbhar 2013). Such restrictions impede the aspirations of women to grow and flourish in their trade, resulting in lowering their motivation to exploit the appropriate opportunities of the twenty-first century.

Influence of gender inequality on education has resulted in decreasing women's productivity, which has an impact on economic growth in many developing and underdeveloped nations, especially in South Asia. These discriminations across gender lines have also impacted work dynamics wherein there is a striking inequality in terms of wage distribution among men and women.

***Lack of Social Capital***: Social capital refers to strength of social ties and norms governing social interaction. It refers to the network of relationships between people residing in society, purposive interaction between whom enables the society to function effectively (Putnam 2000). The structural dimension of social capital reflects impersonal configuration of linkages and networks between people (Uphoff and Wijayaratna 2000). Important aspects of structural social capital are the number of ties a person has, with whom and how strong the tie is (Claridge 2018). Moreover, social capital can be classified as bonding or bridging social capital. Bonding social capital creates horizontal ties between individuals from local communities where many people know many other people within the community. Bridging social capital on the other hand creates vertical ties between individuals from different social groups or communities.

In rural area, individuals are able to create bonding social capital, creating networks within their own rural communities, with their neighbours. The rural people are aware of what the other person in her/his locality is doing. However, individuals from remote rural locales lack the bridging social capital wherein the rural producers are unable to establish connection or network with the urban market

(Debertin 1996). Most marginalized rural communities are disconnected from the local and larger metropolitan area opportunity structure. Owing to these disconnections due to lack of both physical and digital connectivity, the local rural areas have (i) less access to quality training, educational and advisory services (ii) less awareness with regard to the available local opportunities, (iii) less market accessibility, and (iv) less access to any kind of discussion forum where common problems are shared and discussed. Lack of inter and intra communitarian linkage contributes in sustaining social, economic, and civic isolation of rural community. As a result, the rural marginalized are not just deprived to venture in search of additional possibilities, but lack of relevant knowledge alienates them from the extant welfare schemes devised for rural development. These problems are derived from the lack of bridging social capital among the rural mass and create opportunity divide between rural and urban learners.

## 7.3.2  Economic Factors

Economic affordability among specific community members is the most crucial component that influences enrolment and participation in educational institutes. Most rural learners are from lower socioeconomic background, creating economic inequalities and discrepancies, leading to problems in education attainment.

*Financial Affordability*: Maximum rural regions of India are engulfed within the vicious circle of poverty. The socioeconomic status of most rural families being low are unable to access educational resources, resulting in rising rates of illiteracy and school-drop outs. As a result, individuals are unable to rise up the ladder of socioeconomic status or avail better opportunities, resulting in inability to cross the hurdle of poverty trap. This vicious circle of poverty and poor/lack of education continuously sets up a poverty trap for the poor rural mass. As per the Economic Survey 2019–20 (The Hindu 2020), the basic education fee has risen up to newer limits resulting in impending burden on families that are unable to afford the same. Both urban and rural areas are witness to such economic burden. Despite various schemes of "Free Education," the underserved parents have to spend large amount of money against books, stationeries, and uniforms (The Hindu 2020). As studied by Dreze and Kingdon (2001), a large proportion of the population in remote rural areas find it difficult to continue one's education in schools owing to the increasing cost incurred against procurement of different items that are necessary in schools.

*Promise of Economic Return*: Lack of quality education creates opportunity divide, which denies the marginalized population the ability to explore economic prospects (Barton et al. 2016; Park 2007). However, the attainment of education, being directly related to employment probabilities, has made education an investment choice, where people primarily invest in the hope of getting better employment opportunities. Families that value education more than others i.e. families with higher motivation to push their children into learning are more likely to invest more in low-cost private schools and private tuitions. For example, in states of Bihar and Orissa, rural students often tend to spend more on private tuitions rather than their urban counterparts. 24% of rural students spend more on private tuitions as compared to 18% in urban areas. The reason can be cited as the low fees to be paid by the rural students in the rural public schools. (Nagarajan 2011). The motivation of these parents is coming from the expectation of greater returns to education in form of better access to jobs. Education functions as nourishment to the human capital and as a productive component from the nation's perspective. However, from each and every individual's perspective, the meaning of education is just a mean to achieve higher economic benefits in the form of higher wages (Rani and Elliott 2014). However, as mentioned before, parents from different communities have different kinds of motivation with regard to sending their children in schools. Many parents from remote rural areas still feel that sending children to schools is a waste, since it hampers their possibility of earning from their engagement as child-labour.

### 7.3.3 Socio- Psychological Factors

Along with the social and economic factors, individuals' mental or intellectual makeup influences one's interest to take part in an active learning process.

*Motivation of Teachers*: There are some causes behind the consistent irregularity in attendance among teachers in schools. Lack of motivation among teachers is the most important cause. However, the reasons behind this lack of motivation is due to several factors, such as: poorly equipped classrooms, infrastructural limitations, overcrowded classrooms, and unfilled vacancies. Other important factors include teachers' engagement in several non-teaching activities such as preparation of mid-day meal and similar administrative activities. Teachers are not encouraged by the school authority and are rarely given any incentive to work well (Mooij 2008).

Schools in rural areas are either run by the government or by a private body. However, the number of government public schools are much higher than the low-cost private schools. These public schools tend to appoint para-teacher or assistant teachers rather than qualified permanent teachers. These para-teachers are recruited at a much lower cost. Moreover, these non-permanent teachers have no future career prospects and as a result they have least motivation to excel in the profession of teaching. This scenario as a whole demotivates teachers to avail school teaching jobs. Mooij (2008) in this context, studied poor supervision by the school inspectors or educational bureaucrats. This too resulted in lower levels of teachers' motivation.

*Resistance to Change*: Along with the need to motivate students into learning, it is equally important to understand why learners and their parents fail to recognize the importance of learning on the first place. Researchers have come up with the criterion of resistance toward change wherein a large section of the students from remote rural areas choose not to study, reason being their psychological makeup that refrains them from not participating actively in the education process. Students' resistance toward positive change in own life are three folded wherein students believe they can't change, they don't want to change, they don't know what to change, or they don't know how to change (Dembo and Seli 2004).

### 7.3.4  Political Factors

As mentioned toward the beginning of the chapter, Government of India has come up with several policies for the purpose of enhancing access, capabilities, and opportunities among all kinds of learners in the country. In response to the "Education for All" movement and "Education 2030 Goals" launched by UNESCO, India came up with several education policies which were implemented in regions where there is lack of access to quality education and skill-based training. However, several policies recommended or formulated by the Government of India saw limitations at the time of implementation in the remote rural locales of the country resulting in recurrent disadvantages faced by the rural mass. We would now discuss in brief how limitations of few policies impacted learning in rural regions.

*Sarva Shiksha Abhiyan (SSA)* is Government of India's flagship program aiming toward achieving "education for all" in India, focusing on providing free and compulsory education to all children irrespective of their caste, class, race, or religion and also provides teachers' training. In partnership with several state governments, SSA aimed at opening maximum schools with proper infrastructural facilities in areas where there is dearth of schools. However, despite its focus on access, equity, and quality in education for all, SSA has failed in providing quality learning to all learners across public schools in rural regions. Decline in teacher–pupil ratio was not uniform throughout the country. During the SSA decade, central and state expenditures on education increased sharply (UNESCO 2015). This indicates that policy formulation and investment, without considering above-mentioned external factors (social, economic and socio-psychological), is not enough to successfully bridge the education divide.

*National Mid-Day Meal scheme (1995):* Provision of education is not enough in several disadvantaged regions. Focus on health and nutrition becomes the primary objective in several regions where basic subsistence is not met. In that context, the Government of India has come up with the Mid-Day Meal Scheme (MDM) whereby nutritious food is distributed in public schools in disadvantaged regions across the country (Swain and Das 2017; Mandal and Garg 2013). The objective of this Scheme was to ensure maximum enrolment among students. However, there are some problems with regard to its efficacy that leads to recurring disadvantages in rural segments of society:

(a) Problem of hygiene: There are instances in public schools across India where meals are being cooked next to lavatories, abandoned houses, under trees, on roads and even close to drains and meals are served in an unhygienic manner (Sembiah et al. 2019)

(b) MDM in Market Place: Most schools misuse the MDM for their personal gain. MDM comes to school according to the strength of students list, but most of time all students in school are not present every day. The absentee-students' share of MDM is sometimes sold in the market (Swain and Das 2017).

(c) Proportion of Gender for MDM: Persistent gender-related problems in rural areas become evident in Mid-Day Meal Scheme implementation. Owing to "son-preferences" for education, several village public schools see maximum male child enrollment and thus access to mid meals by the male child only.

(d) Caste Discrimination in MDM: Limitations of Mid-meal scheme implementation has been observed with respect to the existing caste-based discriminations in rural schools. In their study, Swain and Das (2017) observed that Children from lower cast groups were made to sit away from upper castes; in some cases, they were not given food or they were served left-over food. There have been instances where food was being rejected by students from upper castes, when they came to know that the cook belonged to lower caste (Swain and Das 2017).

*National Skill Development Mission* (2007) was initiated to inculcate skills that improve employability among the youth. Aiming toward building or updating skills of adults, this Mission focused on providing placements to each one of the trainees after completion of the program. Unfortunately, only 18% got placed, reflecting the discrepancy among pupils to nurture opportunity scopes by virtue of lessons learnt (Makkar 2017). As studied by Makkar (2017), there was no way to find out the impact and outcome of the scheme. There was no evidence as to whether the scheme serves the purpose of facilitating the youth with appropriate employment opportunities. It was also difficult to understand whether the appropriate skill-needs of the industry are met through the trainings. The limitations of this adult learning or skill building programs have left the rural adults with restricted options to explore own capabilities and opportunities within their rural space.

One of the most common political reasons behind failure of implementation of these above-mentioned activities is the persisting corruption prevailing in the education system in India, indirectly supported by political parties in power. Corruption in the education sector can be defined as "the systematic use of public office for private benefit, whose impact is significant on the availability and quality of educational goods and services as a consequence on access, quality or equity in education" (Maheshwari 2019). Corruption in education and political interference can be most commonly found in teacher appointment, posting and transfer. Ignoring their primary activity of imparting quality learning to students in schools, teachers are mostly concerned and apprehensive with regard to their appointments and transfers. The most disturbing fact is that the political leaders or bureaucrats or teacher unions often plays more important role in deciding recruitment and transfer of teachers, wherein the in-service teachers often have to pay bribes in this regard. Thus, favouritism, nepotism, and bribes are some common forms of corruption in our education system. Corruption also prevails through examination and evaluation systems wherein several institutions pay bribe to the external examiners through collections made by students after completion of examinations. Students too pay large amounts to teachers or examiners for making them pass examinations. (Maheshwari 2019). Owing to these corruptive practices, the teachers feel demotivated in teaching students in class-rooms. Huge number of students despite their weak learning backgrounds and poor academic performances often make their way into colleges through age-old political interferences (Aaron 2016). These corrupt practices ultimately influence the quality of education and learning which is disseminated to both school students and adult learners, making learning ineffective and futile. Indian rural schools suffer from a very large amount of teacher absenteeism with minimum teachers in the state of Bihar (Indian state) (Balani 2017). As an evidence of corrupt practices in the Indian education system, there has been huge prevalence of "ghost teachers" who replaces the existing teachers in classrooms (Live Mint 2007). As published by BS (2018), the Human Resource Department Ministry identified 80,000 Ghost Teachers in several colleges and educational institutions across the country after the introduction of the country-wide Biometric Identification System (*Aadhar* card).

To summarize, the extant rural–urban divides in education in terms of access, capability, and opportunity are a result of the hindrances faced by the rural masses due to social, economic, socio-psychological, and political factors. With the aim to address these disadvantages and bridge the extant education divides in the country, several governmental, non-governmental, and private agencies have come up with several ICT-based solutions. In the subsequent section we will discuss in detail those attempts and also critically evaluate them in order to find out the existing gap in all such initiatives.

## 7.4   Attempts to Bridge Education Divide Using ICT: A Critical Evaluation

This extant education divide in terms of access, capability, and opportunity between the rural and urban locales of India has been addressed by several Governmental, non-governmental, and private educational agencies by incorporating ICT or digital technologies in education. For better sustenance and growth of knowledge society, the government of India has formulated the national policy on ICT in education aiming toward enhancing creative participation of learners in their individual processes of learning (Kundu and Nath 2018).

The following section will discuss in brief about these initiatives, how each of the initiatives have played its respective roles in addressing the education divide and problems existing within the rural education scene of India using ICT. We have selected few important initiatives keeping in mind how they address problems in rural education that are influenced by existing social and gender discriminations, problems of economic affordability, resistance to change, politicization and existing corruption in education prevailing in rural regions. However, none of the initiatives is absolutely perfect in terms of its implementation and as a result we critically analyse each of these initiatives and finally propose a framework to address the limitations in order to bridge rural–urban education divide.

### 7.4.1 Government Initiatives

In India, ICT in schools were first introduced in 1984 in form of the Computer Literacy and Studies in Schools (CLASS) project. CLASS was the first to introduce microcomputers in schools. The purpose of the Project was to familiarize all kinds of learners with the function and usage of computers. Owing to its limitations in reach, Government relaunched ICT in Education Programme in schools across India again in 2004 under the Rashtriya Madhyamik Shiksha Abhiyan (RMSA). The government of India has launched "Smart Schools" project in 2005, by approving around 89,000 ICT-enabled schools. This Project has envisioned to positively impact and empower children and youth from both rural and urban areas with holistic learning. The purpose of this project was to help learners solve critical problems independently and inculcate entrepreneurial skills within them (Raghu et al. 2015).

Despite provision of setting computers in all public schools across the country, RMSA and other Governmental initiatives failed to equip public schools with computers. As per the data gathered from the ASER study in 2018, in 596 government schools of 619 districts overall, only 21.3% of the students have access to computers in their schools (ASER 2018). Moreover, most of the computers were left untouched and is in non-working conditions. As per school education statistics, 2016–17, only 14.11% of public schools in India have computers that are in working conditions. In states of West Bengal, Uttar Pradesh, Meghalaya, Rajasthan, and Telangana only 6.38, 3.41, 4.51, 6.60, and 15.49% of public schools have computers that are in working conditions, respectively (NIEPA 2018).

SWAYAM is another ICT-based initiatives of Indian Government to improve formal education and informal learning and skill development. One of the key areas of concern of the "Digital India" Initiative of Government of India is initiation and implementation of "Massive Online Open Courses (MOOCs)." In that context, Ministry of Human Resource Development (MHRD), Government of India has come up with an initiative called "Study Webs of Active Learning for Young Aspiring Minds" (SWAYAM) which is an integrated platform and portal for online courses, covering all higher education and skill sector courses for all kinds of learners having access to computer or smartphone with Internet connectivity. SWAYAM, being an asynchronous learning initiative, is a huge repository of digital learning materials and video lectures that are prepared by teachers from different higher education institutes (Kanjilal and Kaul 2016). However, there are two major issues that need immediate attention and the government has to come up with viable solutions for that: (i) students' enrolment is very restrictive owing to absence of regional language content; and, (ii) limited access to Internet and personal computer in rural parts of India makes it impossible for many underserved learners to access the courses remotely. Additionally, absence of a mobile app of SWAYAM makes the portal accessible to only a handful of students having access to personal desktop computer at home (Kanjilal and Kaul 2016).

Another initiative of "Digital India Programme" is that of the "E-Basta" Scheme which is an online platform bringing together all essential school textbooks in soft copies so that any school can access them when needed. The objective of this scheme is to overcome the challenges of access to physical books by learners, teachers, and schools located in remote rural locations. Thus, this initiative aims to bring together publishers, schools, and students on the same platform. However, this initiative was not utilized sufficiently by schools and educational institutions across the country because of the unavailability of proper ICT infrastructure in schools. Moreover, schools are ill-equipped with proper teachers or trainers who can use the computers to retrieve the digital textbooks. (E-Basta n.d.)

In order to impart and enhance appropriate skills, National Skill Development Corporation (NSDC), India has incorporated e-learning in form of E-Skill India. It is an aggregator platform that consolidates all Business to Consumer Portals operating over internet in the skilling ecosystem. These portals further create and source e-learning content in a hub and spoke manner. Some of the courses available in E-Skill India are Mushroom Cultivation (agriculture sector), Mobile Repairing (electronics), Communicative English, Basic Cutting and Stitching, Computer Basics, and many others. Most of these courses are available free of charge. These courses can be attended by interested learners from anywhere and at any time (ESkill India n.d.).

There are numerous other initiatives, both by central and state government. However, all these initiatives face a common problem with regard to lack of ICT access and absence of user-training in remote rural locations, making it impossible for maximum learners to utilize these opportunities. We will discuss these issues in details in Sect. 7.5.

### 7.4.2 Private or Non-Governmental Initiatives

Several private or non-governmental organizations too have worked toward introducing ICTs among learners (of all age groups and from all socioeconomic backgrounds) to improve learning in rural classrooms or in rural community e-kiosks. Several organizations till date have made relevant contributions in donating computers and facilitating software, internet connectivity in many schools across remote rural areas of the country.

*Evidyaloka* is a not-for-profit organization based in Bengaluru, India, working toward improving quality of education to children in remote rural schools of India through their online live digital classrooms, where learners from rural public schools get connected online in a classroom setting with volunteer teachers from all parts of the world. The NGO either works in public schools that already have workable computers and Internet connectivity. To work with schools having no computers, Evidyaloka collaborates with large corporations who supply schools with workable computers and Internet connectivity.

*Edzilla* is a flagship initiative of a not-for-profit, based in Mysore, India. Focusing on the problem of good quality content in rural public schools, this initiative provides Tablets, computers with digital textbooks in local language to rural public schools. This initiative has benefited more than 2000 upper primary level children.

*E- Prashala* a social enterprise based in Maharashtra, India provides proper hardware integrated with E- Prashala software in rural public and low-cost private schools. The software comprises of regional language educational content and E-Assessment tools. This initiative thus addresses the poor assessment and evaluation patterns conducted in the existing public schools by introducing E-Assessment System.

Along with introducing computers with Internet connectivity in schools, several initiatives are focusing on disseminating mobile-based learning to improve quality of education among the underserved learners (of any age group). Mobile based learning or M-learning is an umbrella term usually used to describe learning that happens through the interaction with content in devices like mobile phones, tablets, palmtops, Personal digital assistants (PDA). McQuiggan (2015) talked about mobile learning being less about physical devices themselves and more about the experience and opportunity afforded by the evolution of education technologies. It was found out that mobile learning encourages collaborative and peer-to-peer learning. Though effective, ICT in schools do not allow learners to fully utilize resources that are available through computer owing to limited school time schedule. Moreover, students face difficulty in using computers in schools as there are very limited trained computer teachers in schools who can help learners to use the same. Nevertheless, the advent of smartphones have made access to online learning and web based content much easy (Boity 2015). Kam et al. (2008) proposed mobile games on cellphones to be effective for learning ESL (English as a second language) in a rural under-resourced setting. Such games had to be educational as well as pleasurable for the target users, who have limited exposure to technology. Thus, in homes where there is a lack of parental support, learners can get sufficient educational support from smartphones that are enabled with Internet connectivity.

Several corporates and social organizations have come up with such M-Learning initiatives oriented toward benefitting the disadvantaged sections of the society and also attempt to bridge the rural–urban education divide:

*Mobile Bus Initiatives*: Despite access to ICT in school education, many teachers and learners remain unconnected. As a result, several countries across the world have come up with "mobile internet computing facilities" to provide access for learners in remote communities to digital teaching and learning resources by launching "internet buses." For some students, "mobile learning" takes place not with the aid of a smartphone, but rather through monthly visits of Internet-connected buses filled with computers. An Indian multi-national conglomerate, namely, Larsen & Toubro in collaboration with Prayas Trust, a non-profit organization (NGO) in Delhi initiated a "mobile classroom" initiative. Colorful vans equipped with innovative teaching–learning materials roam around the roads of Uttar Pradesh and Maharashtra catering to underserved children who otherwise were neglected by the formal education system (Kapoor 2017). The state of Karnataka, India has noticed huge rate of drop outs from school education system despite huge state-spending. In this context, the

state government has come up with the plan of introducing mobile school education system to serve the underserved learners. These mobile learning classes are
conducted also within the Karnataka State Buses (Trucano 2016).

*Project Sakshat Amrita Vocational Education (SAVE)*: This project was conducted
by Amrita Vishwa Vidyapeetham School of Engineering, Amritapuri, India, focusing
on disseminating quality vocational training in rural areas by utilizing the potentials
of haptic digital technologies (3D Technology or virtual reality). This form of technology comprises of multimodal computer interfaces. The objective of SAVE is
to facilitate the rural poor with several vocational training courses such as fabric
painting, household plumbing, etc. Owing to its introduction of 3D technology, this
project was able to do away with the dependency of expert trainers in vocational
training. As a result, the project had to put much more emphasis on standardized
computer-based evaluation methods which helped to reduce time in completing
training courses and foster self-paced, user driven learning and training (Bhavana
et al. 2010).

To critically evaluate each of these ICT-enabled programs, one can observe limitations in terms of digital illiteracy among rural users who are unable to access
the content through mobile Apps without proper support. These Apps mostly lack
regional content, making it difficult for the rural mass to understand. These initiatives
by way of introducing or overemphasizing digital technologies in learning, training
and services often tend to ignore the need to address local context-specific problems
faced by the rural mass on a regular basis.

## 7.5   Limitations of Existing Initiatives to Bridge the Divide

The above-mentioned initiatives, though have been successful in some rural localities, have not been very effective in disseminating quality learning and training in
several other remote rural locations of the country. Edupreneurs, educationists, rural
enablers, and others who are responsible toward implementing these initiatives on
ground level face series of problems due to limitations within biotic and abiotic entities and their constrained interactions and due to impact of external influencers. We
will now summarize these limitations:

*Limitations of ICT Usage*: Despite awareness regarding importance of using ICT
in education and in schools by governmental and non-governmental agencies, many
public schools are lagging behind in computer education. Most rural public schools
face problems with regard to poor electricity supply and the inability to fix technical
glitches along with Internet problems. Owing to the absence of "internet culture" and
realization of the importance of using digital technology for the purpose of improving
life and livelihood among rural youth and children, digital technology is still viewed
as a medium of entertainment and a new toy (Behar 2010). Rural schools with the
access to computers have poorly trained computer teachers to guide students with the
use of computers. Moreover, to observe positive change within each learner through
digital intervention, it is important to have personal access to computers or tablets

or smartphones. Thus, it often becomes challenging and overtly difficult for the government and private bodies to implement their ICT-enabled learning or training programs owing to lack of availability of personalized computer or internet-enabled smartphone facilities in the selected locales.

***Rigid Curriculum and Poor Teaching–Learning Materials***: The above-mentioned initiatives, though focus on disseminating quality learning and training through ICT, hardly question the learning pedagogy and therefore restrain from changing the traditional pattern of training or learning content. Despite focus on twenty-first century learning skills and changing nature of global occupational structure, the school-based curriculum has not quite changed accordingly. Even in 2018, the methodology of teaching is almost a hundred years old, focusing on academic subjects such as reading, writing, math, science, history, and foreign languages. Seldom attention has been paid in developing practical skills among learners, which will attempt in improving their market prospects by empowering them with independent thinking and collaborative problem solving skills. Although several technology-based initiatives have come up to impact change within the learning landscape, very few have been successful in bringing change in the learning content and curriculum which is aligned with the twenty-first century learning skills (World Economic Forum 2018).

***Parents/Family/Peer Groups***: Parents of first-generation learners often express a sense of awe around the use of computers or ICT in education. There is a heightened sense of mystique over technology and its potential (Pal et al. 2009). Despite acknowledging the importance and need of having personal computers at home, many parents are apprehensive with regard to using computers along with their children at home. The reason might be their discomfort with regard to their inflexibility of using ICT (Panagiotes et al. 2008). This leads to problems among enablers (e.g. governmental or non-governmental agencies) to properly motivate or encourage parents or family to incorporate ICT in their daily lives for their own and their children's benefits.

***Teachers and Tutors***: Cleaver (2014) has observed in his studies that a large percentage of teachers find it difficult to integrate technology in their teaching. In spite of their acknowledgement of the positive effects of technology in education dissemination, many teachers find it very challenging to upgrade themselves with changing complexities of technology. The cause behind such apprehension can be their lack of training opportunities. They are often not exposed to developing their professional expertise on new technologies. It is not only with regard to technology upgradation; many teachers are unable to upgrade their teaching pedagogy. Many of them find it challenging to prepare everyday lesson plans owing to lack of time. As a result, teachers often face the problem of "double innovation" wherein they not only have to upgrade their teaching content and methods but also have to integrate their teaching with the newer technology. As pointed out by Johnson et al. (2016), one of the most important reason behind the problem of double innovation is the teacher's lack of time to integrate new technologies in classrooms and further adapt to the change. Several ICT-based initiatives face immense difficulty in convincing teachers, para-teachers, or tutors to give extra time to incorporate digital means in their teaching pedagogy.

## 7.6   Conclusion

This chapter attempts to narrate in detail the education divide, in terms of access, capability, and opportunity that exists between rural and urban India. This chapter is the introductory chapter of part III of our book, which is dedicated to narrate the findings of our empirical interventions conducted to secure effective teaching–learning practices in rural India with the help of our social technology-enabled connected learning framework, as described in the previous chapter. This chapter bears explicit reference of the socioeconomic, political, and psychological intricacies of rural India, which happen to be our practical field site, where we have conducted our empirical studies. While this chapter defines our research context, it also highlights how the socioeconomic, political, and geographical positioning of rural India hinders effective educational practices in terms of providing access, nurturing capability, and securing opportunity for rural learners, thereby sustaining the extant issue of rural–urban education divide.

This is not to imply that the issue of ineffective educational practices in rural India has not attracted adequate attention. The chapter bears explicit reference to the numerous attempts, undertaken both by private and public organizations, to impart effective education to rural learners. These efforts have primarily been dedicated to provide access to educational resources to rural learners, both along physical and digital lines. Apart from being sporadic, such initiatives majorly lack the credibility to enhance the capability of rural learners through disseminated education. While physical measures are restricted by territorial hindrances, digital measures have also been unable to reap desirable results because of the rural target group's alienation from the digital medium.

This marks the incapacitation of these measures, where access to educational resources, without contextual measures adopted to ensure optimal usage of such access, has rendered these initiatives redundant. Instances can be cited, which record how in majority cases, access to educational infrastructure, both physical and digital, have remained underutilized in rural India. As studied by Dreze and Sen (2013), the causes behind possible hindrances in effective learning practices in rural India are poor quality of teaching and learning, absence of good quality teachers, deplorable conditions of teaching–learning materials, irregularity in teacher attendance, absence of child-centric learning environment, and a monotonous daily routine in the remote rural areas. Along digital lines, alienation of the target group from digital technologies, resistance to technology, lack of capability to exploit the digital medium for attracting educational benefits, lack of content in local language in the digital medium and affordability of technology can be cited as major issues limiting ICT's potential in conducting effective teaching–learning practices in rural India (Heeks 2002). The

United Nations Committee (Economic and Financial) is worried about the negative consequences of rural communities as a result of their poor access to ICT. Furthermore, it is concerned about the hindrances faced by the underdeveloped nations as a result of lack of resources (Fenell et al. 2018). Since the extant initiatives majorly remain inadequate in nurturing the capability of rural learners through disseminated education, they subsequently also remain ineffective in securing opportunity prospects for rural learners.

Inefficiency of adopted initiatives in overcoming access, capability, and opportunity divide of rural learners reveal that education divide is still a persistent problem in rural India. Lack of a holistic focus can be identified as a major problem on a macro scale, from which majority of extant initiatives suffer from. The adopted measures although have attempted in improving educational practices in rural India by improving biotic and abiotic parameters, they have mostly remained negligent of the external influencing factors, which critically influence the process of education dissemination in rural India. It is because of these four external influencing factors, urban schools are comparatively in a better position than their rural counterpart. It is these external influencers, namely, social, economic, political, and sociopsychological, that marks the disadvantages of rural India and subsequently hamper rural educational practices. This chapter has helped us in identifying the nature of these external operative hindrances that is marking the poor fate of educational practices in rural India.

A critical understanding of our research context has enabled us to design our research intervention by keeping in mind the specificities of rural India. In the following chapters, we will attempt in implementing our social technology-enabled digital framework as postulated in Chap. 6, to disseminate quality education to rural learners with the help of ICT. The following chapters bear in-depth field insights of our experience in implementing our digital platform to disseminate quality education to rural learners by negotiating with the external influencers operative in rural India.

# References

Aaron, S. (2016). *Rot in education: Students suffer as corruption, politics plague the system.* Retrieved from https://www.hindustantimes.com/india-news/rot-in-education-students-suffer-as-corruption-politics-plague-the-system/story-cNnB8ZoPgXpbVnrZjy0nIM.html.

ASER. (2014). *ASER 2014: Annual Status of Education Report (New Delhi: ASER Centre).* Retrieved from https://img.asercentre.org/docs/Publications/ASER%20Reports/ASER%202014/National%20PPTs/aser2014indiaenglish.pdf.

ASER. (2018). *Annual Status of Education Report (Rural).* New Delhi. Retrieved from https://img.asercentre.org/docs/ASER%202018/Release%20Material/aser2018pressreleaseenglish.pdf.

ASER. (2019). *Annual Status of Education Report (Rural).* New Delhi. Retrieved from https://img.asercentre.org/docs/ASER%202019/ASER2019%20report%20/aserreport2019earlyyearsfinal.pdf.

Balani, K. (2017). *Bihar Short of 280,000 Teachers; Spends Lowest Per Elementary School Student.* Retrieved from https://archive.indiaspend.com/cover-story/bihar-short-of-280000-teachers-spends-lowest-per-elementary-school-student-76265.

Balatchandirane, G. (2007). *Gender Discrimination in Education and Economic Development: A Study of Asia. Institute of Development Economics*, Japan External Trade Organizations. Retrieved from https://www.ide.go.jp/library/English/Publish/Download/Vrf/pdf/426.pdf.

Bandyopadhyay, S., Bhattacharyya, S., & Basak, J. (2020). *Social Knowledge Management for Rural Empowerment: Bridging the Knowledge Divide Using Social Technologies*. Routledge: New York. ISBN: 9780367334949.

Bartels, R. (1968). The general theory of marketing. *Journal of Marketing, 32*(1), 29–33. https://doi.org/10.1177/002224296803200107.

Barton, D., Horvath, D., & Kipping, M. (2016). *Re-Imagining Capitalism*. United Kingdom: Oxford University Press.

Behar, A. (2010). *Limits of ICT in education*. Retrieved from https://www.livemint.com/Opinion/Y3Rhb5CXMkGuUIyg4nrc3I/Limits-of-ICT-in-education.html.

Bhavana, B., Sheshadri, S., & Unnikrishnan, R. (2010). Vocational Education teachnology: Rural India. *In the Procedings of 1st Amrita ACM-W Celebration on Women in Computing in India*. https://doi.org/10.1145/1858378.1858399.

Boity, B. (2015). *Mobile Learning in India Scope, Impact and Implications*. Retrieved from https://canvas.harvard.edu/courses/18484/files/2602766/download/.

Borooah, K. V., & Iyer, S. (2007). Vidya, Veda, and Varna: The influence of religion and caste on education in rural India. *The Journal of Development Studies, 41*(8), 1369–1404. https://doi.org/10.1080/00220380500186960.

BS. (2018). *HRD Ministry Identified 80k 'Ghost' Teachers Through Aadhaar*. Retrieved from https://www.business-standard.com/article/pti-stories/hrd-ministry-identified-80k-ghost-tea chers-through-aadhaar-118010500822_1.html.

Chakravarty, M. (2018). *The Class Divide in Indian Education System*. Retrieved from https://www.livemint.com/Opinion/DuRPMPSqaaqCDLoNMgRAbL/The-class-divide-in-Indian-educationsystem.html.

Chandra, R. (2014). *Role of Education in Rural Development*. SRMU Lucknow. Retrieved from https://www.researchgate.net/publication/260599124_Role_of_Education_in_Rural_Dev elopment.

Chudgar, A, & Quin, E. (2012). Relationship between private schooling and achievement: Results from rural and urban India. *Economics of Education Review, 31*, 376–390. Retrieved from https://sci-hub.tw/http://www.sciencedirect.com/science/article/pii/S0272775711001798.

Claridge, T. (2018). Dimensions of Social Capital-structural, cognitive, relational. *Social Capital Research*. Retrieved from https://d1fs2th61pidml.cloudfront.net/wp-content/uploads/2018/01/Dimensions-of-Social-Capital.pdf?x49412.

Cleaver, S. (2014). *Technology in the Classroom: Helpful or Harmful?*. Retrieved from https://www.education.com/magazine/article/effective-technology-teaching-child/.

Crockett, L., Jukes, I., & Churches, A. (2011). *Literacy is not enough*. Thousand Oaks, CA: Corwin.

Cross, K.P. & McCartan, A. (1984). *Adult Learning: State Policies and Institutional Practices*. Association for the Study of Higher Education and the ERIC Clearinghouse on Higher Education. Retrieved from https://files.eric.ed.gov/fulltext/ED246831.pdf.

CSEI. (2015). Zero Discrimination and Violence. In Educational Institutions in India. *Centre for Social Equity and Inclusion*. Retrieved from https://csei.org.in/zero-discrimination-and-violence-in-educational-institutions-in-india/.

Debertin, L.D. (1996). *A Comparison of Social Capital in Rural and UrbanSettings*, University of Kentucky, Department of Agricultural Economics. Retrieved from https://www.uky.edu/~deb erti/socsaea.htm.

Dembo, H.M., & Seli, P.H. (2004). Students. Resistance to Change in Learning Strategies Courses. *Journal of Developmental Education, 27*(3). Retrieved from https://files.eric.ed.gov/fulltext/EJ7 18559.pdf.

Dixson, C., & Bairamova, N. (2019). Barriers to Learning, Part 2. Retrieved from https://edtech.worlded.org/barriers-to-learning-part-2/.

Dreze, J. (2003). *Patterns of Literacy and Their Social Context. The Oxford India Companion of Sociology and Social Anthropology.* New Delhi: Oxford University Press.

Dreze, J., & Sen, A. (2013). *An Uncertain Glory: India and its Contradictions.* Princeton University Press.

Dreze, J., & Kingdon, G. (2001). School Participation in Rural India. *Review of Development Economics, 5*(1). https://doi.org/10.1111/1467-9361.00103.

E-Basta. (n.d.). Vikaspedia. Retrieved from https://vikaspedia.in/education/interactive-resources/ebasta.

ESkill India. (n.d.). ESkill India. Retrieved from https://eskillindia.org/.

Fenell, S., Kaur, P., Jhunjhunwala, A., Narayanan, D., Loyola, C., Bedi, J., & Singh, Y. (2018). Examining linkages between smart villages and smart cities: Learning from rural youth accessing the internet in India. *Telecommunications Policy, 42*(10), 810–823. https://doi.org/10.1016/j.tel pol.2018.06.002.

FICCI. (2014). *Private Sector's Contribution To K-12 Education in India Current Impact, Challenges and Way Forward.* Retrieved from https://ficci.in/spdocument/20385/ey-ficci-report-edu cation.pdf.

Fox. B.S, & McDermott, L.C. (2015). The Role of 21st Century Skills in Two Regional Areas of Public Education. *Journal of Leadership and Instruction.* Retrieved from https://files.eric.ed.gov/fulltext/EJ1080685.pdf.

GOI. (2013). *Twelfth Five Year Plan 2012–17, Social Sectors* (vol. 3). Government of India, Planning Commission New Delhi: SAGE Publications. Retrieved from https://nhm.gov.in/images/pdf/pub lication/Planning_Commission/12th_Five_year_plan-Vol-3.pdf.

Hasaba, S. (2013). *Making Adult Literacy Learning Sustainable in Rural Areas.* Retrieved from https://ourworld.unu.edu/en/making-adult-literacy-learning-sustainable-in-rural-communities.

Heeks, R. (2002). Information systems and developing countries: Failure, success, and local improvisations. *The Information Society: An International Journal, 18*(2), 101–112. https://doi.org/10.1080/01972240290075039.

Heidi, R., & Lou, J. (2009). Education in Rural China. *Encyclopaedia of Modern China.* Retrieved from https://www.researchgate.net/publication/318969705.

Jimenez, E., & Lockheed, E.M. (1995). Public and Private Secondary Education in Developing Countries: A Comparative Study. In *World Bank. Discussion* [Paper 309]. Washington, D.C.: The World Bank.

Johnson, A.M., Jacovina, M.E., Russell, D.E., & Soto, C.M. (2016). Challenges and solutions when using technologies in the classroom. *Adaptive Educational Technologies for Literacy Instruction.* New York: Taylor & Francis. Retrieved from https://files.eric.ed.gov/fulltext/ED577147.pdf.

Kam, M., Agarwal, A., Kumar, A., Lal, S., Mathur, A., Tewari, A., & Canny, J. (2008). Designing e-learning games for rural children in India: a format for balancing learning with fun. *In Proceedings of the 7th ACM conference on Designing interactive systems.* Retrieved from https://people.eecs.berkeley.edu/~jfc/papers/08/DIS2008.pdf.

Kanjilal, U., & Kaul, P. (2016). *The Journey of SWAYAM: India MOOCs Initiative.* Presented in 8th Pan-Commonwealth Forum on Open Learning (PCF8) [Working Paper]. Retrieved from https://oasis.col.org/handle/11599/2592?show=full.

Kapoor, A. (2017). *Maharashtra, UP introduces mobile-classroom for underprivileged: Hoping to Push for Inclusive Education.* Retrieved from https://mediaindia.eu/society/maharashtra-up-int roduce-mobile-classroom-for-underprivileged/.

Kumar, A.K.S. & Rustagi, P. (2010). *Elementary Education in India: Progress, Setbacks, and Challenges.* Oxfam India [Working Papers Series, OIWPS – III]. Retrieved from https://oxfamilibrary.openrepository.com/bitstream/handle/10546/346628/wp-elementary-education-India-challenges-280910-en.pdf?sequence=1&isAllowed=y.

Kumbhar, V. (2013). Some Critical Issues of Women Entrepreneurship in Rural India. *European Academic Research, 1*(2), 185–192. https://doi.org/10.2139/ssrn.2043821.

Kundu, A., & Nath, D.K. (2018). Barriers to Utilizing ICT in Education in India with a Special Focus on Rural Areas. *International Journal of Scientific Research and Reviews, 7*(2), 341–359.

Retrieved from https://www.academia.edu/37983911/Barriers_to_Utilizing_ICT_in_Education_in_India_with_a_Special_Focus_on_Rural_Areas.

Kurian, N.J. (2007). Widening economic & social disparities: Implications for India. *In Indian Journal Medicine Research, 126*, 374–380. Retrieved from https://medind.nic.in/iby/t07/i10/iby t07i10p374.pdf.

Live Mint. (2007). *Ghost Teachers Main Hurdle in India's Education System.* Retrieved from https://www.livemint.com/Politics/pTqRf6yk7Sn6We9YL4fvlI/Ghost-teachers-main-hur dle-in-Indias-education-system.html.

Madangopal, D., & Madangopal, M. (2018). ICT in education: The Rural Challenge. *Centre for Communication and Development Studies.* Retrieved from https://digitalequality.in/ict-in-educat ion-the-rural-challenge/.

Maheshwari, V.K. (2019). *Corruption Penetration into Indian Education System.* Retrieved from https://www.vkmaheshwari.com/WP/?p=2837.

Makkar, S. (2017). *Why India's skill mission has failed.* Retrieved from https://www.business-standard.com/article/economy-policy/why-india-s-skill-mission-has-failed-117090200098_1. html.

Mandal, K.S. & Garg, M. (2013). Mid-Day Meal for the Poor; Privatised Education for the Non-Poor. *Economic and Political Weekly (EPW), 48*(30). Retrieved from https://www.epw.in/special-articles/mid-day-meal-poor-privatised-education-non-poor.html.

McCannon, R.S. (1983). *Serving Rural Adult Learners. Educational Outreach to Select Adult Populations.* SanFransisco: Jossey-Bass. https://doi.org/10.1002/ace.36719832004.

McQuiggan, S. (2015). *Mobile Learning: A Handbook for Developers, Educators, and Learners.* Wiley Inc. ISBN: 978-1-118-89430-9.

Mooij, J. (2008). Primary education, teachers' professionalism and social class about motivation and demotivation of government school teachers in India. *International Journal of Educational Development*, (Vol. 28, pp. 508–523). Retrieved from https://eric.ed.gov/?id=EJ797447.

Nagarajan, R. (2011). *Tuition often Costlier than Fees.* Retrieved from: https://timesofindia.indiat imes.com/india/Tuitions-often-costlier-than-fees/articleshow/7368611.cms.

Naik, G., Chitre, C., Bhalla, M., & Rajan, J. (2019). Impact of Use of Technology on Student Learning Outcomes - Evidence from a Large-scale Experiment in India. *World Development*, 127(C). Retrieved from https://www.sciencedirect.com/science/article/pii/S0305750X193 03857.

Nambissan, G.B. (2014). *Poverty, Markets and Elementary Education in India* [Working Papers of the Max Weber Foundation's Transnational Research Group India]. Retrieved from https://www. cprindia.org/sites/default/files/events/Geetha%20Nambissan%20paper.pdf.

Narayan. D., & Petesch, P. (2007). Agency, Opportunity Structure and Poverty Escapes. *Moving Out of Poverty. Volume1: Cross Disciplinary Perspectives on Mobility.* New York: Palgrave Macmillan. Retrieved from openknowl-edge.worldbank.org/bitstream/handle/10986/11840/41448.pdf?sequence=1&isAllowed=y.

NIEPA. (2018). School Education In India: U-DISE Flash Statistics 2016–17. *National Institute of Educational Planning and Administration.* New Delhi. Retrieved from https://udise.in/Downlo ads/Publications/Documents/Flash_Statistics_on_School_Education-2016-17.pdf.

Pal, J., Lakshmanan, M., & Toyoma, K. (2009). "My child will be respected": Parental perspectives on computers and education in Rural India. *In Information Systems Frontiers*, (Vol. 11, pp. 129–144). Retrieved from https://doi.org/10.1007/s10796-009-9172-1.

Panagiotes, A., Vitalaki, E., & Nikos, G. (2008). Collaborative learning activities at a distance via interactive videoconferencing in elementary schools: Parents' attitudes. *Computers and Education, 50*(4), 1527–1539. https://doi.org/10.1016/j.compedu.2007.02.003.

Park, H.Y. (2007). Emerging Consumerism and the Accelerated 'Education Divide': The Case of Specialized High Schools in South Korea. *Journal of Critical Education Policy Studies, 5*(2). Retrieved from https://www.jceps.com/wp-content/uploads/PDFs/05-2-14.pdf.

PROBE. (1999). *Public Report on Basic Education in India.* New Delhi: Oxford University Press.

Putnam, R. D. (2000). *Bowling Alone: The Collapse and Revival of American Community*. New York: Touchstone.

Raghu, R., Smrithi, V., Krishnashree, A., & Prema, N. (2015). Computer science (CS) education in Indian schools: Situation analysis using Darmstadt model. *ACM Trans. Computer Education, 15*(2), Article 7. https://doi.org/10.1145/2716325.

Rani, G.P., & Elliott, C. (2014). Disparities in Earnings and Education in India. *Cogent Economics and Finance, 2*(1). https://doi.org/10.1080/23322039.2014.941510.

Satveer. (2017). Challenges In The Implementation Of ICT (Information And Communication Technology) In Rural Areas. *IJESRT, 6*(8). Retrieved from https://www.ijesrt.com/issues%20pdf%20file/Archive-2017/August-2017/54.pdf.

Sein, M. K. (2011). The "I" between G and C: E-government intermediaries in developing countries. *The Electronic Journal on Information Systems in Developing Countries, 48*(1), 1–14. https://doi.org/10.1002/j.1681-4835.2011.tb00338.x.

Sembiah, S., Burman, J., Dasgupta, A., & Paul, B. (2019). Safety of food served in mid-day meal program: An in-depth study in upper primary schools of Kolkata. *Journal of Family Medicine and Primary Care, 8*(3), 938–943. https://doi.org/10.4103/jfmpc.jfmpc_59_19.

Sen, A. (1988). Capability and well-being. *WIDER conference paper.* https://doi.org/10.1093/0198287976.003.0005.

Sen, A. (2003). *Development as Capability Expansion. Readings in Human Development*. New Delhi and New York: Oxford University Press.s.

Sen, A. (1990). *More Than 100 Million Women Are Missing*. Retrieved from https://www.nybooks.com/articles/1990/12/20/more-than-100-million-women-are-missing/.

Singhal, A. (2019). India's Schools Fail to Give Quality Education. Here's Why. Retrieved from https://www.polemicsnpedantics.com/single-post/2019/01/30/indias-education-sector-has-failed-to-give-quality-education-heres-why.

Sreekanthachari, J.G., & Nagaraja, G. (2013). An Overview of Rural Education In India. *Advance Research Journal of Social Science, 4*(1), 115–119. Retrieved from https://www.researchjournal.co.in/upload/assignments/4_115-119.pdf.

Swain, C.S., & Das, S. (2017). A Critical Analysis of Mid-Day Meal In India. *Imperial Journal of Interdisciplinary Research (IJIR), 3*(3). Retrieved from https://www.onlinejournal.in/IJIRV3I3/282.pdf.

Taneja, A. (2018). *The High Drop-out rate of girls in India*. Retrieved from https://www.livemint.com/Opinion/iXWvKng7uU4L8vo5XbDn9I/The-high-dropout-rate-of-girls-in-India.html.

The Hindu. (2020). *Economic Survey 2019–20: High Fees Push Poor out of Education System.* Retrieved from https://www.thehindu.com/news/national/high-fees-push-poor-out-of-education-system/article30705451.ece.

Trucano, M. (2016). *Mobile Internet Buses, Vans and Classrooms to Support Teachers and Learners in Remote Communities, World Bank Blogs*. Retrieved from https://blogs.worldbank.org/edutech/mobile-internet-buses-vans-and-classrooms.

UNESCO. (2015). Promising EFA Practices in the Asia-Pacific Region: India Sarva Sikhya Abhiyan: Case-Study. Retrieved from https://unesdoc.unesco.org/ark:/48223/pf0000233990.

Uphoff, N., & Wijayaratna, C. M. (2000). Demonstrated benefits from social capital: The productivity of farmer organizations in Gal Oya. *Sri Lanka. World Development, 28*(11), 1875–1890. https://doi.org/10.1016/S0305-750X(00)00063-2.

Wazir, R. (2002). *Getting Children Out of Work and Into School: the MV Foundation, Secunderabad (AP): the MV Foundation*. New Delhi. Retrieved from https://www.panchayatgyan.gov.in/documents/30336/104308/4+Getting+childrean+out+of+work+to+school+MV+foundation.pdf/ebacaee5-6925-4ca2-9566-d1e5e75b0088.

Williams, R. (2013). *Why girls in India are Still Missing out on the Education they Need*. Retrieved from https://www.theguardian.com/education/2013/mar/11/indian-children-education-opportunities.

World Bank. (2019). *The Education Crisis: Being in School Is Not the Same as Learning.* Retrieved from https://www.worldbank.org/en/news/immersive-story/2019/01/22/pass-or-fail-how-can-the-world-do-its-homework.

World Economic Forum. (2016). Five Million Jobs by 2020: The Real Challenge of the Fourth Industrial Revolution. Retrieved from https://www.weforum.org/press/2016/01/five-million-jobs-by-2020-the-real-challenge-of-the-fourth-industrial-revolution/.

World Economic Forum. (2018). *Why Schools Should Teach the Curriculum of the Future, not the Past.* Retrieved from https://www.weforum.org/agenda/2018/09/why-schools-should-teach-the-curriculum-of-the-future-not-the-past/.

# Chapter 8
# Online Blended Learning Platform for Educating Underprivileged Children

## Creating Active Learners Using Social Technologies

## 8.1 Introduction

In India, the distribution of educational resources is starkly discriminatory in nature. The education spectrum witnesses excellent urban schools that are comparable to the best institutions in the world, but they are expensive and only a handful. On the other hand, there are low-end Government-aided public rural schools which are in deplorable state. Poor performances of these rural schools are "marked by teacher absenteeism, inadequately trained teachers, non-availability of teaching materials, inadequate supervision, and little support" (Kumar and Rustagi 2010). Children from rural schools often drop out due to factors like an "unattractive classroom environment, teacher absenteeism, teacher-centered teaching, and a stagnant daily routine" (Dreze 2003; Dreze and Sen 2013). Teaching methods predominantly include mindless rote learning, repetition without comprehension, and endless repetition of various tables (Dreze 2003). Teaching methods were often didactic, teacher centric, and repetitive. Limited class time is devoted to activities involving discussion and participation of pupils (Sankar 2009).

However, still the highest number of school enrollments in India is under Government and semi-Government schools and the Government has invested a lot in enhancing school infrastructures to facilitate free and compulsory primary education for all. But investments to improve access and enrolment of poor students were not accompanied by investments in quality, resulting in high dropouts at various transition points in the school system (Dhawan 2014). This poor quality of education gets reflected, when a significant portion of the student population in rural secondary schools is incompetent in simple reading ability and nearly two thirds are not conversant with simple arithmetic (ASER 2014). Additionally, due to lack of proper benchmarking methods, the education standards were never mapped while the government continues to invest on education with no clarity on benchmarking (IANS 2018).

In order to cope up with shortage of school teachers in Government and semi-Government public schools, there is a nationwide practice of recruiting *para-teachers*

© The Author(s), under exclusive license to Springer Nature Singapore Pte Ltd. 2021 191
S. Bandyopadhyay et al., *Bridging the Education Divide Using Social Technologies*,
https://doi.org/10.1007/978-981-33-6738-8_8

with lower academic and no professional qualifications to serve in the formal public school classrooms on a contract basis. The practice of recruiting professionally untrained and academically under-qualified teachers—referred as "Para Teachers" or "Contract Teachers"—to serve in the formal elementary schools of the country has been widespread since the 1990s as part of Universal Primary Education Program of Government of India. Several researchers have raised serious concerns about the capability of para/contract teachers to teach in elementary schools of the country and have warned against the de-professionalization of the teaching cadre (Atherton and Kingdon 2010).

Failures of the public education system in imparting quality education, coupled with a high propensity within India's middle class to spend on education, have resulted in the emergence of private schools. Education is not free in private schools and they are beyond the reach of majority of people. Moreover, good private schools are urban-centric and boast of high-end infrastructure and ICT based support to enhance student learning. These schools are given preference because of their comprehensive curriculum, continuous evaluation, syllabi based on practical applications, interactive skill-based assessments and fun based learning. These schools, in general, ensure better learning levels and better quality of school education compared to public schools in India (FICCI 2014). They boast of higher learning achievement along with high overall development of students, thus proving to be more accountable toward provision of quality. The increase in private school enrolment in India has seemingly sown the seeds of inequality. These schools demand exorbitant fees that are unaffordable for a large section of the Indian population. Such stratification not only perpetuates inequality over generations, but also threatens the ideal of "public schooling" for all students (Muralidharan 2014).

Simultaneously another phenomenon has been observed: the rise of low-cost private institutions in semi urban and rural India (Ohara 2012). However, studies indicate that there are concerns about content, quality, and methods of teaching in both the government and low-cost private school segments and they are not adequate in providing access to quality educations (Sarangapani 2009). In this situation, there is a strong need to identify plausible and sustainable solutions to create educational quality for those underprivileged school students.

In this situation what seems to become pertinent is to actually understand the parameters of quality education and observe the role of social technology-driven digital platform as an important factor in imparting quality education in areas where there is dearth of it. Thus, the objective of this chapter is to develop a social technology-enabled blended learning platform, derived from Connected Learning Framework as postulated in Chap. 6, to improve learning achievements and well-being of rural underprivileged students. More specifically, the objectives of this chapter are: (i) to propose indicators for benchmarking quality of education delivered by Indian school systems; (ii) to identify factors influencing quality of education; and, (iii) using the proposed benchmark, to demonstrate how social technology-driven blended learning platform can improve quality of education for underprivileged and low-performing primary school children.

It is to be noted that pure synchronous and asynchronous e-learning models are not suitable for rural children, since these models assume that each student should have access to a computer or tablet on an individual basis. Smart-class solutions based on blended learning model are also not suitable in rural context, since they are dependent on local teachers at rural classrooms and do not address a major problem: non-availability/lack of accessibility of qualified local teachers at rural classrooms. So, we need to architect a classroom-oriented blended learning model that uses internet to connect remote expert teachers in rural classrooms using social technology-enabled tools and platforms (e.g., online video conferencing, instant messaging system, etc.), thereby reducing dependency on local teachers at rural classrooms.

The chapter is dedicated to explore the effectivity of our proposed blended learning platform in imparting quality education to rural children of underprivileged backgrounds. In doing so, the chapter is divided into three sections. Section 8.2 explains the design and development of an integrated blended learning platform. This section bears explicit reference to the design methodology and functional specifications of our proposed online blended learning platform. The next section, Sect. 8.3, is dedicated to spell out the operational dynamics of our platform. This section narrates the experimentation details of the pilot studies conducted through implementation of our proposed platform in the context of improving educational parameters of underprivileged children of rural India. Finally, the chapter concludes with the findings of the pilot study in Sect. 8.4.

## 8.2 Design and Development of an Integrated Blended Learning Platform

### 8.2.1 The Design Methodology

In this particular research, the concept and consequent design and development efforts need to be tuned according to the learning context and capacities of rural underprivileged students. Several models of blended learning have been tested both globally and locally (PERC 2014; British Council Report 2016). However, all models of blended learning usually assume face-to-face availability/accessibility of qualified teachers, enabling interactions in physical classroom settings as and when needed. However, as discussed before, non-availability/poor accessibility of qualified teachers at rural classrooms is one of the major problems in Indian education system. Moreover, as discussed in Chap. 6, digital maturity of both rural students and rural classroom coordinators are poor and they are alien to computer-based education systems. Additionally, poor economic condition of rural students inhibits them to possess and access any computing device (computer/laptop/smartphone) freely, making them *digitally naïve* compared to the urban students and teachers, who are immersed into the usage of digital technologies throughout the day. Hence, we have to model a different kind of *blended learning practice* in order to improve quality of school education in rural India.

Design science research in Information Technology and Systems focuses on the development of IT artifacts with the objective of improving the performance of the artifact in users' context. Design science research methodology uses a build-and-evaluate cycle keeping the application perspectives in mind (Hevner et al. 2004). However, the exogenous approach of development, which assumes that development can be achieved through acquisition and implementation of technology alone, is also prevalent in traditional Design Science Research (DSR) thinking in the context of Information Systems development. Existing DSR methods "value technological rigor at the cost of organizational relevance, and fail to recognize that the artifact emerges from interaction with the organizational context even when its initial design is guided by the researchers' intent" (Sein et al. 2011). In order to incorporate a user-centric approach in design, Sein et al. (2011) proposes the concept of "action design research (ADR)." ADR reflects the premise that "IT artifacts are ensembles shaped by the organizational context during development and use." ADR method focuses on the "building, intervention, and evaluation of an artifact" that not only captures the intent of the design but also the influence it casts on users.

Our design methodology is motivated by ADR approach and uses the following four *interwoven activities*:

**Problem Formulation**: Problem perceived in practice or anticipated by researchers.

**Building, Intervention, and Evaluation (BIE)**: Testing the initial design of the IT artifact in the context of its usage. This phase "interweaves the *building* of the IT artifact, *intervention* in the organization, and *evaluation*."

**Reflection and Learning**: This is an iterative process to build and refine a solution to make it context-specific and hence applicable to a broader class of problems.

**Formalization of Learning**: Finalizing a solution that addresses the problem.

## 8.2.2   The Proposed Blended Learning Model

The model of blended learning proposed here is an outcome of our design methods discussed in previous section and it takes care of implementation limitations that have been observed during the implementation of traditional model of blended learning, which assumed that the teachers and students are fully empowered to act as active agents in the process. And, it is to be noted that just providing access to technology through computer and internet was not enough to empower them as active agents.

We have architected an online blended learning platform where knowledgeable elderly or senior teachers in the city teach underprivileged children located in remote rural classrooms through Internet. The online teachers use quality digital teaching–learning materials that comprise of audio-visuals and graphical contents in regional language. An on-site classroom coordinator appointed at this rural classroom (e.g. para-teacher, as explained in Sect. 8.1) would schedule classes, coordinate the

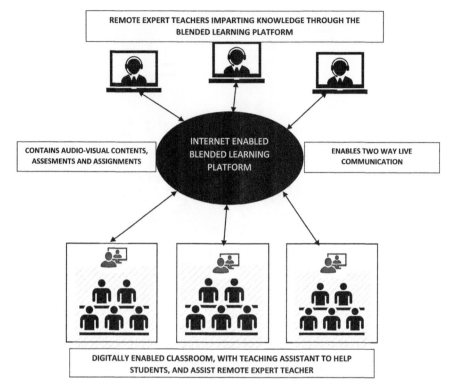

**Fig. 8.1**  The proposed blended learning model

teaching process via this platform, correct homework with the online help of remote expert teachers, manages the classroom and interact with students and the online expert teachers during classroom sessions (Fig. 8.1).

The platform has an inbuilt video conferencing system that also has a provision to share digital content on the computer screen or to use inbuilt digital white board for diagrammatic explanations. The expert online teachers teach from their homes, where they have an ICT setup (laptop/desktop speakers, camera, and headphones) along with high-speed internet connectivity. They use quality digital teaching–learning materials that comprise of audio-visuals contents in regional language.

The students are located in remote classrooms, which is also equipped with a low-cost ICT setup (desktop/laptop, large monitor/screen or projector, camera, speakers, and microphone) and high-speed internet connectivity. The classes are conducted at scheduled times, using the above platform with the help of an on-site teaching assistant/class coordinator (Fig. 8.2).

In this blended learning model, there is a blending of three components: (i) online synchronous learning, where actual teaching is imparted by online remote teachers

**Fig. 8.2** Students studying with remote teacher and local classroom coordinator

through Internet using video-conferencing tools; (ii) online teaching–learning materials available digitally or created by expert teachers; and (iii) offline teaching assistant who manages the learning process physically in the classroom.

As indicated earlier, the concept of blended learning has been new in the rural context of India. In this particular research, the concept is modified according to the learning capacities of rural underprivileged students. The innovative components of our integrated blended learning platform are as follows: i) use of integrated video-conferencing tool to remove the barrier of time and space so that rural students can obtain access to qualified teachers from urban areas; ii) supporting smooth delivery of audio-visual contents in regional language that can make learning enjoyable and engaging; iii) the method of dissemination of knowledge involves not only one-way lecture but also promotes interactions in various forms, which is often lacking in rural education; and, iv) finally, our blended learning platform provides an easy-to-use learning analytics app which is used by the online teachers and the classroom coordinator for easy assessment of students' performance.

### 8.2.3  The Functional Architecture of Proposed Online Blended Learning Platform

This online blended learning platform caters to three user groups who logs in from respective user accounts into the platform for the purpose of synchronous interaction and communication with one another. These users are: online teachers who teaches students remotely, para-teachers or classroom coordinators who manages the remote classrooms, and, the students. In the pilot study, para-teachers or classroom coordinators have been trained to initiate the online classes in a classroom mode with online

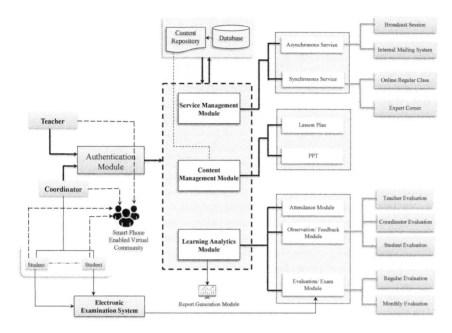

**Fig. 8.3**   The functional architecture of the proposed blended learning platform

teachers at one end and the learners on the other end. Each of the users has specific roles and functions to play in order to make the platform interactive. The objective of the learning platform is to create active learners. The functional architecture of the platform is described below by categorizing the entire system into several modules (Fig. 8.3):

- **_Authentication Module_**: In this module, the three users, such as online teachers, students, and classroom coordinators of the platform, get defined and authenticated. In order to connect with one another and create an active learning environment, the teachers, classroom coordinators, and the rural learners first will have to create their own user accounts by registering to the platform. Once their credentials are authenticated by the system administrator, the users can actively use their accounts for purposes of teaching, learning, and connecting. The registration is validated through offline verification of user credentials. Online teachers are enrolled through interviews and teaching demonstrations. Quality of teaching of teachers is validated extensively by subject matter experts and then eventually are included within the Teacher Panel of the platform. Similarly, credentials of classroom coordinators are properly verified by making offline visits to the rural classrooms or by remotely verifying all their credentials. Since in these rural classes, coordinators are the one-point contact persons, the identities of students are validated through them.
- **Service Management Module**: After authenticating and validating credentials of all the users, the service management module enables them to use several

services related to learning such as synchronous live learning sessions (regular online classes), asynchronous/pre-recorded learning sessions (offline sessions), and synchronous live sessions with experts in different domains (periodical online sessions for getting expert advices). Through their respective user accounts, students or classroom coordinators can attend live/synchronous learning sessions from their designated online teachers at pre-defined time slots. Apart from these live online sessions, learners can participate in the following activities:

- **Internal Mailing System**: It is not always sufficient to connect with mentors or teachers online or live (synchronous). Learners often face problem with their studies when they are preparing at home all by themselves. At that time, learners can send instant messages to their respective teachers/trainers/mentors through the integrated Internal Mailing System. In case of rural classrooms, learners, who do not have direct access to computers, cannot avail the messaging system. Therefore, in that context, classroom coordinators or para-teachers use the internal mailing system on behalf of the learners. Internal Mailing System is integrated within the learning platform through which users can send not only text messages and attachments but also hand-written messages. Users can exchange any diagram, mathematical formula, etc., through these hand-written messages.
- **Pre-recorded Educational Videos**: Apart from attending live online sessions, learners can also watch and learn from pre-recorded educational videos in asynchronous mode. These videos are assorted and collated by content developers from the freely available cyber resource. These educational videos will range from subjects such as history, folk tales, science, general knowledge, geography, current affairs, and many more. These videos will be made in several Indian languages. Learners from any age group can avail pre-recorded educational videos to enhance own skills and knowledge.
- **Expert Corner**: Rural learners can receive counseling services such as career counseling, psychological counseling, financial advices, health and hygiene related advices, etc., from urban experts through this online learning platform. These sessions will be synchronous and live wherein learners can interact with expert advisors on a one- to- one basis, inquiring specific problems.

- **Smartphone-Enabled Virtual Community**: This learning platform not only aims at connecting learners with teachers/trainers/mentors alone, but also encourages parents, content developers, social entrepreneurs/educational administrators, etc., to connect with each other and learners too. Through this particular module, we propose a collaborative learning environment wherein learners (of any age group) can collaborate with any participating entity. Apart from the various functionalities integrated within the platform, we have utilized the potential of WhatsApp communications on smartphones to foster community-connect among entities directly or indirectly involved in the teaching–learning process. WhatsApp is an example of a socially enabled platform through which learners, parents, teachers, social entrepreneurs, classroom coordinators, content developers, etc., can communicate with each other effortlessly. We, as researchers and provider of digital teaching–learning platform, have taken the responsibility to administer these WhatsApp communications by creating different WhatsApp groups where the relevant actors in the teaching–learning process, such as remote online teachers, para-teachers, learners, parents, content developers regularly connect or communicate with each other.

WhatsApp communication is deeply embedded within the operationalization of the Platform. Online expert teachers use WhatsApp to send assignments, study materials, educational videos, etc., to learners after class. The characteristic of instant messaging and communication system of WhatsApp helps teachers to solve learners' queries immediately. Students after completion of their sessions used to get connected with their online teachers using their parents' smartphones, ask them their doubts (if any) or upload their answer sheets. Para-teachers or classroom coordinator too play important role by continuously interacting with the teachers and students by notifying them about their sessions, asking them to login to their respective classes and by continuously following up with the learners to upload their answer sheets for the online teachers to correct. Parents, were not very regular in commenting through WhatsApp. But they observed the WhatsApp interactions between teachers and learners. Also, teachers often play the role of content developers. As content developers, we continuously upload relevant educational content in form of videos, images, or documents through WhatsApp for the learners to watch in their homes after completion of sessions. WhatsApp communication, as an integral part of the system, thus helps us to transcend from e-learning to collaborative learning wherein all biotic components of learning are constantly communicating or collaborating with one another to create a holistic and informal learning environment for each learner along with formal online sessions.

- **Content Management Module**: The System will comprise of the content management module where quality digital content based on school curriculum will be availed by teachers, classroom coordinators, and learners. This repository of digital teaching–learning content consists of everyday lesson plans and audio-visual presentations in regional language, which will be used by online teachers at the time of online delivery to learners. This content repository will be created collaboratively by content developers under the supervision of subject matter experts. This module provides a user-interface that allows a valid user to control the design, creation, modification, and removal of the digital content from the content repository.
- **Learning Analytics Module**: The regular online (synchronous) sessions are monitored, evaluated, and assessed both by online teacher and classroom coordinator. Each learner will be evaluated and monitored with respect to their progress in learning. This module will comprise of regular attendance of learners, daily

class observations, assessments papers, student answer sheets, score records, and feedbacks. The inputs entered by the teachers and coordinators will be compiled, assessed, and interpreted by the system administrator of the platform. The objective of this module is to create a continuous tracking system wherein learners can be tracked at periodic intervals and to understand the effectiveness of learning process. The basic functions of this module are the following:

- **Attendance Module**: Learners' regular attendance is maintained and updated by both online teachers and classroom coordinators from the system. Along with each student's attendance, this module also has a provision to put scores against each student, based on student's classroom participation.
- **Observation/Feedback Module**: Feedback is an essential part of this platform. It helps to track the learning outcomes and also helps learners to maximize their potential at different stages of online classes. To ensure the quality of the entire learning process, the platform will collect feedback from the teachers regarding class observation and evaluation of classroom coordinators. At the same time, it also collects the feedback from the classroom coordinators about class observation and evaluating teachers. While collecting the feedback about class observation, the class coordinators also provide data about students' participation in the class, teachers' teaching pattern in the class, technical problems, if any (e.g., internet problem during class), etc.
- **Evaluation/Exam Module**: This module in the platform allows teachers and class-coordinators to conduct exams remotely. A teacher can upload question paper under a specific course of a specific class. Based on that, the platform will notify and the coordinator downloads the question paper and conduct examinations. It also allows coordinators to upload the scanned answer-sheet in the platform (using coordinator's smartphone) so that the teacher can remotely check the students copy and provide marks on that. This particular module is often functional through WhatsApp wherein students send their test-copies directly to the online teachers who, in turn, correct them and send them back to the learners.

- **Report Generation Module**: This module is designed to provide a feature-rich and user-friendly web interface for managing reports. The report generation module allows to directly extracting all the information from the database based on the requirements and either view it directly online or export it in spread sheets. The reports can be prepared based on the data available in the following modules: (i) Attendance Module; (ii) Evaluation/ Exam Module; and (iii) Observation/Feedback Module.
- **Electronic Examination System**: This module is used to evaluate the performance of each and every individual student through online examination through a smartphone-based application. The subject/class specific questions will be uploaded by expert teachers to the system using their own mobile phones. During the exam, a student will login to the system using the smartphones of their parents and take the online examination through smartphone. Students will also be able

to write the answers in their notebook. They can send a picture of their notebook to the system by using their smartphone camera which will be evaluated by the teachers later on.

### 8.2.4 Discussion

Several studies indicate that most of the underprivileged students are demotivated and have no interest in existing methods of teaching. To provide them with a learning experience that will create in them the zeal to study, one must create a learning environment that is engaging and allows free permeation of knowledge. In this situation, the proposed blended learning model serves multiple purposes. Firstly, the student can freely interact with the online teachers without any fear or stress. In India, there is a strong caste differences that sometimes creates a negative bias in the local teachers' attitude. Thus, such unprecedented situations are avoided through video-conferencing as the subject teacher is remotely interacting with the students. Hence, there is no fear of physical reprimand. Secondly, the audio-visual teaching–learning materials are both interesting and explanatory. Thus, students learn at a better pace without getting bored. Thirdly, the presence of a classroom coordinator not only helps maintain class discipline, but also provides the students with extra attention in their queries, home works, and assessments. This ensures a continuous support present with the students.

## 8.3   Experimentation, Analysis, and Evaluation

### 8.3.1   Objectives

The primary goal of this chapter is to understand the parameters of quality education and observe the impact of social technology-driven blended learning framework in imparting quality education in areas where there is dearth of it. More specifically, the objectives of this paper are: (i) to propose indicators for benchmarking quality of education delivered by Indian school system; (ii) to identify factors influencing quality of education; and, (iii) using the proposed benchmark, to demonstrate how social technology-driven blended learning framework can improve quality of education for underprivileged and low-performing primary school children.

## 8.3.2   Study Design

*Defining the Dependent Variables: Quality of Education, Well-being, and Learning Achievement*

*Quality of Education*: UNICEF defines quality education as "education that works for every child and enables all children to achieve their full potential" (UNICEF 2016). Although quality of education is traditionally measured by student learning achievements, relevance of what is taught and learned and how it associates with the continuous needs of the learner is important (Stephens 2003). Thus, it becomes evident that quality of education is not just dependent on learning achievement of the student but several other factors. A large body of literature states that quality of educational attainments is strongly associated with well-being at school (Mukhopadhyay 2001). Based on these observations, we have tried to measure quality of education outcome with two variables: *Students' Wellbeing* and *Learning Achievement*. In this research, the notion of quality is viewed as a combination of the perception of students' well-being in the schools and their learning achievements or academic performances. The learning achievement of the students has been measured using competency-based grade level questionnaire that have been formulated keeping in mind the heterogeneity of school boards and geographical locations.

***Students' Well-being***: Learning and well-being are closely intertwined, as students learn best when their well-being is at optimal level and eventually, they develop a strong sense of well-being when they experience success in learning. In this context, it has been observed that students themselves identify schooling as significant influencer on their well-being: "be it the positive impact of a great teacher, an inspirational and engaging classroom lesson or that extra support provided at just the right time" (Student Learning and Well-being Framework 2018). It is stated that "more learning occurs in a joyous classroom where children feel safe, secure and accepted, and where they feel the teacher sees them for who they really are" (Diamond 2010). Thus, well-being is a factor that is intrinsically associated with educational quality. A positive school environment augments motivation, increases academic aspirations and improves attentivity and retention, thus fostering well-being and consequently quality of education (Frisco Report 2013).

The four **subcomponents of well-being** considered in this study are:

*Teacher support in school*: The role of teacher is to ensure a safe and conducive learning environment, thereby enabling students to achieve their potential. Several researchers explicitly bring out how interactive teaching can bring in decisive change in the academic and social development of students (Hamre and Pianta 2005).

*Teaching–learning materials*: Most of the time, the teachers focus on finishing the content of the curriculum and less attention is paid on how the content is taught to children. Effective teaching–learning materials enhances the learning process of children, improving their feeling of well-being at classroom (Mayer and Ralph 2008).

*Peer relations*: In the early years of their life, children are inclined to associate and learn from children of the similar age (i.e., their peers). Peer relations are an important facet of human life that helps children grow not only socially but also emotionally (Alward 2005).

*Happiness in learning*: Happiness as an emotion has a very positive effect on learning. Evidences suggest that "periods of happiness are directly proportional to personal growth, health and development." Students who are happy are more receptive to outside stimuli than sad and depressed students (Scoffham and Jonathan 2011).

***Learning Achievement***: Learning achievement is the students' learning performance as reflected in their test scores on different subjects. The National Policy on Education (NPE 1986) emphasizes the importance of Minimum Levels of Learning (MLLs) along with progress measurement to ensure that "all children acquire at least the minimum levels of learning." Learning achievements assesses the "expected levels of learning that children should achieve for that class" (MHRD 2017).

***Defining Independent Variables: Socioeconomic Status, Family Support, and School Environment***

***Socioeconomic Status***: The socioeconomic status defines a family's capacity to afford the basic necessities and remain financially unburdened. Socioeconomic status also highlights the position of "individuals, families, or other units on one or more dimensions of stratification" (Fergusson et al., 2008). In India, students belonging to high socioeconomic status can choose expensive private schools and are more likely to have more exposures that stimulate their intellectual development and well-being. Students from low socioeconomic background suffer from psycho-social problems that include cynicism with low self-esteem" (Blacksher 2002).

***Family Support***: Children's early well-being is primarily dependent on learning environment at home, which "focuses on parents' provision of learning opportunities in the home including both learning materials and their encouragement towards children's learning behavior." Parental involvement has a major impact on children's school performance. Children whose parents are involved in school activities visibly show a higher performance rate both in curricular and extracurricular activities (Khajehpour 2011).

***School Environment***: Once children are enrolled in school, the school environment represents a prominent community space that is likely to influence their well-being. Students spend a considerable amount of time in the classroom and their motivation levels are influenced by the physical learning conditions around them. Several Studies about student academic achievement and building condition conclude that the "quality of the physical environment significantly affects student achievement" (Tafani 2003).

***Research Instrument***

The research undertakes a study on quality of education by interviewing 228 students hailing from 33 schools. The measurement of *quality of education* is a composite score of the measures of two components: *well-being* and *learning achievements*. The pre-intervention study tries to gauge the "as is" situation of the students through the level of perceived quality of education in school. The "as is" study observes the *socioeconomic status*, the *family support*, the *school environment*, the perceived *well-being* and the *learning achievement* of the students, as explained before.

The **socioeconomic status** of the students depicts their capacity to be able to spend on quality of education. The socioeconomic status questionnaire has been derived from the B.G Prasad scales and Udai Pareek scales (Singh et al. 2017). The **family support** questionnaire has been derived partially from Parental Support Scale (P.S.S.), developed by Nandwana and Asawa (2011). However, for the need of the research, the scale has been modified and tailored for open ended answers. The answers have been further coded based on the above scale. The questionnaire on **school environment** is derived from Well-being@School survey on primary students by New Zealand Council of Educational Research (Boyd and Barwic 2011).

The notion of **well-being** is a derived understanding from previous literature that has been referred. The research undertakes its own understanding of the idea of well-being by measuring the following: (a) teacher support in school, (b) peer relations, (c) teaching–learning materials, (d) happiness in learning. The section on **teacher support in school** is also derived from Well-being@School survey on primary students by New Zealand Council of Educational Research (Boyd and Barwic 2011). The section on **teaching–learning materials, peer relation**, and **happiness in learning** has been derived from the following scales—Multidimensional Students Life Satisfaction Scale (MSLSS) (Lani 2010). The **learning achievement** of the students has been measured using competency-based grade level questionnaire that have been formulated by keeping in mind the heterogeneity of school boards and geographical locations. Keeping in mind the research purview and its applications, the questions have been modified according to the geography and language barrier. All the questions have been marked using a five-point Likert Scale.

### Sample and Data Collection

An exploratory study has been conducted into the dimension of quality education through a quantitative survey of 228 students in 33 primary schools, randomly selected across 4 districts in West Bengal, India. These schools are both public and private schools from rural, semi urban, and urban areas. The cost structures of those schools follow a wide spectrum from free schooling to high-cost private schooling. The study will help us to benchmark quality of education in schools and the pertinent factors of what may entail quality education.

After the "as is" study, 79 students from 3 bottom-most school in the "quality" ranking were chosen out of 33 sample schools to conduct a blended learning teaching intervention for a period of 90 days to study impact of this initiative on learning achievements and school well-being on those 79 students. After 90 days, an "after study" was conducted to see changes in the quality of educational outcomes.

### 8.3.3 Analysis

**Analysis I: Benchmarking Quality of Education**

**Benchmarking** is the practice of any organization comparing key metrics of their operations to other similar organizations. Benchmarking aims to answer the following questions (Kempner 1993): "How well are we doing compared to others? Who is doing it the best? How good do we want to be?".

In the context of quality of education in Indian schools, there is no standard metric to judge whether a school is offering quality education and to what extent. In this study, we have made an attempt to evolve a unique metric for the purpose of benchmarking quality of education. It is a composite metric, derived from Well-being score and Learning Achievement score (Sect. 8.3.2). *Wellbeing* is a score derived from students' perception of well-being in the context of their day-to-day life in their respective schools; and, *Learning Achievement* is their test scores obtained in a competency-based grade level questionnaire that have been formulated keeping in mind the heterogeneity of school boards and geographical locations.

The *Quality-of Education* score (average of well-being and learning achievement scores of sample students for each school) is plotted at y-axis in Fig. 8.4 against 33 school-ids at x-axis. In other words, we translate the students' attribute to their schools' attribute by averaging scores of sample students belonging to a particular school against each variable: *wellbeing* and *learning achievement*. As shown in this figure, school S-7 scores the highest in the quality-of education scale, and school S-33 score the lowest. This implies that, on the average, primary students of school S-7 are having a high-Quality-of-Education Score (4.63) compared to those in school S-33 (1.24).

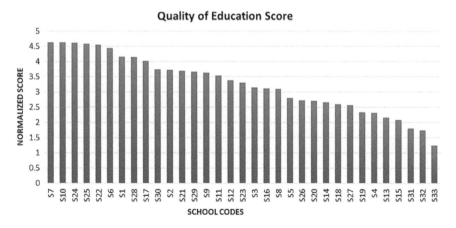

**Fig. 8.4** Benchmarking quality of education: results from 33 schools

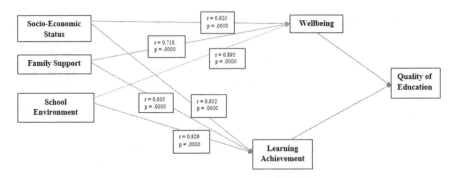

**Fig. 8.5** Correlation between dependent and independent variables

### Analysis II: Factors Determining Quality Educational Outcomes

In order to understand the factors determining quality educational outcome of schools, we use three independent variables described earlier: *Socioeconomic Status* of the students, *Family Support,* and the *School Environment* experienced by the students. The primary focus is to observe if these independent variables have any impact on two dependent variables: Well-being and Learning Achievement.

To do a correlation analysis, first we average the scores of sample students for each school against each variable. In other words, we translate the students' attribute to their schools' attribute by averaging scores of sample students belonging to a particular school against each variable. We redefine the variables at school level as: *Socioeconomic Status* of the students of a school, *Family Support* enjoyed by the students of a school, and the *School Environment* experienced by the students of a school. The correlation analysis between independent and dependent variables is presented in Fig. 8.5.

From the above observations, it can be deduced that quality of education, as captured in two dependent variables (Well-being and Learning Achievement) is heavily dependent on socioeconomic status of the students, the family support enjoyed by the students and the school environment experienced by the students. Hence, those schools where students have low scores on those independent variables are bound to suffer from lack of quality education. In some sense, this is quite intuitive to deduce that rich students who can afford high-cost private schools having good school environment and who get family support toward their academic activities (in the form of encouragement, financing private tuitions, etc.) will, in general, receive better quality of education.

As a consequence, the natural question we need to address is: how poor, underprivileged students, belonging to the bottom-tier schools (Fig. 8.4) can get quality education? We will now address this issue by using blended learning platform in bottom-tier schools.

### Analysis III: Impact of Blended Learning on Quality Educational Outcomes of Underprivileged School Children

Of the 33 schools that were examined in the "as is" study, quality of education scores of three schools were at the lowest (Fig. 8.4). These school students were chosen for the quasi experimental study to observe the effect of blended learning interventions for a period of 90 days. These three schools were also having very low scores in the independent variables of socioeconomic backgrounds, family support, and school environment.

A controlled intervention of online live teaching by quality teachers using quality content and onsite teaching assistant or class coordinator (as explained in Sect. 8.2) was administered on the students for 90 days. After the end of the study, after-study assessments and observations were made to evaluate any change in Well-being and Learning Achievements of those children.

The first study was conducted in a rural school of Burdwan District of West Bengal, India, run by an NGO (School-id: 31). The children participating in the intervention are from class III, aged 8–10 years, hailed from extremely lower socioeconomic backgrounds. Through our blended learning intervention, 29 students have been taught English and Mathematics by an experienced teacher through the online blended learning platform for a period of 90 days.

The second study was conducted in a low-cost private rural school in South 24 Parganas district of West Bengal, India (School-id: 32). The children are from class III, aged 8–10 years and are from lower socioeconomic families. Through the blended learning initiative, 35 students were taught English, Mathematics by two experienced teachers remotely for a period of 90 days.

The third study was conducted in an NGO funded school in the outskirts of Kolkata for the orphan children (School-id: 33). The children hailed from class 1, aged 6–8 years and supported by NGO. Through the online remote teaching initiative, 15 students were taught English, Mathematics by two experienced teachers remotely for a period of 90 days. For the purpose of analysis, we have aggregated the students of all three schools. The descriptive statistical profile is given below in Table 8.1.

Thus, the after-study conducted on the students hailing from these three schools revealed that the students were gradually improving in their overall Quality score (well-being score and learning achievement score). This is depicted in Fig. 8.6.

To ascertain the actual improvement, a paired T-Test was administered on the dependent variables. Paired t-test is used to check statistical significance of the outcomes of a research on the same group or population before and after the research. A paired-sample t-test was conducted on the *Learning Achievement scores* of all the students in these three schools before and after the intervention. There was a significant difference in the scores of pre-intervention study ($M = 27.906$, SD $= 12.185$) and post-intervention study ($M = 57.094$, SD $= 11.338$); $t = 21.239$, $p = 0.000$. There has been an increase of 104.5% of the pre-intervention study score from 27.906 to 57.094 (out of 100).

**Table 8.1** Descriptive statistical profile of selected underprivileged school children

| Variables | Mean score: before-study (in 5-point scale) | | Mean score: after study (in 5-point scale) |
|---|---|---|---|
| | All 228 students from all 33 schools | 79 underprivileged students from 3 bottom-most schools (before intervention) | 79 underprivileged students from 3 bottom-most schools (after intervention) |
| *Independent variables* | | | |
| Socioeconomic level | 3.59 | 1.96 | – |
| Family support | 4.26 | 1.78 | – |
| School environment | 3.35 | 1.88 | – |
| *Dependent variable* | | | |
| Well-being | 3.26 | 1.95 | 3.28 |
| Learning achievement | 3.27 | 1.40 | 2.85 |

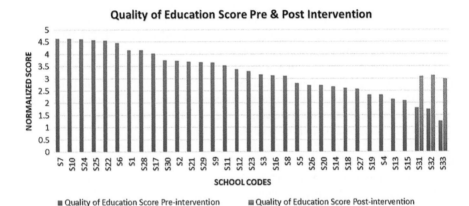

**Fig. 8.6** Improvement of quality score of bottom-most schools after intervention

To study the variations in the **Well-being score**, paired-samples t-test was conducted on well-being scores before and after the intervention. There was a significant difference in the scores pre study ($M = 1.9559$, SD = 0.25117) and post study ($M = 3.2840$, SD = 0.36290); $t = 23.904$, $p = 0.000$. There has been an increase of 67.90% of the Pre-study score from 1.95 to 3.28.

To study the variations in the component of Well-being score before and after interventions, paired-samples t-tests were conducted as shown in Table 8.2.

It is to be noted that students have perceived a remarkable change in *Teacher Support in School* with 84.97% improvement. It must be stated that the online remote elderly teachers created a very positive impact on the students, with their teaching methods and teaching attitudes. There has been a remarkable increase in the perceived student attitude toward *Teaching–Learning Material* (85.94% increase), indicating

**Table 8.2**  T-Tests on components of Well-being on 79 underprivileged students

| Component of well-being score | Mean score before intervention | Mean score after intervention | % increase in mean scores | T value | P value |
|---|---|---|---|---|---|
| Happiness in learning | 2.06 | 3.32 | 61.35 | 14.55 | 0.000 |
| Peer relations | 2.15 | 3.11 | 44.63 | 11.95 | 0.000 |
| Teacher support in school | 1.86 | 3.43 | 84.97 | 20.11 | 0.000 |
| Teaching–learning material | 1.76 | 3.28 | 85.94 | 18.30 | 0.000 |

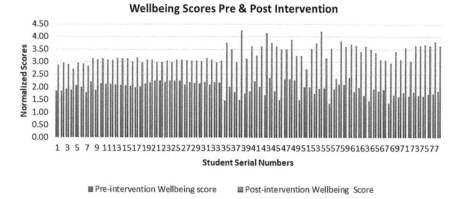

**Fig. 8.7**  Improvement of 79 students in Well-being after Intervention

that the students were extremely receptive to the lesson-wise audio-visual digital content. There has been mentionable increase in student perception of *Happiness in Learning* at 61.35%, indicating that the students perceive such a mode of learning both educational and enjoyable.

Finally, Figs. 8.7 and 8.8 shows the improvement on Well-being score and Learning Achievement score of all those 79 underprivileged students at an individual level. It is to be noted that the improvement is noticeable for each individual student in his/her Well-being and Learning Achievement scores. It must be also stated that there has been a stark improvement in Learning Achievements among the students, indicating a positive impact of our proposed blended learning platform.

### 8.3.4  Discussions

Our after-study has shown remarkable improvement both in academics and in well-being of the underprivileged students. The findings prove our hypothesis that online

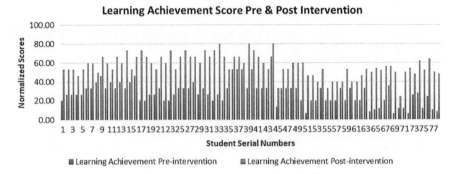

**Fig. 8.8**  Improvement of 79 students in learning achievement score after intervention

blended learning platforms in a classroom setting along with quality digital content, expert online remote teachers and on-site teaching assistants as class coordinator creates a learning environment that can improve learning outcomes and well-being of students drastically, irrespective of their socioeconomic status.

There are some common inferences that can be drawn from this small pilot study:

a.  Steady academic improvement and well-being have been observed due to provision of quality teacher and content, even if it is delivered virtually using online platform. Remote teachers were readily accepted by the students.
b.  Online teachers, with support from on-site classroom coordinator, were able to maintain discipline despite their physical absence and online presence.
c.  There were no dropouts and only 10% of absenteeism was noticed.
d.  The students expressed that they were made aware of a lot of new ideas and concepts that they did not know earlier.
e.  Students were able to express their ideas and opinions more clearly than before.
f.  General aspiration level of the children increased due to their exposure to different cultural perspective from online urban teachers. It enhances the bridging social capital of rural students, as they are now connected to urban teachers.

## 8.4   Conclusion

Since quality education is essentially an expensive service in India, millions of students remain outside the purview of quality education because of their low affordability power. As a result, majority of the underprivileged population of India are compelled to avail the low-quality affordable services provided by public or low-cost private schooling. Lack of necessary infrastructure along with lack of conducive learning environment coupled with a high rate of teacher absenteeism in these schools makes the education delivered ineffective. In this situation, the chapter has tried to create a benchmark of quality education that is measurable and also observable and tries to figure out a solution to improve quality of education in poor schools using online blended learning platform enabled by social technologies.

In the first part of the study, the research has inferred that quality education, as captured in two dependent variables (Well-being and Learning Achievement) is heavily dependent on socioeconomic status of the students, the family support enjoyed by the students and the school environment experienced by the students. Hence, an underprivileged rural school with low scores on these three independent variables would always produce poor learning outcomes and poor well-being scores for its students. In the second part of the study, a controlled intervention using the proposed online blended learning platform was conducted. The after-study reveals that our proposed platform can create measurable difference in the students' scores on well-being and learning outcomes. In other words, students who have low socioeconomic background, poor family support, and deplorable school environment can still have higher scores in well-being and learning outcomes, if they use proposed blended learning methods.

To conclude, this chapter deals with mitigating the access divide and capability divide of rural children using an online blended learning platform. Chapter 9 will deal with mitigating the opportunity divide by connecting the rural adult learners with the expert trainers and mentors from urban areas to improve their skills and competencies, enabling them to improve their market prospects. Chapter 9 will present pilot studies through creation of a collaborative learning environment using the online blended learning platform to witness enhancement of opportunity scopes in rural areas.

# References

Alward, M. (2005). *Friendship: An Important part of your child's development*. Retrieved from www.googobits.com.

ASER. (2014). ASER 2014: Annual Status of Education Report (New Delhi: ASER Centre). Retrieved from https://img.asercentre.org/docs/Publications/ASER%20Reports/ASER%202014/National%20PPTs/aser2014indiaenglish.pdf.

Atherton, P., & Kingdon, G. (2010). *The relative effectiveness and costs of contract and regular teachers in India. Institute of Education*, University of London. Available at: https://2010.economicsofeducation.com/user/pdfsesiones/036.pdf.

Blacksher, E. (2002). On being poor and feeling poor: Low socioeconomic status and the moral self. *Theoretical Medicine, 3*, 455–470.

British Council Report. (2016). *Blended learning, skill, scale at speed: An overview of blended learning in the UK and India, 2016*. Retrieved from https://www.britishcouncil.in/sites/default/files/blended_learning_vol_1_6_april.pdf..

Boyd. S., & Barwic, H. (2011). Wellbeing at school: building a safe and caring school climate that deters bullying. New Zealand Council for educational research. Retrieved from wellbeingatschool.org.nz/about-ws-tools.

Dhawan, A. (2014). *India School Education Vision 2030* [Central Square Foundation Report]. Retrieved from https://www.centralsquarefoundation.org/wp-content/uploads/2015/08/India-School-Education-Vision-2030.pdf.

Diamond, A. (2010). The evidence base for improving school outcomes by addressing the whole child and by addressing skills and attitudes, not just content. *Early Education and Development, 21*(5), 780–793.

Dreze, J. (2003). Patterns of Literacy and Their Social Context. *The Oxford India Companion of Sociology and Social Anthropology.* New Delhi: Oxford University Press.

Dreze, J., & Sen, A. (2013). *An uncertain glory: India and its contradictions.* Princeton University Press.

Fergusson, M. D., Horwood, J. L., & Boden, M. J. (2008). The transmission of social inequality: Examination of the linkages between family socioeconomic status in childhood and educational achievement in young adulthood. *Research in Social Stratification and Mobility, 26,* 277–295.

FICCI. (2014). *Private sector's contribution to K-12 education in India current impact, challenges and way forward.* Retrieved from https://Ficci.In/Spdocument/20385/Ey-Ficci-Report-Education.Pdf.

Frisco Report. (2013). *State of the schools: Frisco independent school district 2013–2014.* Retrieved from https://www.friscoisd.org/docs/default-source/district-publications/state-of-schools_2013-2014.pdf?sfvrsn=2.

Hamre, B. K., & Pianta, R. C. (2005). Can Instructional and emotional support in the first-grade classroom make a difference for children at risk of school failure? *Child Development, 76,* 949–967.

Hevner, A. R., March, S. T., Park, J., & Ram, S. (2004). Design science in information systems research. *MIS Quarterly, 28*(1), 75–105.

IANS. (2018). Retrieved from https://www.maeeshat.in/2018/04/absence-of-benchmarks-impacting-quality-of-education-in-government-schools/.

Kempner, D. E. (1993). The Pilot years: the growth of the Nacubo benchmarking project. *Nacubo Business Officer, 27*(6), 21–31.

Khajehpour, M. (2011). Relationship between emotional intelligence, parental involvement and academic performance of high school students. *Procedia Social and Behavioral Sciences, 15,* 1081–1086.

Kumar, A. K. S., & Rustagi, P. (2010). *elementary education in india: progress, setbacks, and challenges.* Oxfam India [Working Papers Series, OIWPS—III]. Retrieved from https://oxfamilibrary.openrepository.com/bitstream/handle/10546/346628/wp-elementary-education-India-challenges-280910-en.pdf?sequence=1&isAllowed=y.

Lani, J. (2010). *The Multidimensional Students Life Satisfaction Scale (MSLSS).* Retrieved from https://www.statisticssolutions.com/wp-content/uploads/kalins-pdf/singles/the-multidimensional-students-life-satisfaction-scale-mslss.pdf.

Mayer, D., & Ralph, J. (2008). Key indicators of school quality. In B. V. Brown (Ed.), *Key indicators of child and youth well-being: completing the picture* (pp. 279–305). Mahwah, NJ: Erlbaum.

MHRD. (2017). *Draft Learning Outcomes, MHRD, 2017.* Retrieved from https://mhrd.gov.in/sites/upload_files/mhrd/files/Learning_outcomes.pdf.

Mukhopadhyay, M. (2001). *Total quality management in education.* New Delhi: NIEPA Publication Unit.

Muralidharan, K. (2014). *Building an inclusive and high-performing school system.* Retrieved from https://www.Ideasforindia.In/Topics/Human-Development/Building-An-Inclusive-And-High-Performing-School-System.Html

Nandwana, S., & Asawa, N. (2011). *Manual for Parental Support Scale.* National Psychological Corporation.

NPE. (1986). *The national policy on education department of education ministry of human resource development.* New Delhi: Government of India.

Ohara, Y. (2012). Examining the legitimacy of unrecognised low-fee private schools in India: comparing different perspectives. *Compare: A Journal of Comparative and International Education, 42*(1), 69–90. https://doi.org/10.1080/03057925.2011.632537.

PERC. (2014). Blended learning: defining models and examining conditions to support implementation. *Philadelphia Education Research Consortium (PERC). Retrieved from* https://willia mpennfoundation.org/sites/default/files/reports/Blended-Learning-PERC-Research-Brief-Sep tember-2014.pdf.

Sankar, D. (2009). *Teachers' time on task and nature of tasks: evidence from three Indian States.* South Asia Region, World Bank, Washington, DC: Human Development Department.

Sarangapani, P. (2009). Quality, feasibility and desirability of low-cost private schooling. *Economic and Political Weekly, 44*(43), 67–69.

Scoffham, S., & Jonathan, B. (2011). Happiness matters: towards a pedagogy of happiness and well-being. *The Curriculum Journal, 22*(4). Taylor and Francis.

Sein, M. K., Henfridsson, O., Purao, S., & Rossi, M. (2011). Action design research. *MIS Quarterly, 35*(1), 37–56.

Singh, T., Sharma, S., & Nagesh, S. (2017). Socio-economic Status Scales updated for 2017. *International Journal of Research in Medical Sciences, 5,* 3264–3267.

Stephens, D. (2003). *Quality of Basic Education. Background paper prepared for the Education for All* [Global Monitoring Report 2003/4]. Retrieved from https://pdfs.semanticscholar.org/73e7/ 9e261f5dbcf718d376546ee0fb1d684b4be0.pdf.

Student Learning and Wellbeing Framework. (2018). *State Of Queensland (Department Of Education).* Retrieved from https://education.qld.gov.au/schools/healthy/docs/student-learning-wellbe ing-framework.pdf

Tafani, V. (2003). *Language teaching and learning methodology.* Tirana: SHBLU.

UNICEF. (2016). *Quality of education and child-friendly schooling.* Retrieved from https://www. unicef.org/education/bege_61667.htm.

# Chapter 9
# Online Blended Learning Platform for Rural Adult Learners

## Bridging the Opportunity Divide Through Community Formation

## 9.1 Introduction

In India, disparities in education and training can be best understood by studying the extant divides across rural and urban spaces. This has been explicitly studied and discussed toward the beginning of Part III of this book. However, one cannot restrict oneself by just focusing on disadvantages along geographical separations alone; it becomes necessary to explore education divide across three dimensions mentioned earlier in Chap. 7 (Sect. 7.2): access divide, capability divide, and opportunity divide. We have attempted toward bridging access divide and capability divide among learners in the previous chapter using online blended learning platform (Chap. 8) and demonstrated its effectiveness through pilot studies.

This chapter will now explore attempts toward bridging opportunity divide, in addition to access and capability divide that exists between rural and urban population of India. The *opportunity divide* is created between the ones in possession of relevant knowledge and skills needed to improve market performance, and the ones devoid of those relevant knowledge and skills, thereby having poor market performance. The attempt is therefore to enhance rural opportunity scopes by connecting rural adults to the larger available opportunity structure through the online blended learning platform, connecting them with expert trainers and advisors from urban areas. We will present pilot studies where we try to connect rural adults from some villages in West Bengal, India with urban experts, mentors, classroom coordinators, and other agencies through the blended learning platform, enhancing their opportunity scopes.

As mentioned in Chap. 7, there is a large proportion of unorganized laborers working as artisans and craftsperson who stay in the rural fringes. These rural workers are faced with several limitations with regard to sustenance of their life and livelihood in particular rural location. These limitations can be summarized as: (i) limited access to quality raw materials and tools required to compete in global markets (Scrase 2003); (ii) lack of awareness about the wants of people beyond their local markets (Nagori and Saxena 2012); (iii) their limited abilities to satiate the needs of global customers (Shah et al. 2017); and, (iv) their limited access to non-local markets

© The Author(s), under exclusive license to Springer Nature Singapore Pte Ltd. 2021
S. Bandyopadhyay et al., *Bridging the Education Divide Using Social Technologies*,
https://doi.org/10.1007/978-981-33-6738-8_9

(Nagori and Saxena 2012). These limitations are reflections of the extant opportunity divide present between urban and rural locales of India wherein the rural adults are unable to access the larger opportunity scope beyond their locality, whereas their urban counterparts are able to exploit urban opportunity structure within and outside their urban localities more easily (Philip and Williams 2019).

Rural adults have been facing problems with regard to connecting with the larger metropolitan area opportunity structure. These marginalized rural communities face problems such as (i) limitations in access to quality training and advisory assistances, (ii) lack of awareness regarding available local opportunities, (iii) lack of access to the market such as links with buyers, sellers, micro-credits, etc., and (iv) least amount of access to any discussion forum or any support agencies to share personal problems (Bhattacharyya et al. 2020).

The problems related to opportunity divide in rural India have been discussed in details in Chap. 7 (Sect. 7.2.3). These opportunity related problems faced by the rural adults spell out the urgency to upgrade their skills, knowledge, and information capability (capability to use the available information and knowledge: Bhattacharyya et al. 2020) with regard to the changing demands of the global market. In this context, through the online blended learning platform, our pilot studies aspire to disseminate essential lifelong learning skills and practices among all rural adults to explore better chances of employability at any age. Thus, in these pilot studies, we have been trying to connect expert trainers, market experts from urban areas with the rural adults through the digital blended learning platform. Moreover, these rural adults having poor knowledge with regard to usage of smartphone and access to Internet are further trained so that they can get connected to the cyber-world and exploit the potential of online collaborative learning environment in the rural set up.

This chapter has been divided into four sections. Section 9.2 explores creation of collaborative learning space by cultivating communities of practice (Basak et al. 2017) in order to enhance the potentials of rural adults. In this section, we first define communities of practice and then explicate its necessity in creating a collaborative learning space in rural locales. In this context, we aim to cultivate virtual communities of practice through online blended learning platform so that the rural adults with common goals and interest can interact with each other and with those outside their communities to get exposed to larger opportunity structure.

Section 9.3 presents the practical application of cultivating communities of practice through the proposed collaborative learning framework. In this section, we discuss empirical evidences of disseminating competency-based training in a pilot scale to a group of rural adults from three villages of West Bengal, India by connecting them with expert trainers and mentors, both using our online blended learning platform and also by connecting them informally using WhatsApp messaging, enabling creation of online communities of practice. Moreover, this section also presents experiential evidences from the rural adults with regard to their training and learning.

Section 9.4 presents evidences of experiences shared by a group of rural women in a particular village of West Bengal, who were trained to upgrade their skills through the online blended learning platform. These women were engaged in making handmade fashion products and needed to upgrade their fashion design skills and the skills of stitching and tailoring to exploit non-local market opportunities and thereby improve the marketability of their products. In this context, through building communities of practice facilitated by collaborative learning in the form of both formal and informal training processes, these women could nurture their skills and exploit their own potentials. This section ends by explicating the impact of these training in their lives. Section 9.5 concludes this chapter with summary of our findings and with a way forward.

## 9.2  Communities of Practice in Facilitating Collaborative Learning

This section will explore mechanisms of collaborative learning and training within a particular rural community utilizing the potentials of online blended learning platform. The aim is to enhance the basic competencies and skills among the rural adults so that they can successfully exploit available local and non-local opportunities all by themselves.

In order to harness the capabilities of the rural mass, collaborative learning acts as a potential driver. This particular form of learning can help the disadvantaged rural mass with improved levels of awareness and current practices. This collective learning result in practices, which is the property of a kind of community, created over time by the sustained pursuit of shared enterprise. Wenger (1997) calls this as *community of practice*. He defines communities of practice (CoP) as "groups of people who share a concern or a passion for something they do and who interacts regularly to learn how to do it better" (Wenger 1997). Communities of practice can be created and cultivated to attain certain amount of field related knowledge. Moreover, it can evolve naturally owing to members' common interest in a specific domain (Wenger et al. 2002; Basak et al. 2017). In this section, we explore how cultivating communities of practice among the rural adults can create and strengthen the knowledge and information network of the marginalized rural sector. This updated knowledge network can be further exploited by the rural adults to create better opportunities for themselves. Proper functioning of communities of practice in a rural context depends on mutual engagement among not only rural participants but also external mentors/trainers/entrepreneurs/govt. agencies, creating and enhancing bonding and bridging social capital among or between actors.

In our context, the social technology-enabled blended learning platform aims to nurture communities of practice where the rural adults will have a social presence, communicating with expert mentors/trainers and other agencies. Each rural adult in a particular rural community sharing common goals will collaborate with one another and also the external agents to ultimately prosper respective and collective opportunity scopes.

Apart from exploiting opportunity scopes collectively, the attempt is also to enable democratic knowledge and information exchange wherein the rural community members are able to share their indigenous knowledge with their urban counterparts and in exchange acquire appropriate knowledge and information from urban experts and trainers. This creates an environment of collective knowledge and information exchange through collaborative connections among rural and urban actors having common goal. In this context, the technical functionalities of the online learning platform such as discussion forums, expert connect and the community formation through WhatsApp messaging or similar tools (as discussed in Chap. 8) are extensively explored and utilized to perform the above-mentioned activities. In this manner, we attempt to transform physical communities of practice to that of virtual communities of practice facilitated by online collaborative learning. The cultivation of these online communities of practice has been facilitated in terms of both synchronous (live online interactions, e.g., video-conferencing) and asynchronous (offline interactions, e.g., Instant messaging and discussion forums) mode of training and skill development processes that are embedded within the online learning platform.

Active participation of rural population in the process of knowledge exchange, not only within their own communities but also with other communities including urban entities, enables them to apply newly acquired knowledge in pursuit of self and communitarian benefit. This online blended learning environment thus aims at addressing the problems faced by the rural adults in terms of exploiting appropriate opportunities within and outside their local environment. Thus, the focus is not only on increasing access to trainings or improving capability through upgradation of skills among the rural adults; bridging opportunity divide to improve their socioeconomic status also features to be one of the primary objective of undertaken initiative.

The subsequent sections will now present pilot studies wherein we propose to establish online communities of practices with rural adults and urban expert trainers in collaboration with other biotic entities of the education ecosystem. We will categorize these interventions into two sections with respect to two separate rural communities: the first one focuses on competency building and the second one focuses on skill building, both using our online blended learning platform.

## 9.3  Cultivating Communities of Practice for Competency-Building Among Rural Adults

### 9.3.1  Online Collaborative Learning Among the Rural Adults

Pilot studies were conducted with three small groups of rural artisans from three villages from Bardhaman and Birbhum districts of West Bengal, India. These rural adults had common goal of enhancing own competencies in Spoken English and Digital Literacy for ultimately enhancing access to larger opportunities. These rural adults were trained in a digital classroom setting using the proposed online blended learning platform with out-of-classroom communication with experts, research group members, and classroom coordinators. The out-of-classroom communications were facilitated through WhatsApp communication on the adult learners' smartphones. Self-directed learning was also fostered by sharing educational videos via WhatsApp communication.

Training sessions were conducted in a common place such as local community halls or club houses within the villages where rural adults came to take the online trainings from urban expert trainers under our supervision. Each of these online training sessions was coordinated by classroom coordinator at the training centers. Apart from this "fixed time connect" with the urban expert trainers, the rural adults could also connect with them anytime through their smartphones or smartphone of class-coordinator using WhatsApp.

Most rural artisans from these villages practiced particular indigenous art forms and engaged in making handmade products suited for home décor, fashion garments, or jewelleries. Some other artisans were rural theatre practitioners. Rest of the women in these villages were just skilled artisans in basic tailoring and stitching, making bags, baskets, garments, etc. However, these artisans lacked direct market linkages outside their local markets and had to depend on middlemen to access urban markets. Their desire to be self-dependent, to interact with customers and other agents outside their regions and to explore other opportunities for themselves motivated them to learn Spoken English and the use of digital technologies.

Communities of Practice were cultivated and manifested through involvement of the rural adult learners both during the training sessions and after the completion of each session. We would now elaborate on the characteristic of this collaborative learning space created to disseminate the competency-based trainings among the rural artisans.

*Group Participation and Peer-to-Peer Learning*: During Spoken English training sessions, the online expert trainers with the help from classroom coordinators divided the participants into two groups where one group played the role of a rural producer and the other group as consumer. They were asked to initiate conversations in English keeping in mind the situation where a consumer is visiting the producer in his shop for the first time and is inquiring about his displayed products. The participants used simple English words in initiating such conversations. Despite their continuous use of incorrect English sentences, the online trainers encouraged participants to continue conversing in English with their fellow mates. The assignments included explaining the process of making certain product, experience of communicating with consumers, etc. The expert trainers occasionally asked the students to record their English conversations and send it to the teacher for evaluation through WhatsApp. Study materials, important audio conversations were also shared with the participants using WhatsApp. Group participation or peer-to-peer interactions were found to be the most effective forms of learning as it promoted continuous discussions, brainstorming of ideas and a sense of responsibility to learn among the participants. Most of the learning in these sessions focused on the collaborative component of learning where each participant interacted with other participants during the learning process.

**Fig. 9.1** Classroom coordinators conducting group sessions

Figure 9.1. shows evidence of group sessions conducted by classroom coordinators after completion of online sessions.

*Enhancing One's Existing Knowledge*: In the digital literacy sessions, the online expert trainer guided the rural artisans with the process of browsing various websites to gather information on specific art and craft. Both the online trainer and classroom coordinator assisted the participants to search for information using Google where they found out various innovative ways to create and exhibit their indigenous art and craft. The participants learnt to use Skypes/WhatsApp to connect with people located in different geographical locations. Through these video-conferencing tools, the participants would be able to connect with customers or interested individuals with whom they can exchange their creations. During the learning process, they collaborated with one another when in doubt.

*Using Real-life Examples in Trainings*: In a village of West Bengal, most participants didn't know how to speak in English. Through online and offline interventions, these artists were asked to talk in English about their life, their experiences, about their desires, etc. Through real-life examples and role playing, the rural artisans were encouraged to communicate in the language. Even after the conclusion of each sessions, rural adults had to sit in groups with the class-coordinator and talk with each other, sharing their thoughts, their problems with each other in English. Moreover, these conversations were continued over Whatsapp to observe continuity in learning.

*Using Audio-Visual Content*: Online trainers showed videos on art and crafts to enrich the participants' artistic skills. The rural artisans, having no prior experience of having access to such educational videos, are now aware of techniques that were previously unknown to them.

### 9.3.2   Impact Analysis

We have administered pilot training sessions on the online blended learning platform in three villages of West Bengal, where experienced trainers taught the artisans Spoken English for 40 h and Digital Literacy for 20 h online. These sessions were primarily conducted by the online expert trainers and assisted by para-teachers or class-coordinators, thus combining both online and offline components within the training. The offline (face-to-face tutorials/hands-on) component was 80 h for Spoken English and 40 h for Digital Literacy. Based on the level of English and Digital Literacy competencies among the participants in the three villages and their needs, the course structure was designed. Before the beginning of the sessions, a baseline study was conducted to assess the level of competencies among the artisans. Further we conducted two studies: midline and end-line studies to evaluate any growth or development in competencies among the adult participants. All the tests were conducted out of 100 marks to assess their learning performance.

Figure 9.2 shows the pattern of change in the Spoken English training outcome among 17 rural artisans. We try to compare scores of each artisans from baseline study to end-line study. As shown in Fig. 9.2, there has been stark improvement in level of English competencies among the rural artisans. However, as expected, the degree of improvement depends on (i) their baseline status, and (ii) their ability to learn. From the test scores, we can observe improvement in their speaking abilities. After completion of the course, most artisans were able to express themselves and their work in broken English and understand simple stories in simple English.

Figure 9.3 shows the growth pattern in digital literacy training outcomes among the rural artisans. This particular course focused on creating digitally matured citizens wherein the artisans were trained in using a computer, use and exploration of Internet and the use of social media platforms through smartphones. By comparing scores in baseline, midline, and end-line studies, we are able to say that all of the rural artisans now know the computer basics and are able to operate Internet-enabled smartphones (to large extent) for their own benefits. They are now able to explore regional contents of updated designs, products, and several other information from the web for improving individual opportunity scopes.

After completion of the trainings using the online learning platform, some interviews were conducted on the adult learners to understand the impact of these sessions

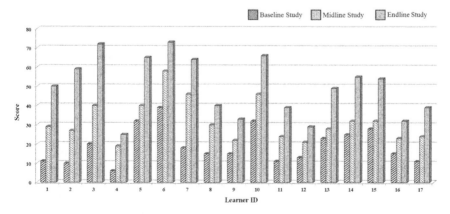

**Fig. 9.2** Improvement in scoring patterns for *spoken english* among rural artisans

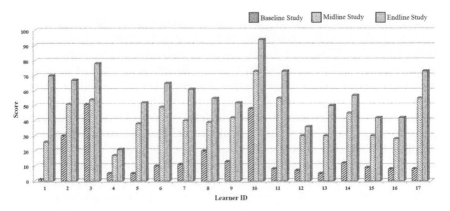

**Fig. 9.3** Improvement in scoring patterns for *digital literacy* among rural artisans

in their lives. This impact study was conducted three months after the completion of the online training with the purpose of evaluating any change or improvement in the lives of the participants. Based on the experiential data collected from the rural adults, the following themes can be derived:

*Capability Enhancement*: As mentioned in the beginning of the chapter, lack of capabilities hinder the rural adults or rural producers to exploit appropriate opportunity scopes. Building competencies can be identified as the first step toward bridging the capability divide among the rural mass. Speaking and communicating in English has become a mandate and necessity for the rural artisans of West Bengal. This is because of the increase in visits of customers outside West Bengal including foreign customers to the villages (as a part of different *village tourism* initiatives) for the purpose of purchasing indigenous handmade products. As a result, the rural artisans need to speak and communicate with them in English. After the three months of blended training of English, these artisans are now able to understand basic conversations in English. Though their English pronunciations and grammar entailed lot of faults, the artisans could express their thoughts in English.

Along with English competencies, it is now a necessity to be digitally competent. The information separation existing between rural and urban locales can be easily bridged if the rural producers becomes capable enough to explore resources on the Internet or to communicate with others using digital tools. Digital literacy is thus vital in the quest to exploit appropriate opportunity scopes. Before initiation of the intervention, the rural artisans unanimously confirmed the need to exploit resources in forms of material and information resources for enhancement of their businesses. Despite presence of Internet-enabled smartphones, the rural adults were unable to exploit the appropriate cyber resources owing to their ignorance in the usage of Internet and lack of understanding about the available digital content. The training sessions helped rural adult learners in self-exploring the information that are available over Internet. As a result, the rural artisans can now explore the world beyond territorial boundaries. Figure 9.4 shows where the rural artisans are trying to explore

**Fig. 9.4**  Rural artisans trying to learn the use of digital technology

the uses of computer by themselves after getting training from the online trainers. Some of the artisans said that they have learnt how to update their art forms in order to increase possibilities of market linkage through explorations over the Internet. They now use WhatsApp for sharing videos or images of their products with potential buyers. Some of them have also confirmed that they are now able to use Internet for financial transactions.

*Enhanced Level of Confidence*: As mentioned in Chap. 7, one of the disadvantages in rural areas is the lack of awareness and motivation among the rural adults regarding the benefits of training, learning and the need to enhance or update knowledge as per the changing demands of the society. Keeping this in mind, the online training sessions focused not only on enhancing ones knowledge in English or Digital Literacy but also to motivate rural adults to enhance or widen one's spectrum of "knowing." This has helped to enhance their level of confidence.

*Promoting a Collaborative and Effective Learning Environment by Fostering Peer-to-Peer Learning*: These blended learning sessions have successfully created communities of practices. Earlier the rural adults rarely met members of their own or across communities to discuss work or future prospects together. Now they interact and communicate more frequently with each other, both face-to-face and through WhatsApp, and discuss studies, practice conversations and push each other to strive for more. Moreover, the informal mode of communication through WhatsApp has created an environment that nurtures collaboration, personalization, and informalization. The expert trainers and classroom coordinators keep on updating the rural artisans with information and resources that might be useful for them. In that context, one of the artisans said "Videos sent through WhatsApp on relevant topics have helped me in revising the lessons taught in class." Thus the learning and training environment is no longer restricted within training hours or within the study centers. One of the rural artisans while sharing his experience of such a unique learning environment said "In WhatsApp, we the students also discuss our doubts and queries, which eases the process of learning." In this context, one of the women participants said "Now, that I can communicate with my trainers through WhatsApp, I find out time in between household chores to work on my English." To facilitate peer-to-peer learning, regular

WhatsApp communications between the rural artisans, expert trainers from urban areas, and classroom coordinators were done, where they attempted in exchanging their thoughts and doubts with each other.

### 9.3.3  Discussions

From time immemorial the Indian rural artisans or producers or the rural adults faced problems pertaining to scarce resources. These resources can be both material and informational. Despite several attempts to increase access to such resources in rural areas, very little progress has been achieved in the domain. In that context, our research group in collaboration with several governmental or non-governmental agencies has demonstrated a pathway in enhancing capabilities of the rural adults through social technology-driven digital interventions. English and digital competencies can be achieved only through continuous, collaborative, informal, and personalized attempts among the rural adults. In this context, a collaborative learning environment becomes important where all rural learners irrespective of their age or gender can participate in a free-flowing process of training and learning. However, the rural disadvantages often hinder these adult learners to participate in training or capacity building programs. In that context, the proposed online blended learning and training platform becomes crucial wherein the digital platform provider, classroom coordinators, online expert trainers, and other local agencies together play collective roles in mobilizing and motivating rural adults to enhance own knowledge and participate in the process of learning.

## 9.4  Cultivating Communities of Practice for Skill-Building Among Rural Women

This section will present evidences of using the proposed blended learning platform for imparting training to rural women by expert trainers, focusing on enhancing the skills of those women so that they can further utilize the same to exploit collective opportunity scopes. In doing so, we cultivate communities of practice through online collaborative learning and training facilitated by our online blended learning platform that engages online expert trainers, classroom coordinators, NGOs, and other local agencies for its operationalization.

This group of women, having basic knowledge of tailoring and stitching, were engaged in making handmade products that include garments, soft toys, fabric painting on clothes, etc., and were interested to earn their own living by exploiting and further updating this particular skill set. Urban expert trainers with experiences in fashion design and fashion marketing trained these women through the online learning platform. The training also includes digital literacy training, especially the use of smartphones. The trainings were provided using both the web-based learning platform and WhatsApp, where the focus was on upgradation of skills on stitching, tailoring, and product designs so that there is a possibility of urban market linkage. The purpose of such an initiative was thus to enhance their existing skills and create sustainable market opportunities through online trainings.

A group of fifty women possessing basic stitching skills participated in the training programs by urban experts through the online blended learning platform. Moreover, the trainings were not only conducted through synchronous mode using the online learning platform, but also through informal communications outside classrooms through WhatsApp in their smartphones. However, most of these rural women do not have access to internet-enabled smartphones. As a result, our research group collaborated with a private organization and disbursed fifty low-cost smartphones with Internet connections to the rural women for the purpose of regularly connecting them with experts from the city who may help them with information regarding better resources, urban marketing strategies, and market-oriented presentation of one's product. After completion of trainings, these women were interviewed where they shared their experiences of training, impact of trainings and how they are utilizing trainings for own benefit.

### 9.4.1 Facilitating Online Collaborative Learning Among Rural Artisans

Aiming toward creating connected learning environment in disadvantaged rural locales of India, this pilot study intended to cultivate virtual communities of practice among the rural women in a village of West Bengal. As already mentioned, the women selected for this study shared similar kinds of expertise in stitching, tailoring and producing garments, soft toys, fabric paining, etc., to sell in local market. Moreover, these women share the common goal of becoming self-sufficient and be able to connect with the urban markets with their handmade products. We will now briefly elaborate the training sessions that helped to cultivate communities of practice among these rural women:

***Online Expert Connect***: Expert trainers with extensive experiences in product making, fashion design, and fashion marketing were connected with those rural women selected for training through the online blended learning platform in a digital classroom setting. In collaboration with content developers and the available content resources in the cyber space, the expert trainers first designed a customized course structure for those rural women. Through these trainings, the women were trained to make designer blouses, handmade bags, home furnishing goods (embroidered bed-covers, pillow covers, curtains, table-cloths, etc.), handmade ear-rings, etc. Expert trainers often shared images of marketable fashion products to create a market-sense among the rural participants. Through continuous hand-holding by classroom coordinators along with online expert trainers, these rural women started to learn

**Fig. 9.5**  Rural women getting online training

not only new and marketable designs but also digital methods for enhancing urban market linkages (e.g., use of WhatsApp and Facebook for product advertisement). Figure 9.5 shows a group of rural women taking training from urban experts from the online learning platform.

*Community Connect Through WhatsApp*: We attempted at cultivating virtual communities of practice through the use of digital platforms (e.g., WhatsApp). Our pilot study utilized WhatsApp to encourage successful virtual exchanges among our research group, rural target group, class-coordinators, and urban professional experts. In addition to online synchronous training, supplementary digital content (mostly in the form of videos) were sent to the rural women through WhatsApp. Following these training videos, the women started learning new design ideas by themselves. Another important component of these WhatsApp exchange is community cohesion and possibility of improving one's social capital. Through continuous communication with the urban entities the bridging social capital of the rural women were enhanced, while communication with other members of the SHG fostered their bonding social capital. Figure 9.6 shows evidences of regular WhatsApp exchanges between the rural women, expert trainers, and classroom coordinators where the rural women have posted the pictures of their created products. The urban experts review these products and give them suggestions.

*Market Linkages Through WhatsApp*: Along with trainings on developing one's existing skills online, the rural adult learners were also given some instances of market connect by their expert trainers from urban areas. These expert trainers have often tried to connect rural artisans with real consumers who might be interested in purchasing their products. WhatsApp was used to exchange messages with regard to order placement, order procurement, logistics, and financial transaction details between the rural producer and urban consumers. Figure 9.7 shows the evidence of an urban customer placing an order of a t-shirt with customized design. The WhatsApp messages show the evidence of customization of design on t-shirt, order

**Fig. 9.6** Rural women interacting with urban experts using WhatsApp in local language

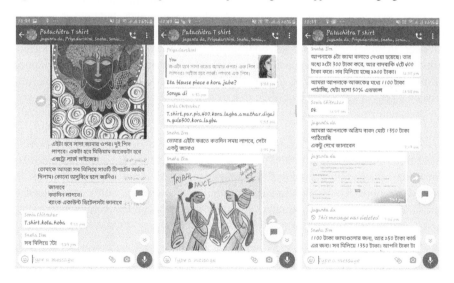

**Fig. 9.7** Market linkage using WhatsApp in local language

**Fig. 9.8**   Rural women taking garment trainings online and their created products

finalization and financial transaction, thereby completing the full transaction cycle. Based on orders, WhatsApp groups were created that were facilitated by the urban expert trainer, para-teacher, and the social entrepreneur. Their role was to guide the rural artisan with the procurement of resources and financial advices.

*Peer-to-Peer Learning*: In the proposed blended learning environment, learning not only happens through online interactions but also through offline/physical interactions with peer group as well as class coordinator. After online training sessions, the classroom coordinators helped them procure raw materials and deliver products to urban market. Figure 9.8 shows groups of rural women working on their individual products in presence of classroom coordinators. These women are collaborating and consulting with each other, facilitating peer-to-peer learning. These are evidence of collaborative creation. The figure also shows evidence of the products that they created after being trained by online trainer and assisted by classroom coordinator. These trainings in blended mode with rural women play important role in establishing the fact that only providing training is not enough, showing the possibility of market linkage is crucial. The purpose of the above-mentioned initiatives of training and market linkage is not limited to marketing or selling the products produced by the women, rather on exposing the women to the wide array of opportunities all around the globe. The market linkage possibilities presented are only examples that these women or other rural women can explore using social technologies under the constant and contextual guidance of instructors and class-coordinators.

### 9.4.2   Impact Analysis

After the completion of the intervention, the rural women were interviewed in detail with regard to their feelings after getting trained through the online platform and also getting connected through WhatsApp. From the interviews certain themes have been explored which are discussed below:

*Enabling Digital Literacy*: Digital literacy enables the rural mass to explore options that are not locally bounded. The rural–urban education, knowledge, and information divide can be diminished by bridging the digital divide that exists between rural and urban actors. The rural women artisans, despite having commendable skills on making handmade products, were limited within their territorial boundaries. They had to depend blindly on the middlemen to sell their products in urban market. This issue has already been discussed under *opportunity divide* (Sect. 7.2.3). As a result, their knowledge and information was limited within the locality. Access to Internet through their smartphones at the time of the trainings helped those women to explore varied options beyond their local context. "I have learned how to weave and stitch bags of different colors and designs by watching YouTube video tutorials," said one of the women who felt greatly benefited from the videos that were shared by the expert trainers. She even explored certain colors which were not so commonly used by rural customers in her local community, but was extensively used in the urban market. This helped her understand the urban market demands. All of them confirmed that the YouTube videos and images they retrieved from online sources have played important roles in assisting them in their regular work. Many of them regularly updated their stitching skills by referring to various training videos on YouTube, shared by online trainers. These training videos shared through WhatsApp groups were regularly watched by those women. In this context, another woman said "Apart from receiving tailoring training, online learning has bought me more close to digital technologies. Now I can use Internet to keep myself updated with latest fashion trends and designer dresses." This form of digital exposure has forced the rural women to explore the cyber-world with their smartphones and find out ways to connect with people, ideas, and resources.

*Fostering Entrepreneurship and Economic Independence*: The skill building trainings and the self-directed learning using the online platform has been successful in cultivating entrepreneurial acumen within the rural women. The rigorous skill trainings to make marketable products have encouraged the women participants to expand their own businesses beyond local boundaries. Majority of our respondents recorded getting more orders after displaying the products that they have learned from the online trainings. "I have learned blouse cutting and designing techniques and is now able to earn more by selling my products," said one woman artisan. The online trainings focused on creating market based products such as making designer blouses, costume jewelries and various other products that have demands in the urban market. With the help of online urban trainers and WhatsApp messaging, some of those artisans were able to showcase their products directly before urban consumers. As a result, customers beyond their localities have started placing orders of such products. This has resulted in expanding their businesses. Engagement in household activities during the day has restricted physical mobility of those women. As a result, it is not possible for them to set up physical businesses outside their locality. Therefore, online training and online market linkages using social media platforms would help them to expand their market beyond their local community.

*Increasing Social Capital*: Social capital is the network of social relations that may provide individuals and groups with access to resources and supports (Policy Research Initiative 2005). In this intervention, social capital has been enhanced using WhatsApp as a supportive and enabling tool of communication. The online sessions conducted by expert trainers have witnessed multiple situations when the women participants have interacted with one another on the lesson learnt from the online trainer. One of the respondents have mentioned in her interview that even after the closure of the online trainings, they continue to interact with each other and also with the online trainers on related issues. She said, "I along with other women in our locality used to take these trainings together and whenever I was unable to understand anything, other fellow trainees would assist me and thus with mutual cooperation everybody learnt." WhatsApp groups and the offline meetings have brought those women together who were not well acquainted with each other before. These collaborative activities have been successful in improving bridging and bonding social capital among those women.

*Recognition from Outside Their Own Locality*: The online expert trainers often helped some of these women to get orders on a specific product with a particular design. These orders were then purchased by the urban buyers who also gave further orders. This has ignited within the women a sense of self-confidence. Earlier their products were confined to the local market. Now with skill upgradation and market exposure, these women are successfully executing orders outside their own localities.

### 9.4.3  Discussions

Women in rural parts of India are experiencing double marginalization wherein on one hand they feel neglected owing to being located in the remote rural areas of the country and away from the global opportunity structure. On the other hand, being women, they are confined within the walls of their houses and have restricted roles in life. In spite of having interest and basic capabilities to earn their own living, most rural women are unable to exploit available opportunities (Kapur 2019). Their male counterparts at home have at least the option to explore opportunities that are outside their particular rural locale. In that context, the proposed online blended learning framework, where a digital platform is at the core, helps rural women to get benefited without physically moving out of their locality. This online platform not only provides them the necessary awareness about the external world but also help them to upgrade their skills to improve their socioeconomic condition. Enhancement of one's social capital through communities of practice in a collaborative learning environment has made the rural women aware of their peers and mentors within and outside their particular rural locale. This has fostered sense of collaborative spirit among the rural women who at the end of the training sessions showed great interest in setting their own virtual shops on social media. Through digital literacy training within the skill development course, the women learned how to use the Internet for their own benefit. They were exposed to upgraded or updated designs, sources of quality raw materials and also digital channels through which they can sell their products to the global market. This demonstrates the effectiveness of online blended learning platform in bridging the opportunity divide prevalent among rural women.

## 9.5  Conclusion

We have indicated earlier that, *education divide* exists not just due to lack of *access* to education but also as a result of improper ways toward disseminating education, which is ineffective in nurturing the *capability* of learners to translate knowledge acquired in pursuit of enhancing *opportunity* scopes. In Chap. 8, we have explored ways to bridge the access divide and capability divide that exist among rural school students by introducing an online blended learning platform that connects rural learners with experienced teachers from urban areas. The present chapter tries to bridge the opportunity divide along with access and capability divides that exists among rural adult learners. We have executed pilot studies to demonstrate how the online blended learning platform can connect the rural adult learners to the larger opportunity structure through the formation of virtual communities of practice.

However, it is to be noted that, this blended learning platform was initially implemented in a pilot scale in three underprivileged schools (in Chap. 8) of West Bengal for a small period of time. Further, it was implemented in a pilot scale to conduct training sessions on skill and competency building among rural adult learners in study centers in three more villages of West Bengal for a similar time-period. Hence, despite the demonstration of positive outcomes of the blended learning platform in mitigating access, capability, and opportunity divide in a pilot scale, issue of sustainability and scaling up of such framework cannot be concluded from this study. From an ecosystemic perspective, these pilot studies, for a short period of time, has only taken into consideration the interaction between biotic and abiotic entities and did not have a scope to experience and analyze the contextual impact of four external influencers (i.e., social, economic, political, and socio-psychological) on a long-term basis. So, further investigations would be needed to understand, whether the positive impact of this blended learning platform is sustainable and scalable.

To do that, we have created a social entrepreneurial venture, NexConnect, which is a start-up venture of our research group. NexConnect has taken initiative to implement this blended learning model in several Indian rural areas in collaboration with several local NGOs and government agencies. This model has been implemented through several rural Internet kiosks which we call as the Internet schools or study centers.

In the next chapter, we will elaborate the scaling up and implementation experience of the proposed social technology-enabled blended learning platform, as initiated by NexConnect, in several remote rural areas where there is dearth of quality learning and training. We will discuss the deployment plans and implementation challenges of the platform wherein the biotic and abiotic components of the education ecosystem interacts with each other effectively by taking into consideration the four influencers of the education ecosystem. We present experiential narratives of the biotic entities in this education ecosystem to better understand problems encountered by them because of the adverse effects of the four influencers on the interactions of biotic-abiotic entities within our blended learning platform and suggest recommendations to mitigate those adversities.

# References

Basak, J., Bandyopadhyay, S., Bhaumik, P., & Roy, S. (2017). Cultivating online communities of practice as rural knowledge management strategy in India. In *Proceedings of the 18th European conference on knowledge management (ECKM 2017)*, Barcelona, Spain.

Bhattacharyya, S., Basak, J., Bhaumik, P., & Bandyopadhyay, S. (2020). Cultivating online virtual community of purpose to mitigate knowledge asymmetry and market separation of rural artisans in India. In*The proceedings of 11th international development informatics association conference (IDIA 2020)*, Macau, China. Retrieved from https://www.idia2020.com/wp-content/uploads/2020/03/IDIA2020-Abstract-Book-Preliminary_Small.pdf.

Kapur, R. (2019). *Problems and challenges in rural areas*. Retrieved from https://www.researchgate.net/publication/332187494_Problems_and_Challenges_in_Rural_Areas.

Nagori, N., & Saxena, K. (2012). Marketing of rural handicraft products through retail format: A synthetic review. *Annals of Management Research, 2*(1), 45–59. Retrieved from https://ijmtpublication.com/files/AOMR_2_1_2012/AOMR_2_1_2012_5.pdf.

Philip, L., & Williams, F. (2019). Remote rural home based businesses and digital inequalities: Understanding needs and expectations in a digitally underserved community. *Journal of Rural Studies, 68,* 306–318. https://doi.org/10.1016/j.jrurstud.2018.09.011.

Policy Research Initiative. (2005). *Social capital as a public policy tool project report.* Ottawa: Policy Research Initiative. Retrieved from https://hdl.handle.net/1880/43196.

Scrase, T. J. (2003). Precarious production: Globalisation and artisan labour in the third world. *Third World Quarterly, 24*(3), 449–461. https://doi.org/10.1080/0143659032000084401.

Shah, A., Vidyapith, G., Patel, R., & Vidyapith, G. (2017). Problems and challenges faced by handicraft artisans. *Voice of Research, 6*(1), 57–61. Retrieved from https://www.voiceofresearch.org/Doc/Jun-2017/Jun-2017_14.pdf.

Wenger, E. (1997). *Communities of practice: Learning, meaning and identity*. Cambridge: Cambridge University Press.

Wenger, E., McDermott, R., & Snyder, W. M. (2002). *Cultivating communities of practice*. Boston: Harvard Business Review Press.

# Chapter 10
# Implementation Challenges of the Online Blended Learning Platform

## An Experiential Analysis from Ecosystemic Perspective

## 10.1 Introduction

In the last two chapters, we have demonstrated positive outcomes of our research experience in mitigating access, capability and opportunity divide of rural learners belonging to different age groups using our proposed blended learning framework. However, it needs to be noted that those positive outcomes of the proposed blended learning platform in rural context are the results obtained from a set of short-duration pilot studies, which has been done in a controlled setup, managed by our research group. Scaling up and sustaining such a venture, by coordinating with biotic and abiotic entities and optimally negotiating with the external enabling factors, is indeed a challenge. In order to study those real-life challenges in rural context, our research group has initiated a social entrepreneurial venture, *NexConnect*. This chapter attempts to present evidences, instances, and experiences of scaling up of our blended learning platform by this social entrepreneurial venture, *NexConnect*.

NexConnect is a social business aiming toward addressing issues of social exclusion by introducing the potentials of social technology and by exploiting the knowledge capital of the crowd. The objective of this social business is to make social technology-enabled tools and platforms available to rural masses residing in remote rural locales of the country where there is serious dearth of access to right kind of knowledge, information, and opportunity. To address poor quality of learning and training in the remotest parts of the country, NexConnect eventually adopted and scaled up the architected social technology-enabled blended learning platform (as described in Chap. 8) by connecting experienced teachers/trainers/mentors from cities with the rural learners (both young and adults). Retired elderly teachers or experienced school teachers and expert trainers from urban locales were used as freelance knowledge resources to address the needs of the rural school students and adults.

NexConnect operates through rural digital classrooms, also called as "NexConnect Internet Schools" (or digital study centers), where community level rural learners (both young and adults) come and take part in the online learning sessions through the proposed blended learning platform. These digital study centers are equipped with the necessary digital infrastructures (explained in detail in Chap. 8). The synchronous learning sessions are coordinated by para-teachers or classroom coordinators who are from the local rural community. These Internet Schools are set up by NexConnect in collaboration with young rural micro-entrepreneurs, or by local NGOs.

NexConnect has been responsible toward observing and implementing this blended learning platform in some rural locales of West Bengal, Bihar and Jharkhand, India where there is serious dearth of education and training. The synchronous learning sessions for school students happen on a supplementary mode wherein they can interact with mentors live/online after their school hours. For the rural adults, sessions are conducted in the digital classrooms or NexConnect Internet School, where the adult learners come to attend the training sessions after completing work. NexConnect implements or executes the design principles of a Connected Learning Environment by instilling active interests among the rural population through promotion of required knowledge and skills, increased levels of participation and most importantly ensuring personal growth in academic, non-academic, vocation, and skill-based competencies. This proposed connected learning environment also propagates shared purpose and common goals among learners (both young and adults), parents, teachers, para-teachers, and local agencies.

Despite focus on both young and adult learning and trainings, NexConnect has made significant interventions in imparting quality education to school students; the progress in the domain of adult skill training and competency building among rural adults is still limited. As a result, the experiential analysis mentioned in this chapter will be mostly limited to accounts of those experienced teachers who have mostly connected with school going students residing in rural localities.

Apart from rural learners, NexConnect has involved six biotic actors within its digital learning ecosystem to improve academic learning and skill building of the rural youth: (i) freelance online teachers or trainers with years of teaching or training experience; (ii) classroom coordinator or para-teacher to physically manage the classroom; (iii) freelance subject matter experts for creating and collating crowd-sourced digital content; (iv) the rural micro-entrepreneur or NGO (who, in collaboration with NexConnect, set up and manage the rural Internet Schools); (v) the parents and family members; and (vi) the social entrepreneur (NexConnect in this case, who provides and manages the digital teaching–learning platform).

To summarize, this chapter will delve deep into the initiatives of NexConnect, a social entrepreneurial venture of our research group, in improving rural learners' access and usage of social technology-enabled blended learning platform. This will eventually help the rural learners to exploit necessary resources and opportunities for knowledge and skill acquisition and livelihood enhancement using the proposed digital platform. Aimed at improving learning and acquisition of appropriate skills, observing consistency in learning and training and most importantly witnessing twenty-first century oriented holistic development among underserved students and adult learners in remote rural regions, this social entrepreneurial venture attempts to guarantee successful interaction and interrelationship between the biotic and abiotic entities in the education ecosystem under the contextual influence of four external influencers. We will discuss the issues and challenges faced in implementing this initiative in subsequent sections.

Section 10.2 of this chapter will discuss the detailed roles, functionalities, and activities performed by the six biotic entities in our education ecosystem in the context of implementing the blended learning platform in some Indian rural locales by NexConnect. Each of these biotic actors connect with each other, collaborate and utilize certain necessary abiotic components of learning such as digital teaching–learning materials or training content, innovative assessment tools and other digital infrastructures to ensure quality learning and training among learners (both young and adults) within the rural study centers or Internet Schools. Section 10.3 tries to explicate both limitation and positive aspects of the implementation by analysing experiences of each of the biotic actors in specific operating contexts, impacted by four external influencers (social-economic-psychological-political). Keeping in mind the limitations of the execution owing to the presence of the four influencers, we have also come up with certain mitigation plans so that one can observe an equitable, uniform, and collaborative learning ecosystem that would benefit the learners at remote locales where there is serious dearth of education and training.

## 10.2  Implementing Collaborative Connections Among Biotic and Abiotic Entities

NexConnect is currently operating in some selected rural regions of West Bengal, Bihar, and Jharkhand (three states in India) by nurturing collaborative connections among the biotic and the abiotic entities of the education ecosystem in specific operating contexts, influenced by four external influencers (social-economic-psychological-political). In this section, we will discuss the roles, functionalities, and activities of six biotic actors and how they are interacting with the abiotic components of learning through our social technology-enabled blended learning platform resulting in a collaborative education ecosystem which is aligned to meet twenty-first century learning needs and philosophy of Connected Learning.

### 10.2.1  Online Teachers and Expert Trainers

NexConnect uses the dormant knowledge capital of the urban retired elderly, often ignored by the society, to provide online education to the rural children from marginalized communities, who often do not have access to quality teachers to learn from (Parthiban et al. 2020). Additionally, NexConnect also identifies expert trainers and mentors, who are capable of giving training and sharing advices to upgrade skills and expertise of rural adults. More than fifty elderly or retired teachers, trainers, mentors from different metropolitan cities of India, having experiences of teaching and training for many years in respective subjects, are part of a robust panel of online teachers and trainers. Most of the teachers and trainers are retired school or college teachers and professional subject experts, having strong motivation to devote time to improve quality of learning and skill development among rural learners. These teachers and trainers get engaged with the learning platform after a couple of screening interviews by subject matter experts. This screening includes demo teaching sessions and personal interviews that determines capabilities of respective teachers and trainers. Keeping in mind the twenty-first century learning needs, these trainers, mentors, or teachers, apart from teaching curriculum-based subjects, also focus on disseminating values, logical reasoning and critical thinking among learners, aiming toward holistic development of learners. These teachers act as additional support to the rural school students, thus not replacing the existing school teachers. In case of adult learners, the expert trainers act as personal guides and mentors for the rural adults, advising them on accounts of improving personal skills and expertise to exploit appropriate opportunities within and outside their local village community. Following are some of the activities performed by the online experienced teachers and trainers through the online teaching–learning platform, administered by NexConnect:

*Sharing Innovative Digital Content*: Online teachers and trainers often prepare innovative digital teaching–learning materials and training content for the rural learners by collaborating with digital content developers from NexConnect. Predominantly, the learners' cognitive profiles are taken into consideration while preparing innovative digital content. Moreover, in a collaborative learning environment, the online teachers and trainers make use of the huge free cyber resource curated by content developers, teachers, or educators from all across the world. These audio-visual materials aim to match the in-school and out-of-school learning, focusing on academic as well as holistic learning among students. For skill building trainings, training contents available on the cyber space are customised by the trainers according to the specific needs of the rural adults. Teachers contextualize the illustration of concepts in the teaching–learning materials, so that the students can understand those concepts from the perspective of their day-to-day context. The idea behind each of the digital content is to ignite within each learner interest and curiosity to know more and explore the unknown by themselves. The digital academic content prepared in regional languages comprises of everyday lesson plan and audio-visual based power point presentations. For vocational trainings, the digital training contents are categorized into several levels such as beginners, intermediate, and advanced, catering to the varied categories of adult learners. The online teachers with support from content developers keep on updating content by continuously collaborating with NexConnect (the platform provider), the local school teachers, parents and rural students, making content interactive and context specific. As shown in Fig. 10.1, an online teacher was sharing audio-visual digital content online while taking remote classes.

*Regular Communication with Learners Through WhatsApp*: NexConnect has adopted a collaborative learning ecosystem where the focus is to move beyond an e-learning system and incorporate a connection-centric and learner-centric education ecosystem. The digital platform architected and implemented by NexConnect

**Fig. 10.1**  Online experienced teacher sharing digital content in remote session

is connected to other socially enabled digital platform and services, e.g., WhatsApp. To keep learning active and continuously upgraded, the online teachers and trainers interact and connect with their students through WhatsApp. School students use the smartphones of their parent's or class-coordinator's to communicate with their respective online teachers. For the rural adult learners, those who are having their own smartphones, they use them to connect with their respective expert trainers and para-teachers through WhatsApp. Through WhatsApp instant messages, teachers and trainers send educational and training videos, assignments, and study materials to learners. Learners post queries and also upload answers to assignments through WhatsApp. NexConnect moderates these conversations between the experienced teacher/mentor and the learners by forming a common WhatsApp group. This creates a combination of "in-schooling" and "out-of schooling" where learners keep on learning and exploring new and innovative concepts beyond learning hours.

*Creating Active Learning Environment*: Focusing on creating active learners in the selected rural areas, the online teachers and trainers, with help from para-teachers or class-coordinators, have conducted several cultural programs, product exhibits, workshops, competitions with both young and adult learners. The idea was to inculcate within the learners sense of confidence, self-belief, and participation. Few of the workshops, moderated by NexConnect, happened in the rural Internet schools in virtual presence of online teachers and physical presence of school teachers, para-teachers, and the learners. Several sit-and-draw competitions, go-as-you-like programs were conducted for school children. As a virtual collaborative learning environment, most rehearsals prior to any cultural programs are conducted by the experienced virtual teachers through the online platform. Figure 10.2 is an exhibit of drawings done by the students after being told by the online teacher. It is always the collaborative effort that makes learning interesting and innovative. These drawings have been put up at the Internet School by the class-coordinator.

In case of product exhibits for rural adults, online expert trainers ask the participants to create sample products prior to their exhibits. The urban experts often ask

**Fig. 10.2** Students engaged in different kinds of activities

them to send their handmade products, wherein the former tries to sell their product among friends and colleagues in city. This infuses enthusiasm among the rural adults.

### 10.2.2   Para-Teachers or Classroom Coordinators

Another important participating entity within our proposed collaborative learning environment is Para-teachers or classroom coordinators. NexConnect has tried to implement the two-teacher system or dual teacher model in the selected rural locations of India. Two-Teacher or Dual Teacher System, mostly prevalent in China, is a blended learning model wherein both remote online teacher and the offline or on-site coordinator/assistant teacher play important role in imparting quality learning to the students (Medium 2017). In such a dual model teaching set up, an online expert teacher delivers lecture and interacts with learners through the online platform. He or she is usually a senior teacher or mentor having years of teaching experience. Along with this remote teacher, there is also a classroom coordinator or para-teacher, who may not be an experienced teacher, but must have basic educational qualification to be able to assist the online senior teacher. He/she will be monitoring the learners during class hours to ensure their participation in classroom activities.

In our context, more than ten para-teachers were identified by NexConnect from the selected rural locales. Most para-teachers were either looking for a work opportunity after completion of their formal education or were school teachers in rural low-cost private schools, looking for additional work and engagement. The minimum qualification and criteria of becoming para-teachers in the rural learning centers (Internet schools) were completion of high schools, ability to speak in English and guide learners with basic levels of learning and training. Keeping in mind the basic concept of dual teacher model, NexConnect has come up with several activities assigned to these para-teachers or assistant teachers which is explained in detail below:

*Teaching Assistance and Class Monitoring*: Each learning center (the Internet School) follow a regular class schedule. Depending on the class schedule, the live/online classes take place. Each of these centers in rural locations is governed by a para-teacher who looks into daily class activities, which includes both administrative and academic. These para-teachers assist young and adult learners with learning and training (as and when required) both during and after completion of online sessions taken by the experienced online teachers and expert trainers. At the time of online sessions, these para-teachers continuously check on the learners' work to ensure that they are following the online lectures. Whenever there is any audio/video problem, these para-teachers help learners understand what the teacher or trainer is saying. After the sessions, they often follow up with the already taught topic and help learners to further understand or even help connect them with the online teacher or trainer through WhatsApp if required. Evaluations in the form of oral tests and written exams are conducted both weekly and monthly, where teachers share question papers through the internal messaging system or WhatsApp group to the para-teacher, who in turn shares the same with the students during exams. After exams, the answer sheets are sent back to the teachers. The scores are shared by the teachers in a score sheet. Moreover, in the skill development sessions, online expert trainers ask adult learners to prepare a product by themselves at home and exhibit in class. The classroom coordinators are also responsible toward recording the classes and sharing with the NexConnect Team for future reference. Often these para-teachers assist the rural adults in sending their sample products to the expert trainers in city.

*Data Gathering and Documentation*: Apart from assisting in academic and non-academic activities, these para-teachers also play important role in administrative work such as preparing class schedules in consultation with the representatives of NexConnect, taking class attendance of students for each class, maintaining class observation sheets and feedback documents. This helps NexConnect in evaluating the performance of this teaching–learning process through data analytics.

### 10.2.3 Parents, Family, and Peer Group

Successful implementation of this collaborative learning framework is possible only when there is a support from parents, family members, and the peer groups surrounding the learners. It has been observed that, parents of rural learners often feel demotivated to send their children to the Internet Schools because of two reasons: (i) they are totally unfamiliar with internet based online learning and, therefore, skeptic about the usefulness of this teaching method; (ii) from their lack of exposure to learning and education at large, some of them fail to understand the problems of local education and the need for *quality* education. Many students being first-generation learners fail to get assistance from parents at home. In this context, NexConnect has come up to inculcate a sense of collaboration by including parents and students' family members within the proposed collaborative education ecosystem. These parents attended motivational workshops organized by NexConnect (both online and offline). Few sessions were designed to cater to the needs and desires of the parents. Mothers were given more importance, motivating them and making them involved in the learning process of their children. Moreover, these parents were given several digital literacy workshops wherein they were trained on how to use WhatsApp or other social technology-enabled platforms for the purpose of enhancing learning and skills among their children. Eventually, parents having smartphones started interacting with online teachers and members of NexConnect, highlighting the difficulties faced by their children. WhatsApp communication between learners and teachers is only possible if there is strong support rendered by parents. Thus, the parents started to contribute as mediators in the path of their children's exploration to education and learning.

Family members also play important roles in supporting the rural adults to pursue skill based or competency based trainings after reaching an age when opportunities of formal learning gets practically closed and one gets entwined into household and familial responsibilities. Women in villages despite having desire to enhance own skills for the purpose of working independently are often restricted by their husband or family members (Raj et al. 2019). In this context, NexConnect tries to motivate the husbands in order to send their wives for the online training sessions.

### 10.2.4  Edupreneurs, Government Agencies, and NGOs

As indicated in Chap. 6, the proposed framework is a transition from a face-to-face, centralized, teacher- and content-centric learning environment to a virtual, decentralized, connection-centric and collaborative, digital learning environment. This *socio-technical transition,* which influences not only user practices but also formal and informal institutional structures (including sociocultural, economic, regulatory, etc.) needs to be managed properly so that technology can be smoothly integrated with the extant social system (Markard et al. 2012). In order to manage a socio-technical transition for underprivileged community involving multiple agents, *transition intermediaries* play an important role to speed up transitions. In our context, transition intermediaries can be defined as actors that positively influence transition processes by linking actors and activities, and their related skills and resources, with existing regimes in order to create momentum for socio-technical system change (Kivimaa et al. 2019). An intermediary facilitates and enables use of the digital platform, as well as takes an active role with the aim of empowering disadvantaged groups.

Edupreneurs, Government Agencies, and NGOs in our context are not only supporting infrastructures of Internet Schools, but also playing the role of *transition intermediaries.* NexConnect, as social edupreneur, is providing the digital platform, administering Internet schools, managing relationships and interaction dynamics within all biotic entities in given contexts, moderated by socio-economic-political-psychological influencers. As a transition intermediary, NexConnect plays pivotal role to mobilize the disadvantaged sections of society to use digital platform in order to get exposed to available teaching–learning resources. NexConnect, with local NGOs and governmental agencies have played vital roles in ensuring realization of a digital connected learning environment in specific rural context. In all of the rural regions where we have worked, NexConnect has taken help from the local NGOs or local government bodies. Following are the activities performed by these three agencies in a collaborative manner:

*Community Mobilisers*: After coming across the deplorable state of learning in a particular region of rural West Bengal, NexConnect approached a century-old NGO in that region. This particular NGO has been trying to improve skill and basic learning among the rural population. However, they were facing limitations in terms of quality teachers or trainers in their rural localities. In this context, NexConnect collaborated with the NGO to mobilize children from the community and provided them quality teaching through the online blended learning platform. Similarly, NexConnect collaborated with a Delhi based NGO along with a rural NGO to create online connected learning environment in an Indian village of Bihar. Figure 10.3 shows how the NGO owners, rural NGO, and NexConnect are organizing an online demonstration session to mobilize rural students and motivate their parents. NexConnect has also established Internet Schools in rural Jharkhand in collaboration with local NGOs, who acted as community mobilizer.

NexConnect has collaborated with several governmental entities such as the District Industrial Centre (DIC) under Micro Small and Medium Enterprises (MSME), Government of India to mobilize the rural artisan community in a district of rural West Bengal. With intervention from government officials from DIC, several workshops have been conducted with the rural artisans within the government office to mobilize and motivate artisans to participate in online learning activities within the Internet Schools. NexConnect has also collaborated with some rural public school, where some online classes were conducted within the premises of these public schools after school hours for the purpose of disseminating quality education to the learners. Thus, mobilization of rural learners, who are completely new to this online teaching–learning platform, is only possible if edupreneurs, government agencies, and NGOs

**Fig. 10.3** Local NGO mobilizing the rural learners and their parents with demonstration

collaborate with each other and play an active role to manage this socio-technical transition.

*Facilitating Infrastructure*: To observe a socio-digital education ecosystem in specific rural localities, it becomes pertinent to first ensure access to computer, smartphones, and internet connectivity. NexConnect, in collaboration with NGOs or corporates, acts as infrastructure facilitator by way of ensuring high-speed internet connectivity and also facilitating the rural study centers with appropriate infrastructures that are needed to ensure quality learning. These infrastructures include table, chairs, electricity, power-banks (because of the recurrent power cuts) and most importantly computer and projector set up. Thus, apart from becoming the community mobilizers, social edupreneurs, government agencies, and NGOs need to play the crucial role in becoming the mediators and facilitators in each rural locality where we desire to implement a connected learning environment.

*Impact Assessment and Monitoring*: Apart from managing the online learning sessions in the Internet Schools, NexConnect also monitors, evaluates, and assesses the quality of teaching–learning processes happening in the Internet Schools, including tracking the learners' improvement in that regard. In this context, a Learning Analytics mobile App has been designed and implemented by NexConnect specifically for regular usage by online teachers and para-teachers. This App comprises of the following functionalities: (i) recording student attendance by both online teachers and para-teachers on a regular basis; (ii) regular class observation and evaluation given by both online teacher and para-teachers; and (iii) uploading test papers for students by online teachers and uploading of answer sheets by para-teachers.

On a regular basis, each of the online teacher and the para-teacher has to fill up a class observation sheet separately on their respective Learning Analytics App after each session where they can comment on different classroom conditions such as electricity, digital infrastructure, etc., that has hindered the ongoing class. Additionally, both teacher and para-teacher can evaluate one another on their respective performances in classrooms. Both these actors also have the option in the Analytics App to evaluate the conduct of each learner by putting scores and commenting against their names in each and every session. These data are recorded and later analysed by NexConnect to understand and evaluate the effectiveness of online blended learning happening in the Internet Schools. Apart from regular session-wise evaluation, NexConnect also conducts Before Study, Midline Study, and End-line Study to evaluate learners' improvement in learning outcome and subjective well-being, as illustrated in Chaps. 8 and 9. The results of these regular monitoring and frequent assessments are further codified and analysed in form of Impact Assessment Reports.

## *10.2.5   Content Developers*

We have utilized the potential of the "crowd knowledge" in preparing updated teaching–learning materials (TLM) which are used by the online experienced teachers while teaching-learners online. These crowd-sourced TLMs are recreated or updated by a huge pool of freelance content developers. Within a span of three years, NexConnect has come in contact with several individuals such as students, teachers, professors, professional content developers, etc., who had immense interest and enthusiasm in exploring innovative educational content for the underprivileged learners. These individuals in coordination with NexConnect initiated the process of co-creating educational content matching the exact needs of rural learners. These contents were prepared in forms of regular lesson plans and audio-visual based Power Point presentations.

### 10.2.6 Abiotic Components in the Education Ecosystem

Each of the above stated biotic actors of the learning ecosystem plays respective roles and functions by successfully utilizing and managing necessary abiotic components of learning such as the necessary infrastructures in rural classrooms, digital teaching–learning materials, and innovative assessment tools. The *classroom infrastructures* are either sponsored by NGOs, Corporate Houses or are procured by the local rural micro-entrepreneur. These infrastructures may include sitting arrangements for students, large screen TV or projector, Computer, internet connectivity, solar power (if needed in areas where there is persistent problem of electricity), smartphones (if needed) etc. Para-teacher or classroom coordinator manages this infrastructure by ensuring security of the Internet Schools. Owing to several instances of theft in several rural localities, the local agencies and para-teacher make it a point to safely secure the classroom infrastructures properly.

The *digital teaching–learning materials* in forms of lesson plans, power point presentations (as prepared by freelance content developers or online teachers with support from NexConnect) and digital training contents become crucial at this point to deliver updated content which is in alignment with the learning needs of the rural learners. These digital contents are regularly shared by the online teachers and trainers during remote sessions to complement training sessions. NexConnect has also tried to train some of the para-teachers to use of these digital TLMs, so that in absence of the online teacher, he or she can use them in classes. Some of the para-teachers being local tutors themselves are encouraged to co-create digital TLMs and use them personally for dissemination of quality learning and training.

For the purpose of effective evaluation, NexConnect uses App-based *assessment tools* to monitor not only learners' performance but also the performance of teachers and trainers and classroom coordinators on a regular basis. NexConnect has incorporated the use of WhatsApp within their blended learning platform. Through regular informal usage of the WhatsApp, learners are regularly assessed and evaluated by the trainers and teachers. Online teachers and para-teachers are able to correct home-assignments through WhatsApp messages and also share necessary educational videos, images, or documents with learners all the time; making learning informal and collaborative. During skill building training sessions, online expert trainers too are able to correct assignments and also review sample products made by the rural adults at home, images of which are uploaded by them and sent through WhatsApp.

## 10.3  Contextual Impact of Four External Influencers on Teaching–Learning Process

Although pilot-scale implementation of the proposed online blended learning framework has demonstrated improvement in the learning outcome and well-being of students in remote rural areas (as described in Chap. 8) and improvement in life and livelihoods of some rural adults (as described in Chap. 9), the scaling-up process of the said framework in different rural locations has revealed that there has been lack of consistency in the number of learners coming to the study centers and in the regularity of the number of sessions been conducted in the Internet Schools. The causes behind such irregularities are the following implementation challenges:

- *Student Drop-outs*: Learners in the Internet Schools that are run by the rural micro-entrepreneurs often drop-out from Internet schools because of the fee that they cannot afford. However, the Internet School run by NGOs are free and those schools observe less drop-outs.
- *Obligations of Rural Adult Learners*: Most of the rural adult learners are women and they have responsibilities at home, which hinder their coming to the Internet Schools for taking trainings. Many a times excessive pressure at home makes it difficult for them to attend the remote sessions, resulting in drop-outs. Moreover, the rural males too find it difficult to manage time for the training sessions owing to their work-related obligations.
- *Student Absenteeism*: Many a times, some students, especially girl students, get engaged in household works, assisting their parents, resulting in their absence from the online sessions.
- *Apprehension of Rural parents*: Many rural parents are unable to understand the benefits of learning through online teaching–learning process. As a result, some of them often seem to discourage their children to participate in such online learning activities.
- *Lack of Support at Home*: The women in rural locales often do not find enough support from their family members to pursue vocational or skill development courses in order to exploit own opportunity scopes. Such non-formal trainings are often not considered lucrative and time-worthy by their family members, thus resulting in the women not attending the remote training sessions.
- *Problem Created by Local Tutors or School Teachers*: Local tutors and school teachers often discourage parents to send their children to the Internet Schools. Reasons can be their feeling of being threatened by the increasing popularity of the online sessions been conducted in the Internet schools.

- *Lack of Interest Among Para-Teachers*: Para-teachers, who are the backbone of Internet Schools in rural locales, often find it difficult to stay motivated all the time. One of the reasons behind them feeling demotivated is the low remuneration they receive, unless supported by some NGOs.
- *Infrastructure Related Issues*: Disruptions in terms of power failure, unstable internet connectivity, and poor transport facilities to Internet Schools from students' homes are some important causes behind the inconsistency in conducting online sessions in some Internet Schools.

We will now present experiences of each of the participating entities within the education ecosystem which would further explain the contextual influence of four external influencers on the teaching–learning process. Moreover, how the participating entities of the education ecosystem manage the rural disadvantages in terms of those four influencers and ultimately help in enhancing holistic learning and skill development among the learners using our digital framework is the focus of this section. However, the subsequent experiential analysis concentrates primarily on the biotic actors' engagement with rural school students. This is because of the inadequate experience till date on rural adult training done by NexConnect.

### 10.3.1  Impact of Social Factors on the Teaching–Learning Process

**Social Discrimination**

*Online Teachers' Perspectives*: The retired, experienced teachers shared their experiences of connecting with the learners from remote rural areas through the online learning platform and how prevailing social distance and discrimination in the rural locations influenced the activity of disseminating learning. One of the online teachers said "I believe there still exists caste based discriminations in the particular rural location where I teach. While interacting with the students during class hours, I came to know that many of them have been exposed to differential treatments in terms of corporal punishments based on their particular caste affiliations by their local school teachers. This has very much saddened me and as a result I have tried to eradicate this sense of discrimination from the mind of my students. I have always treated each of them equally, never asked their caste or class background." Most of the online elderly teachers expressed their deep grievances against the prevailing social discriminations in some remote rural locales. However, none of them have faced any social discriminatory practices among students within their respective online learning sessions owing to their conscious attempt to create an equitable learning environment.

*Learners' Perspectives*: There are evidences of social discrimination and abuse operating in remote locales. The local school teachers enforce social distance between students from varied caste and religious backgrounds. In one such rural school in

West Bengal, the students said "We are beaten up by the class-teacher owing to our affiliation with the Tribal Caste." However, the same children feel much more comfortable while interacting with their online teachers, since they never use any abusive language and are unable to beat them. Unfortunately, the blended learning model acts in a supplementary mode, not a replacement of the local school teachers in formal schools. As a result, the students have to face these abusive class-teachers in their schools. Occasionally, it has been observed that some students were beaten up so badly by their local school teachers that it became difficult for them to get up and attend the online sessions.

From the adult learners' perspective, some adults from lower caste backgrounds have said that they cannot sit side by side with other adults from a higher caste. They prefer to sit with those who are affiliated within his/her own caste group.

*Para-Teachers' Perspectives*: Para-teachers act as the bridge between the online teachers/trainers and the learners in the blended learning model. They have shared their experiences of observing social discrimination and distance in their specific rural locales, where learners from different social groups are disallowed to even sit together and learn. "Though online learning is effective, learners after the online classes have to deal with lot of discriminations in their day-to-day life based on their class, caste, religion. As a result, although they receive equitable treatment in the online sessions, it becomes meaningless after the online sessions."

### Social Capital

*Online Teachers'/Trainers' Perspectives*: Unlike the existing rural school teachers, the online teachers encouraged students to participate, interact with peers, read story books, poems, sing and dance in class to make the classroom environment learner-centric and devoid of the monotony of a regular classroom. One of the online elderly teachers had asked the students to organize a cultural function where all of the students rehearsed online and staged a play scripted by the elderly teacher himself. "Participation in cultural events in group help them to nurture the spirit of collaborative activities"—said one of the elderly retired teachers. This, in turn, helps to develop bonding social capital within the learning communities. In another context, one of the online teachers said "The students from the rural communities were not exposed to the world outside. They felt social isolation and unawareness to what is happening outside because they were restricted to mix up with people from other communities within their village boundaries." Through the blended learning platform, the online teachers from different locales took the opportunity to bridge the social distance virtually by introducing the learners to unfamiliar urban environments, showing them their urban surroundings. A teacher from Boston, USA said "I once showed the children the snow-fall and streets and buildings of Boston from my window. Each one of them irrespective of their class or caste affiliations, saw them. They were elated and asked me many questions afterwards." These instances of effortless interaction and communication between online teacher from an urban area and learners from a rural locale are evidence of increasing bridging social capital.

The online expert trainers while training the rural adults witnessed absence of bonding social capital among one another before the initiation of the remote sessions.

However, the informal collaborative learning environment and informal communications with the expert trainers, classroom coordinator, and fellow trainees through WhatsApp communications have increased their bonding social capital (This has been discussed in detail in Chap. 9).

*Learners' Perspectives*: One of the school student said "We are asked to help our peers with studies, to talk and interact with them in classes by the online teachers. But when we go to our local tuitions and schools, we are scolded for talking with our peers." Similarly, as mentioned in Chap. 9, the rural adults have collaborated with their peers after the remote sessions and have created products collectively. The blended learning model has promoted collaborative learning, resulting in increasing one's bonding social capital. Unfortunately, traditional rural schools and local tuition centers do not promote or nurture the habit of collaboration among learners.

*Para-teachers' Perspectives*: One of the para-teachers from an Internet School shared his experience of assisting the online teachers, wherein he observed high level of interest, participation, and interaction among learners. He also said that students in rural locales hardly get the opportunity to communicate with people from outside their immediate community. Another para-teacher said "It is the first time that I am getting to see these rural kids interact and communicate with someone who is not from the same community and from different socioeconomic and cultural background." These instances have a positive impact on improving bridging social capital of learners.

### Gender Discrimination

*Online Teachers'/Trainers' Perspectives*: The online teachers teaching students from a village of West Bengal said "the girls refuse to sit with the boys in my class." Some other teachers teaching in another village of West Bengal complained about the continuous absence of girl students from the study center. Despite continuous dialogue with the para-teachers, the elderly teachers have witnessed regular absenteeism of girl children in the classes. This issue is more prominent among girl children who are more than 12 years of age. One of the teachers observed "I have seen some of the girls only attended the first day of my class. I have observed that the absenteeism is more common in the evening sessions." In case of training sessions for adults, online expert Trainers too have observed frequent absenteeism among rural women in some of the training sessions owing to their responsibilities at home.

*Learners' Perspectives*: "We are not allowed to attend the online classes conducted in the evenings by our Hostel Warden," said one of the residential girl students from the study center in a village of West Bengal. The girl students conveyed their deep interest in attending online classes. But, their social conditions restrain them from going out of their hostels to the study center for attending the online classes as there they have to sit beside boy students. In case of training sessions for adults, as already mentioned in the beginning of this sub-section, many rural women are restricted by their husbands and family members to pursue such vocational training courses.

*Para-teachers' Perspectives*: One of the para-teachers narrated that gender based role divisions exist in the remote rural locales. Even the local school teachers have an inclination toward segregating a girl child from a boy child, focusing more on the boy students than the girls. In stark contrast, the online urban teachers do not instigate any gender discrimination among leaners during the teaching–learning process.

To mitigate the problem of gender discrimination in the remote rural locales, NexConnect joined hands with local NGOs and local government agencies in organizing workshops wherein members of local communities including parents, local teachers, and others are given awareness sessions. In these workshops, the experts and mentors tried to counsel them against their beliefs toward gender discrimination. As a result of these workshops, there was a noticeable improvement in the attendance of girl students.

## 10.3.2   Impact of Economic Factors on the Teaching–Learning Process

### Financial Affordability

Primarily there are three cost components associated with this online blended learning model: cost of teaching (online teachers/trainers and para-teachers), cost of service (provided by platform provider: NexConnect in this case), and cost of infrastructure (Internet, electricity and set up and running cost of study centers). Since the paying capacity of most of the rural population are extremely low, these cost components need to be supported (by NGO, for example) or subsidized (by engaging volunteer teachers, for example).

*Online Teachers'/Trainers' Perspective*: NexConnect primarily recruits teachers having intense desire to serve underprivileged children or the underserved rural adult learners. At the same time, they also need to earn something for their service. Some of these teachers have expressed their struggle to teach students at a much subsidized rate. One of the teachers said "I started to teach these children knowing that their paying capacity is extremely low. However, after teaching for two months through the online learning platform, it became difficult for me to manage my time toward low-paying activities. As a result I had to leave this activity despite my immense love toward these children." In this context, the social enterprise is engaging volunteer teachers who may be interested to teach these rural children free of cost. However, this may not a sustainable solution because of lack of sustained commitment and occasional irregularities of volunteer teachers.

*Para-Teachers' Perspective*: Most of the para-teachers in Internet Schools that are operated by local rural entrepreneurs (in collaboration with NexConnect) get paid at the end of every month from the collected fees from the students who study in those Internet Schools. One of the para-teachers shared her grave experience by saying "I often do not get paid or get less paid owing to less amount of fees been collected from the parents. These parents, mostly agricultural labourers or house-maids, earn very less amount. As a result, after paying for their children's school fee or other stationary items, they often do not have anything left with them to pay for our online sessions." In another context, one of the para-teachers in an Internet School in rural

Jharkhand said, "We know most of the children and their families as they are from my community. As a result, they take advantage of the familiarity and refrain from paying fees, making it difficult to sustain the study centres."

*Parents' Perspectives*: Some of the parents in remote rural locales of West Bengal tried to engage their children both in Internet School and their local tuition centers. They are enthusiastic about online teaching, but at the same time, they do not want their children to leave existing tuition centers. As a result, some parents said "Though teachers are very good in the Internet Schools, we are unable to pay fees for the same as we have to simultaneously pay for the local tuitions."

Problem related to financial affordability of this platform is one of the many reasons behind drop-outs of students from several Internet Schools, unless it is fully supported by NGOs. Owing to problems of financial affordability of the rural parents, it is either the online teacher or the para-teacher who refrain from continuing the online sessions. NexConnect has come up with several mitigation plans in this context. One of them is to identify an NGO or local agencies (government or non-government) or corporates who can sponsor those children who are unable to pay fees. Another initiative is to engage committed volunteer teachers in this platform. NexConnect has also collaborated with several social organization and corporate houses to procure the required digital and physical infrastructure for some rural Internet Schools.

### Promise of Economic Return

*Online Teachers'/Trainers' Perspective*: In this context, the online teachers pointed out the limitations in existing curriculum that refrain a learner to imbibe skills that may be useful in their future career. They felt the need to focus more on career counseling, skill development of each learner along with their academic syllabus. The limited connection of most of the rural learners with rest of the world makes them unaware of opportunities that are available around them outside their rural home. This also restricts their career aspirations to the available ones within their own surroundings. "When I started teaching the children online, many of them said they want to become a farmer like their father or home-maker like their mothers. With the increasing exposure with the cyber-world and the career counselling sessions online, the students started to explore other career opportunities." The focus should be more on the awareness of available opportunities and, as a result, there is a serious need to conduct sessions that are more related with skill-based development of learners. Unfortunately, the teachers said the local schools focus more on academic subjects than on counseling services.

*Learners' Perspectives*: Underserved learners have grown up seeing their parents pursuing activities such as daily labor services, farming, home-making, shop-keeping, and similar low-paying jobs within their village locality. As a result, they tend to focus on a similar career from childhood. An upper-secondary school student conveyed: "Owing to my grave family background with both parents dead and no one to fall back on, I thought of myself ending up to be a manual labourer. However, the Internet schools acted as a blessing to me. I met some very inspiring elderly online teachers who kept on pestering us to think of professions that can both earn us money and also respect in society." Unfortunately, the students also mentioned the lack of career counseling and skill-building sessions conducted in their local school.

Some adult learners also conveyed their previous lack of awareness with regard to the available work opportunities. However, online interactions with the expert trainers and explorations through Internet have enabled them to find appropriate opportunities for themselves.

*Para-Teachers' Perspective*: In many study centers, the para-teachers are also the owners of the study centers who invest some money on procuring the necessary infrastructures for the classrooms. They often feel apprehensive with regard to the economic return against such investments. One of them said "Taking loan from the bank is a huge risk. If by chance I am unable to return back the money. Since this online teaching is very new, parents feel apprehensive to send their children to such study centres. And if they do not come, how will I procure my invested money." These para-teachers and local level entrepreneurs are mostly rural youth who are eager to find employment for themselves within the boundaries of their village locality. In that context, many rural youth in quest for better opportunities on one hand get very much interested with this particular idea of starting own business in one's locality. On the other hand they feel anxious with regard to the financial return in such business. As a result, some of these local entrepreneurs themselves stall the ongoing classes on account of non-payment by parents.

### 10.3.3   Impact of Socio-Psychological Factors on the Teaching–Learning Process

#### Motivation of Learners

*Online Teachers'/Trainers' Perspective*: The online teachers or trainers shared their initial experiences of interacting with learners who were not quite aware of the need to study or the need to imbibe skills that are necessary to exploit appropriate opportunity scopes. One of the teachers teaching secondary school students online said "It is not the student who needs motivation and push, it is the parents who needs counselling because they finance the students' education and training." Many of the online teachers have even interacted with the parents through the online learning platform, where they found out that they lack motivation to send their children to the study centers. For many of the parents, it is more important for their children to support them in the household works rather than studying for themselves.

*Learners' Perspectives*: The learners shared insights behind their lack of motivation to study. A girl student from upper primary school said, "When I go back home from the study centres, I see my mother either watching TV or chatting with the neighbourhood lady. My father who comes late from work is so tired that he goes off to sleep. There is no one to even ask me whether I have done my home-work properly."

*Resistance to Change*

As indicated in Chap. 7 (sec. 7.3.3), students' resistance toward positive change in own life are three folded wherein students believe: they can't change, they don't want to change, they don't know what to change, or they don't know how to change (Dembo and Seli 2004). Below are some examples of students' resistance toward positive change:

*Online Teachers'/Trainers' Perspective*: This is an example of learners' belief that "they can't change." In the context of an online class on spoken English, one of the online senior teacher said "The other day, I asked a student to explain a paragraph in English. I asked him to forget about the incorrect pronunciations, to forget about the incorrect grammar and to just focus on the essence of the sentences. I knew, he would be able to say those sentences in English. Unfortunately, he chose not to utter a single word in English. Rather, he just stood by and looked at me for several minutes. When I asked him the reason, he said, he knew that he won't be able to speak." The concern these teachers raised is the psychological mindset of the learners that refrains them from learning new things.

*Learners' Perspectives*: This is an example of students' belief that "they don't want to change." The learners in this context, said they do not feel confident enough to stand up in front of everyone and to answer. It is primarily because they feel scared. One of the students in a study center in a rural location of West Bengal said "I am scared of punishments. Though I know the online teachers won't punish us from the screen, I feel scared anyway. The reason can be the prevalence of corporal punishments in my schools."

*Para-teachers' Perspective*: This is an example of students' belief that "they don't know how to change." The para-teachers said the fluctuations in the number of students' enrolment is primarily because of the fact that the students are not motivated. They are extremely pessimistic and have low opinions about themselves. One of the para-teachers said, "For years, these students are prey to demotivating words from their parents, neighbours, school teachers. This has shattered their morale and self-belief, making it difficult for the online teachers to reconstruct the same again."

To address the issues of lack of motivation and resistance to change among learners and other community members, NexConnect has organized workshops and awareness campaigns in the local community. The purpose of these workshops is to make them realize the need to learn, to feel motivated, and to learn to explore available options on the cyberspace.

## 10.3.4   Impact of Political Factors on the Teaching–Learning Process

*Learners' Perspectives*: The students in a village of West Bengal attended ten sessions in the beginning at the Internet school. But, they were prevented from attending the online classes thereafter by their local tuition centers and school teachers. The local school teachers, who run local tuition centers also, feel threatened by the experienced online teachers. In spite of improving own teaching standards, these local teachers spend time in stopping the Internet schools.

*Para-teachers' Perspective*: In this context, the para-teachers too have raised their concern with regard to the oppositions created by the local tuition teachers and school teachers. One of the para-teacher shared her experience: "When I wanted to start the online Internet school for the first time, local tutors came up to me and asked not to run such online study centre. Few of them also threatened the parents from the locality not to send their children to my online study centre." As experienced by the para-teachers in some remote rural locales, "the local school teachers have created huge problems during the running of the online learning sessions in the study centres. They have even restricted students from going to the online study centres."

To overcome this problem, NexConnect aims to collaborate with civic societies, local teachers, administrators, local political parties for the purpose of mobilizing, stabilizing, and improving quality learning in the remote rural areas. In some places, NexConnect has engaged local school teachers as para-teachers at the Internet Schools.

## 10.4   Conclusion

This chapter highlights several implementation challenges from different perspectives, which we have faced and tried to mitigate while implementing the proposed blended learning platform in rural context. A coordinated and collaborative effort among different participating entities is needed to combat these challenges. Keeping in mind the limitations pointed out by the online teachers/trainers, learners and the para-teachers, our social entrepreneurial venture, NexConnect, has come up with several mitigation measures. To enhance the degree of participation in online classes and holistic growth among rural learners, NexConnect, in collaboration with local NGOs and local civic agencies, has initiated the following additional activities:

- Conducting regular workshops with the parents and the learners' family members to motivate them regarding the importance of quality learning and training and the use of ICT in education and training.
- Conducting digital literacy training and motivational programs for the para-teachers who runs the study centers.
- Involving local school teachers as para-teachers to make them directly involved in the day-to-day learning activities within the study centers.

These mitigation activities are showing positive impact wherein all the participating entities are acting their respective roles in enhancing knowledge and skills among the rural learners, incorporating both curricular and non-curricular activities in the teaching–learning process.

The experiential analysis of participating entities in the teaching–learning process reflects effectiveness of the proposed platform and the challenges they face toward bringing change in the learning environment. Each rural location has its unique social, economic, political, and socio-psychological characteristics that influence the functioning of the specific learning environment in the particular geographical region. The central force that binds the components of the education ecosystem is the social technology-driven online blended learning platform that is architected based on Connected Learning Framework and fostered through social entrepreneurship venture. To summarize, the problems of education divide can only be solved if collaborative relationship among participating entities can be established and sustained by utilizing the potentials of a social technology-enabled platform, nurtured by social entrepreneurs or similar agencies.

As mentioned in previous chapters, several organizations, both governmental and non-governmental, are working toward disseminating quality learning among those who need them. Unfortunately, most of those initiatives focus on development from exogenous points of view where the learners are provided access to digital learning resources from outside through several digital platforms. However, in rural context, providing access is not enough to bring changes in the teaching–learning process. We propose to nurture an endogenous approach, driven by an online blended learning platform, which can nurture coordination and collaboration among all biotic and abiotic entities within an education ecosystem by keeping in mind the contextual specificities of the four external influencers of the education ecosystem.

In this context, the role of a social enterprise, who takes the responsibility of managing the social technology-enabled blended learning platform, becomes important. To improve the learning environment in a remote rural locale and bridge the extant education divide, a social entrepreneur plays the crucial role to bring together all necessary biotic and abiotic components within the virtual learning platform, where participating entities collaborate with one another in bringing changes in the learning environment of the rural learners.

# References

Dembo, H. M., & Seli, P. H. (2004). Students resistance to change in learning strategies courses. *Journal of Developmental Education, 27*(3). Retrieved from https://eric.ed.gov/?id=EJ718559.

Kivimaa, P., Boon, W., Hyysalo, S., & Klerkx, L. (2019). Towards a typology of intermediaries in sustainability transitions: A systematic review and a research agenda. *Research Policy, 48*(4), 1062–1075.

Markard, J., Raven, R., & Truffer, B. (2012). Sustainability transitions: An emerging field of research and its prospects. *Research Policy, 41,* 955–967.

Medium. (2017). *Two-teacher system, the new model for the education training market in China?* Retrieved from https://medium.com/@EdtechChina/two-teacher-system-the-new-model-for-the-education-training-market-in-china-63da97df0d4b.

Parthiban, R., Qureshi, I., Bandyopadhyay, S., Bhatt, B., & Jaikumar, S. (2020). Leveraging ICT to overcome complementary institutional voids: Insights from institutional work by a social enterprise to help marginalized. *Journal Information Systems Frontiers, 22*(3). https://doi.org/10.1007/s10796-020-09991-6.

Raj, A., Salazar, M., Jackson, E. C., et al. (2019). Students and brides: a qualitative analysis of the relationship between girls' education and early marriage in Ethiopia and India. *BMC Public Health, 19.* https://doi.org/10.1186/s12889-018-6340-6.

# Chapter 11
# Conclusion

## 11.1 Summary of our Work

The book attempts in providing both theoretical postulations and practical demonstrations of a social technology-enabled digital framework for addressing the issue of education divide. In doing so, it first starts by conceptually clarifying education divide from an ecosystemic perspective by defining and explaining chronological development of education ecosystem. It then proceeds on to explore the potential of contemporary digital technologies in enabling purposive collaborations between biotic, abiotic, and external influencers within an education ecosystem, which has the potential in addressing the issue of education divide on a holistic scale. In this context, we have designed a social technology-enabled online blended learning framework, derived from Connected Learning Theory, to facilitate effective collaborations between different agents within an education ecosystem, which has been subsequently implemented to improve educational practices of rural India, where learners' marginalized status has compelled them in being on the disadvantageous side of education divide.

In this context, it needs to be remembered that our research endeavour embraces a holistic focus of mitigating the education divide of marginalized learners. We have conceptualized education divide along three dimensions of access divide, capability divide, and opportunity divide. This implies that in the process of addressing the education divide of underprivileged learners, it is mandatory to overcome the divides in these three dimensions. It is with this intention, this book highlights our research efforts in equipping marginalized rural Indian learners with digital infrastructure, improving their capability to acquire effective knowledge by virtue of the medium and finally improving their opportunity prospects with the help of acquired education. Our initiative of addressing the issue of education divide is not only restricted to rural Indian children but has also been extended to address the issue of opportunity divide of rural adult learners, thereby having a holistic focus toward rural community empowerment. One of the primary reasons for rural marginalization in the context of developing nations owes its origin to the deplorable standards of rural literacy and the rural community's lack of knowledge regarding issues of importance. This proves that rural community is not just exposed to ineffective educational practices, but their poor market performance is also derivative of improper teaching–learning methods to which they are conditioned. This makes addressing the issue of education divide, by overcoming rural learners' access, capability and opportunity divide, a crucial component in the process of achieving rural community empowerment on a holistic scale.

Given the importance of improving rural education in the context of overall rural community empowerment, several measures have emerged across time to address the issue of education divide. However, if a critical investigation is done, it can be noted that majority of these initiatives are restricted in providing formal access to physical and digital educational resources to learners belonging to the disadvantageous side of the education divide. The book discusses at length how different attempts undertaken across the globe to provide access to educational resources to marginalized learners have remained largely ineffective due to the negligence of the contextual specificities of a given scenario. Negligence of local dynamics in the process of implementing initiatives dedicated to address the issue of education divide has made the undertaken attempts exogenous in nature, which has been externally imposed on the target groups without taking into account the contextual specificities. It is because of this, majority of undertaken initiatives have remained inadequate in enhancing the capability of marginalized learners and the ability to nurture their acquired knowledge in pursuit of improving opportunity prospects. Non-contextual application of undertaken measures not only contributes to their exogenous nature, but they have also disallowed optimal participation of marginalized learners in the process of learning.

To address the limitations of conventional attempts undertaken to bridge education divide, our solution rests on imparting education to marginalized learners by securing active collaboration between different participating entities within an education ecosystem with the help of social technologies. Steiner and Farmer's (2017) EPE model (Engage-Participate-Empower) of community empowerment forms the ideology of our research intervention. Our research endeavor of addressing the issue of education divide of marginalized learners with the help of social technology is premised on first engaging, then securing participation of marginalized learners in the education process, and finally achieving their empowerment in the process. The engagement and active participation of marginalized learners is derivative of adequate access to educational resources and enhanced capability of learners to improve self-prospects through acquired education. However, it needs to be remembered that it is only when the learners develop the applicability of their acquired education, by virtue of which they will derive the ability to improve their opportunity prospects, they can be truly identified as empowered. In this context, to achieve active engagement, participation and empowerment of marginalized learners, we have attempted in facilitating effective educational practices through our proposed framework by enabling purposive collaboration between biotic and abiotic parameters of an education ecosystem.

We have done pilot studies by practically implementing our proposed digital framework in a few villages of rural India to improve educational practices for marginalized rural Indian learners. Our empirical insights highlight that the external influencers (social, economic, political, and socio-psychological factors) operative in the rural Indian scenario often act as hindering factors in the process of disseminating technology-enabled quality education to rural Indian learners. Also, a critical investigation of our empirical study indicates that, although our research study has been successful to demonstrate improvement in the educational practices of marginalized rural Indian learners using online blended learning platform, it has been able to do so in a controlled environment managed by our research group. From an ecosystemic perspective, these pilot studies, for a short period of time, has only taken into consideration the interaction between biotic and abiotic entities and did not have a scope to experience and analyze the contextual impact of four external influencers (i.e., social, economic, political, and socio-psychological) on a long-term basis. In order to scale up and sustain such educational practices, this book narrates the experiences of the social entrepreneurial journey of NexConnect in disseminating quality education to rural Indian learners with the help of the designed digital platform. NexConnect has been mentioned in this book as an example of a social entrepreneurial venture whose presence and involvement is crucial in the pathway of scaling up and sustaining implementation efforts in marginalized and remote rural locales of the country.

The experiential narratives of NexConnect's journey highlight how the external influencers, along social, economic, political, and socio-psychological dimensions, act as impediments in the process of scaling up and sustaining quality educational practices in rural India through the proposed framework. When NexConnect attempted in imparting quality education with the help of technology in rural India, it had to counter several operative hindrances. This implies that adopting a technological solution to the problem of education divide is not sufficient, until and unless such a solution is designed contextually keeping in mind a socio-technical framework, by taking into consideration the local specificities, which crucially impact the process of education dissemination. Hence, implementation of this platform in rural areas is not a technology-implementation exercise alone, since it heavily relies on underlying social process, requiring a socio-technical approach to system design and implementation (Baxter and Sommerville 2011).

The introduction of such socio-technological innovations in society to solve social problems require a deep transition from older system to a new technology-mediated system and it entails simultaneous development (co-evolution) of technologies, service operations, and people's practices and mindsets (Kivimaa et al. 2019; Geels 2002; Department for Education 2019). In our context, it is a transition from a face-to-face, centralized, teacher-and content-centric learning environment to a virtual, decentralized, connection-centric, collaborative, personalized, and digital learning environment. These *socio-technical transitions* should take care of changes in user practices and formal and informal institutional structures (including socio-cultural, economic, regulatory, etc.) so that technology can be smoothly integrated with the extant social system (Markand et al. 2012). Socio-technical transition can be achieved by securing interdependence and mutual adjustment between technological, social, cultural, and political dimensions (Smith et al. 2010).

In order to manage this socio-technical transition for underprivileged community involving multiple agents, *transition intermediaries* play an important role to speed up transitions. In our context, transition intermediaries refer to entities endowed with the capacity to positively influence the transition process by connecting actors and activities, their related skills and resources with extant operations in order to facilitate socio-technical system change (Kivimaa et al. 2019). An intermediary facilitates and enables use of the digital platform, as well as takes an active role with the aim of empowering disadvantaged groups.

In the previous chapter of this book, we have investigated the role of our social entrepreneurial venture, NexConnect, as a transition intermediary to scale up and sustain the implementation of this socio-technical venture using digital teaching–learning platform. We have also explored the challenges and mitigation efforts of those challenges from the perspective of NexConnect. This research has demonstrated that the social entrepreneur, as a transition intermediary, can cultivate valuable relationship through building networks among participating agencies. The primary challenge is to include new users in the system and to combat external skepticism toward online teaching–learning methods.

We have used the concept of *user intermediary* suggested by Kivimaa et al. (2019) in order to demonstrate the role of NexConnect in this context as an intermediary. User intermediaries are "user support organizations who connect new technology and practices to citizens." It is crucial for user intermediaries to maintain its community or network in order to scale up and sustain (Kivimaa et al. 2019). NexConnect, as a social entrepreneur, is providing the digital platform, administering Internet Schools, managing relationships and interaction dynamics within all biotic entities in given contexts, moderated by socio-economic-political-psychological influencers. As a transition intermediary, NexConnect plays pivotal role to mobilize the disadvantaged sections of society to use digital platform in order to get exposed to available teaching–learning resources. NexConnect, with local NGOs and governmental agencies have played vital roles in ensuring realization of a digitally connected learning environment in specific rural context. In all of the rural regions where we have worked, NexConnect has taken help from the local NGOs or local government bodies.

## 11.2   The Way Forward

NexConnect's entrepreneurial journey highlights experiential insights of the venture in addressing the issue of education divide of rural Indian learners by contextually moderating the collaboration between different entities of the education ecosystem. Through the blended learning framework, NexConnect not only attempts in helping marginalized learners to acquire education by collaborating with the teachers, exogenous agencies like edupreneurs, government agencies, NGO, content developers, and others, it also strives to facilitate the endogenous development of rural learners in terms of capability and opportunity expansion by virtue of established social technology-driven collaborations.

However, it is not the job of one single social venture like NexConnect to create an impact on education divide holistically. We need several social entrepreneurs like NexConnect that would not only provide and manage the digital platform but also act as transition intermediaries to facilitate technology adoption and to manage the socio-technical transition process. The roles and responsibilities of these social entrepreneurs as transition intermediaries are however not linear and simplistic by nature. They have to take into consideration several factors while optimally moderating the collaborations between different entities within an education ecosystem. Some of those factors are:

- *Inclusion of the Marginalised Community*: Most of the target areas of interventions are impoverished, underserved, and inhabited by individuals who belong to the lower socioeconomic strata of the society. The backwardness is not only in terms of their poor accessibility to materials and informational resources, but also their socioeconomic incapability to utilize and exploit resources, even if they are accessible, which hinders their participation in the mainstream socioeconomic activities. In this context, the social entrepreneurs are expected to design innovative solutions to include these marginalized learners into new educational practices using digital teaching–learning platform and to sustain their motivation in the process.

- *Social Sustainability through Community Formation*: One of the major goals of the social is to cultivate socially sustainable communities that are equitable, democratic, and connected in order to sustain the ecosystemic relations existing between biotic and abiotic entitles of the education ecosystem even under the adverse contextual influences of external socio-economic-political influencers. To achieve this sustainability, the social entrepreneurs must come up with several strategies of incentivizing the online senior teachers, motivating local micro-entrepreneurs and classroom coordinators to run local Internet schools as their franchisees, instigating local government and non-government agencies for extending their support and above all convincing parents or family members of school children and adult learners regarding the benefits of the digital platform toward disseminating quality education and training. Additionally, the social entrepreneurs should take an integrated approach to addressing local issues at the local level by creating locally responsive services that fit the given context.

- *Increasing Popularity among Village Level Entrepreneurs*: One of the village level micro-entrepreneurs, who is running a NexConnect Internet School in remote locales of Birbhum, India said: "When I divorced my husband because of domestic violence, I had to leave my native village because of the social stigma. One day I got a call from my sister who shared an opportunity to earn by helping underprivileged rural students in the locality. This got my interest and I took that leap to return back to my village and eventually to open a NexConnect Internet school for imparting quality education to local children." NexConnect's entrepreneurial journey reveals similar such success stories, where several village level entrepreneurs got interested in taking up such initiatives of setting up Internet schools that can not only fetch them some money but also earn them respect in their community. Initially, they were very skeptical with regard to taking up such an initiative in their locality primarily because of the relatively new concept of "online learning." Return on investment was low too. But perseverance and success of the online classes after running of the study centers for several months with support from NexConnect restored interest among those village level entrepreneurs. In this context, social entrepreneurs, like NexConnect, must work for motivating community members into being successful village level entrepreneurs, so that effective educational practices can get eventually conducted by community members, thereby making the initiative sustainable.

- *Financial Sustainability*: Young adults after completing basic education often search for work opportunities for themselves within their local context. Unfortunately, they mostly have to look for one outside their locality and may often have to migrate to other cities due to unavailability of suitable job prospects in their immediate context. The social entrepreneurs in this scenario can tap this opportunity, where they can engage these youths in the activity of imparting quality education in their given locale as para-teachers by setting up Internet schools and help them in earning a livelihood from the same. Earning an income out of such an activity will motivate the community members to work toward improving the educational practices of their own community, thereby making the role of external funding agencies redundant in the process and making the undertaken effort financially self-sustainable.

- *Ensuring Digital Infrastructure Including Internet Connectivity*: The central key to success of the proposed online teaching–learning platform is not only the affordable availability of digital infrastructures including internet connectivity but also digital literacy among community members to be able to use the same. Although in contemporary world, internet penetration has been successful in most regions, in cases where they have not been, it often becomes necessary for the social entrepreneurs to mobilize resources to establish digital connectivity in remote areas. Moreover, ensuring availability of smartphones among rural learners with the help from government agencies or corporate bodies will ensure faster penetration of the online blended learning platform within rural community members.

- *Managing Interventions in Coordination with the Local Agencies*: In order to implement online blended learning platform in the underserved localities, the social entrepreneurs must coordinate with online teachers, local class coordinators who would run the Internet schools, local school teachers, parents, government agents, NGOs and most importantly the local government and civil agencies. To include students from a community into the online platform, the social entrepreneurs must realize the requirement for collaborative support from all these individuals and agencies that forms the biotic components of the education ecosystem. Apart from contributions made by the online teachers and offline para-teachers in disseminating effective learning among underserved rural learners, it becomes equally important to harness potentials of local school teachers by training them with updated teaching pedagogy and the use of digital content in classrooms. NexConnect thus has played this role of uplifting the teaching skills and motivations of these local school teachers who otherwise had lost interest in the process of teaching owing to several factors (as discussed in Chap. 7). Before establishing Internet schools or digital study centers in different remote and underserved locales, it becomes important to take care of all dimensions and influences of participating entities. What becomes important for the social entrepreneurs is the need to mobilize and make the community members aware of the benefits of online teaching–learning platform. In order to have a scalable and sustainable entrepreneurial venture, the social entrepreneurs, with the collaborative support from other biotic entities, must work toward creating a local network conducive for conducting effective educational practices in marginalized locales. They must motivate individuals, local club members, and local government agents in taking up the task of setting up study centers in remote locations.

A social entrepreneur must take into account the above-stated factors while moderating collaborations between different entities in the education ecosystem in order to facilitate effective educational practices in underserved locales. It is only by encouraging engagement and participation of rural learners along with other participating agencies in the proposed platform, effective education can be delivered that would eventually help empower the marginalized learners by bridging access, capability, and opportunity divide.

# References

Baxter, G., & Sommerville, I. (2011). Socio-technical systems: From design methods to systems engineering. *Interacting Computing, 23*(1).

Department for Education, UK. (2019). *Realising the potential of technology in education: A strategy for education providers and the technology industry.* Retrieved from https://assets.publishing.service.gov.uk/government/uploads/system/uploads/attachment_d ata/file/791931/DfE-Education_Technology_Strategy.pdf.

Geels, F. (2002). Technological transitions as evolutionary reconfiguration processes: A multi-level perspective and a case-study. *Research Policy, 31,* 1257–1274.

Kivimaa, P., Boon, W., Hyysalo, S., & Klerkx, L. (2019). Towards a typology of intermediaries in sustainability transitions: A systematic review and a research agenda. *Research Policy, Elsevier, 48*(4), 1062–1075.

Markard, J., Raven, R., & Truffer, B. (2012). Sustainability transitions: An emerging field of research and its prospects. *Research Policy, 41,* 955–967.

Smith, A., Voss, J., & Grin, J. (2010). Innovation studies and sustainability transitions: The allure of the multi-level perspective and its challenge. *Research Policy, 39*(4), 435–448.

Steiner, A., & Farmer, J. (2017). Engage, participate, empower: Modelling power transfer in disadvantaged rural communities. *Environment and Planning C: Politics and Space, 36*(1), 118–138. https://doi.org/10.1177/2399654417701730.

Printed by Books on Demand, Germany